10/08

D0857416

A New Orleans Voudou Priestess

UNIVERSITY PRESS OF FLORIDA

Florida A&M University, Tallahassee
Florida Atlantic University, Boca Raton
Florida Gulf Coast University, Ft. Myers
Florida International University, Miami
Florida State University, Tallahassee
University of Central Florida, Orlando
University of Florida, Gainesville
University of North Florida, Jacksonville
University of South Florida, Tampa
University of West Florida, Pensacola

A NEW ORLEANS
Voudou Priestess

The Legend and Reality of Marie Laveau

CAROLYN MORROW LONG

University Press of Florida
Gainesville · Tallahassee · Tampa · Boca Raton
Pensacola · Orlando · Miami · Jacksonville · Ft. Myers

11 10 09 08 07 06   6 5 4 3 2 1

A record of cataloging-in-publication data is available from the
Library of Congress.
ISBN 0-8130-2974-0

The University Press of Florida is the scholarly publishing agency
for the State University System of Florida, comprising Florida A&M
University, Florida Atlantic University, Florida Gulf Coast University,
Florida International University, Florida State University, University
of Central Florida, University of Florida, University of North Florida,
University of South Florida, and University of West Florida.

University Press of Florida
15 Northwest 15th Street
Gainesville, FL 32611-2079
http://www.upf.com

Atibô-Legba, l'uvri bayé pu mwé, agoé! Papa-Legba, l'uvri bayé pu mwé pu mwé pasé—remove the barrier for me so that I may pass through. (Song for Papa Legba, guardian of the crossroads, opener of the way for all human endeavor, and keeper of the gate to the spirit world.)

I dedicate this book to the unacknowledged interviewers and researchers of the Louisiana Writers' Project: Hazel Breaux, Edmund Burke, Catherine Dillon, Robert McKinney, Henriette Michinard, Zoe Posey, Jacques Villere, Maude Wallace, and Cecile Wright. Their work opened the way and removed the barrier for me.

Contents

Figures

Tables

Acknowledgments

A grant from the Office of Curatorial Affairs, National Museum of American History, Smithsonian Institution, enabled me to make the first of many extended research trips to New Orleans. After my retirement in 2001 the Museum allowed me to retain the position of Research Associate, giving me access to the collections and the Smithsonian Institution library system.

I was assisted in my work by many wonderful people. Mary Linn Wernet, archivist at the Cammie G. Henry Research Center, Northwestern State University Library in Natchitoches, Louisiana, provided hundreds of photocopies from the Louisiana Writers' Project Collection. Dr. Charles Nolan, archivist of the Archdiocese of New Orleans, allowed me access to the sacramental registers, and Janet Adams, Connie Birabent, and Jack Belsom cheerfully hauled these heavy tomes out of the cold-storage vault. Sally Reeves and Ann Wakefield of the Notarial Archives Research Center, and Wayne Everard, Greg Osborn, and Irene Wainwright of the Louisiana Division, New Orleans Public Library, not only helped me find what I needed, but even answered my desperate long-distance requests for photocopies of documents and newspaper articles. Marie Windell, Louisiana and Special Collections, Earl K. Long Library, University of New Orleans, made photocopies of Louisiana Supreme Court documents. Mary Lou Eichorn and Pamela Arceneaux of the Historic New Orleans Collection Williams Research Center were of great assistance as was Dr. Wilbur Menary at Special Collections, Howard-Tilton Memorial Library, Tulane University. Dr. Alecia Long, historian, and Adrienne Berney, special projects curator, at the Louisiana State Museum, gave me valuable information on nineteenth-century domestic life, and Nathaniel Heller, assistant registrar, allowed me to spend a day searching the museum's accession files. Liz Good and Jennifer Lushear, curators at the New Orleans Pharmacy Museum, provided information on epidemics.

New Orleans cemetery historian and preservationist Robert Florence, tour guide Mary Millan, and Laveau scholars Barbara Trevigne, Martha Ward, and Ina Fandrich added their expertise. Nancy Ochsenschlager allowed me to live in her home during my lengthy research trips. Paula Artal-Isbrand, Christine Barollier, and Nancy McKeon helped with translating long and complicated Spanish and French documents that were beyond my ability. Stephen Hank sent me a videotape of his film, *The Widow Paris*. Jazz historian Tad Jones guided

me to the magical key to all nineteenth-century New Orleans business transactions, the Conveyance Office Index to Vendors and Purchasers. I especially
appreciate the efforts of the volunteers of the USGenWeb Orleans Parish Archives Index Project, who have transcribed birth, marriage, and death records
and city directories and made them available on the Web.

Dr. Judith Schafer, an expert on nineteenth-century civil law governing slavery, miscegenation, and inheritance, patiently answered my many questions.
Judge Steve Ellis also provided information on Louisiana's changing defini-
tions of race. Dr. Virginia Gould, writer on the free woman of color Henriette
Delille who founded the Sisters of the Holy Family, offered insights into the
intricacies of nineteenth-century race relations. My friend Erin Loftus read the
entire manuscript and made valuable suggestions. The critiques of Dr. David
Estes and Dr. Vaughan Baker helped to improve the final product.

It was Meredith Morris-Babb, who, in her capacity as acquisitions editor at
University of Tennessee Press, encouraged me to begin writing my first book,
Spiritual Merchants, in 1995. Now, as director of the University Press of Florida, Meredith, editor-in-chief John Byram, and project editor Susan Albury
have made the publication of *A New Orleans Voudou Priestess* as smooth as
possible.

Finally, my utmost gratitude goes to my husband Douglas Wonderlic for his
unfailing love and support, and for making it possible for me to "quit my day
job" and devote my full attention to this project.

Introduction

My love affair with New Orleans—and my obsession with Marie Laveau—
began in the spring of 1978. A Florida/Georgia native and longtime denizen of
Alabama and Mississippi, I was living at the time in rural Vermont, terminally
sick of the six-month winter and the dismal cold and slush of "mud season."
I escaped to New Orleans for a two-week visit and wanted to stay forever—I
had never felt so at home. This "Crescent City" on the Mississippi River was
the South and yet not the South, close to my roots and yet irrevocably foreign.
People said "ya'll" and called me "dawlin" just like they did where I came from,
but the similarity ended there. In New Orleans, there were fortune tellers and
fire eaters at the cathedral; second-line parades and jazz funerals; nuns on the
bus; John the Conqueror and Stop Evil Floor Wash in the grocery store; chic-
ory coffee and *beignets* at the French Market and okra gumbo at the Napoleon
House; St. Expedite in the mortuary chapel and the Blessed Virgin Mary in
the front yard. You could buy beer in a go-cup and drink it on the street, sit
on the stoop and eat crawfish out of a paper bag and listen to the calliope from
the riverboat. It was funky and decadent and beautiful and slightly dangerous.
It was Bourbon Street, the Cities of the Dead, and Voodoo—or *Voudou*, as
it was spelled in the nineteenth century. I have returned to this magical city
again and again.

On August 29, 2005, just as this book was going to press, Hurricane Katrina
struck New Orleans, causing unprecedented damage, flooding, and misery. In
the days that followed, I listened in horror to news reports of the devastation
of my beloved city and its people. As I write this, the future of the place I knew
remains uncertain.

Back in 1978, like most other first-time visitors, I made the obligatory pil-
grimage to New Orleans' oldest aboveground cemetery, St. Louis No. 1, paying
my respects at the three-tiered, white-stuccoed brick tomb inscribed "Famille
Veuve Paris née Laveau" (Family of the Widow Paris born Laveau). A bronze
plaque states cautiously that this is the "reputed burial place of Marie Laveau,
the notorious Voodoo Queen." Tourists and locals alike visit the tomb to carry
out the prescribed ritual—rap three times on the wall, draw a cross mark with
a bit of soft red brick, place your hand on the marble slab, ask Marie to grant
your wish, and leave a small offering of coins, fruit, candy, or flowers.

* * *

According to the legend told and retold in newspaper and magazine articles, popular histories, tourist guidebooks, three novels, an opera, a film, a play, a musical, and on the World Wide Web, Marie Laveau was an extraordinary woman, a Voudou priestess and a highly successful entrepreneur capable of both good and evil. Descended from foremothers who served the Voudou deities, her combination of spiritual power, clairvoyance, healing abilities, beauty, charisma, showmanship, intimidation, and shrewd business sense enabled her to assume leadership of a multiracial religious community and accumulate wealth and property. Her influence is said to have extended to every segment of New Orleans society, from slaves to upper-class whites, and she is believed to have controlled the actions of policemen, judges, and city officials through magic or blackmail. She supposedly acquired her cottage on St. Ann Street by extricating a client from the clutches of the law. It is claimed that she led the Voudou dances in Congo Square and the orgiastic St. John's Eve ceremonies on the shores of Lake Pontchartrain, kept a gigantic snake named Grand Zombi, and procured young women of color for white men at an infamous house of assignation. On the other hand, we hear of her devotion to the Roman Catholic Church, her kindness and charity, her nursing of yellow fever victims and ministry to condemned prisoners, her antislavery activism, and her leadership in the struggle by women of African descent against the hierarchy of white men.

The legend tells us that Marie Laveau was the daughter of a wealthy white planter and his beautiful mulatto mistress, that she was married first to Jacques Paris and then to Christophe Glapion, and that she was the mother of fifteen children. She is said to have been nearly a hundred years old at the time of her death in 1881. As she aged, one of her daughters, known as "Marie II," is supposed to have secretly taken her place, giving the impression that the Queen of the Voudous reigned, perpetually beautiful, until the end of the nineteenth century.

*   *   *

Standing before the tomb of Marie Laveau, the curious visitor is moved to question just whose bones are interred here and why, more than a century after her death, she has become an internationally renowned cult figure. Looking for answers, I read everything available on the famous priestess. Although a great deal had been written, I found nothing of substance. Finally, in 1995, I decided to undertake this project myself.

I began my research with the reports and interviews submitted in the late 1930s and early 1940s by the Louisiana Writers' Project (LWP). The LWP was a local branch of the Federal Writers' Project, created during the Great Depression under the auspices of the Works Projects Administration to provide employment for journalists, creative writers, and other white-collar workers. Under the leadership of project director Lyle Saxon, LWP fieldworkers made the first serious attempt to uncover the true story of Marie Laveau. They located and transcribed civil and ecclesiastical records relating to Marie, her family, and her associates, translating those written in French or Spanish into English. They made typed copies of nineteenth-century newspaper articles on Voudou and compiled a bibliography of hundreds of others.

Most significantly, LWP fieldworkers interviewed seventy mostly black New Orleanians, born between 1853 and 1878, who remembered the famous Voudou priestess or her successor. Forty-seven of the interviews were of sufficient substance to be usable in this study. These informants are listed in the appendix, with date of birth (if known), address, association with Marie Laveau, and category of information provided. In the interest of clarity, I have converted the "Negro dialect" in which the interviews were transcribed by Writers' Project workers to standard English spelling.

The interviews vary considerably in quality. These elderly people were recalling events fifty to sixty years past; they sometimes contradicted each other or even contradicted themselves. They held widely divergent opinions of Marie Laveau's character. The Writers' Project fieldworkers did not have the use of sound recording equipment, but took notes and wrote their reports from memory. Many of the informants spoke Louisiana Creole as their first language, and their English might have been difficult for the LWP workers to understand. Some errors undoubtedly crept in due to the interview methods. The best of the interviews nevertheless have a definite ring of authenticity. The descriptions of Voudou ceremonies can be correlated with newspaper reports and other printed sources, and information about Marie Laveau's extended family is substantiated by archival evidence.

In 1940, Writers' Project employee Catherine Dillon drew upon the archival documents, newspaper stories, and interviews collected by LWP fieldworkers to produce a 700-page "Voodoo" manuscript. In the most important chapters, "Marie the Great" and "Marie the Mysterious," Dillon interpreted these primary sources to create a narrative of the original Marie Laveau and her successor. Another book-length manuscript, a history of African Americans in Louisiana, was compiled by researcher Marcus Christian, director of the LWP's "Negro Unit" at Dillard University. Christian's chapter on "Voodoo-ism and Mumbo-Jumbo" was based primarily on newspaper articles and other printed accounts.

The Louisiana Writers' Project, along with other Works Projects Administration programs, was abruptly shut down in 1943 after the United States entered World War II. Most of this valuable data remains unpublished and is not readily accessible to the general public. The greater part of the LWP collection, including Dillon's "Voodoo" manuscript, resides in the Cammie G. Henry Research Center at the Watson Memorial Library, Northwestern State University of Louisiana at Natchitoches. Duplicates of some of the reports and interviews are found in the Robert Tallant Papers at the New Orleans Public Library. A small amount of material is included in the Lyle Saxon Papers in Special Collections at Howard-Tilton Memorial Library at Tulane University. Marcus Christian's manuscript, "A Black History of Louisiana," is housed in the Archives and Manuscripts Division, Earl K. Long Library at the University of New Orleans.

Armed with clues from the LWP files, I proceeded to Louisiana's archival repositories. I consulted primary documents at the Archives of the Archdiocese of New Orleans, the City Archives in the Louisiana Division of the New Orleans Public Library, the Notarial Archives Research Center, the Conveyance Office in New Orleans' Civil District Court building, the Historic New Orleans Collection, the Louisiana State Museum's Historical Center at the Old Mint Building, Special Collections at the libraries of Tulane University and the University of New Orleans, and at the Louisiana Division of Archives in Baton Rouge. I also found primary data at the Moreland-Springarn Research Center at Howard University and at the National Archives and Records Administration in Washington, D.C. Gwendolyn Midlo Hall's CD-ROM, *Databases for the Study of Afro-Louisiana History and Genealogy 1699–1860*, was essential to my location of documents regarding slave sales, purchases, and emancipations. In later years I was able to do considerable research via the World Wide Web, particularly at Ancestry.com, the USGenWeb Orleans Parish Archives Index Web site, and at NUTRIAS, the Web site of the New Orleans Public Library.

I heard repeatedly that no accurate history of Marie Laveau could be recovered, that no records were kept for people of color, and that any Laveau documents that might have existed have been lost, destroyed, or stolen. This, like much of the Laveau Legend, is not true. Owing to the meticulous documentation of baptisms, marriages, and funerals in the sacramental registers of the Roman Catholic Church, and the obsessive record keeping required by French and Spanish civil law and continued under the American administration, I was able to find a prodigious quantity of information on Marie Laveau, her ancestors, and her descendants. While my research has gone far beyond that of the Louisiana Writers' Project, I would not have known how to begin were it not for the foundation provided by LWP fieldworkers almost seventy years ago.

The purpose of this research has been to disentangle the complex threads of the "Laveau Legend," separating verifiable fact from semifiction and complete fabrication. I have attempted to trace the evolution of the legend and uncover the truth regarding the life of the original Marie Laveau and her associates, and to identify her successor, the elusive "Marie II." This story is told against the backdrop of eighteenth- and nineteenth-century New Orleans, the unique social, political, and legal setting in which the lives of Marie Laveau's African and European ancestors became intertwined and Voudou evolved from the religious traditions of enslaved Africans, flourished in the early nineteenth century, was exploited for the denigration of black people during and after Reconstruction, and was eventually suppressed.

In the prologue I outline the development of the Laveau Legend in print and performance. The numerous permutations of this legend are woven throughout the subsequent chapters, where they are balanced against the LWP interviews and the archival evidence. Part one concentrates on Marie Laveau's personal life—her ancestors, parents, domestic partners, and children—and her place as an ordinary citizen of New Orleans. Part two examines New Orleans Voudou as an Afro-Catholic religion and Marie Laveau's role as a leader of the Voudou community. Part three deals with the final years of the Voudou Queen and the fate of her descendants and reflects on the identity of her successor.

Because Marie Laveau was illiterate, this cannot be a typical biography based on the writings of its illustrious subject. Marie left no letters or diaries and granted no interviews. She never speaks to us in her own voice. All we know is what was said of her by others: the journalists, popular historians, and novelists who spun ever more extravagant yarns about the celebrated priestess; the members of her own community who shared their remembrances with Louisiana Writers' Project fieldworkers; and the priests, clerks, notaries, and census enumerators who recorded the usual milestones of her life and the lives of her relatives and associates. Through a process of creative detective work I have attempted to construct an accurate narrative from the sources available, but gaps in the evidence have sometimes necessitated an educated guess about what *might* have happened. My speculations are always identified as such and are never presented as fact. Marie Laveau's thoughts and feelings, her religious convictions, her motivations and ambitions, her triumphs and bereavements, remain unfathomable. She is a blank slate, a receptacle for our prejudices, our fantasies, and our desires.

Definitions

In Louisiana, as in all French and Spanish New World colonies, the term *Creole* meant any person, regardless of race, who was native born (excepting indigenous Indians), as opposed to one born in Europe or Africa. Creoles were French-speaking, Roman Catholic, and most importantly, they were established in Louisiana before the arrival of the Americans. In this text I occasionally distinguish between white Creoles and Creoles of color, or Afro-Creoles.

In nineteenth-century Louisiana, an individual referred to in English as *black* or *negro* (*nègre/négresse* in French) was a person of pure African descent and was assumed to be a slave. A *free black* or *free negro* (*nègre/négresse libre*) was a free person of unmixed African blood. A *free man/woman of color* (*homme/femme de couleur libre*) meant a free person of mixed race. Collectively, they were *colored* or *gens de couleur libres*. These men and women were further classified as *free mulatto* (*mulâtre/mulâtresse libre*), of half African and half European ancestry, or *free quadroon* (*quarteron/quarteronne libre*), of one-quarter African and three-quarters European blood. While one hears of *octoroons*, who had one part African and seven parts European ancestry, the term is never found in the sacramental records or civil documents. The word *griffe* could refer to an individual of mixed African and Native American ancestry or could mean yet another gradation between black and mulatto. *Métis/métisse* also indicated Indian ancestry and was applied to mixtures with both blacks and whites. These words were simply descriptors and were not capitalized. I use *people of African descent* to mean all people, black and colored, with any degree of African ancestry.

The reader must bear with my insistent documentation of addresses. I wanted not only to be able to stand on the spot where Marie Laveau lived—this is known to every tourist—but also to see where other members of her family had their residence, where the African conjurer Doctor John and lesser-known priests and priestesses lived and did their work. For those who wish to share this experience, I have provided house numbers and cross streets. Because New Orleans streets follow the Mississippi River and do not run strictly north, south, east, and west, New Orleanians designate an address as being on the uptown, downtown, riverside, or lakeside of the street. *Uptown* means up the Mississippi River, *downtown* means down the river, *riverside* means toward the river, and *lakeside* means toward Lake Pontchartrain.

One of the greatest challenges to the researcher is the fact that a person often was known by several different names. New Orleanians usually had two or three given names, as well as a nickname, any one of which might be used. During the colonial period and continuing into the nineteenth century, a name might be rendered in French, Spanish, or English, depending on the native language of the clerk or the priest. In the interest of consistency, I have used the French spellings, assuming that these are the names by which these French-speaking individuals actually called themselves. Certain names reoccurred within families; children were named for their parents, aunts, uncles, grandparents, or godparents, and almost every female child was given the first name Marie, for the Blessed Virgin. Surnames were equally confusing because of fantastic variations in phonetic spelling. Marie Laveau's father signed his name *Laveaux*, but one finds numerous other permutations (Lavoz, Labeau, Leveau, Lavan, Lavou, Levaux, and Lavo, to name a few). Marie herself could not write, and presumably had no opinion about the spelling of her name. Since *Laveau* is most commonly used today, I have chosen to stay with that spelling.

Prologue

The "Laveau Legend" in Print and Performance

On June 15, 1881, the Voudou priestess Marie Laveau died from the complications of old age at her home on St. Ann Street in the original French Quarter of the city and was interred in the Widow Paris tomb in St. Louis Cemetery No. 1. Although Voudou had been a favorite topic of nineteenth-century New Orleans journalists, Marie was seldom the subject of newspaper stories during her own lifetime. In her infrequent appearances in the local press she was nevertheless referred to as "the head of the Voudou women," "the Queen of the Voudous," "the celebrated Marie Laveau," "the Priestess of the Voudous," or "Queen Marie," indicating that her exalted position was widely recognized. It was only after her death, beginning with the obituaries and remembrances that appeared in almost every New Orleans newspaper and even in the *New York Times*, that the tales about her grew ever more fantastic and the name *Marie Laveau* became synonymous with Voudou.

All of New Orleans' English-language dailies noted the passing of the Voudou Queen. Reporters for the *Picayune*, the *City Item*, and the *States* treated Marie Laveau as the cherished relic of a more romantic past, portraying her as a traditional herbal healer and a Christian woman of unfailing charity. The *Democrat* presented a dissenting view, and the *New Orleans Times* printed one of its typical "Voudou orgy" stories. The French-language newspaper, *L'Abeille de la Nouvelle-Orléans* (published in English as the *New Orleans Bee*), made no comment beyond a simple death notice.

The longest of the obituaries, titled "Death of Marie Laveau— A Woman with a Wonderful History, Almost a Century Old, Carried to the Tomb Yesterday Evening," appeared in the *Daily Picayune* on June 17, 1881. On the same day the *City Item* included a shorter but almost identical piece, now attributed to the journalist and fiction writer Lafcadio Hearn, in its "Wayside Notes" column. These articles, the source of some of the most tenacious elements of the Laveau Legend, present a remarkable combination of truths, semitruths, and outright fantasy—probably a journalistic embellishment of family history incorrectly remembered or deliberately falsified by Marie's daughter, Marie Philomène Glapion Legendre.

According to the newspapers, Marie Laveau's unidentified father was "a rich planter, who was prominent in all public affairs and served in the Legislature of this State." Her mother's name was given as Marguerite Henry, and her grandmother was said to be Marguerite Semard—both were described as "beautiful women of color." The obituaries promoted the notion that Marie was much older than her actual seventy-nine years. Both the *Picayune* and the *City Item* reported that she died at the age of ninety-eight, from which has been calculated the birth date of 1783 cited by some writers. The newspapers also told of her marriage to the carpenter Jacques Paris at the age of twenty-five, from which is deduced the more frequently cited birth date of 1794. They told of Jacques' mysterious disappearance and Marie's second marriage to Christophe Glapion. The *City Item* reported that from her union with Glapion she "became the mother of fifteen children, only one of whom now lives—a very estimable widow." About five years after Glapion's death in 1855, said the *Picayune*, "Marie Laveau became ill and has been sick ever since, her indisposition becoming more pronounced and painful within the last ten years."

The *Picayune* obituary went on to describe Marie's many admirable traits—her charity to the poor, who were "welcome to food and lodging at any time of night or day," and her abilities as a yellow fever and cholera nurse and her knowledge of "the valuable healing qualities of indigenous herbs." She was said to have known Père Antoine, the beloved pastor of St. Louis Cathedral, "better than any living in those days—she to close the faded eyes in death, and he to waft the soul over the river to the realms of eternal joy." Marie, it was noted, "labored incessantly" to comfort condemned prisoners, praying with them in their last moments and endeavoring to rescue them from the gallows.

Neither the *Picayune* nor the *City Item* mentioned Marie Laveau's role as a Voudou priestess. It was hinted by the *Picayune* that her skill and knowledge were attributed by the ignorant to "unnatural means," that she was held by such people "in constant dread," and that she often met with "prejudice and loathing" while "doing good for the sake of doing good alone." The *City Item* protested that "whatever superstitious stories were whispered about her, it is at least certain that she enjoyed the respect and affection of thousands who knew her, of numbers whom she befriended in times of dire distress, of sick folks snatched from the shadow of death and nursed by her to health and strength."

The *Picayune* obituary ended on a sentimental note: "Her last days were spent surrounded by sacred pictures and other evidences of religion, and she died with a firm trust in heaven. While God's sunshine plays around the little tomb where her remains are buried, by the side of her second husband and her sons and daughters, Marie Laveau's name will not be forgotten in New Orleans." The *City Item* was only slightly less effusive: "Marie Laveau was one of the kindest women who ever lived, and one who probably did more good to a greater number of people here than any other who lived to her great age."[1]

A writer for the *New Orleans Daily States* supplemented the *Picayune* and *City Item* obituaries with his "Recollections of a Visit on New Year's Eve to Marie Laveau, the Ex-Queen of the Voudous." The reporter had been taken to the famous cottage on St. Ann Street by a friend who was a frequent visitor. The two men entered the gate and made their way to the front door, through which were heard the sounds of music and dancing. They were greeted by "a middle-aged, light-visaged woman [Marie Laveau's daughter Philomène], a lady in all her motions and conversation." The guests were shown through the house and across the back yard to an outbuilding, where, in a large walnut bed, lay her "ancient majesty," the former priestess of the Voudous. After visiting for a short time, the reporter and his companion said their goodbyes, "kissed the 'old lady' on her forehead, and wishing her many returns of the new year, retired from the room."[2]

The politically conservative *New Orleans Democrat* printed a short piece on June 17, 1881, that differs sharply from the laudatory eulogies of the *Picayune*, the *City Item*, and the *States*: In "Marie Lavaux—Death of the Queen of the Voudous," Marie was described as the leader of "that curious sect of superstitious darkies who combined the hard traditions of African legends with the fetish worship of our creole negroes." The *Democrat* made much of the fact that she died a few days before St. John's Eve, "the anniversary of the Voudous, commemorated by the sect under her regency for the last forty years on the twenty-third of June." "Now Marie Lavaux is gone," said the *Democrat*, and with her "vanishes . . . the last representative of that class whose peculiar idiosyncracies were derived from the habits and environs of old Louisiana. Much evil dies with her, but should we not add, also a little poetry?"[3]

On the following day, the *Democrat* issued a rebuttal to the *Picayune*, the *City Item*, and the *States*, sarcastically titled "A Sainted Woman." The *Democrat* noted that the reporters for these newspapers "consist admirably in their uniform departure from historical fact" by portraying Marie Laveau as one who "had spent a life of self-sacrifice and abnegation in doing good to her fellow mortals, and whose immaculate spirit was all but too pure for this world. One of them even goes so far in his enthusiasm as to publish a touching interview with the sainted woman, in which the reporter boasts of depositing a chaste kiss on her holy forehead." In opposition to its "esteemed but deluded contemporaries," the *Democrat* characterized Marie Laveau as "the prime mover and soul of the indecent orgies of the ignoble Voudous; to her influence may be attributed the fall of many a virtuous woman." She may have been "kind-hearted and charitable," conceded the *Democrat*, but "talk about her morality and kiss her sainted brow—pouah!!!"[4]

On June 23, 1881, the *New Orleans Times*, ever the purveyor of scandal and sensationalism, ran one of its standard St. John's Eve items, titled "Voudou Vagaries—The Spirit of Marie Laveau to be Propitiated by Midnight Orgies on the Bayou." Following a harangue about "weird fetish worship" and "lewd women and worse men," the article announced that "Tonight is St. John's Eve, and on the banks of Bayou St. John . . . all that is left of the old Voudou clan will convene to honor the memory of their late Queen Marie Laveau . . . by a series of drunken orgies around a bonfire."[5]

On June 24 the *Times* published "The Departed Voudou Queen," an interview with "Doctor J. B. Bass, the New York practitioner of Voudouism," said to be reprinted from the *New York Sun*. According to Doctor Bass, Marie Laveau "knew all the secrets of Voudouism, including the charms, the influences, and the rites. In the days of slavery she made a powerful sight of money selling charms to protect runaway slaves while they followed the North Star." She "saved the lives of hundreds of people" during the cholera epidemics and "was very powerful in yellow fever too, and in fact was a mighty helpful woman in the community." In a similar article, which appeared in the *New Orleans Daily States* of August 26, 1881, Doctor Bass was quoted as saying that "before the war, [Marie Laveau] made piles of money by selling [herbal charms] to runaway slaves to prevent them from being captured."[6]

The *New York Times* printed a lengthy obituary for Marie Laveau on June 23, 1881, titled "The Dead Voudou Queen—Marie Laveau's Place in the History of New Orleans—The Early Life of the Beautiful Young Creole—The Prominent Men Who Sought Her Advice and Society—Her Charitable Work—How She Became an Object of Mystery." Like the New Orleans *Picayune*, *City Item*, and *States*, the *New York Times* dismissed the idea that Marie was actually a Voudou priestess, portraying her instead as a woman of great beauty, intellect, and personal magnetism who was also pious, charitable, and a skilled herbal healer. In her modest cottage, said the *New York Times*, Marie received "Louisiana's greatest men and most distinguished visitors . . . lawyers, legislators, planters, and merchants, [who] all came to pay their respects and seek her offices." She soon "possessed a larger *clientele* than the most astute legal counselor." The public, of course, attributed her success to Voudou, and Marie "delighted to cover her actions with an air of mystery." Echoing the New Orleans newspapers, the *New York Times* concluded that Marie Laveau was "one of the most wonderful women who ever lived," lamenting that "Now her lips are closed forever . . . and as she could neither read nor write, not a scrap is left to chronicle the events of her exciting life."[7]

* * *

Later nineteenth-century literary representations of Marie Laveau augmented the 1881 obituaries and remembrances and further laid the groundwork for the Laveau Legend. New Orleans, like the rest of the South, had undergone tremendous social upheavals following the end of the Civil War, the emancipation of the slaves, and the legislation of the Reconstruction era that supposedly gave equal rights to all. When Reconstruction ended in 1877, New Orleans was engulfed by a backlash of racism that resulted in a rigid segregation previously unknown in the Crescent City. The newspapers missed no opportunity to ridicule persons and institutions of African origin, and even the more benign of the local-color writers distanced themselves from such associations. Whites felt the need to reestablish their racial superiority and make clear the difference between themselves, as rational and literate authors, and the superstitious, uneducated, black "others" who were their subject. Voudou was a favorite target of late nineteenth-century writers, and ever more fantastic descriptions of naked, drunken orgies were used to bolster claims that people of African descent were unfit to vote, hold office, or associate with white people.[8] But even during these racially charged times, Marie Laveau was—with a few exceptions—untouchable.

The New Orleans writer George Washington Cable (1844–1925) was immensely popular in the 1880s, and it was his fiction and local-color sketches that brought Marie Laveau to national prominence and popularized New Orleans Voudou. Cable, born in the Crescent City to American parents, specialized in documenting New Orleans' rapidly disappearing Afro-Latin culture, considered exotic by out-of-state readers. Cable's works were offensive to white Creoles because he portrayed them as a vain and pleasure-loving population who spoke a quaint, nearly unintelligible form of English. He also suggested that they gave credence to Voudou superstitions, and worse still, he implied that some Creoles who called themselves white were not of pure Caucasian ancestry. One of his detractors, in an anonymous pamphlet, accused him of consorting with "the voudou queen Mari Lavo [*sic*] to beget a numerous progeny." Cable's later advocacy of equal rights for black people provoked such an uproar in the South that he, with great sadness, left New Orleans to spend the rest of his life in Massachusetts.[9]

Cable's 1880 novel *The Grandissimes* has as one of its most interesting characters a free colored hairdresser and Voudou priestess called Palmyre la Philosophe, "a woman . . . of superb stature and poise, severely handsome features, clear, tawny skin and large, passionate black eyes . . . a barbaric and magnetic beauty, that startled the beholder like the unexpected drawing out of a jeweled sword." It was widely believed that Marie Laveau was the prototype for Palmyre.[10]

Although Cable included numerous Voudou references in his literary and historical works, he concurred with the negative opinion of the white mainstream in his 1886 *Century Magazine* piece, "Creole Slave Songs." Here he characterized the religion as "dark and horrid as bestialized savagery could make the worship of serpents. So revolting was it, so morally hideous, that even in the French West Indian possessions a hundred years ago . . . the orgies of the Voudous were forbidden." He reassured readers that "this worship . . . in comparison to what it once was [in New Orleans], has grown to be a rather trivial affair. The practice of its midnight forest rites seemed to sink into inanition along with Marie Laveau."

Cable was nevertheless sympathetic when describing a visit with the Voudou Queen just before her death, declaring that he "once saw, in her extreme old age, the famed Marie Laveau." She was, wrote Cable, "over a hundred years old . . . yet withal one could hardly help but see that the face, now so withered, had once been handsome and commanding. There was still a faint shadow of departed beauty on the forehead, the spark of an old fire in the sunken, glistening eyes, and a vestige of imperiousness in the fine, slightly aquiline nose, and even about her silent, woe-begone mouth." Cable tells us that Marie Laveau was cared for by her only surviving daughter, "a woman of some seventy years, and a most striking and majestic figure. In features, stature, and bearing she was regal. One had but to look on her and impute her brilliancies—too untamable and severe to be called charms or graces—to her mother . . . to understand how the name of Marie Laveau should have driven itself inextricably into the traditions of the town and the times."[11]

Lafcadio Hearn (1850–1904), like George Washington Cable, promoted the concept of New Orleans as a place of exoticism and mystery. Hearn was not a native New Orleanian, but was born on the Greek island of Lefkas, son of an Irish father and a Greek mother. He arrived in New Orleans in 1877, having been sacked from his job with the *Cincinnati Enquirer* because of his brief marriage to a woman of mixed race. He was employed until 1881 by the *City Item*, where he wrote a daily column, at first called "Odds and Ends" and later "Wayside Notes," illustrated with charming woodcuts based on his own sketches. Between 1882 and his departure from the city in 1887 he was a reporter for the *Times-Democrat*. While in New Orleans, Hearn, like George Washington Cable, became fascinated by the history, customs, and language of the Creoles of African descent. Some of his favorite informants were the black market women, attired in their "ample skirts of guinea-blue cotton, spotless white fichu across their bosoms, and brilliant plaid tignons."[12] Lafcadio Hearn wrote several Voudou-related stories for local and national publications, but none of his literary output refers specifically to Marie Laveau. He did contribute a detailed article on another famous nineteenth-century Voudou personage, Doctor John, published by *Harper's Weekly Magazine* in 1885.

Rather than contributing to the Laveau Legend through his published works, Hearn actually became a character in it. After his death in 1904, there was gossip about an alleged sexual relationship between Lafcadio Hearn and the Voudou Queen. The rumor began when Alethea Foley, the African American woman to whom Hearn had once been married, came forward as his widow to claim a share of his estate. This sparked sensationalized reports of his "lapses from conventional standards." The *New York Sun* asserted that Hearn "consorted with colored people only.... When in New Orleans, he lived with Congo priestesses and prophetesses, including Marie Laveau."[13] Hearn's former employer Page Baker, owner and editor-in-chief of the *Times-Democrat*, refuted the tale, saying that "Hearn, like every other newspaper man in New Orleans who thought there might be a story in it, entered into communication with a Negro woman who called herself Marie Levaux [*sic*] and pretended ... to know something of the mysteries of Voodooism. ... What the *Sun* states ... would have been impossible in a Southern city like New Orleans, where the color line is so strictly drawn."[14] Lafcadio Hearn may well have been acquainted with Marie Laveau, but the story of their "affair" is obviously nonsense. Marie was an old lady when Hearn arrived in New Orleans in 1877 and was dead by the summer of 1881. Later biographers implied that it was her daughter and successor, "Marie II," who became Hearn's mistress.[15]

Henry Castellanos (1828–1896), a lawyer and local-color writer from a distinguished Creole family, proved to be Marie Laveau's chief detractor. Castellanos made frequent contributions to the local newspapers, and it may have been he who, following Marie's death, wrote the vicious rejoinder to the eulogistic obituaries of the *Picayune*, the *Item*, and the *States*, saying that the "fictions" published by the other dailies "created a vast amount of merriment among the old creole residents." His denunciations exhibit a particularly personal tone. Was Castellanos motivated by some disagreeable encounter with the Voudou priestess, or was he simply distancing himself from anything of African origin in reaction to the perception by outsiders that all New Orleans Creoles were people of mixed race who dabbled in Voudou?

Castellanos' article "The Voudous: Their History, Mysteries, and Practices" appeared in the *Times-Democrat* of June 24, 1894, and was reproduced in his 1895 collection of vignettes, *New Orleans As It Was: Episodes of Louisiana Life.* Here, perhaps inspired by Cable's character Palmyre from *The Grandissimes*, Castellanos initiated the idea that Marie Laveau had been a hairdresser. He also characterized her as a procuress: "In her youth," Marie Laveau was "a woman of fine physique and a noted procuress. Introducing herself into families as a hairdresser, she would assist in the clandestine correspondence of sweethearts and aid youthful lovers—and old coquettes as well—in their amours." By this he seems to have meant that Marie was a matchmaker and facilitator of relationships, both licit and illicit. Castellanos' remark was later interpreted to mean that she was an actual "procuress" of young women of color for the sexual pleasure of white men.

In the opinion of Castellanos, Marie's reputation as a worker of magic was based on illusion: "Such was the superstition of our people . . . that her apartments were thronged with visitors from every class and section . . . ladies of high social position . . . politicians and candidates for office . . . and sports . . . [all] in search of aid from her supposed supernatural powers. Is it needless to say that she was an arrant fraud? Yet money poured into her purse." Castellanos also credited Marie Laveau with instituting the worship of the African deities along with the Catholic saints: "She exercised the ritual of the original creed, so as to make it conform to the worship of the Virgin and other saints. To idolatry she added blasphemy."

Castellanos not only fulminated against Marie Laveau; he also railed against Voudou in general, that "mysterious sect of fanatics, imported from the jungles of Africa and implanted in our midst," who with their "stupid creed and bestial rites, made considerable progress among the low and ignorant of our population in the early period of the present century. . . . The tribe of Voudous . . . deserves to be stamped out . . . and with the advances of our superior civilization it is to be hoped that the hour is not far distant when the last vestige of its degrading and dangerous influence will forever be wiped out of existence."[16]

Information on Marie Laveau and Voudou was also included in nineteenth-century guidebooks for tourists. In the *Historical Sketch Book and Guide to New Orleans and Environs*, written for the 1884–85 World's Industrial and Cotton Centennial Exposition, visitors were directed to the former home of "the Voudou Queen, Marie le Veau [*sic*], who before she died turned from the superstitions of her life and died in the church." In the *Picayune's Guide to New Orleans*, first published in 1896 and "revised and enlarged" in 1900, 1903, 1904, 1906, and 1913, two new elements of the Laveau Legend were introduced. We hear for the first time of Marie's gigantic snake called Grand Zombi, and we are told that she was descended from a line of Voudou priestesses.[17]

By the end of the nineteenth century, most of the elements of the Laveau Legend were firmly established: the extraordinary beauty of the Voudou Queen, her wealthy white planter father and her lovely mulatto mother, her profession as a hairdresser, her marriage to the carpenter Jacques Paris and his subsequent disappearance, her second marriage to Christophe Glapion, their fifteen children, her special friendship with Père Antoine, her repudiation of Voudou and return to the church, and the idea that she was nearly one hundred years old at the time of her death. Opinions about the character of Marie Laveau were already divided. We hear of her exemplary benevolence, but we are told that she preyed upon the superstitions of the gullible and effected the downfall of innocent females through her activities as a procuress. Never, in any of these nineteenth-century sources, is there any indication that Marie Laveau was succeeded by her daughter.

*   *   *

The first half of the twentieth century saw more fantastic embellishments and reiterations of the legend. Voudou was perceived as irresistibly scary and enticingly erotic. Marie Laveau, a tempting combination of black magic with beauty and sexuality, was an ideal subject, and it was during the 1920s–1940s that her evil reputation really evolved. Sensational stories concocted by newspaper reporters of the 1870s–1890s were avidly incorporated into the Laveau Legend, and the works of Cable, Hearn, and Castellanos were freely interpreted.

Between about 1915 and the mid-1930s there was a resurgence of interest in Marie Laveau and Voudou, which by then had come to be spelled *voodoo* (usually not capitalized), a term encompassing everything from the African-based religion in Louisiana and Haiti to Southern hoodoo and European-style black magic. This renewed focus on New Orleans Voudou coincided with the U.S. Marine occupation of Haiti between 1915 and 1934. The marines were deployed for the stated purpose of "stabilizing" Haitian politics and protecting American interests during World War I. They were soon engaged in quelling an indigenous rebellion and suppressing "voodooism." Shocking reports of zombies and human sacrifice began to flow out of Haiti. Public fascination was fueled by a number of travel memoirs, written by marines and others, that range from paternalistic to scurrilous.[18] New Orleans journalists jumped on this bandwagon, producing some highly imaginative articles illustrated with lurid depictions of "voodoo orgies," while more serious authors added their efforts to this genre as well. These writers eschewed the zombie-cannibal theme and concentrated on Marie Laveau. It is also during this period that we first hear of the alleged "Marie II." The most influential contributors to the Laveau Legend during these years were G. William Nott, Lyle Saxon, Herbert Asbury, and Zora Neale Hurston.

The New Orleans journalist George William Nott (1869–1946) first wrote about Marie Laveau in 1915 in a *New Orleans American* article, and in 1922 the *Times-Picayune* Sunday magazine printed Nott's "Marie Laveau, Long High Priestess of Voudouism in New Orleans." This piece was subtitled "Some Hitherto Unpublished Stories of the Voudou Queen," and one suspects that they were unpublished because Nott invented them. Nott proposed that the real Queen of the Voudous was born in 1827 to the first Marie Laveau and Christophe Glapion. Nott is also responsible for the tale of Marie's acquisition of her home on St. Ann Street by magical means and of her nearly drowning in Lake Pontchartrain in the mid-1880s. Many writers have repeated Nott's comment, credited to "an old gentlemen who remembers her from childhood days," that Marie Laveau had a "Voltairian look, penetrating and taking in everything at a glance." She was "held in dread by many of the residents below Canal Street. . . . Enlightened people have dismissed her as a crass imposter, though not denying . . . the prestige she held among her own race."[19] Nott's articles were not generally known outside New Orleans, but they were incorporated into other works of local color and popular history that saw national distribution.

Lyle Saxon (1891–1946) was affectionately known as "Mr. New Orleans," a man of great personal charm and a consummate raconteur. He established his literary reputation in the 1920s and 1930s, first as a journalist, then as a writer of local-color sketches and fiction, and became director of the Louisiana Writers' Project in 1936. Saxon had a particular interest in the folklore of black New Orleanians. He was fascinated by tales of Marie Laveau and Voudou, and both were included in his 1928 "series of impressions," *Fabulous New Orleans*. Marie was said to be "the subject of hundreds of tales of terror and wonder," and her name was "used to frighten children." Inspired by G. William Nott, Saxon proclaimed that the original Marie Laveau was succeeded by the daughter who was born in 1827.[20]

Herbert Asbury (1891–1963) was a New Yorker whose "informal histories" include *The Gangs of New York* (1926) and similar volumes on San Francisco and Chicago. In 1935 Asbury arrived in New Orleans to research the "criminal history of the wickedest city in the world." *The French Quarter: An Informal History of the New Orleans Underground* was published in 1936. It is here that the Laveau Legend really took shape, and Asbury's imaginative rendering of the story greatly influenced later writers. In this work Asbury gathered together snippets of material from various printed sources and fashioned them into an entertaining and highly readable product. He not only recycled nineteenth-century newspaper articles and elements introduced by earlier writers, he embellished stories already in circulation and created new ones.[21]

The first serious study of New Orleans' magico-religious practices was undertaken by the African American anthropologist and novelist Zora Neale Hurston (1891–1960), who referred to the Crescent City as the "Hoodoo Capital of America." Her use of the term *hoodoo* instead of the earlier *Voudou* or even *voodoo* is indicative of the twentieth-century concern with magical spells and charms rather than devotion to the spirits, the saints, and the ancestors. Hurston made several extended trips to New Orleans between 1928 and 1930, where she sought out hoodoo workers and asked to be taken as an apprentice. In an August 6, 1928, letter to her colleague Langston Hughes, Hurston announced that "I have landed in the kingdom of Marie Laveau and expect to wear her crown someday." A page from Hurston's personal expense notebook listed "materials for altar—candies 40¢, flowers 50¢, incense 10¢, cantaloupe 25¢, candles $1.60."[22] Unfortunately, Hurston's New Orleans field notes have been lost. Her findings were published in the October–December 1931 *Journal of American Folklore* as "Hoodoo in America," and a shorter version appeared in her 1935 book *Mules and Men*. Although much of Hurston's Marie Laveau material was gleaned from earlier published sources, in *Mules and Men* she creatively transformed it into a history recounted by the mentor she called "Luke Turner," supposedly Marie's grandnephew.[23]

* * *

The archival documents, newspaper articles, and oral histories collected by the Louisiana Writers' Project were also absorbed into the Laveau Legend. After the shutdown of the Federal Writers' Project, the state offices were instructed to transfer all of their data to the Library of Congress. LWP director Lyle Saxon, however, retained the folklore files for his personal use.[24] Before Saxon had a chance to undertake the project for which he planned to use this material, he was stricken with cancer and died in 1946. In that same year, with Saxon's apparent endorsement, Robert Tallant published his flamboyant and sexually titillating *Voodoo in New Orleans*, replete with lurid tales of nudity, drunkenness, devil worship, snake handling, blood drinking, the devouring of live chickens and dead cats, and interracial sexual orgies. Tallant skillfully reworked the "Voodoo" manuscript created by LWP employee Catherine Dillon, combining bits and pieces of the oral histories, changing the names of informants, and concocting fictitious interviews when needed to prove some point. To this he added dubious "facts" culled from the earlier works of Cable, Hearn, Castellanos, Nott, Saxon, and Asbury (he ignored Hurston), and stirred it all together into a smoothly written mélange, seldom citing his sources. *Voodoo in New Orleans* has been the primary vehicle for the perpetuation of the Laveau Legend, influencing virtually everything written in the latter half of the twentieth century.

An interesting variation on the Laveau Legend was proposed by Helen Holdredge, a writer of popular history in the tradition of Herbert Asbury and Robert Tallant. In her 1952 book *Mammy Pleasant*, Holdredge created a fictionalized biography of Mary Ellen ("Mammy") Pleasant, a free woman of color now called the "mother of civil rights in California." Pleasant became widely known in nineteenth-century San Francisco as a highly successful entrepreneur, an abolitionist, and a supporter of John Brown's attempted slave revolt. Holdredge's *Mammy Pleasant* is an assemblage of source material of variable credibility, fleshed out with imagined incidents, conversations, and steamy love scenes. She postulated that Mary Ellen Pleasant, while involved with antislavery activities in New Orleans, served an apprenticeship with Marie Laveau. Here, according to Holdredge, Pleasant not only gained knowledge of Voudou theology, but also absorbed Marie's method of using secrets to manipulate the holders of social, political, and financial power.

Holdredge appears to have extracted some of her material from Tallant's *Voodoo in New Orleans*. Her description of a ceremony allegedly conducted by Mary Ellen Pleasant at a rural site outside San Francisco is suspiciously close to Tallant's portrayals of New Orleans Voudou rites. The entertainments said by Holdredge to have been held by Pleasant, in which she provided young women of color for wealthy white San Franciscans—and subsequently blackmailed them—are too close to Tallant's representation of Marie Laveau's "orgies" to be coincidental.[25]

In addition to these popular histories, Marie Laveau has been the subject of three novels—*The Voodoo Queen* (1956) by Robert Tallant, followed by Francine Prose's *Marie Laveau* (1977), and *Voodoo Dreams: A Novel of Marie Laveau* by Jewell Parker Rhodes (1993). Tallant's novel, while full of inaccuracies, at least has some basis in the archival evidence and oral histories collected by the Louisiana Writers' Project. Prose has written a work of pure fantasy in which Marie is envisioned as a mythic and magical figure, a combination of spirituality and eroticism. Rhodes' *Voodoo Dreams* is a historical bodice-ripper oozing gratuitous sex and violence. All of these authors rely on the popular conception of the Laveau Legend, with which they have sometimes taken great liberties. In these novels we find the evolution of the supposed relationship between Marie Laveau and the renowned New Orleans conjurer Doctor John, said to have been her teacher, her lover, or her bitter adversary.

The Laveau Legend naturally lends itself to dramatization and has re-emerged as a "Voodoo opera," composed as a Ph.D. dissertation by John Carbon (1983), a film by Stephen Hank titled *The Widow Paris* (1991), the play *Gris-Gris* created in 1998 by Daniel Du Plantis, and the still-evolving and as yet unperformed musical, "Voodoo on the Bayou," by Wendy Mae Chambers. In all of these works, the legend has been creatively altered to suit the requirements of the art form.

*   *   *

Throughout most of the twentieth century, an astonishing number of academics accepted the Laveau Legend without question, quoting the usual sources—particularly Tallant's sensationalized rendition of the Louisiana Writers' Project interviews from *Voodoo in New Orleans*—and even incorporating "information" gleaned from the works of fiction discussed above. Apparently Marie Laveau was considered too trivial a subject to merit the arduous research necessary for discovering the truth.[26]

This changed in the 1990s, when scholars in the fields of folklore, anthropology, and religious studies began to move beyond the stereotypes and re-examine the role of Marie Laveau as a female religious leader. Some of these writers have analyzed the work of earlier authors, while others have conducted primary archival research and made use of the Louisiana Writers' Project interviews. Nineteenth-century journalists and popular historians could not reconcile the idea of Marie Laveau as a virtuous and exemplary Christian with her leadership of the Voudou congregation. If she were indeed good, she could not have been the Queen of the Voudous; if she were the Queen of the Voudous, she could not have been good. Today's writers, such as Barbara Rosendale (Duggal), Ina Fandrich, Rachelle Sussman, Susheel Bibbs, Martha Ward, and Barbara Trevigne, are able to see her as both.[27]

Returning to the laudatory obituaries and remembrances that followed her death, the Voudou Queen is now visualized as a traditional healer, a kind and charitable woman, a devout Roman Catholic, and a Voudou priestess. In addition, she is characterized as an abolitionist and community leader and a role model for her race and gender. In the current zeal to portray Marie Laveau as the quintessential "strong black woman," new elements have entered the legend.

Ina Fandrich completed her Ph.D. in religious studies at Temple University in 1994. Her dissertation, "Mysterious Voodoo Queen Marie Laveaux: A Study of Female Leadership in Nineteenth-Century New Orleans," was the first treatment of Marie Laveau based on archival research since the work of the Louisiana Writers' Project. Here Fandrich introduced the idea that Marie was an antislavery activist, stating that although she and Christophe Glapion "occasionally engaged in buying and selling enslaved persons," this was "not an investment strategy, but was always connected with a stipulation to liberate their 'purchase.'" Although Fandrich's revised dissertation was not published in book form until 2005, her theories had already been widely disseminated through lectures and interviews.[28]

Susheel Bibbs, in her 1998 publication *Heritage of Power: Marie LaVeau—Mary Ellen Pleasant*, explored the legendary relationship between Laveau and Pleasant, offering a rebuttal to Helen Holdredge's negative portrayal in *Mammy Pleasant*. While Holdredge used the association between Marie Laveau and Mary Ellen Pleasant to bolster her assessment of Pleasant as an evil- doer, Bibbs cast it in a positive light, as the pivotal occurrence in Pleasant's career. Mary Ellen Pleasant, wrote Bibbs, became the pupil of the "humane and powerful leader" Marie Laveau, who used her religion "to aid the disenfranchised of New Orleans." Using Marie as her role model, Pleasant "learned to mentor her people and to effect methods of gaining and using the secrets of the powerful to garner their aid of the powerless." Following Fandrich's lead, Susheel Bibbs also characterized Marie Laveau as an abolitionist who helped slaves to escape from bondage.[29]

Anthropologist Martha Ward authored the 2004 study, *Voodoo Queen: The Spirited Lives of Marie Laveau*. Ward presented Marie Laveau as "two women with the same name—a mother and daughter," who led "dangerous and secret lives" as leaders of the Afro-Creole community. Both, according to Ward, "helped slave families disappear, defied the pro-slavery laws about 'illegal assembly,' and hypnotized, blackmailed, or bribed judges and policemen on behalf of people of color."[30]

*　*　*

In keeping with the African tradition by which powerful and honored ancestors are accorded the status of a deity, Marie Laveau is now experiencing a sort of Voudou canonization. In 1999 the contemporary New Orleans Voudou priestess Sallie Ann Glassman announced in an interview with the *Times-Picayune* that the spirit of Marie Laveau had "entered her own body the evening before during a ceremony on Bayou St. John." Glassman's book, *Vodou Visions: An Encounter with Divine Mystery* (2000), is a series of "visions" of the Haitian Vodou deities called *lwa*. Marie Laveau is saluted as a "historical lwa of New Orleans; Vodou Queen; strong, intelligent, wise and powerful woman. . . . Hear her drum rhythms pulsing like blood. It is the ongoing passage of the bloodline in the eternal feminine."[31]

Table 1. Evolution of the Laveau Legend

Date	Element of Legend	Source
1850	First mention of Marie Laveau in local newspaper; referred to as "head of the Voudou women."	"Curious Charge of Swindling," *Picayune*, July 3, 1850.
1869	Marie said to have retired.	"Voodooism," *Commercial Bulletin*, July 5, 1869.
1871	Marie's ministry to condemned prisoners.	"The Condemned," *Picayune*, May 10, 1871.
1872	First mention of the Maison Blanche/White House.	"Making a Night of It," *Times*, June 26, 1872.
1873	Mamma Caroline takes Marie's place on St. John's Eve.	"St. John's Eve—The Voudous," *Picayune*, June 4, 1873.
1875	Madame Frazie takes Marie's place on St. John's Eve.	"Fetish Worship," *Times*, June 25, 1875.
1875	Sanité Dédé cited as reigning Voudou priestess of the 1820s; wore her tignon in seven points; ceremonies held in an abandoned brickyard.	Williams, "A Night with the Voudous," *Appleton's Journal*, March 27, 1875.
1875	Marie said to have abandoned Voudou and joined the Catholic Church.	"Fetish–Its Worship and Worshipers," *Picayune*, June 24, 1875.
1880	Palmyre la Philosophe, a character based on Marie Laveau, portrayed as a hairdresser and a Voudou priestess.	Cable, *The Grandissimes*, 1880.
1881	Marie died at age 98. Father, a white planter, was member of the state legislature; mother was Marguerite Henry; grandmother was Marguerite Semard. Jacques Paris, a carpenter, disappeared one year after marrying Marie. Christophe Glapion was captain of the colored Men of Santo Domingo in the War of 1815; Marie and Christophe had fifteen children.	Obituaries, *Picayune* and *City Item*, June 17, 1881; *New York Times*, June 23, 1881.
1881	Story about a sorceress and her daughter, possible inspiration for idea of Marie I and II.	Hearn, "El Vomito," *City Item*, March 21, 1881.
1883	Introduction of Moreau de Saint-Méry's description of a Vodou ceremony in eighteenth-century Saint Domingue.	Allain, *Souvenirs d'Amérique*, 1883.

Date	Element of Legend	Source
1885	First mention of Doctor John in a national publication.	Hearn, "The Last of the Voudoos," *Harper's Weekly*, November 7, 1885.
1886	First mention of Marie Laveau in a national publication; illustration of Marie and her daughter; first English translation of Moreau de Saint-Méry's description of a Vodou ceremony in Saint-Domingue.	Cable, "Creole Slave Songs, *Century Magazine*, April, 1886.
1894–95	Marie said to be a hairdresser and a procuress; "poisoned gumbo" administered to condemned prisoner Antoine Cambre; Doctor Jim Alexander and "Pedro Prince of Darkness" cited as Marie's successors.	Castellanos, *New Orleans As It Was*, 1995.
1900	Marie's mother and grandmother said to be Voudou priestesses; the "Congre Noir" cited as Marie's successor; introduction of the snake deity "Grand Zombi."	*Picayune's Guide to New Orleans* for 1900.
1920	Marie's near-drowning in Lake Pontchartrain.	"A Sketch of Marie Laveau," cited by Dillon as *City Item*, December 12, 1920.
1922	Marie's daughter, born Feb. 2, 1827, was the Voudou Queen; Marie received her house from a grateful client.	Nott, "Marie Laveau, Long High Priestess of Voudouism" *Times-Picayune*, Nov. 19, 1922.
Before 1927		Introduction of the "Marie Laveau Routines." Hurston, *Mules and Men*, 1935.
1828	Marie succeeded by her daughter.	*Life and Works of Marie Laveau*, n.d.
1931	There were three Marie Laveaus: grandmother, mother, and daughter; Marie could control the behavior of policemen; Marie rose out of Lake Pontchartrain and walked across the water on St. John's Eve.	Saxon, *Fabulous New Orleans*, 1928; Hurston, "Hoodoo in America," 1931.

continued

Table 1—*Continued*

Date	Element of Legend	Source
1935	Doctor Jim Alexander was Marie's mentor; Marie kept a rattlesnake.	Hurston, *Mules and Men*, 1935.
1936	Slave Pauline Rebennack was a client of Doctor John; introduction of Marie's rival, Rosalie; Marie ministered to the prisoners Adam and Delille, Mullen, Haas, Smith, Lindsay, and Bazar; Marie was consulted by the Basin Street madam Fanny Sweet.	Asbury, *The French Quarter*, 1936.
1940	Introduction of names "Marie I" and "Marie II."	Catherine Dillon, "Voodoo" manuscript.
1946	Concept of "Marie I" and "Marie II" more fully developed; Marie and Jacques lived in a house given to Marie by her father as a part of her dowry; Marie wore her tignon in seven points; Marie was the successor of Sanité Dédé and Marie Saloppé.	Tallant, *Voodoo in New Orleans*, 1946.
1956	Marie's mother and grandmother were Voudou priestesses in Saint-Domingue; Doctor John was Marie's rival; Marie Philomène succeeded her mother.	Tallant, *The Voodoo Queen*, 1956.
1991	Role of Marie Laveau as a female religious leader is reexamined.	Rosendale, "The Voodoo Queen Repossessed," 1991.
1994	Marie and Christophe were antislavery activists.	Fandrich, "Mysterious Voodoo Queen," 1994.
2000	Marie is elevated to the status of a lwa.	Sallie Ann Glassman, *Vodou Visions*, 2000.

Part I

The Colonial Past

Marie Laveau's genealogy serves as a paradigm for race relations during the first two hundred years of Louisiana's history. Born around 1801, she was descended from French colonists, from Africans who had the misfortune to be slaves, and from racially mixed free people of color. These men and women crossed the color line to form domestic partnerships and employed strategies to circumvent the increasingly repressive laws against the amalgamation of African and European blood and the flow of white prosperity into black hands. In each generation born in the New World during the eighteenth and nineteenth centuries, at least one of Marie's kinswomen had children by a white man. Within seven generations, the lineage founded by ancestors of pure African origin had produced descendants who were legally classified as white.

The French Settlement

Marie Laveau's family history begins in the earliest days of the Louisiana colony. The Louisiana Territory was claimed by France in 1682, during the reign of King Louis XIV. Louisiana originally consisted of a vast swath of land from Canada to the Gulf of Mexico, lying between the Mississippi River and the Rocky Mountains and extending along the Gulf Coast from Spanish-held Florida to what is now Texas. In 1712 Louis XIV granted a fifteen-year proprietary contract to the merchant Antoine Crozat, but within a few years Crozat realized that nothing was to be gained in Louisiana and opted out of the bargain. In 1717 the territory came under the administration of the Company of the West, later called the Company of the Indies. The Company was the creation of John Law, a Scots gambler and financial speculator, who with the backing of the French crown promised investors huge profits from thriving tobacco plantations, gold and silver mines, pearl fisheries, and a lucrative fur trade.

In 1718 the Canadian-born explorers Pierre Le Moyne, Sieur de Iberville, and his brother Jean Baptiste Le Moyne, Sieur de Bienville, selected a location about one hundred miles from the mouth of the Mississippi, where the river makes a majestic crescent, coming within five miles of the lake the French called Pontchartrain. There they established the "Crescent City" of *La Nou-*

velle Orléans as the capital of the Louisiana colony. In 1721, the French military engineer La Tour de la Blond drew the plan for the original town in a perfect grid pattern, nine squares wide by six squares deep, and his assistant Adrien de Pauger laid out the streets. The parish church of St. Louis (now St. Louis Cathedral) and the Place d'Armes (the public square and military parade ground now called Jackson Square) were given the most prominent location, front and center facing the river. A portage route connected the rear of the town to Bayou St. John and thus to Lake Pontchartrain and the Gulf of Mexico. A rudimentary levee was built to contain the Mississippi River. The town was surrounded by rough wooden ramparts, and outside this barrier lay the wilderness. The area known today as the French Quarter or *Vieux Carré* (Old Square) was bounded by the Mississippi River and what is now Esplanade Avenue on the downtown side, Canal Street on the uptown side, and Rampart Street (named for the ramparts that once protected the settlement) toward the "back-of-town" stretching away to Lake Pontchartrain.

Although it was depicted by its promoters as "the New Paris," New Orleans was a miserable place during most of the French colonial period. Situated in the middle of a swamp and subject to periodic flooding from the Mississippi River, it was little more than a huddle of wooden shacks in a sea of mud, plagued by insects, tropical diseases, poor sanitation, and food shortages. The town was occupied by government and military officials, a contingent of soldiers, members of Roman Catholic religious orders, a raggedy collection of white male settlers and indentured servants, a few white women of questionable virtue, some indigenous Indians, and enslaved Africans.

By 1731 the speculative bubble created by the Company of the Indies had deflated, and Louisiana reverted to the French crown. The colony was thereafter directed by a military governor, a civilian administrator called the *commissaire-ordonnateur*, and a *Conseil Supérieur* (Superior Council) of leading planters and merchants. It was regulated by French civil law, known as the *Coutume de Paris* (Custom of Paris), which had its origin in Roman law.[1]

As was the case elsewhere in the Americas, the French first attempted to enslave native peoples. Most of these Indian slaves were women, who grew and prepared food, performed domestic tasks, and served as sexual partners. But when the colonists required workers to construct buildings, clear swampland, build levees, dig drainage ditches, cut firewood, cultivate cash crops, and tend livestock, they wanted Africans. As one government official put it, the Indians "only cause us trouble and [we receive from them] very little service since they are not appropriate for hard labor like the blacks."[2] Soon the first enslaved Africans began to arrive, and the struggling colony became increasingly dependent on their knowledge and abilities.

Between 1719 and 1731 the Company of the Indies was licensed by the French government to control the commerce between France and the African slave-trading nations. An internal slave trade already existed in West Africa, where prisoners of war were enslaved by the victors, criminals were punished by enslavement, and debtors were sold to pay their obligation. But the demand for unfree labor for the European colonies, which had grown insatiable by the eighteenth century, prompted African potentates to wage war and conduct raids against their neighbors to procure captives for the Atlantic slave trade.

From the French port cities of Nantes, Bordeaux, Rouen, St. Malo, Le Havre, La Rochelle, and Lorient, ships stocked with trade goods sailed for the west coast of Africa, stopping to transact business at the infamous "slave forts." These were actually fortified warehouse complexes, established by the Portuguese, Dutch, Danish, Swedish, English, and French with the cooperation of African rulers who grew rich from this traffic. There, captive men, women, and children were held in dungeons awaiting the arrival of European ships, and goods such as textiles, firearms, iron, brandy, and tobacco were bartered for Africans destined for bondage in the Americas. The slave ships also carried thousands of pounds of cowrie shells from the Maldive Islands off the coast of India. The shells, almost worthless to Europeans, were originally employed as ballast and packing material. The Africans, however, considered them a desirable commodity, and European slave traders began to use cowries as currency for paying workers, buying food, and purchasing human beings. After trading their goods for a full contingent of "cargo," the slavers embarked on the "middle passage" to the Americas. Although ships' captains tried to make the trip in about seven weeks, it often took much longer, and captives and crew alike died of starvation, bacterial infections, and deficiency diseases. The Africans who survived the voyage were exchanged in the French colonies for sugar, rice, indigo, cotton, and tobacco that was subsequently exported to Europe.[3]

Twenty-three slave ships landed in Louisiana during the French colonial period, delivering a total of 5,951 men, women, and children. Sixteen of the ships traded goods for captives at the Senegal Concession at Gorée Island, conveying to Louisiana 3,909 Wolofs, Bambaras, Foulbes, and Mandingas from the region between the Senegal and Gambia rivers, now the nations of Senegal, Gambia, Sierra Leone, Guinea-Bisseau, Ghana, and Mali. These Senegambians were sometimes referred to in old records as "Guinea negroes." Six of the ships conducted their unsavory business at Whydah (also called Juda or Ouidah) on the Bight of Benin, delivering 1,748 enslaved Fon and Yoruba from what are now the nations of Benin, Togo, and Nigeria. One other ship took on human cargo from the fort at Cabinda, delivering 294 Kongo and Angolan captives from what are now the Central African nations of the Democratic Republic of Congo, Cameroon, Congo-Brazzaville, Gabon, Cabinda, and Angola. Some slaves from the French colonies of Saint Domingue (now Haiti), Martinique, and Guadeloupe also entered Louisiana, and a few were seized from the ships of other nations and sold in Louisiana.[4]

The acquisition of slaves necessitated laws to regulate their management. Louisiana's 1724 *Code Noir* (Black Code) was modeled after a set of ordinances already in place in the older French colonies. It consisted of fifty-four articles. The first three articles established Roman Catholicism as the only religion permitted in the colony and excluded Protestants and Jews. Six articles set forth the harsh rules by which slaves had to abide. Enslaved persons were prohibited from carrying weapons or gathering in large groups. They could not conduct business on their own account, receive donations of money or goods, own property, or will it to their heirs, nor could they sue in court or testify against a white person. The law specified punishments—flogging, branding, bodily mutilation, and death—for theft, running away, or assaulting a free person. The balance of the articles governed the treatment of slaves and free Negroes. Masters were required to instruct their human chattel in the Roman Catholic faith, to have them baptized, and to encourage slave marriages. Enslaved women were protected from the sexual advances of their owners, and sexual relations between Europeans and free people of African descent were forbidden. Slaves were exempted from labor on Sundays and religious feast days. The restrictions and privileges of the Code Noir were loosely enforced. Some owners gave their slaves a great deal of autonomy, and others disregarded the humane provisions of the code and severely mistreated their bondspeople. The provision against concubinage between masters and slaves, and between white and nonwhite persons, was consistently ignored.[5]

In 1758 Antoine-Simon Le Page du Pratz, employed in the 1720s by the Company of the Indies as overseer of their plantation outside New Orleans, published the first history of the colony, *Histoire de la Louisiane*. Le Page counseled in his chapter on the treatment of slaves that masters who purchased captives directly from Africa must treat them kindly, lest they commit suicide or run away, but that the prudent slave owner should also "distrust them without seeming to fear them." Following the dictates of the Code Noir, he advised that slaves should be given nourishing food, adequate rest, appropriate clothing, a

CODE NOIR,

OU

RECUEIL D'EDITS,

DÉCLARATIONS ET ARRETS

CONCERNANT

Les Esclaves Négres de l'Amérique,

AVEC

Un Recueil de Réglemens , concernant la police des Isles Françoises de l'Amérique & les Engagés.

A PARIS,

Chez les LIBRAIRES ASSOCIEZ.

M. DCC. XLIII.

1. Title page of the *Code Noir*, Paris, Chez les Librairies Associez, 1743. (The Historic New Orleans Collection, accession no. 80-654-RL.)

place to bathe, and a plot of ground to cultivate "for their own profit"; that they should not be punished unjustly; that enslaved men and women should be encouraged to marry, and that child-bearing women should be cared for in "everything that their condition makes necessary." As Christians, admonished Le Page, slave owners "ought to take care that the children be baptized and instructed, since they have an immortal soul."[6]

* * *

Out of this chaotic past Marie Laveau's maternal grandmother, Catherine Henry, emerges from the archival record with great clarity. At the end of a long and eventful life, Catherine made her will, stating herself to be "a free negress about seventy-seven years of age [born in 1754], a native of New Orleans, daughter of Marguerite and of Jean Belaire, both dead a long time." She listed her four natural children, Marguerite, Joseph, Celestin, and Narcisse, as well as her grandchildren, one of whom was Marie Laveau. Finally, Catherine declared that she was "formerly the slave of Françoise Pomet, free woman of color."[7] These few lines provide the key to Marie Laveau's ancestry.

By tracing the sequence of slave ownership backward from Françoise Pomet through two interim owners, we learn that Catherine's original master was the white Creole Henry Roche *dit* (known as) Belaire.[8] Roche's signature on official documents shows that he spelled his given name *Henry*, rather than the French *Henri*. Years later, as a free woman, Catherine would take Henry as her surname.

The archival evidence shows that Henry Roche also owned Catherine's mother, Marguerite, and that Catherine was raised in the Roche household. When Roche, a widower, contracted a second marriage on February 26, 1756, an inventory was made of his goods and chattels. Roche was a master shoemaker and a man of some wealth, owning property valued at 5,349 French livres. The contents of his home on Royal Street near the corner of St. Peter included walnut and cypress furniture, bed sheets, coverlets, a lace canopy, embroidered table linens, china, silver, and kitchen utensils. Adjacent to the house was his shoemaking shop, and listed among the tools of his trade were knives, a sharpener, patterns for shoes, and a supply of leather. Most significantly, Henry Roche owned "une négresse nommée Marguerite agée d'environ vingt ans et son enfant nommée Catherine" (a negress named Marguerite aged about twenty years and her child named Catherine), valued at 900 livres.[9] Such inventories often indicated whether the slave was a Creole of Louisiana or a native of Africa, sometimes even specifying his or her African nation, but the Roche inventory is disappointingly silent regarding Marguerite.

Marguerite's age at the time of the 1756 inventory indicates that she was born about 1736. She might have been born in Louisiana to an African mother, or she herself might have been born in Africa. If so, she was probably transported to Louisiana in 1743 on the last of the French slave ships, the *St. Ursin.* The previous ship, the *St. Louis,* had left the Senegal Concession on Gorée Island in 1730, before Marguerite was born. After this the Company of the Indies was no longer licensed to import slaves. The shortage of labor eventually became so acute that two Louisiana colonists, Dubreuil and Dalcourt, entered the slave trade on their own. Their ship the *St. Ursin* sailed from the French port of La Rochelle to Gorée Island, where 220 captives were taken on board. The goal of bringing able-bodied male laborers to Louisiana was not realized—according to the pilot's log, "we found ourselves with many women and few men." There is no numerical breakdown by age and gender for the "cargo" of the *St. Ursin,* so it cannot be determined if Marguerite, who would have been seven years old, was on board. The vessel departed the African coast on June 5 and arrived in Louisiana on August 23, 1743. The Atlantic passage had taken seven weeks, and thirty of the captives died on the way.[10]

Marguerite (or her mother) was most likely a Wolof from present-day Senegal. The Wolofs were a tall, dark-skinned people, noted for their trading and marketing traditions and considered to be extraordinarily intelligent and handsome. The French colonist Le Page du Pratz, in his 1758 *Histoire de la Louisiane,* offered advice on the suitability of the slaves of various nations for certain tasks. For "any sort of service . . . about the house," he recommended "Doilaufs" (Wolofs), because they "have the purest blood. . . . They have more fidelity and greater understanding than [slaves of other nations], and are consequently fitter for learning a trade. . . . They are good commanders over other negroes." While only one-third of the Africans brought to Louisiana by the French were women, almost all of those women were Wolofs, chosen for their desirability as domestic servants.[11]

Marie Laveau's great-grandfather, Jean Belaire, remains a mystery. He may have been African-born, he may have been a Louisiana Creole, and there is even the possibility that he was an Indian, accounting for the frequently repeated story of Marie's African, European, and Native American ancestry. The fact that Catherine Henry knew her father's identity indicates that her parents were an established couple. The name Belaire suggests that Jean was the bondsman of Henry Roche or of Henry's father, Arnaud Roche *dit* Belaire, but Jean

Belaire appears nowhere in the inventories of the Roche family or in the eighteenth-century records of slave purchases and sales.

* * *

The Sundays and holidays granted to the slaves by the Code Noir, and the additional time off allowed by some masters, were not only devoted to rest and recreation. Enslaved men and women also used the time to cultivate their own gardens, hunt and fish, trap fur-bearing animals, harvest wild plants, gather firewood, and otherwise provide for themselves and have surplus goods to sell in New Orleans. By around 1740 an area located just outside the ramparts at the end of Orleans Street was being used as a Sunday market. Originally designated the *Place des Nègres*, it later became famous as Congo Square, where Voudou dances were allegedly presided over by Marie Laveau. Despite the prohibitions of the Code Noir that forbade slaves to gather in large groups or conduct trade on their own, Africans and people of African descent congregated at the Place des Nègres to sell their produce and crafts, to socialize, and to participate in dance circles accompanied by drumming and chanting after the manner of their African nations. It is easy to imagine that Marie Laveau's ancestors were among them.

Le Page du Pratz was probably referring to this aspect of the Sunday market when he wrote, in his *Histoire de la Louisiane*, that "the negroes assemble together on Sundays.... Under pretext of the calinda [a dance], they sometimes get together to the number of three or four hundred, and make a kind of Sabbath." These "tumultuous meetings," he advised, were potentially dangerous, because the slaves "sell to each other what they have stolen . . . commit many crimes . . . [and] plot their rebellions."[12]

* * *

As soon as New Orleans was established, members of Catholic religious orders arrived to attend to the spiritual needs of the colonists. French Capuchin friars came in 1723, and by 1727 they had established the parish church of St. Louis of France and its adjacent ecclesiastical residence and administrative office called the *Presbytère*. Ursuline nuns arrived in 1727. The mission of the Ursulines was the propagation of Christianity through the instruction of women. In New Orleans, they turned their attention not only to white females but also to enslaved and free Negro and Indian women and girls. They established a school and an orphanage, and by 1730 had founded a lay confraternity called the Children of Mary, who were active in proselytizing their household slaves.

2. The Ursuline Convent. Built in 1745, the convent still stands at the corner of Chartres and Ursulines streets and is the oldest building in the Mississippi Valley. Illustration by Joseph Pennell for George Washington Cable's "Who Are the Creoles," *The Century Magazine*, January 1883, p. 388. (Author's collection.)

As required by the Code Noir, these pious women saw to it that bondspeople, adults as well as children, were baptized, that they attended Mass, and that they were given a Christian burial.[13] We know from the sacramental records of St. Louis Cathedral that Marie Laveau's grandmother, Catherine Henry, was a practicing Catholic; she may have been brought into the faith through the efforts of the Ursulines or the Children of Mary.

We can have no certain knowledge of the spiritual beliefs held by Marie Laveau's enslaved ancestors. They might have been Muslim or even Christian, but they more likely practiced one of the many variations of African traditional religion. Upon arrival in Louisiana, they would have become at least nominally Roman Catholic. When enslaved Africans were exposed to Catholicism, they found many elements to which they could relate. The supreme being common to most indigenous African belief systems was analogous to God the Father, and the deities and ancestors who serve as intermediaries between men and the supreme being became identified with Mary the Blessed Mother and the legion of saints. The rituals, music, vestments and miracle-working objects of the Catholic Church seemed intrinsically familiar to Africans whose religious ceremonies stressed chanting, drumming, dance, elaborate costumes, and the use of spirit-embodying charms. Through a process of creative borrowing and adaptation, they reinterpreted Roman Catholicism to suit their own needs, occasioning the evolution of the New World Afro-Catholic religions of Haitian Vodou, Cuban Santería, Brazilian Candomblé, and New Orleans Voudou. Marie Laveau's ancestors would have discovered the compatibility of African religious beliefs with Catholicism, moving easily between the two as the occasion required.

*   *   *

Catherine Henry, Marie's grandmother, is described in the archival record as a *négresse*, a woman of pure African descent, not as a *mulâtresse*, a woman of mixed race. We therefore know that she was not fathered by a white man, a frequent occurrence in colonial New Orleans. The development of a population of biracial *gens de couleur libres*—the free people of color—began in the earliest days of the Louisiana colony. The pioneering French settlers usually did not bring wives, and the white women who departed for Louisiana were often prostitutes and other less-than-respectable females from the houses of correction. As a result, there were frequent sexual encounters between white men and enslaved women. Even when the ratio of white women to white men became more equal, slave owners continued to form sexual liaisons with their bondswomen and to father their children. While most of these relationships are now defined as coercion or rape because of the unequal balance of power between the man and woman, there may have been some instances of mutual attachment. The status of a child followed that of the mother at the time of birth. The child of a slave mother was automatically a slave, and the child of a free mother was automatically free. The status of the father was of no consequence.

Some slaves were freed voluntarily out of affection and gratitude for faithful service, a process that required the permission of the Superior Council. This did not necessarily indicate a sexual or familial bond between the slave and the owner, but when we find a negress and her mulatto children being emancipated by a white master, we can reasonably infer that a more intimate relationship existed. Adult men were also emancipated by both male and female owners, and some men earned their liberty by serving in the militia. In addition, slaves could be purchased and freed by some other interested party. Self purchase, by means of which enslaved persons literally "bought themselves," was possible, but the practice was discouraged because slaves had no legitimate means of earning money, and it was feared that they would resort to thievery to obtain their purchase price. If an owner refused to manumit his or her bondspeople or allow them to be bought by a third party or to purchase their own freedom, there was no recourse. Faced with this dilemma, slaves sometimes escaped into the cypress swamps and bayous to form settlements with other fugitives and local Indians. These runaways were called *marrons*, or, in English, *maroons*.

The Spanish Town

Compared to Canada and the highly remunerative Caribbean colonies, the French government considered Louisiana a dead weight. In 1763 the king of France was happy to unload Louisiana onto the Spanish as "compensation" for Spain's loss of Florida in the Seven Years' War, in which the French and Spanish fought as allies against England. Faced with Spanish domination, the inhabitants of Louisiana petitioned the king to take them back, but France had no wish to retain a colony that had never been anything but a financial drain. Louisiana existed in a state of uncertainty for the next six years. The newly appointed Spanish governor, Antonio de Ulloa, lacked the will and the resources to assume leadership, and French Creole merchants, planters, and officials finally banished him from the colony. In 1769, Captain-General Alejandro O'Reilly, an Irish mercenary in the employ of the Spanish crown, was sent to New Orleans with a contingent of 2,100 troops to impose control. The leaders of the rebellion against Spanish rule were executed and their fellow conspirators were sentenced to prison in Havana's Morro Castle.[14] The French governor was superseded by a Spanish governor, and the Superior Council was replaced by the *Cabildo*, composed of twelve prominent citizens called *regidores* who served as city councilmen and judges.

The French clergy remained in New Orleans until 1772, when Spanish Capuchin friars arrived to replace them. In 1793, the Diocese of Louisiana and the Floridas was created, a bishop was installed in New Orleans, and the Church of St. Louis became St. Louis Cathedral. The Spanish Capuchin Fray Antonio de Sedella, known as "Père Antoine," served for the rest of his life as a priest of the cathedral. Over 3,500 baptisms, marriages, and funerals were performed by Père Antoine and entered, in Spanish, into the sacramental registers in his tiny, almost medieval script. He officiated at many of the important rites of passage for Marie Laveau and her kin.[15]

*   *   *

The French ceased to import enslaved Africans after 1743. With the exception of those who were smuggled into the colony, no new workers arrived directly from Africa until 1776, when the slave trade was reopened under the Spanish administration. While the captives came from the same African nations as those arriving during the French colonial period, the percentages were different. There were some Senegambians and more Kongo people from Central Africa, but the greatest number were Fon and Yoruba from the Bight of Benin. In addition to bondspeople brought directly from Africa, enslaved Africans were also reexported to Louisiana from the islands of Jamaica, Dominica, Cuba, Saint Domingue, and Martinique by English, Spanish, and French traders.[16]

Spanish laws regarding slavery and manumission would have a profound effect on Marie Laveau's grandmother, Catherine Henry. Like the French legal system, Spanish law was derived from Roman civil law. The Spanish, however, introduced a new and considerably more liberal black code, the *Codigo Negro*, based on *La Recopilación de Castilla* (the law of Castile), *La Recopilación de leyes de las reynos de las Indias* (the law of the Spanish West Indian colonies), and *Las Siete Partidas* (the law of seven parts). Enslavement of Indians was forbidden. The slavery of people of African descent was not considered to be a permanent condition, and Spanish law provided many avenues by which a bondsperson could obtain his or her *carta de libertad* (certificate of liberty). Slave owners were no longer required to obtain government approval for manumission. Masters could free their slaves voluntarily, either during their lifetimes or in their wills, with no financial compensation. Also included in the Spanish Codigo Negro was the practice known as *coartación*, the right of slaves to purchase their freedom for a price agreed upon by their masters. If the slave owner refused or set the price unreasonably high, the enslaved person could petition the governor's tribunal to assess his or her monetary value, and a carta de libertad was issued upon receipt of this sum. The same procedure applied to third-party purchase by a relative, lover, or friend.

In contrast to the restrictive provisions of the French Code Noir, which prohibited slaves from conducting business, receiving donations, or owning property, during the Spanish colonial period slaves could legally accumulate wealth. Skilled artisans hired themselves out for wages; others marketed their crafts or produce. They were allowed to keep a portion of their earnings and could use this money to purchase their freedom or the freedom of a loved one. Sometimes individuals who were themselves still enslaved used their pay to liberate another slave. Toward the end of the eighteenth century, self purchase and third-party purchase became more common than voluntary manumission, indicating that people of African descent had greater opportunities to earn money and more highly developed networks of support among kinsmen and friends. Over eight hundred slaves were freed between 1769, when the Spanish arrived to govern the colony, and 1803, the date of the Louisiana Purchase. The number of free people of African descent increased from 7.1 percent of the population of New Orleans in 1769 to 33.5 percent in 1805, when the first census was taken after the transfer of Louisiana to the United States.[17]

The change from French to Spanish rule occurred as Catherine Henry was growing up in the household of Henry Roche *dit* Belaire. In 1770 Roche turned his house and shoemaking shop on Royal Street over to his adult son and moved with the rest of his family to the corner of Bourbon and St. Louis. His wife Catherine Laurandine made her will on August 26, 1782, and died on September 11 of that year. Included in her succession is an inventory of the property acquired during her marriage to Henry Roche and held jointly with her husband—the house at Bourbon and St. Louis, furniture, clothing, and five slaves. Among the Roches' bondspersons were "una negra nombrada Cathalina criolla de edad de veinte y ocho anos con su hijo Josef, mulato de quatro meses" (a negress named Catherine, Creole of the age of twenty-eight years, with her son Joseph, a mulatto of four months). Catherine was specified as a "lavandera, cocinera, y planchadera" (laundress, cook, and ironer). Together, Catherine and Joseph were valued at 750 pesos (the Spanish peso was equivalent to the American dollar). Also listed was "una mulata de edad dies años criollo" (a Creole mulatress age ten years) valued at 400 pesos. Although this girl is not named, she was probably Catherine's daughter Marguerite. Catherine's mother, who would have been around forty-six by then, had disappeared from the Roche family inventory.[18]

All of Catherine's children were born in slavery, and all were classified as mulattos, indicating that they were fathered by one or more white men—possibly Henry Roche, his son, or a subsequent owner. While many white men freed their slave concubines, acknowledged their biracial offspring, and provided for their future security, no such solicitude was bestowed on Catherine. Rather than being liberated, she was sold and separated from her children.

Catherine's first two children, Marguerite and Joseph, were born while she was the slave of Henry Roche *dit* Belaire. On September 30, 1784, when she was thirty years old, Roche sold Catherine, along with two-year-old Joseph, to Bartolomé Magnon for 750 pesos.[19] He retained possession of Catherine's daughter Marguerite, by then about twelve years old. Magnon, who was related to Roche by marriage, only served as a middleman. Five days later he sold

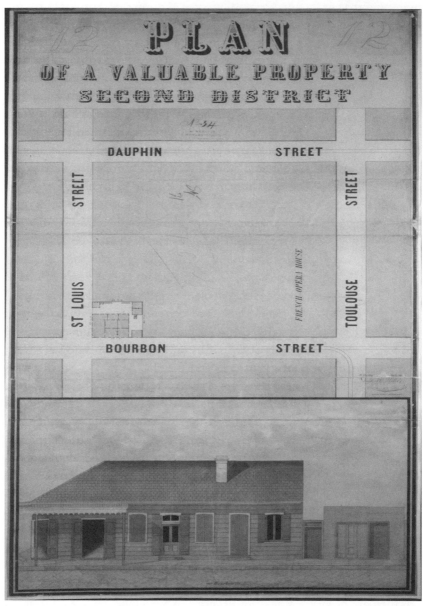

3. Home and shoemaking shop of Henry Roche *dit* Belaire, corner of Bourbon and St. Louis (now 501-507 Bourbon Street). In 1770 Roche moved to this location with his family and his slaves, one of whom was Marie Laveau's grandmother Catherine. Catherine's children, Joseph and Marguerite (Marie's mother), were born in this house. (Notarial Archives Research Center, Plan Book 100, folio 11.)

Catherine and her little boy to the merchant Jean Joseph Bizot for 800 pesos, making a small profit. Roche and Bizot were neighbors, living a few blocks from each other in the Vieux Carré, and had served together as *fusileros* in the Company of Grenadiers under General Bernardo de Galvez against the English.[20]

Catherine remained the slave of Joseph Bizot for four years, giving birth to another child in early 1788. On August 12 of that year, Bizot sold Catherine and her unidentified eight-month-old mulatto son (probably Celestin) to Françoise Mazan Pomet, a free woman of color. It must be kept in mind, when discussing Louisiana slavery, that as the community of free people of color increased in size and wealth, they also owned slaves. While some purchased their loved ones in order to free them, others bought and sold slaves for the same reasons as whites. Françoise Pomet was not a kinswoman of Catherine's but a hard-headed business woman who was actively engaged in slave trading.[21] She appears to have purchased Catherine as an investment.

The transaction, enacted before the notary Raphael Perdomo, specifies the sale of the thirty-three-year-old Creole negress and her nursing infant, who "has no proper name because he is not yet baptized." Bizot guaranteed Catherine to be free of vices and maladies and to be a woman of good character. The sale price for Catherine and her son was 850 pesos; Françoise Pomet gave 400 pesos in cash and agreed to pay Bizot the remainder by the end of the year.[22] Joseph Bizot kept Catherine's older son, Joseph, finally freeing him gratis on July 4, 1791, at the age of ten years. This act, according to Bizot, was performed in fulfillment of "a promise to the child's mother, Catalina [Catherine], who was sold."[23]

On January 13, 1795, Catherine, by then age forty-two, appeared with her mistress Françoise Pomet before the notary Carlos Ximines to purchase her freedom for 600 pesos cash. Pomet stated that she entered into the emancipation of Catherine "voluntarily and out of charity."[24] It was common for slave owners to deploy their bondswomen to sell merchandise and foodstuffs on the street or in the city's markets, extracting a portion of their earnings and allowing the slaves to keep the balance. Françoise Pomet might have been running such an operation, which enabled Catherine to earn her purchase price. Later, as a free woman, Catherine was listed in the city directory as a *marchande* or trader.

Three years after her emancipation, on March 23, 1798, Catherine Henry bought a piece of property on the uptown side of St. Ann between Rampart

4. *Marchande des Calas*. Marie Laveau's grandmother, Catherine Henry, was listed in the city directory as a marchande, meaning that she sold foodstuffs or merchandise on the street or at the French Market. Illustration by Edward W. Kemble for George Washington Cable's "The Dance in Place Congo," *The Century Magazine*, February 1886, p. 527. (Author's collection.)

and Burgundy, and here she commissioned the construction of a simple Creole cottage that would later become famous as the home of Marie Laveau.[25]

Catherine's daughter Marguerite, who would become the mother of Marie Laveau, remained the slave of Henry Roche *dit* Belaire. On April 26, 1788, Roche made his will before the notary Pedro Pedesclaux. After a lengthy salutation to the Trinity and the Holy, Catholic, and Apostolic Church, he directed a prayer to "Mary, Mother of God, with your Most Precious Son," asking them to "pardon the gravity of my faults," and ordered that masses be said for his soul. He listed his real estate and movable property and his only remaining slave, the sixteen-year-old mulatress Marguerite. Instead of freeing this young woman, whom he may have fathered with his slave Catherine, Roche directed that Marguerite was to continue in the service of his legitimate daughter Elizabeth.

When the succession of Henry Roche was opened on March 23, 1789, Marguerite was listed in the inventory as a "lavendera, planchadera, cocinera muy poco" (laundress, ironer, cooks very little), valued at 800 pesos. The conditions of the will were not carried out, and Marguerite was sold to François Langlois for 913 pesos. On October 16, 1790, Langlois gave Marguerite her freedom for "good services and various particular deeds."[26] The relationship between Marguerite and François Langlois is unknown, and he plays no further part in her story.

*   *   *

In contrast to the exploitative sexual relationships between masters and slave women, white men and free women of color formed liaisons that, although unlawful, often resembled true marriages. Legally, this was termed *concubinage* (which refers to any domestic partnership outside of marriage regardless of the race of the parties), but in common parlance the practice was known as *plaçage*, from the French verb *placer*—to place (under a man's protection). The woman was called a *plaçée*. In contravention of laws forbidding whites to make donations to persons of color, the man would provide a small cottage and support his plaçée and their children for life, even if he also established a white family. The house became the property of the woman and could be passed on to her heirs.[27]

The prevalence of concubinage, and the elegant clothing lavished on the colored plaçées by their protectors, prompted the Spanish governor Estebán Miró to include sumptuary laws in his 1786 *Bando de Buen Gobierno* (Proclamation of Good Government). In articles 5 and 6 Miró railed against the

5. *Madame John's Legacy.* This house, built in 1788, was the setting for George Washington Cable's story of plaçage, "Tite Poulette." It still stands at 632 Dumaine Street and is now the property of the Louisiana State Museum. Illustration by Joseph Pennell for Lafcadio Hearn's "The Scenes of Cable's Romances," *The Century Magazine*, November 1883, p. 41. (Author's collection.)

"idleness" of the free women of color, who "subsist from the product of their licentious life." Miró required that these females dress in a manner befitting their subordinate status. He admonished them "to drop all communication and intercourse with vice, and go back to work," with the understanding that he would be "suspicious of their indecent conduct [as evidenced by] the extravagant luxury in their dressing." Any free woman of color, according to Miró, who arrayed herself in beautiful gowns, bonnets, jewels, and elaborate hairstyles, could not have gotten such finery through her own industry or from a legitimate husband. Women of color were ordered not to "wear feathers, nor curls in their hair, combing same flat or covering it with a tignon," the head wrap worn by slaves. Although the language of Governor Miró's proclamation indicates that his concern was with "idle" colored mistresses being opulently supported by white men, most writers have interpreted the "tignon law" as an attempt to distinguish women of color from white women and render them less attractive.[28]

Instead of being considered a badge of dishonor, the tignon, traditionally made from a large plaid scarf imported from Madras, India, became a fashion statement. The bright reds, blues, and yellows of the scarves, and the imaginative wrapping techniques employed by their wearers, are said to have enhanced the beauty of the women of color, who ranged in complexion from a rich brown to the palest ivory.

Even when the "tignon law" became obsolete under the American administration, many Afro-Creole women still wore the traditional Madras head wrap. In *Voodoo in New Orleans* Robert Tallant introduced the notion that Marie Laveau always arranged her tignon in seven points—this is now considered to be her signature costume. To his fictitious informant, "Gerald July," the "mulatto porter in a downtown office building," Tallant ascribed the statement that Marie Laveau "always wore . . . a tignon tied wit' seven knots and the points stickin' straight up." The idea of the "tignon with seven points" comes from an 1875 *Appleton's Journal* article, "A Night with the Voudous," where an earlier Voudou priestess, Sanité Dédé, is described as wearing "the traditional Madras handkerchief, with its . . . seven points upturned to heaven."[29]

* * *

It should not be assumed that every free woman of color formed a sexual liaison with a white man—many chose legal marriage or domestic partnership with men of their own caste. In this way, strong family networks were created, leading to the formation of a free colored elite who embraced French culture and education, were devoted to the Roman Catholic Church, served in the military, and owned businesses, real estate, and slaves. Over many generations the free people of color were increasingly removed in worldview and physical appearance from their African origins. They were neither black nor white, but "colored," definitely not slaves but not quite full citizens. They constituted the middle tier in New Orleans' tripartite society.

Catherine Henry's daughter Marguerite made a choice between concubinage with a white protector and marriage with a man of color. Sometime after her emancipation from slavery in 1790, she became the plaçée of the Frenchman Henri D'Arcantel, a bachelor old enough to be her father. During the Spanish colonial period, D'Arcantel occupied the prestigious position of chief official for the accounting office of the army and royal household.[30]

The Spanish census of 1795 listed "Hy. D'Arcantel" sharing his home in the Vieux Carré with a free mulatress named Marguerite, along with a girl and two boys of mixed race.[31] These children would have been Marie Louise and

Antoine D'Arcantel and the couple's newborn infant son. A free quadroon boy named Miguel Germelo, son of Don Enrique D'Arcantel and Margarita San Marre, free mulatress, was baptized at St. Louis Cathedral on July 30, 1795. Marguerite ordinarily used D'Arcantel as her surname; the fact that in this baptismal record she was called Marguerite San Marre brings to mind Marie Laveau's 1881 *Daily Picayune* obituary, where it was stated that Marie's "mother was Marguerite Henry and her grandmother was Marguerite Semard [San Marre]." Miguel Germelo D'Arcantel died at the age of six months.[32]

At some point Marguerite became involved in a relationship with Charles Laveaux, resulting in the birth of a daughter, the future Voudou Queen Marie Laveau. On September 16, 1801, a six-day-old infant named Marie (no surname) was baptized by Fray Antonio de Sedella, the beloved Père Antoine, and entered in the sacramental register of St. Louis Cathedral as "una niña mulata libre, que nacio el dia dies de este presente mes, hija de Margarita, mulata libre, y de un padre no conocido" (a free mulatto girl born the tenth day of this present month, daughter of Marguerite, free mulatress, and an unknown father). The godfather was José Joaquin Velasquez, a white man who frequently stood as godfather for slaves and free people of color. The godmother's name was only given as Catalina (Catherine), the name of Marie's grandmother. Girls were often named for their godmothers, and as an adult Marie occasionally appeared in the archival record as Catherine Laveau.[33]

Almost every telling of the Laveau Legend, from the time of Marie's death until the present, has repeated the line from the 1881 *Daily Picayune* obituary stating that "her father was a rich planter, who was prominent in all public affairs, and served in the Legislature of this State." Most writers have concluded that Laveaux was a white man and Marie's mother was his plaçée. Louisiana Writers' Project fieldworkers uncovered overwhelming evidence to the contrary. Robert Tallant certainly knew better, having had access to the LWP files in which Marie Laveau's parentage is clearly documented, yet he did nothing to correct the error. In *Voodoo in New Orleans* he said only that "newspaper reporters later wrote of her father as having been a wealthy white planter, of her mother as a mulatto with a strain of Indian, and though these accounts may not have been accurate, the racial mixture sounds logical." In his novel, *The Voodoo Queen*, Tallant depicted Marie's father, Charles Laveau, as a white planter and her mother, Marguerite, as his beautiful but pathetic mistress. In Francine Prose's 1977 novel *Marie Laveau*, Marie's mother, here renamed Delphine, is the plaçée of the fictional Victor Laveau, a white immigrant from the island of Saint Domingue. Jewell Parker Rhodes, in her 1993 *Voodoo Dreams*,

6. *Charles Laveau Trudeau*. Portrait by José Francisco Xavier de Salazar y Mendosa, 1795. Oil on canvas. The portraits of Laveau Trudeau and his wife, Charlotte Perrault, depict the couple engaged in a game of backgammon. (Tulane University Art Collection, gift of the children of Mrs. Angelina Labatut Puig, New Orleans, Louisiana.)

makes "Monsieur Laveau" the owner of Marie's grandmother and father of her children. Marie's own father is dismissed as "some [anonymous] white man my mother whored with."[34]

In actuality, Charles Laveaux was a prosperous free man of color who traded in real estate and slaves and owned several businesses. Archival records indicate that Laveaux was born around 1774, the natural son of a free negress named Marie Laveaux. She appears in the Spanish census of 1791 as Maria Lavoz, *negra libre*, living on Dumaine Street. Included in the household is a young adult mulatto male, possibly her son Charles, who would have been about sixteen at the time.[35] Nothing further is known of this Marie Laveaux.

Since Charles Laveaux was always designated as a mulatto, we can assume that his father was a white man. From several sources one hears that his unidentified progenitor was Charles Laveau Trudeau.[36] Laveau Trudeau, usually called Carlos in official documents, was a trained engineer and draftsman who served as surveyor general of Louisiana under the Spanish government. His signature appears on many of the elegantly drawn and inscribed maps found in New Orleans' archival repositories. A 1795 portrait by José Francisco Xavier de Salazar y Mendosa, now in the collection of Tulane University, depicts this handsome gentleman with a long, straight nose, dressed in a military jacket with epaulets and brass buttons and a lace cravat.[37] In 1809 he became president of the New Orleans City Council. William C. C. Claiborne, governor of the Territory of Orleans after the Louisiana Purchase, described Laveau Trudeau as "a man of some science, great integrity of character, and possessing much local knowledge."[38]

Charles Laveau Trudeau died October 6, 1816, at the age of seventy. He never acknowledged Charles Laveaux as his son during his lifetime or in his will, and the archival record reveals no social or business interactions between the two and no connection between Laveau Trudeau and the negress Marie Laveaux.[39] The absence of direct evidence does not mean that Charles Laveau Trudeau was not Charles Laveaux's father, only that we cannot say with certainty that he was.

If the September 16, 1801, baptismal record for the mulatto infant Marie, natural daughter of Marguerite, is indeed that of Marie Laveau, it is somewhat curious that Charles Laveaux's name was omitted. He later declared Marie to be his daughter and had a close relationship with her throughout his life. Because of Marguerite D'Arcantel's dependence on her white protector, and because of Charles' own commitment to the woman he would soon marry, he may have wished to keep his paternity secret at the time.

On August 12, 1802, Charles Laveaux wed Marie Françoise Fanchon Dupart, a free woman of color who brought considerable wealth to the marriage. The ceremony was performed by Père Antoine: "Carlos Labeau, mulato libre . . . hijo natural de Maria Labeau, negra libre, y de un padre no conocido, con Maria Francisca, grifa libre . . . hija natural de Francisca Dupart y de un padre incognito" (Charles Laveau, free mulatto . . . natural son of Marie Laveau, free negress, and an unknown father, [married] with Marie Françoise, free griffe . . . natural daughter of Françoise Dupart and an unknown father).[40] The fact that Marie Françoise was referred to as a *griffe* (a term signifying the offspring of a black and a mulatto) indicates that she was a darker-skinned woman.

*   *   *

While these personal dramas were playing themselves out, the struggling settlement of New Orleans was evolving into a real town with a busy port, substantial buildings, and a sizable population that included professionals, merchants, and artisans, set in a countryside dotted with plantations. Under Spanish laws that facilitated emancipation from slavery, the free nonwhite community had grown and prospered. A central market, now known as the French Market, was constructed along the Mississippi River. A waterway, the Carondelet Canal, had been dug to connect the town to Bayou St. John and Lake Pontchartrain; its turning basin gave its name to Basin Street. The Spanish added more levees against flooding, building massive earthen barriers fifteen feet high by thirty feet at the base. Two fires, one in 1788 and one in 1794, wiped out the center of the Vieux Carré. The rebuilding of St. Louis Cathedral, its adjoining Presbytère, and a new administrative office for the Cabildo, was financed by Don Andrés Almonester y Roxas, a wealthy landowner and regidor of the Cabildo. Some of the finer private residences were also built after fire destroyed the ramshackle structures surrounding these edifices of church and state. The rest of New Orleans still consisted of small houses, like that of Marie Laveau's grandmother, set back from the street and surrounded by yards in which the residents raised vegetables and kept livestock.

During the Spanish administration the inhabitants of New Orleans retained their French culture and spoke French as their first language, although official business was conducted and recorded in Spanish, as were the sacramental records of St. Louis Cathedral. Despite the change in government, New Orleans remained a colonial French city.[41] It is in this environment that Marie Laveau would begin her life.

The Antebellum City

In 1800 Napoleon Bonaparte negotiated the secret Treaty of San Ildefonso with Spain's Charles IV, by which he received the Louisiana colony in exchange for a small kingdom in northern Italy; Louisiana was formally retroceded from Spain to France on November 30, 1803. But the political situation had changed in the intervening three years, and the defeat of Napoleon's troops in the thirteen-year slave revolt in Saint Domingue had made France wary of additional commitments in the New World. Without Saint Domingue, Louisiana was of little value. Instead of resuming responsibility for this burdensome colony, Napoleon sold Louisiana to the United States for fifteen million dollars. With this purchase, the United States acquired not only the present state of Louisiana, but all of the land from the Gulf Coast to the Canadian border between the Mississippi River and the Rocky Mountains—a third of North America.

On Monday, December 20, 1803, a silent crowd gathered in the Place d'Armes, the public square and military parade ground overlooked by St. Louis Cathedral, the Presbytère, and the Cabildo, to witness the transfer of Louisiana to American rule. The documents were signed by representatives of France and the United States in the *Sala Capitular*, the council chamber of the Cabildo, and the keys to the city were turned over to the new American owners. Outside in the square, accompanied by rifle salutes and the roll of drums, the French tricolor was lowered and the American stars and stripes flew over New Orleans. Representing the French government at these ceremonies was Colonial Prefect Pierre Clément Laussat, who recorded in his journal that the Creoles wept. Their cherished language, laws, religion, and cultural practices would soon be under attack.[1] As Marie Laveau grew to womanhood, married, and raised her children, she would see New Orleans change from a close-knit, racially integrated, French-speaking, Roman Catholic Creole community to an increasingly segregated city dominated by English-speaking Protestant Anglo-Americans.

Newcomers swarmed into New Orleans in the decades following the Louisiana Purchase. The worst were the unwashed and uncouth riverboat men, known as Kaintucks, who came down the Mississippi to New Orleans in increasing numbers to drink, carouse, and pillage. Most, however, were merchants and professionals from the mid-Atlantic states and New England who went there to make a quick financial killing. The New Englanders, schooled in the Puritan tradition of hard work, austerity of religious observance, and strict morality, were especially critical of New Orleans and its culture. They looked upon the white Creoles as indolent, uneducated to the point of illiteracy, lacking in business sense, and incapable of self-government. They were horrified by the racial mixing of New Orleans society, the prosperity and privilege of the free people of color, the relatively permissive form of urban slavery, and the continued existence of African music and dance traditions. They regarded Roman Catholicism as idolatry; Voudou, in no way recognized as a religion, was perceived as an ominous manifestation of African "savagery."

Lower Louisiana, including the city of New Orleans, became the Territory of Orleans. President Thomas Jefferson appointed William C. C. Claiborne, a twenty-eight-year-old Tennessean, as the first territorial governor. Claiborne was a lawyer by training, having previously served as Tennessee's representative to Congress, and most recently as governor of the Mississippi Territory. This young American was, in the words of an influential Creole planter, "a stranger here, a stranger as far as the soil itself is concerned, its local interests, the customs, habits, and even the language of the inhabitants."[2]

President Jefferson had two strategies for integrating the Territory of Orleans into the United States and turning the Creoles into Americans. He initially proposed annexing the territory to Mississippi. When that failed to materialize, he had a bill introduced in Congress that would transport thirty thousand able-bodied white male settlers to the territory, where they would be awarded 160 acres of land in return for a promise to reside there for seven years, giving two of those years to military service. Two birds could thereby be killed with one stone: the Creoles—with their French language, their Roman Catholicism, and their Afro-Latin culture—would be overwhelmed by the influx of Anglophone white American Protestants, and the Territory of Orleans would be defended by this resident militia against reclamation by the French or Spanish. This would undoubtedly elicit protests from the Creoles, but after all, said Jefferson, "in making this acquisition we had some view to our own good as well as theirs," and in the end "the greatest good of both will be promoted by whatever will amalgamate us together."[3] Neither of these schemes succeeded.

Jefferson also failed in his attempt to replace the Territory's Roman-derived European civil law with the Anglo-American system of common law, which evolved from English feudal tradition. The differences between the two systems had significant implications for the status of women in Lower Louisiana. Common law vested authority and property ownership in the male head of the household, and the bulk of a man's estate usually went to his first-born son. Under both civil and common law, single women and widows could conduct business without male interference, but under common law a married woman took her husband's surname and ceased to exist as a legal entity. Under civil law, a married woman kept her maiden name and could have considerable control over wealth and property. A wife retained possession of money, real estate, slaves, or movable goods that she brought to the marriage, and earnings and property acquired by a couple during their union was held jointly. This "community of goods" was administered by the husband during the marriage, but a wife could declare herself separate in property, gaining the right to conduct business in her own name and insulating herself from her husband's debts. When the husband or wife died, his or her half of the estate was divided equally between all their children, regardless of gender.[4]

Just as President Jefferson and Governor Claiborne were devising schemes to Americanize Louisiana's anomalous Creole population, an even more alien and potentially more dangerous group of immigrants arrived in New Orleans in the wake of the slave revolt in the French colony of Saint Domingue that culminated in the founding of the Republic of Haiti. During the 1790s and into the first decade of the nineteenth century, thousands of refugees, among them Marie Laveau's future husband, Jacques Paris, and other relatives and associates, fled the fighting and political upheaval. Some left Saint Domingue for the Atlantic seaboard ports of New York, Philadelphia, Baltimore, Norfolk, Charleston, and Savannah, eventually making their way to Louisiana. Some fled to Jamaica, but were expelled by the British; these also landed in Louisiana. In 1803, following the final defeat of Napoleon's troops, thirty thousand sought shelter in the vicinity of Santiago de Cuba, hoping eventually to resume their lives in Saint Domingue. After the French invasion of Spain in 1809, those who refused to swear allegiance to the Spanish government were forced out of Cuba and made their way to Louisiana. It is estimated that nearly ten thousand immigrants arrived in 1809 alone, more than doubling the French-speaking population of New Orleans.

The refugees who arrived in New Orleans—the former sugar and coffee planters and slave masters of Saint Domingue—included natives of France and whites and free people of color born in the Americas. The immigrants also brought their slaves, many of whom were African-born Fon, Yoruba, and Kongo. Although the law barred free nonwhite persons and slaves from the French

Caribbean islands from entering the Territory of Orleans, a special dispensation was made in the case of the Saint Domingue refugees. The newspaper *Le Moniteur de la Louisiane* announced on January 27, 1810, that the refugees arriving from Cuba numbered 2,731 whites (1,373 men, 703 women, 655 children); 3,102 free people of color (428 men, 1,377 women, 1,297 children); and 3,226 slaves (962 men, 1,330 women, 934 children). Notice the preponderance of females among the free people of color and slaves, augmenting an already powerful community of women of African descent in New Orleans.[5]

The arrival of the immigrants from Saint Domingue, so similar in culture to the native New Orleanians, lifted Creole spirits and added reinforcements in the face of Anglo-American aggressiveness. They received a chilly reception from the Americans. Governor Claiborne, in a letter of 1809, complained that "The native-born Americans . . . appear to be prejudiced against these strangers, and express great dissatisfaction that an asylum in this territory was afforded them." He was especially worried about the presence of so many free people of African descent. In 1810 he confided that "I must confess I am not without apprehensions that disorders and disturbances may arise. The free men of color [who are] capable of bearing arms cannot be less than eight hundred. Their conduct has hitherto been correct. But in a country like this, where the negro population is so considerable, they should be carefully watched."[6] Blind to the subtleties of race, Claiborne failed to realize that these free people of color did not identify with the slaves and did not consider themselves "negroes." The Saint Domingue refugees, both white and nonwhite, eventually established plantations, businesses, schools, theaters, newspapers, and Masonic lodges. They also joined Louisiana Creoles and Anglo-Americans to fight against their common enemy, the British, under Andrew Jackson in the Battle of New Orleans in 1815.

The Territory of Orleans was entitled to statehood when its population reached sixty thousand. The citizens had petitioned for this privilege in 1809, but Governor Claiborne was opposed because such a small percentage of them were American-born. The Territory finally entered the Union as the state of Louisiana in 1812. The debate in the House of Representatives hinged primarily on whether or not the Constitution allowed admission of lands outside the boundaries of the original thirteen colonies. Other objections were raised because the people of the Territory of Orleans were perceived as "French," and because a "large proportion" had African blood. It was argued that the Union was "never intended to include the people of the Territory of Orleans, who are foreigners, subject to a foreign government at the time of the adoption of the

Constitution." Some members of the House of Representatives, concerned by the fact that *all* free male property owners were granted the right to vote under the terms of the Louisiana Purchase, specified that suffrage should be restricted to *white* male property owners. The sizeable "mixed population" in the Territory, "a goodly number [of whom] are wealthy and respectable people," raised the possibility that a man of color might be elected to Congress. "In that event," said the representative from Tennessee, he would "feel no inclination" to associate with such a person while conducting the nation's business. The Enabling Act for the Territory of Orleans, including the motion to deny suffrage to free men of color, eventually passed by a vote of seventy-seven to thirty-six.[7]

* * *

While these important events were taking place, Marie Laveau was growing up in the still-insular world of the Vieux Carré. Nothing is known of her childhood. If the 1881 *Picayune* obituary is to be believed, Marie was "born in the house where she died [and] her mother lived and died there before her." This would indicate that she was brought up in the St. Ann Street cottage of her maternal grandmother, the market woman Catherine Henry, and that her mother, Marguerite D'Arcantel, resided there at least part of the time.

Marguerite maintained her relationship with the white Frenchman Henri D'Arcantel, with whom she had two surviving children, Marie Louise and Antoine. In 1809 Marguerite gave birth to a daughter named Adelaide D'Arcantel, presumably the child of Henri; Adelaide died in 1815.[8] When Henri D'Arcantel wrote his will on October 22, 1817, he stated that 3,300 *piastres* (the French piastre was equivalent to the American dollar) were owed him by the Spanish Royal Treasury for eleven years of service as head of the accounting office. He left 100 piastres to "the mulattress Marguerite who cared for me well in my illness," and 200 piastres each to Marguerite's daughter Marie Louise and her son Antoine. This was a common method by which a white man could circumvent the laws against miscegenation and concubinage and leave money to his colored family. At the end of the will he reiterated that a total of 500 piastres was to be given to these three individuals. D'Arcantel instructed his testamentary executor, his brother Paul D'Arcantel, to make every effort to recover the money owed him by the Royal Treasury. If these funds were not forthcoming, Paul was to sell Henri's movable property to raise the cash for these bequests.[9]

Louisiana civil law governing inheritance favored marriage and the legitimate family and, although color blind, particularly served to obstruct the inheritance of property by the nonwhite partner and children of a white man. The Civil Code of 1808 stated that "those who have lived together in open concubinage are respectively incapable of making to each other any universal donation when alive (*inter vivos*) or by will (*mortis causa*)," meaning that Henri D'Arcantel could not have left all of his assets to Marguerite and their children. He could, however, leave them one-third of his estate, so he was legally entitled to make them the bequest of 500 piastres provided this did not exceed the stipulated one-third. Since D'Arcantel had no legitimate wife or progeny, his brother Paul would have inherited the rest.[10]

Henri D'Arcantel died on December 8, 1817. The entry in the St. Louis Cathedral funeral register describes him as a sixty-three-year-old bachelor, who "died suddenly in the Chantilli [Gentilly] residence about one league distant from this capitol." Maps of the period show the D'Arcantel family owning land on both sides of Bayou Sauvage and Gentilly Road. On April 8, 1818, Paul D'Arcantel and Judge James Pitot met at the Gentilly plantation to inventory Henri's movable goods: a desk, an armoire, a bed, a few clothes, and 210 books, including an *Atlas of the Voyage of Captain Cook*—a library of this size is remarkable in an age when few people were literate. D'Arcantel's possessions were valued at only 129 piastres, not sufficient to cover the 500-piastre bequest to Marguerite, Marie Louise, and Antoine.[11] During the chaotic period following the Louisiana Purchase, as the Territory of Orleans was transferred from Spanish to French to American administrators, many of the debts of the Spanish government went unpaid. It is unlikely that Henri D'Arcantel's back wages from the Spanish Royal Treasury were recovered in order for his plaçée and his mixed-race children to receive their inheritance.[12]

Marguerite died on July 31, 1825, at the age of about fifty-three. Her funeral is recorded under the name Marguerite D'Arcantel, *mulâtresse libre*, in the sacramental registers of St. Louis Cathedral.[13] Her continued use of the surname D'Arcantel indicates that she considered herself to be the "widow" of Henri D'Arcantel. This term was used by the concubines of white men not only when their protectors were actually deceased but also when they had been deserted in favor of a legitimate wife.

Marie Laveau's father, Charles Laveaux, had become the head of a family and a prosperous entrepreneur. Charles and his wife, Marie Françoise Dupart, had three children. Four months after they were married, in November 1802, Françoise gave birth to their first son. The baby, named Charles, died at the age of twelve days. Marie de los Dolores, born January 3, 1804, and Laurent Charles, born July 30, 1805, survived to adulthood.[14] Between 1805 and 1833,

7. Signature of Charles Laveaux, Acts of Narcisse Broutin, March 30, 1807. (Courtesy of the Notarial Archives Research Center, New Orleans, Louisiana.)

Charles Laveaux was actively engaged in lending money and dealing in land and slaves.[15] He signed the notarial acts in which these transactions were recorded in a bold, flowing hand, indicating that he was well educated. Charles probably received his elementary instruction at one of New Orleans' private academies for free children of color. He may have been sent to France to continue his schooling, as were many young men of his caste. Both of his legitimate children were literate, and it is surprising that a man of his resources did not provide an education for his natural daughter, Marie Laveau. Perhaps she declined his offer.

* * *

The city in which Marie Laveau lived as a young woman was a place of great ethnic diversity, characterized not only by beauty and gaiety but by squalor and disease. Early nineteenth-century travelers commented on sights and phenomena that New Orleanians considered unremarkable: the "exoticism" of the city and its varied inhabitants; the rather independent circumstances of the slaves; the education, property-holding, and privileged status of the free people of color; the prevalence of interracial domestic partnerships; the survival of African cultural practices; and the perceived eccentricities of the Creoles.

One of the most perceptive observers was the architect and engineer Benjamin Henry Boneval Latrobe. In 1819, the year in which Marie Laveau married Jacques Paris at St. Louis Cathedral, Benjamin Latrobe was in New Orleans to oversee the building of the municipal waterworks. During his stay, he kept a journal and sketch book, now published as *Impressions Respecting New Orleans*.

Latrobe arrived by way of the Mississippi River on January 12, 1819. His first sight was of the French Market. "Everything," he wrote in his journal, "had an *odd* look . . . it was impossible not to stare at a sight wholly new even to one who has traveled much in Europe and America." Along the levee he observed the rows of market people: "The articles to be sold were not more various than the sellers. White men and women, & all hues of brown, & of all

8. *Market Folks*. Watercolor sketch by Benjamin Henry Latrobe, January 13, 1819, from the Diary and Sketchbook of Benjamin Latrobe. (Maryland Historical Society, Baltimore, Maryland, accession no. 1960.108.1.14.17.)

classes of faces, from round Yankees to grisly & lean Spaniards; black negroes and negresses; filthy Indians half naked; mulattoes, curly & straight-haired; quarteroons [quadroons] of all shades, long-haired and frizzled, the women dressed in the most flaring yellow and scarlet gowns, the men capped and hatted." So fascinated was Latrobe with this diverse assembly that he returned the next day to make a watercolor sketch of the "market folks," which includes two black women in long skirts, shawls, and tignons.

Latrobe also noted that women of color, both slave and free, sold their wares from door to door: "In every street, during the whole day, women, chiefly black women, are met carrying baskets upon their heads and calling at the doors of houses. . . . It [is] not the fashion for Ladies to go shopping." These female vendors sold dry goods, foodstuffs, and other merchandise.[16] One of the market women observed by Benjamin Latrobe might have been Marie Laveau's grandmother, Catherine Henry.

On April 18, 1819, Latrobe wrote an account of a Sunday walk around the city. His description again highlights the great racial and national diversity of the population and the ease with which they interacted, as well as their Sunday activities. On the levee, he bought some oranges from a black woman and watched the unloading of a basket of pecans, a quantity of wild ducks, carrots, sugar cane, and corn from a market boat, by "two old black men in blanket frocks with pointed hoods." On the boat, he noted, were "two black women in Madras turbans, & gowns striped with scarlet and yellow. Round their necks a plentiful assortment of bead necklaces." The owner of the boat was "an old sunburnt [white] Creole, slovenly in his appearance." Further on he saw "two drunken Indians, who afforded sport to several boys who surrounded them. Then half a dozen Kentuckians [the infamous Kaintucks], dirty, savage, & gigantic, who were selling a horse to a group of genteel-looking men who spoke English." Near the steamboats Latrobe observed many well-dressed ladies and gentlemen strolling "without any apparent object but to take the air."

Leaving the levee, Latrobe saw that the stores were open for business, despite its being Sunday. In one, some sailors were trying on pantaloons with the help of a black shopwoman. On the steps of another store lay two boatmen, "drunk & half asleep, swearing in English at some boys who were teizing [sic] them." A group of Creoles of color, coming from Mass at St. Louis Cathedral, were debating in French over which of the priests had the finest voice. On Bourbon Street, Latrobe peeped into the shop of a white cooper who was "at work with some mulatto boys. He was scolding them in very good English." In a shoemaker's shop, a "broad-faced dark mulatto" and a "well-dressed white man" were playing checkers—"they seemed to be arguing, on terms of perfect equality, some knotty problem of the game." A white woman stood by and watched, while "four boys & an enormous man, all black, [were] hard at work at their trade." On St. Louis Street he noticed a horse-drawn cabriolet "in which were a white man & a bright [light-complexioned] quadroon woman. . . . A ragged black boy sat at their feet and drove, & a girl of 13 or 14 years old sat upon the trunk board behind."[17]

Choctaw Indians were a frequent sight in antebellum New Orleans, where they came to sell their wares on the street. Their presence was noted by Dr. Paul Alliot, who arrived in New Orleans from Saint Domingue in 1803 and later composed his *Historical and Political Reflections on Louisiana*. Alliot records that "Some hundreds of savages with their wives and children live apart in the huts which they have constructed on the vacant lands on the outskirts of New Orleans." The men, noted Alliot, sold wild game, and the women sold handcrafted reed baskets and firewood gathered in the forest. "The savages . . . always go bareheaded. They have magnificent long black hair which they color red and which falls almost to their heels. To their hair they fasten feathers of various colors."[18] The Louisiana Writers' Project interviews indicate that in

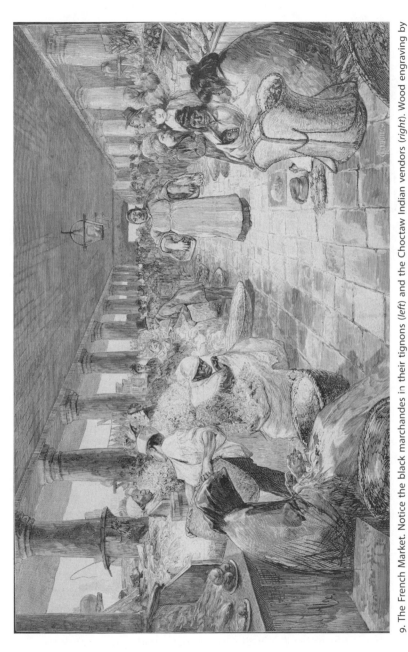

9. The French Market. Notice the black marchandes in their tignons (*left*) and the Choctaw Indian vendors (*right*). Wood engraving by H. Claudius from a drawing by John W. Alexander, *Harper's Weekly Magazine*, January 21, 1882. (Author's collection.)

10. A quadroon mother and daughter. Illustration by Albert Herter for George Washington Cable's "Tite Poulette," in *Old Creole Days*, 1897 edition. (Author's collection.)

later years Marie Laveau allowed the Choctaw women to camp in her yard on St. Ann Street. She may have been continuing a practice started by her grandmother, Catherine Henry, who would have worked alongside the Indian market women as she plied her trade as a marchande.

*   *   *

When the Americans arrived after the Louisiana Purchase, the majority of New Orleanians had some degree of African blood. The first American census, taken in 1805, recorded 8,212 inhabitants, of whom only 3,551 were classified as white. They were outnumbered by 3,105 slaves and 1,556 free people of color. Many urban slaves enjoyed a considerable degree of independence, living away from the premises of their owners and hiring themselves out for wages. Most of the free colored community owned their homes and earned modest livings as laborers, carpenters, masons, plasterers, house painters, iron workers, cigar makers, militiamen, shop keepers, tailors, barbers, street vendors, laundresses, boarding house managers, seamstresses, nurses, and hairdressers. The wealthier Creoles of color were well educated and successful, controlling extensive real estate in New Orleans or plantations in the countryside, and were themselves slaveholders. An unusually high percentage of free colored business people and property owners were women.[19]

None of this could be swallowed by the Anglo-Americans, who were accustomed to the concept of slavery as a permanent condition appropriate to an inferior race and who considered free people of African descent an anomaly that threatened the stability of society.[20] New Orleans' tripartite racial structure of black, colored, and white was, in fact, identical to that found in Latin America and the Caribbean. It was the rest of the United States, with its "rigid, two-tiered structure that drew a single unyielding line between white and non-white," that was deviant.[21]

Despite laws to the contrary, interracial domestic unions were still commonplace in early antebellum New Orleans. Of the 1,391 households enumerated in the 1805 census, 8.6 percent consisted of a white man and a nonwhite woman, often with racially mixed children.[22] Archival evidence shows that in many instances these were long-term relationships that resembled legal marriage, belying the popular notion of the white man living with his legitimate family and visiting his colored mistress and children on the sly. Some women of color became the plaçées of white men strictly for financial security, and some men chose plaçage over marriage to a white woman because it was more

11. Père Antoine.
Illustration from George
Washington Cable's
"Plotters and Pirates of
Louisiana," *The Century
Magazine*, April 1883,
p. 826. (Author's collection.)

convenient; others entered into these relationships out of mutual affection and respect.[23] Plaçage arrangements were said to have been made at New Orleans' legendary "quadroon balls," where white gentlemen met and courted young free women of color and later entered into financial negotiations with their mothers or guardians.[24] Because these agreements were outside the law, enacted verbally and in private, they will not be found in the notarial records.

*   *   *

Virtually all of the Creole population were Roman Catholic. The clergy of St. Louis Cathedral, still recording baptisms, marriages, and funerals in French or Spanish, viewed Anglo-Americans as aliens, referring to states other than Louisiana as though they were in some foreign country called "the United States" or "North America."[25]

The Catholic Church in Louisiana had always been racially integrated and remained so until after the Civil War. The majority of the congregants of St. Louis Cathedral were females of African descent. The pastor, Père Antoine, was especially sympathetic to these women. Although those who lived in extramarital domestic partnerships were technically in a state of sin, Père Antoine allowed them to receive communion and baptized their natural children. In 1819 Benjamin Latrobe reported that on Sunday, high Mass at St. Louis Cathedral was attended by "all the beautiful girls in the place, 2 or 300 quateroons, negroes, and mulattoes, and perhaps 100 white males." In a later entry, he mentioned that "the congregation consisted of at least 4/5ths women, of which number one half at least were colored." One of these women could conceivably have been Marie Laveau, by all accounts a regular worshiper at St. Louis Cathedral. "On each of the side altars," Latrobe continued, "were half a dozen candles stuck upon the steps by old colored women, who seemed exceedingly devout."[26]

Some Afro-Catholics were undoubtedly synthesizing Roman Catholic ritual and the veneration of sacramental objects with traditional African religion. The English social reformer Harriet Martineau remarked in her 1838 *Retrospect of Western Travel* that Catholicism, as practiced by black New Orleanians, constituted "the most abject worship of things without meaning . . . an unintelligible and ineffectual mythology."[27] Other Afro-Catholics embraced the teachings of the church wholeheartedly. Henriette Delille, daughter of a white man and a free woman of color (who may have been distantly related to Marie Laveau), became the foundress of an order of nuns called the Sisters of the Holy Family. Delille's work began in the mid-1830s, when she and two other young women of color, Juliette Gaudin and Josephine Charles, began to

PRAYER
FOR THE BEATIFICATION OF
HENRIETTE DELILLE

O good and gracious God, you called
Henriette Delille to give herself in service and i
love to the slaves and the sick, to the orphan an(
the aged, to the forgotten and the despised.
    Grant that inspired by her life we migh!
be renewed in heart and mind. If it be your will,
may she one day be raised to the honor of saint
hood. By her prayers may we live in harmony a:
peace. Through Jesus Christ our Lord. Amen

Nihil Obstat: Rev. Msgr Franz Graef, S.T.D.
Imprimatur: Most Rev. Francis B. Schulte
Archbishop of New Orleans. August 23,1997

12. Prayer card for the beatification of Henriette Delille, 1997. (Author's collection.)

aid, educate, and minister to poor people of African descent. After overcoming many obstacles owing to their race, Delille, Gaudin, and Charles took their vows in 1852.[28]

* * *

One of New Orleans' most famous attractions was Congo Square, site of the Sunday slave dances.[29] Since all traditional African music and dance is sacred in nature, Congo Square could justifiably be called a venue for what came to be known as Voudou. The area behind the Vieux Carré called the Place des Nègres had been used since the mid-1700s for marketing, socializing, and for African-style singing and dancing accompanied by drums and musical instruments. Shortly after the Louisiana Purchase, Governor Claiborne ordered the removal of New Orleans' old ramparts and forts to open the city up to the surrounding countryside, after the manner of other Anglo-American urban centers. The demolition of Fort St. Ferdinand, adjacent to the site of the slaves' market and dance space at the Place des Nègres, created an open, grassy area bounded by Rampart, St. Claude, St. Ann, and the Carondelet Canal turning basin. This was designated the *Place Publique* or Public Square.

The American administration allowed the slaves' market activities and dances "only on Sundays, and solely in such open or public places as shall be appointed by the Mayor." The Place Publique became the designated location.[30] For an undetermined period of years ending in 1817, Gaetano Mariatini's traveling "Congo Circus" from Havana set up in the Place Publique during the winter season, and it was then that the site came to be called Circus Square or Congo Square.[31] The weekly phenomena at Congo Square drew many white spectators and became a tourist attraction for American and European visitors, for whom traditional African music, dance, and costume was a great curiosity.

The published impressions of these travelers bear a striking resemblance to a 1735 report from Sierra Leon written by John Atkins, a surgeon in the British Royal Navy. Atkins described dancing as the "great diversion" of the people: "Men and women make a ring . . . and one at a time shows his skill in antick motions and gesticulations with a great deal of agility." Music was provided by the spectators "clapping their hands . . . helped by the noise of two or three drums made of a hollowed piece of tree and covered with kid-skin."[32]

The German-American traveler Christian Schultz, visiting New Orleans in April 1808, commented on the typical Sunday, which, after Mass, was given over to a degree of commerce and pleasure that was shocking to American visitors: "In the afternoon, a walk to the rear of the town will still more astonish their bewildered imaginations." At the Place Publique, wrote Schultz, the stranger will encounter "twenty different dancing groups of the wretched Africans, collected together to perform their *worship* after the manner of their country." Shultz noted that the dancers were accompanied by "a long kind of narrow drum of various sizes, from two to eight feet in length, three or four of which make a band." They were "dressed in a variety of wild and savage fashions, always ornamented with a number of the tails of the smaller wild beasts, and those who appeared most horrible always attracted the largest circle of company." The "amusements" continued until sunset, when the crowd was dispersed by the city patrol.[33]

On February 21, 1819, Benjamin Latrobe made a journal entry on the "Mode of Keeping Sunday in New Orleans and Reasonings Thereon," contrasting it with the Anglo-Protestant manner of observing the Sabbath as a day of strict abstinence enlivened only by churchgoing. This "dissertation," wrote Latrobe,

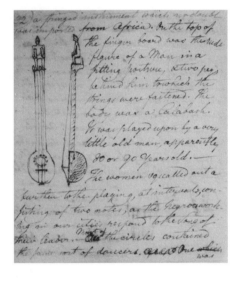

13. African instruments observed at Congo Square. Sketch by Benjamin Henry Latrobe, February 21, 1819, from the Diary and Sketchbook of Benjamin Latrobe. (Maryland Historical Society, Baltimore, Maryland, accession no. 1960.108.1.14.17.)

was "suggested by my accidentally stumbling upon the assembly of negroes which I am told every Sunday afternoon meets on the Common [Congo Square] in the rear of the city." Upon approaching the square he heard "a most extraordinary noise, which I supposed to proceed from some horse mill, the horses trampling on a wooden floor."

Drawing near enough to see the performance, Latrobe observed that the crowd of five or six hundred were formed into circular groups of about ten feet in diameter. In one ring, two women were dancing: "They held each a coarse handkerchief extended by the corners in their hands & *set* to each other in a miserably dull & slow figure, hardly moving their feet or bodies." He also described the musical instruments: "An old man sat astride of a cylindrical drum about a foot in diameter, & beat it with incredible quickness with the edge of his hand & fingers. The other drum was an open staved thing held between the knees and beaten in the same manner.... The most curious, however, was a stringed instrument which no doubt was imported from Africa. On the top of the finger board was the rude figure of a man in a sitting posture, & two pegs behind him to which the strings were fastened. The body was a calabash." The women, according to Latrobe, "squalled out a burthen [refrain] to the playing at intervals, consisting of two notes."

In another circle Latrobe saw a dozen women who "walked, by way of dancing, round the music in the center." He observed that this group had instruments of a different construction: "One, which from the color of the wood seemed new, consisted of a block cut into something of the form of a cricket bat with a long & deep mortise down the center. This thing made a considerable noise, being beaten lustily on the side by a short stick. In the same orchestra was a square drum, looking like a stool, which made an abominably loud noise; also a calabash with a round hole in it, the hole studded with brass nails, which was beaten by a woman with two short sticks. A man sung [*sic*] an uncouth song to the dancing which I suppose was in some African language, for it was not French, & the women screamed a detestable burthen on one single note."

While Latrobe defended the slaves' right to their Sunday amusements, he did not admire these African cultural practices, remarking that he had "never seen anything more brutally savage, and at the same time more dull and stupid, than this whole exhibition." When he returned after sunset by a different route, he could still hear the noise from Congo Square. With some surprise he noted that "there was no disorder among the crowd, nor do I learn on enquiry that these weekly meetings of the negroes have ever produced any mischief."[34]

Congo Square was fenced and gated in 1820, the year after Latrobe's visit. In 1822 John Adem Paxton, newly arrived from Philadelphia, published the first English-language city directory in New Orleans. In his introductory "Notes on New Orleans," he wrote disapprovingly: "The Circus Public Square is planted with trees and enclosed, and is very noted on account of its being the place where the . . . negroes dance, carouse, and debauch on the Sabbath, to the great injury of the rising generation. It is a foolish custom that elicits the ridicule

14. *The Bamboula.* Slave dance in Congo Square. The Congo Square dances had ended decades before this representation was created. Illustration by Edward W. Kemble for George Washington Cable's "The Dance in Place Congo," *The Century Magazine*, February 1886, p. 524. (Author's collection.)

of most respectable persons who visit the city, but if it is not considered good policy to abolish the practice entirely, surely they could be ordered to assemble at some place more distant from the houses, where the evil would be measurably remedied."[35]

Later travelers were not as puritanical as Paxton, and recommended the Congo Square dances as one of the "sights to see" in New Orleans. James R. Creecy, who visited the city in 1834, gave an effusive account of the "groups of fifties and hundreds" that could be seen in different sections of the square, with "banjos, tom-toms, violins, jawbones, triangles, and various other instruments." The dancers, he wrote, "are most fancifully dressed, with fringes, ribbons, little bells, and shells and balls, jingling and flirting about the performer's legs and arms, who sing a second or counter to the music most sweetly." Creecy praised the Congo Square observances as "a certain cure for ennui, blue-devils, mopes, horrors, and dyspepsia. Hundreds of nurses, with children of all ages, attend, and many fathers and mothers, beaux and belles, are there to be found. . . . Every stranger should visit Congo Square when in its glory. . . . The gaieties continue till sunset; and at the gun-fire the whole crowd disperse."[36]

* * *

Every description of New Orleans, from colonial times through the end of the nineteenth century, commented on the city's lack of sanitation, lingering in nauseating detail over the filth, the mud, the mosquito-infested swamps, the stench of the cemeteries, the reeking markets, the dead animals, the rats and cockroaches, the malodorous garbage and human waste thrown into the street to decompose in the hot weather, and the dogs and livestock that roamed at will, rooting through this disgusting accumulation. The city's efforts to keep the thoroughfares clean were of little avail, and refuse and sewage were dumped into the river, which also supplied drinking water for the citizens. The detriment to public health can well be imagined.[37]

New Orleanians suffered from small pox, bronchitis, tuberculosis, malaria (a parasitic infection spread by the *anopheles* mosquito), dysentery (an intestinal disorder caused by bacteria or parasites), and typhus (carried by fleas and lice). There were periodic scourges of deadly yellow fever and cholera. The first recorded yellow fever epidemic in New Orleans occurred in 1796, and from then on the infection returned almost yearly during the hot months from June through September. The symptoms were a yellow or bronze discoloration of the skin and regurgitation of blackened, partially digested blood caused by internal hemorrhaging—thus the nicknames "Yellow Jack," "Bronze John," and "the black vomit." Yellow fever was spread by a virus carried from one infected person to another by the *Aëdes aegypti* mosquito. Asiatic cholera, characterized by severe diarrhea and vomiting, was spread by bacteria in drinking water and food.

It was universally believed that the sickness came from miasmatic emanations from the swamp. City officials and citizens went to great extremes to dissipate this "bad air" and managed to create quite a stench of their own. They burned animal skins, horns, hoofs, and tar, carried cloves of garlic, soaked themselves with vinegar, and added to the discomfort by shooting off the cannons at intervals. Sufferers were often done in by physicians who so weakened their patients by bleeding and administering emetics and purgatives that death was inevitable. Those cared for by the Afro-Creole fever nurses, such as Marie Laveau is said to have been, were treated with herbal teas, cooling baths, massage, and nourishing broths, and were more likely to survive.

During the summer of 1832 over eight thousand New Orleanians out of a population of 55,000 died from a combination of yellow fever and cholera. A later epidemic, in 1853, accounted for eleven thousand fatalities. The death-cart drivers made their daily rounds, calling for residents who were still on their feet to "bring out your dead." Bodies were hauled to makeshift cemeteries and dumped into mass graves. Most of the people who died in the yearly epidemics

15. Charles Laveaux's store building, formerly corner of Grands Hommes and Histoire, now 1801 Dauphine, corner of Kerlerec, Faubourg Marigny. (Photograph by author, November 15, 2004.)

were new arrivals from Europe or from the northern cities of the United States. Because those who survived even a minor case of yellow fever acquired lifetime immunity, native New Orleanians were not as susceptible. Previous exposure did not offer protection against cholera. While it is generally believed that people of African descent were less likely to succumb to yellow fever, cholera, and other tropical diseases, this has no medical basis.[38]

*   *   *

By 1836 the ongoing antipathy between Creoles and Americans resulted in a division of the city into three municipalities. The Vieux Carré and the "back-of-town" beyond Rampart Street were designated as the First Municipality. The Second Municipality—the "American Quarter"—was above Canal Street. There the Americans built their homes, established their churches and schools, and located their retail businesses, banks, insurance companies, warehouses, and the offices of their commodity brokers and commission merchants. The Third Municipality consisted of the *faubourgs* (suburbs) below the Vieux Carré, where land formerly occupied by large plantations was subdivided into building lots. Census records show that these downtown neighborhoods were racially integrated and that the residents were a mixture of Louisiana Creoles and immigrants from Europe and the Caribbean islands.

Much of the property owned by Marie Laveau's father, Charles Laveaux, was located in the Faubourg Marigny, a new suburb in the Third Municipality created from the plantation of Bernard de Marigny. This pie-shaped tract just below the Vieux Carré has its point at the river, bounded by Esplanade and Elysian Fields and extending back to St. Claude Avenue. The squares and lots were laid out in 1806, and Marigny chose whimsical street names like Rue des Grands Hommes (great men), Rue d'Amour (love), Rue des Bons Enfants (good children), Rue Bagatelle (trifle), and Rue de Craps (a game of dice).[39]

A map of the new suburb drawn by Barthélemy Lafon shows the lot numbers and original property owners. Charles Laveaux owned two large adjacent lots at the corner of Grands Hommes and Histoire, where he erected an imposing store building. This structure, now 1801 Dauphine, corner of Kerlerec, is on the National Register of Historic Places and bears a bronze marker declaring that it was "built in 1817–1833 for Charles Laveaux, a free man of color, said to be the father of the Voodoo Queen, Marie Laveaux." Charles Laveaux also owned lot 207 on Rue d'Amour, the second from the corner of Union (now North Rampart near Touro), on the river side of the street.[40] This property was later given to Marie by her father on the occasion of her marriage to Jacques Paris.

Charles Laveaux's wife, Françoise Dupart, died on June 23, 1824, at the age of forty.[41] The couple's community property, valued at $10,631, consisted of ebony, cherry, and mahogany furniture, silverware, china, household linens and utensils, wearing apparel, a horse, three milk cows and their calves, two houses on Dauphine Street between St. Philip and Dumaine, a house at the corner of Grand Hommes and Mysterious in the Faubourg Marigny, a tract of land with buildings on Gentilly Road, and fourteen slaves—eleven adults and three children.[42] The extent of the personal property and real estate and the number of slaves held by the Laveaux family is indicative of the high status achieved by free people of color in early antebellum New Orleans. Some free Afro-Creoles were far more affluent, and many people of European descent were far less so.

Domestic Life

Marie Laveau's grandmother may have been the slave concubine of one or more of her white owners. Marie's mother was freed from slavery at the age of eighteen and subsequently became the plaçée of a well-situated white government official. Marie, who was born free, chose legitimate matrimony with a man of her own caste.

Jacques Paris

The first verifiable appearance of Marie Laveau in the archival record is her marriage contract with Jacques Paris, enacted before Notary Hugues Lavergne on July 27, 1819. Here she was referred to as a minor under the age of twenty-one, the "natural daughter of Marguerite D'Arcantel, free woman of color, and of Charles Laveaux, also a free man of color residing in New Orleans." Jacques Paris was a free quadroon from Saint Domingue, probably one of the refugees who came to New Orleans as a result of the Haitian Revolution. Jacques was "above the age of majority" and had sufficient means to bring to the marriage $500 "derived from his economy and thrift."

Marie and Jacques stated that "having the intention of being married together," they promised to "comply with all the civil provisions and agreements of their marriage contract" and to "have one partnership of assets and gains, which are settled according to the laws of the state." Charles Laveaux provided Marie with a dowry "because of the attachment he bears for her as his natural daughter whom he acknowledges," giving to the future husband and wife "a donation *inter vivos* and irrevocable . . . of that half lot belonging to him situated in the Faubourg Marigny in Rue d'Amour . . . numbered 207." All parties declared themselves "content and satisfied," and "St. Yago" Paris, Charles Laveaux, Notary Lavergne, and the other witnesses affixed their signatures; Marie did not sign, indicating that she could not write.[1]

On August 4, 1819, Marie Laveau and Jacques Paris were married at St. Louis Cathedral by Fray Antonio de Sedella (Père Antoine). The venerable Spanish priest recorded their marriage in the sacramental register: "Santiago Paris, free quadroon, native of Jeremie on the Island of Santo Domingo, resident of this city, natural son of Santiago Paris and Sanité Bleon, was married . . . to Maria Labeau, free woman of color, native and resident of this parish, natural daughter of Carlos Labeau and Margarita D'Arcantel." The witnesses included Charles Laveaux's brother Chardy (Jardet) Laveaux, his brother-in-law Paul Cheval, and the prominent white Creole attorney Christoval de Armas.[2]

Both of the documents above were discovered and translated by Louisiana Writers' Project fieldworkers. Robert Tallant was obviously aware of the Laveau-Paris marriage contract, by which Charles Laveaux gave Marie a half lot on Rue d'Amour (later renamed Love Street and then North Rampart). Although the contract refers only to an undeveloped lot, not "a lot with buildings and improvements," Tallant fostered the legend that Marie and Jacques resided in a comfortable cottage provided by Marie's father. According to *Voodoo in New Orleans*, "The newly married couple lived in a house in what is now the 1900 block of North Rampart Street, in a house given to Marie by her father, Charles Laveau, as a part of her dowry." In his novel, *The Voodoo Queen*, Marie loses this home when Laveau, a white planter, dies, and his wife claims the property.[3] We cannot assume that Charles Laveaux gave Marie and her future husband a house or that they ever lived at 207 Rue d'Amour. A search of city directories for the 1820s shows that address as unoccupied.[4]

The archival evidence indicates that Marie and Jacques first resided on Bayou Road. On July 20, 1820, a year after they were married, we find Santiago Paris and Marie Catherine (no surname) standing as godparents at the St. Louis Cathedral baptism of the free mulatto child Eugene Foucher. Eugene was the son of Marie's maternal half-sister Marie Louise D'Arcantel and her husband Louis Foucher. The fact that Jacques and Marie were chosen for this role demonstrates that they met the canon law requirement that godparents be baptized and confirmed in the Roman Catholic faith and demonstrate a commitment to the church. While the baptismal register does not usually give the address of parents and godparents, this entry records that all were "residents of Bayou St. John Road in this parish."[5] By 1822 Marie and Jacques were living at 122 Dauphine between Dumaine and St. Philip, where "St. Yague Paries" was listed in the city directory as a cabinetmaker. Marie's father owned property on both sides of this block.[6]

*   *   *

Almost everything written about Marie Laveau, scholarly works as well as popular treatments of her history, state unequivocally that no children were born of her marriage to Jacques Paris. A search of the St. Louis Cathedral baptismal registers, however, uncovered entries for two daughters. Marie Angèlie Paris, *mulâtresse libre*, was born November 27, 1822, and baptized on February 14, 1823. She was recorded as "fille légitime de Jacques Paris et de Marie Laveau, gens de couleur libres" (legitimate daughter of Jacques Paris and Marie Laveau, free people of color). Felicité Paris, *mulâtresse libre*, was baptized on November 17, 1824. Felicité was stated to be seven years old, daughter of the late Jacques Paris and Catherine "Lilavoix." Given the mangled phonetic spellings employed by the priests of St. Louis Cathedral, plus the possibility that Marie was using her middle name, "Catherine Lilavoix" was almost certainly Marie Laveau. Seven-year-old Felicité would have been born in 1817, when Marie was only sixteen, two years before her marriage to Jacques Paris. Although baptismal records usually specify whether the baptizand was a natural or a legitimate child, this one does not. Felicité would have been legitimized by Marie's subsequent marriage to Jacques.[7] I found no further reference to Marie Angèlie and Felicité in the archival record. The girls most likely died in childhood, but this cannot be verified because the St. Louis Cathedral funeral registers for 1825–1829 have been lost.

Marie Laveau's *Daily Picayune* and *Daily City Item* obituaries declared that Jacques Paris "disappeared" a year after their marriage, and "no one knows to this day what became of him." Lyle Saxon, in *Fabulous New Orleans*, and Herbert Asbury, in *The French Quarter*, stated authoritatively that Jacques died in 1826. In *Voodoo in New Orleans*, Tallant wrote, with no citation of the source, that "there is a record of his death some five or six years after the wedding." In *The Voodoo Queen*, Tallant has Jacques leave Marie in disapproval of her Voudou practice, take employment on a ship traveling between New Orleans and Marseille, and die in a storm just as the vessel enters the mouth of the Mississippi River on its return trip. In Francine Prose's *Marie Laveau*, Jacques is possessed on their wedding night by Ezili-Freda, the Haitian Vodou spirit of love and femininity, who takes him for her own. Jewell Parker Rhodes, in *Voodoo Dreams*, neatly eliminates Jacques by having the African conjurer Doctor John turn him into a zombie.[8]

The fate of Jacques Paris remains a mystery; no documentation of his death has been discovered. His daughter Marie Angèlie would have been conceived in March of 1822 and his demise or disappearance could have occurred at any time between that date and November 1824, when Felicité's baptismal record declared him to be deceased. The absence of a death certificate or funeral record has led to the supposition that Jacques deserted Marie, perhaps to return to Haiti. But few deaths were reported to the Recorder of Births and Deaths during those early years, and, if Jacques Paris died in one of the fatal yellow fever epidemics, he could have been buried in a mass grave with no notation in the sacramental registers. Whatever happened to her husband, Marie was henceforth designated in official records as "the Widow Paris" and went by that name for the rest of her life.

The Laveau Legend maintains that after becoming a widow Marie Laveau supported herself as a hairdresser, being called to the homes of wealthy white women to arrange their coiffures. It is said that family secrets learned from these patrons during her hairdressing days later proved useful in her Voudou practice. The memoir of the free colored hairdresser Eliza Potter, published in 1859, attests to the intimacy of the relationship between hairdresser and client, and to the confessions and gossip that she was likely to hear: "My avocation calls me into the upper classes of society . . . and there reigns as many elements of misery as the world can produce. . . . Nowhere do hearts betray themselves more unguardedly than in the private boudoir, where the hairdresser's mission makes her a daily attendant. . . . Indeed, I have often wished I could absent myself from conversations that I knew ought to be confidential and that I had no business to hear."[9]

George Washington Cable's character Palmyre la Philosophe, from his novel *The Grandissimes*, was both a hairdresser and a Voudou priestess. Palmyre was said to have been modeled after Marie Laveau. Henry Castellanos was perhaps inspired by *The Grandissimes* when, in *New Orleans As It Was*, he characterized Marie herself as a hairdresser. This statement was repeated in Herbert Asbury's *The French Quarter*, turns up in Robert Tallant's *Voodoo in New Orleans* and *The Voodoo Queen*, and has found its way into subsequent portrayals of Marie Laveau.[10] Many free women of color indeed followed this profession, but Marie was never listed as such in the city directories or the U.S. Census.

The hairdresser story is given some credibility by a couple of Louisiana Writers' Project interviews. Theresa Kavanaugh, born about 1860, said that Marie Laveau "called herself a hairdresser, and that's how she got in the good graces of the fine people." Mary Washington was born in 1863. As a young woman, she operated a fruit and oyster stand on the corner of Rampart and St. Ann streets, steps away from Marie Laveau's cottage. She claimed to have been a Laveau disciple, telling her interviewer that she "often visited the home of the Voudou Queen." Mrs. Washington recalled that Marie "was some kind of a hairdresser and seamster, but she did all that in her early days. Shucks, she soon cut that stuff out. Her associating with the white people made her know how to fool them."[11]

Christophe Glapion

Sometime after the disappearance of Jacques Paris, Marie Laveau entered a domestic relationship with Louis Christophe Dominic Duminy de Glapion that lasted until his death in 1855. Her 1881 obituaries from the *Picayune* and the *City Item* stated that Marie "married Captain Christophe Glapion . . . [who] served with distinction in the [free colored] battalion of men of Santo Domingo, under D'Aquin, with Jackson in the war of 1815." This gave rise to the erroneous belief that Glapion was a person of mixed race from Saint Domingue.

The statement regarding Christophe Glapion's ethnicity first appeared in Lyle Saxon's *Fabulous New Orleans*: "shortly after [the death of Jacques Paris] his widow formed a liaison with Christophe Glapion, another mulatto." The notion was repeated in Robert Tallant's *Voodoo in New Orleans* and *The Voodoo Queen*, where Glapion was characterized as "a quadroon from Santo Domingo." Francine Prose, in her novel *Marie Laveau*, portrayed him as the owner of a bookshop, a "tall, saffron-colored mulatto" with "almost-Arab features, [and] a neat black moustache and goatee." Marie finds him as "dignified as a cavalry officer on horseback" and remembers him as the leader of Andrew Jackson's Ninth Native Regiment.[12] Glapion does not appear as a character in Jewell Parker Rhodes' *Voodoo Dreams*.

Christophe Glapion's baptismal entry, military service documents, his death certificate and property succession, plus a wealth of civil and ecclesiastical records relating to his grandparents, parents, and siblings, indicate that he was born in Louisiana, the legitimate son of white parents and descendant of an aristocratic French family. Just as the Louisiana Writers' Project researchers knew that Marie Laveau's father was not a wealthy white planter, they knew perfectly well that her domestic partner was not a man of color. LWP workers discovered many of the documents relating to Christophe Glapion in the course of their research in city and archdiocesan archives and placed typed translations in the files.

The Glapion family originated in the French parish of Sainte Scholastique in Normandy. Christophe Duminy de Glapion's grandfather was the Chevalier Christophe de Glapion, Sieur du Mesnilgauches—later shortened to Duminil or Duminy. The title of *Chevalier*, literally "horseman," is the French equivalent of the English knight; de Glapion was a Knight of St. Louis. The Chevalier de Glapion came to Louisiana in the early eighteenth century and settled in St. John the Baptist Parish on the *Côte d'Allemande* (German Coast) up the

Mississippi River from New Orleans.[13] Don Cristobal, as he was referred to in Spanish documents, held the respected position of regidor of the Cabildo, having purchased the office of "receptor de penas de cámera" (receiver of court fines) in 1776. His duties involved collecting and recording fines imposed by the civil courts, of which he was entitled to 10 percent.[14]

The Chevalier Christophe de Glapion and his wife were the parents of four children, one of whom was Denis Christophe Dominic Duminil de Glapion, born in 1764.[15] Denis Christophe married Jeanne Sophie Lalande Ferrier, daughter of a French military officer and his Louisiana-born wife. Among the couple's twelve children was Louis Christophe Dominic, who became the domestic partner of Marie Laveau. Louis Christophe was born in 1789 and baptized on January 18, 1790, at the Church of St. Charles Borromeo in St. John the Baptist Parish.[16]

As Marie Laveau's obituaries correctly state, Christophe Glapion was a veteran of the Battle of New Orleans, which took place below the city at Chalmette on January 8, 1815. A search of the military records at the National Archives and Records Administration reveals that he was mustered into service on December 23, 1814, the day of the English invasion. He was not, however, the captain of the free colored Battalion of Men of Santo Domingo. This position was held by Charles Savary, a man of color, under the command of a white officer, Major Louis D'Aquin. Both were Saint Domingue immigrants. Christophe Glapion served for approximately three months as a private in the all-white Cavellier's Second Regiment of Louisiana Militia under Captain Barthélemy Fabré Daunoy.[17]

In 1817 Christophe's mother, the Widow Jeanne Sophie Lalande Ferrier Duminil de Glapion, moved from St. John the Baptist Parish to New Orleans. She settled at 25 Bayou Road between Rampart and St. Claude, now the 1100 block of Governor Nicholls, just outside the Vieux Carré. Christophe, by then a young bachelor, may have shared this home with his mother and sisters. As we have learned, Marie Laveau and her husband Jacques Paris were also living on Bayou Road. Catherine Dillon, in her "Voodoo" manuscript chapter "Marie the Great," noted that "After their marriage, Jacques Paris and his beautiful young wife made their home on Bayou Road, just off Rampart Street. . . . Their next-door neighbor was the Widow Glapion." Dillon conjectured that the love affair between Marie and Christophe began at this time: "Thus Marie Laveau Paris came to know and cast longing eyes toward Christophe Duminy Glapion, and he, like so many others, could not resist the magnetism of her gaze."[18] In reality, we have no idea where or how Marie and Christophe met.

Interracial relationships such as that between Marie Laveau and Christophe Glapion were common in early nineteenth-century New Orleans. What makes this alliance exceptional is that Marie was not a typical plaçée, an exquisite and charming companion comfortably provided for by her white protector. Such women were usually "placed" when in their early teens; if her partner eventually left to take a wife of his own race, the plaçée might then marry a man of color. But Marie had already been married to Jacques Paris, borne two children, and was a widow in her mid-twenties when she and Christophe Glapion began their relationship. More significantly, she was no ordinary young woman—she would eventually become the city's most celebrated Voudou priestess. Glapion appears to have played no role in Marie's religious vocation.

Most of the Louisiana Writers' Project interviewees were born after Glapion died in 1855; thus he is never mentioned in the oral histories. The archival evidence indicates that, like most racially mixed couples, Marie and Christophe socialized with Marie's family and friends within the free colored community and chose them as godparents for their children. Christophe had both colored and white business associates. He maintained at least some contact with his mother and sisters, although Marie and their biracial offspring would not have been acknowledged by his kin, and especially not by his female relations. As the free nonwhite community began to coalesce and marriages between men and women of African descent became the norm, some Creoles of color looked down on their peers who cohabited with white men. We have no way of knowing if Marie and Christophe were affected by these attitudes.[19]

Children

Marie Laveau and Christophe Glapion probably became a couple in the mid-1820s. The *Daily Picayune* obituary declared that "Fifteen children were the result of this marriage. Only one of them is now alive." Although this number is likely an exaggeration, the story has been repeated by most subsequent writers.

Documentation exists for seven children born to Marie Laveau and Christophe Glapion: Marie Heloïse Euchariste, Marie Louise Caroline, Christophe, Jean Baptiste, François Maurice Christophe, Marie Philomène, and Archange Edouard. In addition, Marie raised at least three of her grandchildren. The *Picayune's Guide to New Orleans* for 1897 also reported that she "used to gather from the streets the young orphans whom no one else laid claim to and give them the shelter of her charitable roof."[20] This statement is supported by archival evidence. In 1852 Marie sponsored a seven-year-old boy named François, referred to as her *protégée*, at the *Institution Catholique des Orphelines Indigents* (Catholic Institution for Indigent Orphans), a school established with funds bequeathed by an African-born former slave, Marie Justine Couvent.[21]

Marie and Christophe's first child, Marie Heloïse, was born February 2, 1827. This is the daughter designated by twentieth-century writers as "Marie II." Heloïse was baptized on August 19, 1828. Her name was entered in the baptismal register as "Marie Heloïse fille naturelle de Marie Lavau," followed by an asterisk that refers to Christophe Glapion's name added in the margin. Glapion also signed the register, acknowledging Heloïse as his daughter. Most baptisms were signed only by the priest, not by either parent.[22] Heloïse also appears in the archival record as Eloise, Eloisa, Epicaris, and Euchariste.

Marie Louise, probably named for Marie's maternal half-sister, was born August 10, 1829. Her baptismal entry for September 10, 1829, refers to her as "enfant libre et natural de Marie Laveaux, Veuve Jacques Paris" (free natural child of Marie Laveau, Widow of Jacques Paris). On December 9, 1829, the funeral of Caroline Laveau Glapion was recorded; she was described as "enfant de colour libre, ageé de cinq mois, fille naturelle de Marie Laveaud, Veuve Jacques Paris" (a free child of color, age five months, natural daughter of Marie Laveau, Widow of Jacques Paris). This is undoubtedly the same girl as Marie Louise, who would have been five months old at the time.[23]

The third of the Laveau-Glapion children was a son named Christophe, who died at the age of eight days on May 21, 1831. The funeral register refers to him as the "natural son of Marie Laveau."[24] Another son, Jean Baptiste, died the following year, on July 12, 1832, also at the age of eight days.[25]

François Maurice Christophe was born September 22, 1833. Six months later Marie went in person to the Recorder of Births and Deaths to register the boy, stating herself to be thirty-three years old, a resident of St. Ann Street between Rampart and Burgundy. She signed with an X. François was baptized on May 13, 1834; his godfather was François Auguste, the husband of Marie's paternal half-sister Marie Dolores Laveaux. Marie and Christophe also lost this child, at the age of eight months, on May 18, 1834. The register for St. Louis Cathedral records the funeral of François, the "son of Dominique Glapion and Marie Lavaud [*sic*]."[26]

Marie Philomène's April 1, 1836, baptism was entered into the sacramental register under the name Phélonise Lavan, "fille natural de Marie Lavan et père inconnu" (natural daughter of Marie Lavan and an unknown father) born March 6, 1836. Marie again went to the Recorder of Births and Deaths to report Philomène's arrival. She stated her own age to be thirty-five and declared that

Table 2. Marie Laveau's Maternal Line

First Generation—Great-Grandparents

Marguerite
  enslaved negress, possibly African; born ca. 1736, died before 1782
Jean Belaire
  enslaved negro, possibly African; dates unknown

Second Generation—Grandmother

Natural daughter of Marguerite and Jean Belaire
Catherine Henry
  negress, born enslaved, purchased freedom 1795; born 1754, died 1831 (market woman)

Third Generation—Mother

Natural daughter of Catherine Henry, possibly fathered by Catherine's white owner, Henry Roche *dit* Belaire (master shoemaker)
Marguerite Henry/D'Arcantel
  mulatress, born enslaved, freed gratis in 1790; born 1772, died 1825

Fourth Generation—Marie Laveau and Surviving Siblings

Natural daughter of Marguerite Henry and Charles Laveaux (merchant), free mulatto
Marie Catherine Laveau
  free mulatress; born 1801, died 1881 (Voudou priestess)

Natural children of Marguerite Henry and Henri D'Arcantel (chief accounting office of the Spanish army and royal household), white
Marie Louise D'Arcantel
  free quadroon; born ca. 1796, died ?
Antoine D'Arcantel
  free quadroon; dates unknown

Legitimate children of Charles Laveaux and Françoise Dupart, free mulattos
Marie Dolores Laveaux
  free mulatress; born 1804, died in Paris 1839
Laurent Charles Laveaux
  free mulatto; born 1805, died ?

Fifth Generation—Children

Legitimate children of Marie Laveau and Jacques Paris (carpenter), free quadroon
Felicité Paris
  free quadroon; born 1817, died ?
Angèlie Paris
  free quadroon; born 1822, died ?

continued

Table 2—*Continued*

Natural children of Marie Laveau and Christophe Glapion (real estate speculator), white

Marie Heloïse Euchariste Glapion
    free quadroon; born 1827, died 1862
Marie Louise Glapion
    free quadroon; died in infancy 1829
Christophe Glapion
    free quadroon; died in infancy 1831
Jean Baptiste Glapion
    free quadroon; died in infancy 1832
François Maurice Glapion
    free quadroon; born 1833, died 1834
Marie Philomène Glapion
    free quadroon; born 1836, died 1897
Archange Edouard Glapion
    free quadroon; born 1839, died 1845

Philomène Glapion was "the natural daughter of the said Deponent . . . [and] Mr. Christophe Duminy Glapion" born in "a house situated on St. Ann Street between Burgundy and Rampart Streets." As usual, Marie signed with an X. A second baptismal record for Philomène appears in the St. Louis Cathedral register for 1838. In this version she is called Philomène Glapion, "fille natural de Christophe Glapion et de Marie Laveau." Her parents were sufficiently concerned with establishing Christophe's paternity and acknowledgment of Philomène as his daughter that they returned to the church office to have the baptismal record corrected.[27]

Archange Edouard was born June 5, 1838, and baptized on May 7, 1839. He died on January 6, 1845, at the age of seven years and six months.[28] The loss of this son, the only one to have survived infancy, must have been particularly tragic for Marie and Christophe. Archange was interred in the Widow Paris tomb in St. Louis Cemetery No. 1. His name and death date are inscribed below that of Christophe Glapion on the middle tablet and again on a marble plaque set into the ground.

Representations of Marie Laveau

What was Marie Laveau's physical appearance during the antebellum years, as she married, raised her family, and began her Voudou practice? Her daughter Philomène Glapion Legendre declared, when interviewed by a *Daily Picayune* reporter after Marie's death, that her mother never sat for an artist or allowed herself to be photographed.[29] Nevertheless, almost every nineteenth-century portrait of a woman of color is said to represent the Voudou Queen.

The image of Marie Laveau most often reproduced is the painting that now hangs in the Louisiana State Museum in the old Cabildo on Jackson Square. The woman in this portrait appears to be in her middle thirties, with a rounded face, full lips, a rather flat nose, dark, penetrating eyes beneath gracefully arched brows, and a light complexion. She wears a plain black dress, a red shawl embellished with a delicate leaf pattern, gold hoop earrings, and a yellow and red plaid tignon from beneath which peep a few curls. According to the label, this is "Marie Laveau, legendary African American Voodoo Queen of New Orleans during the early nineteenth century." When Louisiana Writers' Project interviewees were asked by fieldworkers if the portrait resembled the Marie Laveau they remembered, they uniformly agreed that it did not.[30]

The original canvas was purportedly executed in 1837 by George Catlin (1796–1872). Catlin, noted for his portrayals of Native Americans, traveled the Mississippi River by steamboat during the 1830s, frequently stopping in New Orleans. Although he is not known to have depicted people of African-European heritage, Catlin may have been intrigued by New Orleans' famous free women of color.[31] The painting belonged at one time to Gaspar Cusachs, a New Orleans merchant, collector of antiquities, and a past president of the Louisiana Historical Society. The Catlin portrait was loaned by Cusachs to the Louisiana State Museum between 1911 and 1922. During this time a copy was made by museum employee Frank Schneider. In 1922, Cusachs reclaimed the portrait and sold it for $1,000 to Simon J. Schwartz, owner of the Maison Blanche Department Store, where Schwartz exhibited it in his "gallery" on the fourth floor. Schwartz sold the canvas to the Louisiana Historical Society in 1933. Although a *Times-Picayune* article of August 24, 1933, proclaimed that the Historical Society intended to return the portrait to the museum, this did not occur, and it was last heard of in 1947 in the possession of the Society's president, Edward A. Parsons.[32] The present whereabouts of the original painting is unknown, and it is Schneider's copy that hangs in the Louisiana State Museum.

An 1860s canvas, attributed to François Fleischbein and now in the collection of the New Orleans Museum of Art, represents a young woman in the black dress and white lace collar and cuffs characteristic of nineteenth-century mourning attire. She holds a slip of paper and a watch and wears a brooch, two strands of garnet beads, and a pair of pearl and garnet earrings. On her right

16. Alleged portrait of the first Marie Laveau. Oil on canvas. The original is said to have been painted in 1837 by George Catlin; the copy on display at the Louisiana State Museum was made in the early twentieth century by Frank Schnieder. (Collection of the Louisiana State Museum, accession no. A-02-11537.)

hand are two rings; her left hand is hidden. Her appearance is quite different from the subject of the Catlin portrait. Her eyebrows are heavy and straight; her hair is parted in the middle and braided; she does not wear a tignon. G. William Nott's highly imaginative *Times-Picayune* article of November 19, 1922, is illustrated with a reproduction of this painting, subtitled "Marie Laveau, high priestess of voudooism in New Orleans for many years, from an oil painting made when she was a young woman." Nott obviously decided that this unidentified lady would serve admirably for his depiction of Marie Laveau. The painting was subsequently copied by the late Charles Gandolfo, founder of the New Orleans Historic Voodoo Museum, and is displayed there as a likeness of Marie Laveau.[33]

Two lesser-known paintings of women of color are also said to depict the Voudou Queen. An undated miniature, signed A. Alaux, portrays a woman wearing a flower-print dress, several necklaces and lockets, earrings, and a yel-

17. *Portrait of a Free Woman of Color*. Oil on canvas. Attributed to Franz (François) Fleischbein sometime after 1860, this work is alleged to be a portrait of the second Marie Laveau or possibly of Marie Laveau's daughter. (New Orleans Museum of Art, gift of William E. Groves, accession no. 66.29.)

low and red plaid tignon. The miniature, part of the Gaspar Cusachs collection, is on permanent loan to the Louisiana State Museum.[34] An 1844 portrait signed by A. D. Rinck shows a darker-skinned woman wearing a simple dress and shawl, a bead necklace, earrings, and a tignon. This painting, according to an April 18, 1937, article in the *City Item*, was discovered in a secondhand store by the New Orleans collector Dr. Isaac Cline. It was said to have been exhibited in Rinck's Paris salon and was subsequently purchased by New Orleans chess champion Paul Morphy. Later it "passed into the hands of Negro devotees to the cult of Voodoo, who scratched out the eyes." The newspaper photograph of the portrait shows damage from abrasion and flaking over much of the canvas, not only the eyes, which do not appear to have been deliberately obliterated. Cline, an amateur conservator, cleaned the surface and restored the missing areas. The painting now belongs to the University of Southwestern Louisiana at Lafayette.[35]

The Cottage on St. Ann Street

Tour guides still point out the site of Marie Laveau's home on the uptown side of St. Ann Street between Rampart and Burgundy, at the edge of the Vieux Carré. This was a short walk from St. Louis Cathedral, Congo Square, the St. Louis Cemeteries, and the Parish Prison, all of which Marie frequented in her work and daily life. Here she performed her duties as a Voudou priestess, raised her family, and it was here that both she and Christophe Glapion died. Like most of the older dwellings in the neighborhood, the house was a Creole cottage of the type built in the Vieux Carré from colonial times through much of the nineteenth century. These one- or one-and-a-half-story houses consisted of four main rooms with doors opening to the outside. They were constructed of *bousillage* (a combination of clay or plaster and Spanish moss) or soft brick between wooden posts, covered with stucco or cypress weatherboard, and had overhanging side-gabled roofs covered with shingles, slate, or half-round earthenware tiles.[36]

Throughout the nineteenth century it was generally accepted that this cottage had been Marie Laveau's ancestral home. This perception changed with the publication of G. William Nott's 1922 *Times-Picayune* Sunday magazine article, "Marie Laveau, Long High Priestess of Voudouism." Nott was the first to relate the tale, supposedly learned from an "octogenarian mammy," of how Marie saved a young man from being convicted of a crime and received the house in payment from his grateful father. "When the day set for the trial came round," wrote Nott, "the wily 'voodoo,' after placing three Guinea peppers in her mouth, entered Saint Louis Cathedral, knelt at the altar rail, and was seen to remain in this posture for some time. Leaving the church, she gained admittance to the Cabildo [where criminal trials were held until the 1890s] ... and depositing the three peppers under the judge's bench, lingered to await developments." When the jury found the youth innocent, his father, "as a recompense for her miraculous intervention ... gave [Marie Laveau] the deed to a small cottage."[37]

Nott's relatively obscure article was appropriated by later twentieth-century writers and has become firmly embedded in the Laveau Legend. Herbert Asbury, in *The French Quarter*, and Robert Tallant, in *Voodoo in New Orleans*, retold the story almost verbatim, without acknowledging the source. Later, in *The Voodoo Queen*, Tallant has Marie and her domestic partner Christophe Glapion move into a house given to Marie by a client as a reward for securing the acquittal of his only son, accused of killing a man in self-defense during a

18. Creole cottage at 915–917 St. Ann between Burgundy and Dauphine. This house is of the same type as Marie Laveau's home on St. Ann between Rampart and Burgundy; the bricks are exposed instead of being covered with stucco or weatherboard. (Historic American Building Survey 36-NWOR, 79-1, Library of Congress, Division of Prints and Photographs. Image courtesy of the Library of Congress photoduplication service.)

barroom altercation. Francine Prose, in her novel *Marie Laveau*, eschews this tale, as does Jewell Parker Rhodes in *Voodoo Dreams*. Prose has Marie buy the cottage with money inherited from her parents. In Rhodes' *Voodoo Dreams*, the house, called the Maison Blanche, belongs to the African conjurer Doctor John. It is to this home that he takes Marie after seducing her away from her husband, Jacques Paris.[38]

In the case of Marie Laveau's cottage on St. Ann Street, the nineteenth-century accounts are true. The house was built for Marie's grandmother, Catherine Henry, sometime after she bought the lot in 1798. The 1822 city directory shows Catherine residing at 57 St. Ann; in 1823 the numbering had changed and her address was 179 St. Ann. After 1861 the house number became 152 St. Ann.

On March 19, 1831, Catherine Henry summoned Notary Octave de Armas and three witnesses to her home for the purpose of making her will. De Armas noted that they "found the said Catherine Henry sitting in a chair, ill in body but sane in spirit and memory and understanding." Catherine stated

19. *Voudou Quarters.* An artist's conception of Marie Laveau's cottage, *Picayune's Guide to New Orleans* for 1900, p. 65. (The Historic New Orleans Collection, Williams Research Center, accession no. 71-63-L.)

that, although she had never been lawfully married, she had four natural children named Marguerite, Joseph, Celestin, and Narcisse. All except Joseph were dead, "but Marguerite has left three children named Marie Louise, Antoine, and Marie, and Narcisse has left one small daughter named Catherine." Catherine Henry declared that "her property consists of the lot of ground and house in which she resides . . . and the little furniture for her particular use." She appointed her son Joseph Bizou, who shared her home and cared for her in her old age, as her testamentary executor.[39]

Catherine Henry died a few months later, on June 18, 1831. In the entry for her funeral in the sacramental register of St. Louis Cathedral, she is referred to as a "free negress aged about seventy-eight years, born in this city and died the day of her interment at half-past-six in the morning."[40]

Catherine Henry's property succession was opened in probate court on June 28. Included in this lengthy document is the claim of a creditor, who declared that the estate was indebted to him for the sum of $1,200 loaned to the deceased on January, 24, 1824, as well as for $81.02 for her funeral and doctor bills. Present at the customary "family meeting" regarding settlement of Catherine's estate were Catherine's son Joseph Bizou and her grandchildren Catherine Narcisse, Marie Louise and Antoine D'Arcantel, and Marie Laveau. It was decided by the heirs that the property on St. Ann Street should be sold at public auction and the proceeds used to pay the debt.[41] As we will see, Christophe Glapion bought the cottage, which continued to house the Laveau-Glapion family until the end of the nineteenth century.

*   *   *

At this time Marie Laveau and Christophe Glapion began a sequence of maneuvers by which they put their real estate holdings in the names of their minor children, evidently hoping to hide their property from possible creditors and circumvent the laws that prevented a white man from leaving wealth to his nonwhite family. While these mundane transactions were being enacted in the quiet of the notary's office, the horrors of the 1832 fever season—the evil-smelling smudge fires, the ominous booming of the cannons, and the rattling of the death carts—were taking place throughout the city. Eight thousand New Orleanians, possibly including Marie and Christophe's infant son Jean Baptiste, perished from cholera and yellow fever that summer. One wonders how anyone had the presence of mind of attend to business.

On July 25, 1832, Marie and Christophe appeared before the notary Louis T. Caire to donate to their five-year-old daughter, Marie Heloïse Euchariste Glapion, the lot at 207 Rue d'Amour given to Marie by her father in 1819 on the occasion of her marriage to Jacques Paris. In this document Marie is referred to as the "widow without children of Santyaque Paris," indicating that Feliticé and Angèlie, the daughters from her first marriage, were dead. Marie Laveau made the *inter vivos* donation of her "one-half lot of ground" on Rue d'Amour, valued at $1,000, "as a mark of tenderness to her daughter Epicaris [*sic*] Glapion, free female of color, her minor daughter, born since her widowhood to herself and Christophe Glapion by whom she is acknowledged." The donation was "accepted for the child . . . by her natural father Christophe Glapion dwelling in this city, here present." Notary Caire, the witnesses, and Christophe Glapion signed the document, and Marie, "declaring that she has no knowledge of writing," signed with an X.[42]

Marie Laveau had always maintained friendly relations with her father, Charles Laveaux, and over the years the two were involved in various business transactions. Laveaux's financial affairs had taken a downward turn after the death of his wife Françoise Dupart, and he was even sued by the couple's legitimate children, Marie Dolores and Laurent Charles, for allegedly defrauding them of their inheritance.[43] On September 28, 1832, Marie Laveau appeared before the notary Theodore Seghers to assign power of attorney to Charles Laveaux, authorizing him to mortgage her property at 207 Rue d'Amour. It

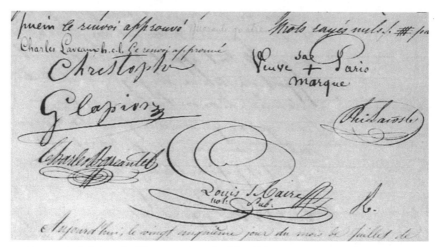

20. Signature of Christophe Glapion and mark of the Widow Paris. Donation by Marie Laveau to her daughter Heloïse Euchariste Glapion, Acts of Louis T. Caire, July 25, 1832. (Courtesy of the Notarial Archives Research Center, New Orleans, Louisiana.)

was described in this document as "a half lot with buildings and dependencies situated on Rue d'Amour in the Faubourg Marigny," meaning that a house and outbuildings had been erected since Marie acquired the vacant land in 1819.[44]

On the same day, the cottage of the late Catherine Henry was auctioned, by order of the probate court, at the new Exchange Coffee House. Christophe Glapion bought Marie's ancestral home for $3,355, "payable one third at nine months and the balance at eighteen months."[45]

Two months later the once-prosperous businessman Charles Laveaux declared bankruptcy "owing to the pressure of the times and to various losses in business." Sixteen creditors presented their claims—totaling almost $10,500— against the estate of the "insolvent debtor." Laveaux listed his assets as a boat valued at $450; $500 worth of movable furnishings from his tavern; two slaves worth $350, on whom there existed a mortgage; and property in the Faubourg Marigny worth $6,000, also mortgaged. These assets, plus $273.43 in debts owed to him, amounted to $7,573.43. Most of his holdings, including his corner store building, were subsequently sold, and when he died three years later there was nothing left for his children.[46]

On November 28, 1832, Marie Laveau and the other heirs of Catherine Henry received their bequests. One third of the estate, $363.41, went to Catherine's son Joseph Bizou; one third went to Catherine Narcisse, minor daughter of her deceased son Narcisse Henry; and one third was equally divided between the three children of her late daughter Marguerite D'Arcantel, "Marie Louise D'Arcantel widow of the late Louis Foucher [Foucher had died in 1824], her brother Antoine D'Arcantel, and Marie Laveau widow of Jacques Paris."[47]

On August 11, 1836, Christophe Glapion used the St. Ann Street property as security for the purchase of $5,000 worth of stock in the Citizens' Bank of Louisiana.[48] Two years later, on June 8, 1838, Glapion sold the house for $1,500, less than half the price he paid for it, to the free man of color Pierre Charles Marioux. Glapion was granted use of the property during his lifetime. On September 23, 1839, Marioux, who was ill, summoned the notary Theodore Seghers to his home to enact an *inter vivos* donation to Marie Laveau and Christophe Glapion's three-year-old daughter Marie Philomène and their one-year-old son Archange. Philomène and Archange were referred to as "the children of Marie Laveaux f.w.c., the widow of Saint Yague Paris . . . here present to accept for the two children."[49] Louisiana law was making it increasingly difficult for a white man to give such a donation to his nonwhite family, but donations between persons of color were perfectly legal. This sale and donation was obviously a tactic to ensure that the Laveau-Glapion children could inherit the family home.

Although Christophe Glapion bought the St. Ann Street property in 1832, it was only in 1841 that the family began to appear at this address in the city directories. Christophe, who dabbled in stock speculation, money lending, real estate, and slave trading, was listed in 1841, 1842, 1846, and 1853; his occupation was never specified. Marie, on the other hand, turned up in almost every city directory—also with no stated occupation—from 1841 until her death in 1881. Over the years she was listed as Marie Lavaud Widow Paris, Mrs. Laveau Paris, Widow Mary Paris, Marie Laveau, Marie Paris Widow of Christophe, and Mrs. Lavan Paris. In 1880 she was Mary Glapion, and in 1881 she was listed as Marie Glapion, Widow of Dominick. Although some people of African descent were designated in the city directories as f.m.c. or f.w.c. before the Civil War and later as "col'd," Marie Laveau was not.[50]

The Laveau-Glapion family was enumerated for the first time in the U.S. Census of 1850. Marie Laveau, here called "Mrs. Widow Paris," was listed as the head of household, with family members C. Glapion, Heloïse Glapion, and Philomène Glapion. Also included were two children called Malvina and Henieta, with no surname. All household members, even Glapion, were designated as mulattos born in Louisiana. Christophe may have had a tawny complexion and was either mistaken for a man of color or represented himself as such to the census enumerator.[51]

The two little girls residing with the Laveau-Glapion family in 1850 were probably the daughters of Marie Heloïse Euchariste Glapion. At a young age Heloïse had entered a long-term relationship with the free man of color Pierre Crokère (usually anglicized as Crocker), a well-to-do commission broker, builder, and architect. His father, Bazile Crokère, was characterized as "one of the handsomest men in New Orleans," and was a respected free colored militia officer, fencing master, and professor of mathematics. Pierre was twenty-four years older than Heloïse and had been married since 1827 to Rose Gignac, with whom he had ten children. He died in 1857 at the age of fifty-six.[52]

Heloïse gave birth to her first child with Pierre Crocker when she was seventeen years old. The baptismal register of St. Augustine's Church records that Joseph Eugene Crocker, natural son of Eloise Glapion and Pierre Crocker, was born February 28, 1844, and baptized on May 18 of that year. Crocker acknowledged the child in the presence of two witnesses, and all three signed the baptismal book.[53] Joseph Eugene died at the age of one year on May 5, 1845. He was interred, along with his sister Esmeralda Crocker, in the Widow Paris tomb in St. Louis Cemetery No. 1. The marble tablet bears the inscription "Jph. Eugene Crocker décédé le 5 Mais 1845/ Esmeralda Crocker décédé le 8 Janvier 1850."

Two more children, both referred to in the sacramental registers as "daughter of the free mulatress Eloise Glapion," were baptized at St. Louis Cathedral. Adelai Glapion was born December 25, 1847, and baptized on February 3, 1848. Adelai would be the girl referred to in the 1850 census as "Malvina," probably a misspelling of Aldina, the name she used in later life. Marie Glapion was born June 12 and baptized on July 9, 1850; her godmother was Marie Laveau.[54] Marie may have been the one-year-old child called "Henieta" in the 1850 census. Although Pierre Crocker's name does not appear on the baptismal register for either of these girls, they later used the surname Crocker.

On November 8, 1853, at the end of the worst yellow fever epidemic in New Orleans history, Heloïse gave birth to another son, Victor Pierre Duminy Dieudonné de Glapion, known as Victor Pierre Crocker. His middle name, *Dieudonné*, means "God has given."[55] Victor Pierre was raised in the Laveau-Glapion household, along with his sisters Aldina and Marie.

Marie Heloïse Euchariste Glapion disappears from the archival record after this, and her name occurs nowhere in the Louisiana Writers' Project interviews. Her whereabouts remain a mystery. Only in 1881, when Victor Pierre Crocker petitioned the Civil District Court for possession of "all the effects belonging to the succession" of his deceased mother, was it revealed that Heloïse had died in 1862. Victor Pierre's petition was accompanied by the affidavits of Philomène Glapion Legendre and four family friends, all of whom signed before Notary Charles Rolle. Philomène testified that "Eloise Euchariste Glapion was her natural sister . . . that she is the godmother of the petitioner [Victor Pierre Crocker] . . . [and] that her sister presented the said child to the officiating priest at his baptism, which was celebrated at no. 152 St. Ann Street." All verified that Heloïse had "departed life in this city in the month of June, 1862."⁵⁶

*   *   *

Louisiana Writers' Project informants who had grown up in the St. Ann Street neighborhood in the 1860s–1880s offered their recollections of Marie Laveau's home. It had probably changed little since the antebellum years when it was occupied by Marie, Christophe, their children, and grandchildren. The cottage was described in the interviews as a "little old time wooden shack with the paint wore off," having "two rooms and then a gallery and then two more rooms." The roof "came way down on the side, and there was no roof in the front." Most of the LWP narrators said the house was set back in a big yard, with a flower garden and pomegranate and banana trees. All mentioned the "high closed fence in the front" that protected the family home from curious eyes.⁵⁷

Several of the LWP interviews mentioned the Choctaw market women who were allowed to camp in the yard. The Choctaws lived at the reservation on Bayou Lacombe, across Lake Pontchartrain, and came into New Orleans by boat or train to sell herbs, fruits, and vegetables at the French Market. One neighbor remembered that they "would sleep on the ground . . . with their babies in their baskets and all their wares." Another said that Marie "had lots of Indians living with her and some [former] slaves." An unattributed report in the LWP files noted that "There was a room off to itself in the back yard where [Marie Laveau] gave shelter to [the] . . . Indian women."⁵⁸

The LWP interviews are verified by Sanborn Fire Insurance maps of the 1880s, which show the cottage at 152 St. Ann as a square one-story structure with a back gallery and four outbuildings, one of which is one-and-a-half stories. Unlike the other houses on the block, which front directly on the street, this one is set back on the lot with an ample yard on the left and in the rear.⁵⁹

Marie Laveau's family occupied the cottage on St. Ann Street for nearly a hundred years (1798–1897). During this time living conditions remained generally unchanged for people of modest means. Most of the domestic activity took place in the backyard. Because of the danger of fire, cooking was done in a detached kitchen. Daily trips to the market were necessary owing to the lack of refrigeration, although by the later nineteenth century steam boats were bringing in great blocks of ice from the North. A vegetable garden and hen-house were usually located in the yard near the kitchen, and some people also kept a few pigs and a milk cow. There were cypress cisterns for collecting rain water. When the cisterns ran dry, residents could buy from carts that made the rounds of the city with hogsheads of purified water; they also attempted to treat river water with alum or clarify it by filtering. Bathing was done in a large metal tub into which heated water was poured. Laundry was washed in an iron pot in the yard, although some families sent their clothes out to a laundress. There was a privy in back for daytime use; at night residents used a chamber pot, which was emptied into the street in the morning. In winter, homes were heated by small coal- or wood-burning fireplaces. The unscreened windows were left open for ventilation in summer. Mosquitoes were a constant plague, and beds were equipped with mosquito bars and netting. If the family owned slaves, the endless tasks of caring for children, cooking, marketing, gardening, feeding the chickens and other livestock, gathering eggs, milking the cow, transporting and heating bath water, tending the fireplaces, washing and ironing clothes, house cleaning, and emptying chamber pots was performed by bondswomen. Otherwise this work was done by the wife and older children of the household.

4

Slaves

The institution of slavery in Louisiana underwent great changes under the American administration. As business and agriculture began to flourish, citizens clamored for additional workers. The revolt in Saint Domingue, which culminated in the overthrow of white rule and the establishment of the Republic of Haiti, had made Louisianians even more wary of slaves originating in the Caribbean islands. They preferred captives brought directly from Africa, presumably uncontaminated by revolutionary ideas. But an 1804 act banned the importation of "foreign" slaves into the Territory of Orleans, and in 1808, when the United States ceased to participate in the African slave trade, it became illegal to bring Africans into *any* state of the Union. The citizens of the Territory protested that their sugar and cotton plantations would become valueless without an adequate labor supply.[1]

Slave smuggling was therefore rife, and the illegal trade in enslaved persons from Africa flourished during the early antebellum period and continued sporadically until the eve of the Civil War. As late as the 1850s there were occasional reports of shipments of Africans, with filed teeth and "the brands and marks of the tribe from which they came," being unloaded and offered for sale in Louisiana and surrounding states.[2]

Slaves who legally entered Louisiana during the antebellum period were brought from Maryland, Virginia, and the Carolinas to be sold in the slave "depots" of New Orleans. The first of these clusters of slave pens evolved in the 1830s on the edge of the Vieux Carré at the corner of Chartres and Esplanade. After 1840 another slave market was located above Canal Street in the central business district. Many of these "American" slaves were destined for the ever-expanding sugar and cotton plantations. Newspapers carried advertisements for "Carolina Cotton Field Negroes, ages 15 to 21, boys and girls," or "Just arrived, one hundred Virginia and Carolina Negroes consisting of plantation hands, blacksmiths, carpenters, cooks, washers, ironers, and seamstresses." Traders sought to present their "merchandise" as healthy, clean, good-looking, personable, and willing to work. Those who did not make themselves agreeable to prospective buyers were beaten after the customers had departed.[3]

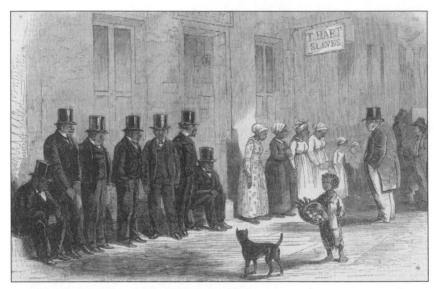

21. A slave market in New Orleans, *Harper's Weekly Magazine*, January 24, 1863, p. 61. The accompanying text gives a description by the unidentified artist who made this sketch before the war: "The men and women are well clothed in their Sunday best—the men in blue cloth of good quality, with beaver hats; the women in calico dresses, of more or less brilliancy, with silk bandana handkerchiefs bound round their heads. Placed in a row in a quiet thoroughfare . . . they stand through a great part of the day, subject to the inspection of the purchasing and non-purchasing crowd. They look heavy, perhaps a little sad, but not altogether unhappy." (Author's collection.)

Slaves were also sold in the rotunda of New Orleans' fashionable St. Charles Hotel. This practice was documented by the free colored hairdresser Eliza Potter. During the winter social season Potter served the wealthy patrons of the St. Charles, where she was horrified to come upon a slave auction: "I stood for some time watching this market. I saw people, both young and old . . . as white as white could be and as black as black could get, put up and sold to the highest bidder in this elegant hotel. . . . Some seemed satisfied with their lot, and others . . . grieved to death. . . . I have often wondered to myself how men can speak so much on the glorious cause of freedom and talk of this as the land of liberty, while they are daily and hourly trafficking in human beings."[4]

In 1806 the Louisiana Territorial Legislature had enacted a Black Code governing slaves and curtailing the rights of free people of color. This was reinforced by the Act of 1807, the Digest of 1808, and the 1825 Civil Code. The new laws eliminated the liberal provisions of the Spanish Codigo Negro and were even harsher than the French Code Noir. The American Black Code required judicial permission for voluntary manumission. During the years between en- actment of the Black Code and the final emancipation of all slaves after the Civil War, various requirements were added, such as minimum age, proof of good conduct, and birth in Louisiana, and schemes were proposed to expel newly freed slaves from the state or deport them to Liberia. Slaves still had the right to sue in court to claim a promise of freedom or to contest being wrong- fully held in slavery.

While some who were voluntarily emancipated were the sexual partners and children of white owners, Eliza Potter observed that slaves who were freed gratis were often "those who were too bad to keep" and therefore impossible to sell because of their intractable behavior or were "too old to be made any longer useful." Potter was especially outraged by owners who liberated aged slaves who had no means of support: "These poor creatures are worked to death, and when [they are] worn out and good for nothing, all at once a charitable feeling rises up in the master's breast, and he gives them free papers, puts them on the [train], and sends them off to Cincinnati" where they end up "in the pest-house or in jail."[5]

Although self-purchase was not prohibited, the new law included provi- sions intended to make this virtually impossible by eliminating the slaves' abil- ity to acquire their purchase price. Enslaved persons could no longer receive donations of money or property. They were required to live on the premises and under the supervision of their owners and were prohibited from hiring themselves out or marketing their handiwork and produce without permis- sion. These regulations were often ignored, and it was still common for urban slaves to find their own accommodations and hire their own time, paying a por- tion of their wages to the master. Third-party purchase was possible, but only if the slave owner agreed to the sale. The records of the Orleans Parish Court show that white men continued to buy their concubines and children out of slavery, and free nonwhite husbands, parents, siblings, aunts, grandmothers, and godmothers also purchased their kin.[6]

On March 6, 1857, the Louisiana Legislature flatly prohibited all manumis- sions, declaring that "From and after the passage of this act, no slave shall be emancipated in this state." In 1859 a law was enacted requiring all free persons of African descent to choose a master to whom they would be enslaved for life—this, of course, was unenforceable.[7]

Despite these increasingly repressive laws, travelers' accounts show that ur- ban slaves, employed as personal attendants, domestics, vendors, and skilled artisans, enjoyed a fair amount of autonomy and were not as harshly treated as those in other parts of the South. An English abolitionist, visiting New Orleans in 1842, observed that "their labour is light, they are well fed, well clad, and do almost as they please within the limits of reasonable service." The lot of plantation field hands, most of whom had been imported from the Upper South, was a different matter entirely, and some were worked very hard.[8]

Virtually all well-to-do New Orleanians, including free people of color, owned slaves. Some used enslaved people as household servants and some hired them out for wages. According to data for the year 1830, free people of color comprised a little over 25 percent of the population of New Orleans; there were 1,645 free colored families, and 753 of these households (almost 46 percent) owned an average of 3.14 slaves per household. Many of the men of color who became community leaders after the Civil War were former slave owners.[9]

*   *   *

A recent addition to the Laveau Legend portrays the Voudou Queen as a social activist, an early advocate for the abolition of slavery, and a champion of civil rights for people of African descent. Scholars Ina Fandrich ("Mysterious Voodoo Queen," dissertation 1994, book 2005), Susheel Bibbs (*Heritage of Power*, 1998), and Martha Ward (*Voodoo Queen: The Spirited Lives of Marie Laveau*, 2004) contend that Marie Laveau and her domestic partner Christophe Glapion bought slaves in order to liberate them, helped others to "disappear" by providing them with charms "to protect them on their journey north to liberty in Canada," and that the Laveau-Glapion home might have been "a Southern terminus for the Underground Railroad."[10]

As much as we might like to believe that Marie and Christophe strove to subvert the institution of slavery, the archival evidence proves otherwise. Christophe was engaged in buying and selling slaves before beginning his relationship with Marie. He bought Michaux, age sixteen, and Catherine, age twenty, on May 1, 1810, for a total of $1,300, and bought fifty-year-old Jacques Congo for $350 on November 12 of the same year. He sold Michaux for $700 one month after acquiring him and sold Catherine for $680 in 1815. Nothing further is known of Jacques Congo.[11]

After becoming a couple, both Marie and Christophe were involved in slave trading. Between 1828 and 1854 they bought and sold eight slaves: Eliza, Molly and her sons Richard and Louis, Peter, Irma and her son Armand, and Juliette. The notarial acts show that in most cases Marie and Christophe, like other

New Orleanians, bought slaves, kept them for a while, and sold them. Eliza, Molly, and Molly's sons served the Laveau-Glapion household for many years, but they too were eventually sold.

The archival record conveys the bare facts of these purchases and sales, but it does not tell us whether Marie and Christophe treated their bondspeople liberally or harshly, what sort of work they performed, and whether they lived in the St. Ann Street cottage or made their homes elsewhere. We do not know if they assisted Marie in her Voudou practice or were members of her congregation.

* * *

The Laveau-Glapion family acquired their first slave on March 14, 1828, when Christophe paid $215 cash for "an orphaned negress named Eliza aged eight years" to the professional slave trader John Woolfolk of Augusta, Georgia. Because the Black Code forbade separating children under ten from their mothers, a young slave like Eliza was usually classified as an orphan. It is more likely that she was sold away from her family in the Upper South.[12] Eliza was with Marie and Christophe for twenty-four years. She grew up in the Laveau-Glapion household and probably helped raise their children and grandchildren.

* * *

On February 7, 1838, Marie Laveau bought a thirty-eight-year-old slave negress named Molly and her son Richard, age eighteen months, from Christophe's brother-in-law, Pierre Joseph Tricou. Molly's English name indicates that she was also an "American Negro." Marie paid $400 cash with a promissory note to Tricou for an additional $400. Christophe's sister, Arthemise Glapion Tricou, signed the form renouncing her rights to the slave as part of the couple's community property. Marie Laveau signed with an X. Shortly after this purchase, Molly gave birth to another child named Louis.[13]

* * *

On August 10, 1838, Marie Laveau purchased the slave Irma from the merchant Pierre Oscar Peyroux for $750 cash. Irma was described in the act of sale as a twenty-year-old quadroon, designated as *statu liber*. This term is defined in the Louisiana Civil Code of 1825: "Slaves for a time or *statu libri* [the singular is *liber*] are those who have acquired the right of being free at a time to come, or on a condition that is not yet fulfilled, or in a certain event that has not happened, but who, in the mean time, remain in a state of slavery."[14] Along with Irma came her twenty-one-month-old daughter, Coralie, who was already free. In conformity with the stipulation of the Black Code against separating children under ten from their mothers, Coralie was to stay with Irma until her tenth birthday. No instructions regarding Irma's manumission were included in the act of sale, but it was specified that she was not to be mortgaged or sold.[15]

The Peyroux family, including Pierre's wife Eulalie, his children, and his unmarried sister Constance, lived around the corner from Marie Laveau and Christophe Glapion on the corner of Burgundy and Dumaine. We learn from a notarial act of February 13, 1838, that Pierre Oscar Peyroux had acquired Irma from Constance Peyroux for $1,500, paying her half the price and owing the remainder. It was stated that the child Coralie's freedom had been purchased by "une personne qui ne désire pas étre connu" (a person who does not wish to be known). Peyroux subsequently made a "promesse de liberté" (promise of freedom) to the slave Irma, in which he agreed, as a "marque de bienveillance" (mark of his benevolence) that Irma would be free when she reimbursed him for her purchase price of $1,500 plus the legal fees for her emancipation—and Peyroux in turn repaid the $750 owed to his sister Constance.[16]

While in the possession of Marie Laveau, Irma gave birth to a son, Armand, who, following the status of his mother, was also *statu liber*.[17] Marie subsequently used Irma and Armand as collateral for a loan, violating the terms of her purchase agreement with Pierre Peyroux. On October 21, 1839, she returned Irma, Coralie, and one-year-old Armand to Peyroux's sister Constance for a refund of $750. It was again stipulated that Irma's daughter Coralie, now almost three years old, would stay with her mother until age ten, at which time Peyroux would legalize her manumission. As soon as Irma, or a third party acting on her behalf, paid the other half of her original $1,500 purchase price, she and all her children—Coralie, Armand, and any others to whom she might give birth—would be free.[18]

Irma never raised the funds to procure her freedom. Three years later, on March 22, 1842, Irma died, still a slave, "at the home of her mistress [Constance Peyroux] corner Dumaine and Burgundy." She was only twenty-four years old. The St. Louis Cathedral funeral record describes her as: "Irma, American quadroon, natural daughter of an unknown father, and Hélène, mulatress slave of Mademoiselle C. Peyroux."[19] The Peyroux family did liberate Irma's children. In the record of Slaves Emancipated by the Council of the First Municipality, we discover that Constance Peyroux freed Coralie, by then age thirteen, on May 7, 1850, and Madame Oscar Peyroux freed two adult slaves and three children, including a boy named Armand, on the same day.[20]

* * *

On August 17, 1843, Christophe Glapion purchased the eighteen-year-old mulatress Juliette from Leonard Lévesque for the bargain price of $210. The notarial act refers to this young woman as "Juliette—called Nounoute—born September 1, 1825, and baptized with the name Cleménce, daughter of Alexandrine, slave of Jeanne Gabrielle Redonne, the Widow of Jean Baptiste Montignac." Like Irma, Juliette was designated as *statu liber*. Glapion bought her with the understanding, resulting from the promise of her deceased mistress, the Widow Montignac, that Juliette was to be emancipated on her twenty-fifth birthday, September 1, 1850. In the first version of her will, Madame Montignac had granted immediate freedom to Juliette and her brother Oscar. A revised version, dated July 19, 1841, stipulated that Juliette and Oscar were each to be freed upon reaching the age of twenty-five.[21]

Juliette made repeated attempts to escape from bondage. When she was acquired by Christophe Glapion, having already passed through two owners after being sold from the succession of Madame Montignac, she was described as being prone to *marronage* (running away). Three months later, on November 11, 1843, Christophe sold Juliette to Gustave Ducros of St. Bernard Parish, revealing, when required to list her defects, that "the slave absented herself while in his possession."[22]

Juliette changed hands twice more before she was purchased by Marie Laveau from the free man of color Pierre Monette on November 15, 1847. Marie paid $210 cash for Juliette, assuming the obligation to free her on September 1, 1850.[23] One wonders why Marie would again introduce this chronic *marron* into her home. True to form, Juliette ran away and was discovered in the home of Charlotte Miles, a free woman of color. According to Miles, "Nounoun" represented herself as free and had formed an alliance with a "white Frenchman named Jean who walked arm in arm with her in the street." Juliette had been missing for most of the time that Marie Laveau owned her. On April 27, 1848, Marie made a ninety-dollar profit when she sold Juliette for $300 to Sanité Couvreure, a free woman of color who owned several other slaves.[24] As we will learn, Couvreure was among the women arrested in the summer of 1850 at a Voudou ceremony on the shores of Lake Pontchartrain.

Sanité Couvreure kept Juliette for a little over a year, and on March 24,

1849, sold her, still *statu liber*, to Augustus Reichard.[25] The terms of sale again stipulated that "when the said mulatress *statu liber* Juliette attains the twenty-fifth year of her life [on September 1, 1850], she will be given her liberty." Nevertheless, Juliette was not formally emancipated by Reichard until May 22, 1852, in an act before the notary Achille Chiapella.

Freeing a slave had become a complicated process. Reichard first had to petition the Third Municipality Council, stating that Juliette was "sober, honest, industrious, competent to provide for her wants and sustenance; that she is of good conduct, honest, respectful towards the whites, and that she has never committed any crimes." Reichard asked that Juliette be allowed to remain in the state. Notary Chiapella, acting as attorney for Reichard, then petitioned the First District Court, saying that his client had fulfilled the requirements of law and asking that the sheriff be authorized to post "the usual notices." These notices, printed in English and French, stated that Augustus Reichard, inhabitant of the Parish of Orleans, intended to manumit "the mulatress statu-liber named Clémence alias Juliette, aged about 27 years." Persons having reason to legally oppose the emancipation were "required to file said opposition in the office of the Clerk of the First District Court of New Orleans within forty days." At the end of this time the emancipation was finalized before the notary and endorsed by all parties. Juliette signed with an X.[26]

* * *

On April 12, 1848 Christophe Glapion bought "a negro named Peter, aged thirty-one," from Arnold Bodin for $400. Bodin had acquired this slave two weeks earlier from *la failtite* (bankruptcy—literally "failure") of the free man of color Pierre Crocker, father of Heloïse Glapion's children. Christophe kept Peter for a little over a year, selling him on October 24, 1849, for a profit of fifty dollars.[27]

* * *

The 1850s were a time of financial and personal difficulty for Christophe Glapion. He had mortgaged the family home to the Citizens' Bank of Louisiana, and he also may have been in poor health and feared that his death was imminent. Anxious to put his affairs in order, he sold the family's remaining slaves. On March 8, 1850, Glapion sold Molly's son Richard, by then a "likely" young man of fifteen, to the notorious slave trader Elihu Creswell for $450.[28] The Conveyance Office Index to Vendors and Purchasers reveals that Creswell made hundreds of such transactions, buying and selling young adults and teen-

agers—even children as young as eleven—as "slaves for life." Although a boy
like Richard would have been worth between $650 and $850, I found no record of Creswell's having resold him.

Elihu Creswell died of typhoid fever on May 29, 1851. In his will, written
several years before his illness, he stated that "the uncertainty of life is very
great and is not to the time and choice of human beings." He granted freedom
to his manservant, Gabriel, with a bonus of fifty dollars, followed by an amaz-
ing proviso for "the freedom of all slaves that may belong to me at the time of
my death." The slaves were to be "sent to one of the free states of the United
States of America and there liberated, and their names shall be registered in
the court as free persons no longer to be held in bondage." The slaves were to
work for wages until arrangements could be made to transport them north,
and the executor of Creswell's estate was to receive "great compensation for
his trouble." Creswell stated that he had written his last will and testament "in
a state of sound mind" and hoped that no one would interfere with its execution. He ended by asking that his body receive a respectful burial; his soul, he
said confidently, "belongs to the Supreme Being and I with pleasure submit it
to his will."[29]

But, as might be expected, there were problems. Creswell's mother—his
only legal heir—attempted to prevent the emancipation of the slaves, and for
some time the executor of the estate kept them in rented lodgings and paid
for their care, compensating the estate by hiring them out and collecting their
wages. According to one witness, the slaves were mostly a bad lot. Creswell had
"bought them out of prison and picked them up wherever he found them."
They were "very troublesome, and hardly a week passed that an officer of the
police did not come with a warrant and take some to jail for stealing, running
away, or some other difficulties."

On November 8, 1851, the slaves petitioned the Fourth District Court to
allow them to be liberated in Louisiana. They testified, through their attorney,
that they were "peaceable, orderly, obedient, and industrious." They argued
that they had been "born and have always lived in the State of Louisiana and
City of New Orleans, where their husbands and wives and children, fathers
and mothers, brothers and sisters, and other relations and friends live." They
were "accustomed to southern labor and a southern climate," and they dreaded
the cold of Massachusetts, "the state to which they have been informed they
will be removed." They asked that the money saved by freeing them in Louisiana instead of transporting them north be paid to them, and that they be
compensated for "the amount of wages which they have earned since the death

of the said Elihu Creswell." Their request came to nothing. When the estate was finally settled in 1853, fifty-one slaves, valued at $33,900, were transported to New York. All of the Creswell slaves were inventoried and listed by name and age in the succession documents, but there is no young man fitting the description of Molly's son Richard. His fate is unknown.[30]

Two years after selling Richard, on April 26, 1852, Christophe Glapion sold Richard's mother Molly and her eleven-year-old son Louis for $700. The purchaser was the free colored watchmaker Philippe Ross, a friend of the Laveau-Glapion family.[31] On April 26, 1854, Christophe finally sold thirty-two-year-old Eliza to the free man of color Pierre Monette, for $600.[32] Monette might also have been a family friend. I found no evidence that Molly, Louis, and Eliza were resold. Presumably they were freed in 1864 when the state constitution put an end to slavery in all of Louisiana.[33]

Hard Times

By the spring of 1854 Christophe Glapion was ill and in debt. In desperate need of cash, he applied for the forty acres of bounty land to which he was entitled as a veteran of the War of 1812. Glapion had served for three months in Cavellier's Second Regiment of Louisiana Militia under Captain Barthélemy Fabré Daunoy. On March 17, 1854, he appeared before Robert Ker, notary public, and Daniel Scully, clerk of the First District Court of New Orleans, declaring that "he was a private in the company commanded by Fabré Daunoy . . . and that he was mustered into service . . . on the 23rd day of December, 1814, and continued in active service until the end of the hostilities, when he was honorably discharged at New Orleans sometime during the months of February or March, 1815 . . . as will appear by the muster rolls of said company." On April 17, 1854, Robert Ker received the reply from the commissioner of pensions in Washington that "There are no rolls of Capt. Fabré Daunoy on file in this office."

On May 1, 1854, two of Glapion's former military comrades, Jean Jacques Isnard and Hugues Pedesclaux, gave statements before Robert Ker and Daniel Scully. Both swore that they were "well acquainted with Christopher Glapion, a resident of this City, and . . . know that the said Glapion was a private in Captain Fabré Daunoy's Company of Louisiana Militia, the same company in which these deponents themselves served." On April 30, 1855, Glapion appeared before Edwin L. Lewis, notary public, again trying to claim his bounty land on the grounds that he had received a warrant for forty acres.[1]

Why was Glapion, whose petition was obviously valid, being given such a runaround by the commissioner of pensions? Apparently the idiosyncracies of Louisiana's French double names, plus the fact that the name of Glapion's commanding officer was rendered as both "Fabré" and "Favré," were incomprehensible to the bureaucracy in Washington. To Glapion and his friends Isnard and Pedesclaux, it was sufficient to say they served under Fabré Daunoy. But to the American military establishment, he was Captain Barthelemy Favre—there was no such person as Fabré Daunoy. Glapion's petition was ultimately rejected, even though documents showing his name on the muster roll of Barthelemy Favre's company are filed with his military records at the National Archives and Records Administration in Washington, D.C.

A case brought before New Orleans' Fifth District Court reveals Christophe Glapion's precarious financial situation. On August 11, 1836, Glapion had used the St. Ann Street property as collateral for the purchase of $5,000 worth of stock in the Citizens' Bank of Louisiana. On May 3, 1853, he also used the family home as collateral for a two-hundred-dollar loan, agreeing to repay in fifty-dollar installments in 1854, 1855, 1856, and 1857, and for two stock notes amounting to $1,240, which were due May 1, 1855. Glapion dutifully paid the first fifty dollars in 1854. But on May 4, 1855, when he had failed to make his next fifty-dollar payment plus the $1,240 repayment of the stock notes, the Citizens' Bank petitioned the Fifth District Count to give notice to Glapion and order the sheriff of Orleans Parish to seize and sell the property at 152 St. Ann. This petition was granted.[2] On May 30, 1855, Glapion made a final attempt to raise cash, disposing of a lot he owned in the Faubourg Marigny to his friend Philippe Ross, a free man of color.[3] One can well imagine that financial worries and harassment from his creditors helped send Glapion to his grave.

Christophe Glapion died on June 26, 1855, just two days after St. John's Eve. His passing was reported to the Board of Health by the father of Heloïse Glapion's children, Pierre Crocker, described in the record as "a broker of New Orleans, aged fifty-two years, residing on St. Philip between Robertson and Villere." According to the death certificate, "On the 26th of June, 1855, at one o'clock p.m., Christophe Glapion, a native of the Parish of St. John the Baptist, Louisiana, aged 66, departed this life in a house situated on St. Ann between Burgundy and Rampart. . . . Deceased was a bachelor, and the son of Christophe Duminy Glapion and Sophie Lalande Duferriere, both natives of New Orleans." No cause of death was given.[4]

Christophe Glapion's funeral announcement appeared in the Bee of June 27, 1855: "His friends and acquaintances are asked to attend, without further invitation, at his burial, which will take place this evening at precisely five o'clock. The company will leave from his home at St. Ann Street between Burgundy and Rampart."[5] Funeral arrangements were made by Pierre Casenave, a free colored undertaker, who charged $150 for his services. This included twenty dollars for the least expensive "fourth class interment" in the Widow Paris tomb in St. Louis Cemetery No. 1.[6] The inscription on the middle vault reads, "Cphe Duminy De Glapion, décédé le 26 Juin 1855." Marie Laveau and Christophe Glapion were a couple for approximately thirty years. Marie was in her mid-fifties when Christophe died in 1855; she lived for another twenty-six years and is not known to have taken another partner.

*　*　*

Not only had Marie Laveau lost her beloved companion, she was in danger of losing her home. The Citizens' Bank of Louisiana continued to pursue its lawsuit against Glapion's estate. The bank's attorney sent a memorandum to the court, informing the judge that: "The defendant is dead, and according to their charter the Bank has the right to proceed with the sale of the property seized prior to [his] death. . . . No administrator has been appointed to the succession of the deceased . . . so that there is no actual proprietor of the property on whom notice . . . can be served." The court therefore appointed its own curator to carry out the terms of the settlement. Christophe Glapion had sought to protect his family from such an eventuality by selling the house to the free man of color Pierre Charles Marioux in 1838; the following year Marioux donated the property to Marie and Christophe's children and granted usufruct to Glapion during his lifetime. Seizure of the Laveau-Glapion home was possible because of one fatal provision in this document, which stated that "The donation is made with the understanding that the mortgage to the Citizens' Bank of Louisiana still exists in full force and that there is no guarantee against foreclosure."

In order to pay Glapion's debt to the Citizen's Bank, the cottage on St. Ann was auctioned at a sheriff's sale on July 17, 1855. Newspaper advertisements in English and French gave the location and dimensions of the property with the additional information that the "buildings consist of a one-story frame house, shingle roofed, having four rooms and gallery, three small one-story kitchens, one well, &c." The sheriff stated in a memorandum to the court that "On the day fixed for the sale . . . I did, at the hour of twelve o'clock, repair unto the Rotunda of the City Exchange . . . and announced the terms and conditions of sale on the said property, and read the certificate of mortgage in a loud and audible voice, showing the mortgages and liens existing at the time of sale on the property in the name of said defendant."[7] Friends of the family came to the rescue, and the house was purchased for $1,880 by Pierre Crocker, acting as agent for Philippe Ross.[8] Ross never occupied the property and generously allowed Marie Laveau, her daughters, and her grandchildren to remain in residence.

Christophe Glapion's three surviving sisters, Elizabeth Heloïse (wife of Jean Baptiste Durel), Elizabeth Hortense (wife of Thomas Casey), and Jeanne Azelie (wife of Felix Plumard), came forward as his legal heirs. Glapion's succession was opened in Second District Court on June 29, 1855, and the proceedings dragged out until February 4, 1856. First there was a wrangle over who was to be the administrator of the estate. The attorney Pierre Sylvestre Biron, to whom Glapion owed a small sum of money, declared that he should have the position, while the undertaker Pierre Casenave presented himself as the logical person to assume these duties. Biron and Casenave were opposed by Glapion's brother-in-law, Felix Plumard. Plumard particularly objected to Pierre Casenave, protesting that Casenave was "a man of color who has no right to the administration of said succession, and that your petitioner, who is a white man and the husband of one of the heirs, is entitled in preference to all other persons." It should be pointed out that Pierre Casenave was a man of substantial wealth and standing, a Saint Domingue immigrant who owned a successful undertaking establishment and claimed assets worth approximately $40,000.[9] Rather than seeking the administration of Glapion's estate for financial gain, as a family friend he perhaps hoped to protect the interests of Marie Laveau and her daughters.

In the end, Biron, the attorney, was named administrator. An inventory of Glapion's property was taken on August 30, 1855, at his former residence. In attendance were a notary, the undertaker Pierre Casenave, Glapion's brother-in-law Felix Plumand, an attorney representing Glapion's other sisters, the justice of the peace, and a team of appraisers. One wonders if Marie Laveau was present during this invasion of her family home. Glapion owned almost nothing of value. The entire estate, after satisfying the claim of the Citizens' Bank of Louisiana, amounted to only $286.50. After payment of funeral expenses, court costs, and other debts, there was nothing left.

Final judgment was handed down with the "account of distribution rendered by P. S. Biron, curator of the succession of C. Glapion, deceased." The debts were listed on the right, and on the left, in the assets column, we find the following curious statement: "There is some old wearing apparel . . . belonging to the deceased which is in the possession of an old woman who always attended on him during his sickness. The curator did not think it proper to cause said articles to be sold as the costs of court incident to such sale would be greater than the proceeds thereof. They are worth about seven dollars." Was Marie Laveau the "old woman," and did the heirs and the lawyer—in their "generosity"—see fit to let her keep Glapion's used clothing?[10]

The Civil Code of 1808 forbade donation of a man's entire estate to his concubine, but he could bequeath to his partner and their children one-third of his holdings. The revised Civil Code of 1825, in order to keep immovable property (real estate and slaves) out of the hands of colored plaçées, decreed that those who have lived together in concubinage "cannot donate to each other immovable property, and are only allowed to donate one-tenth of their mov-

able property (money, jewelry, clothing, furniture, livestock, and such) by gift."
If Christophe Glapion had made a will, and if he had not been in debt to the
Citizens' Bank of Louisiana, he could have bequeathed one-tenth of his movable property to Marie Laveau (his concubine), and one-fourth of his entire
estate, movable or immovable, to his daughters Heloïse and Philomène Glapion, whom he had acknowledged as his natural children. The rest would still
have gone to his sisters as his legal heirs, and a squabble over ownership of the
St. Ann Street cottage would certainly have ensued. Glapion probably assumed
that the family was protected by his sale of the house to Pierre Charles Marioux
and Marioux's subsequent donation to the Laveau-Glapion children.

* * *

The Laveau Legend tells us that Marie was not only beautiful and charismatic,
she was also shrewd, powerful, and rich. It is said that through blackmail she
exercised control over the white elite and that city officials, the police, the sheriff, and the courts acquiesced to her in everything. She supposedly knew their
secrets from her hairdressing days, from her network of informants among
their servants, and because they came to her for consultations and believed in
and feared her magic. Castellanos reported that aristocratic ladies, politicians,
and "sports" relied on her "supposed supernatural powers" and that from this
commerce "money poured into her purse." Zora Neale Hurston claimed that
Marie could make policemen run in circles, bark like dogs, and beat each other
with their night sticks.[11]

In *Voodoo in New Orleans*, Tallant has one of his fictitious informants, "Pop
Abou," declare that Marie Laveau was "the real boss of New Orleans." She
could "have a policeman fired with one snap of her fingers and she could get
one promoted with two snaps. . . . She just walked into a big politician's office
and said 'Do it! I is Marie Laveau and I wants it done.' And he knew better 'n
not to do. If he didn't something awful bad was sure gonna happen to him."[12]

Tallant had access to the Louisiana Writers' Project files, and while the
statements he attributed to "Pop Abou" do not exist, he appears to have drawn
inspiration from the narratives of two men, Joseph Alfred and James Santana,
interviewed by LWP fieldworkers. Both were probably speaking of the "Marie II" of the 1870s and 1880s. According to these informants, "Marie Laveau
never went to jail. . . . She was in with all of the lawyers, policemen, judges, and
big city officials. . . . If you committed a crime and asked her to get you out of
trouble, she would go to the high sheriff and tell him you was her friend and
he'd set you free. The judge and sheriff . . . submitted to her in anything."[13]

The Writers' Project interviews also lend support to the idea that Marie acquired a degree of wealth from an elite white clientele—again, some of these informants may have been speaking of the second Marie Laveau: "She worked mostly for white people, and she made piles of money.... Sometimes she got as much as a thousand dollars, but five hundred, two hundred, and one hundred dollars were her popular prices.... [Clients] paid her plenty ... to win cases in the courts.... There was always a line of carriages in front of her house, and the [white] ladies who entered were heavily veiled.... [They] did not hesitate to consult Marie Laveau, who would give them powders to use on their husbands and bones ... to put in their pockets."[14]

Where was Marie Laveau's alleged power and wealth in 1855, when Christophe Glapion plunged the family into financial crisis by his wheeling and dealing with their assets and died before the problem could be resolved? She apparently lacked the funds to make the required payment to the Citizens' Bank of Louisiana, reimburse the undertaker for Glapion's funeral, or reclaim her home from the sheriff's auction. The Citizens' Bank, the judge of the Fifth District Court, the sheriff, and the white Glapion heirs were obviously not intimidated; they either did not know or did not care that Christophe Glapion's domestic partner and the mother of his children was the famous priestess of the Voudous.

On the other hand, Marie was not totally impoverished. Both before and after Christophe died, she apparently had sufficient funds to furnish security for free women of color who were arrested for minor crimes. No money actually changed hands in these cases—Marie simply pledged that the defendants would appear for trial. On September 4, 1850, she guaranteed a security bond of $500 for her neighbor Julia Evans, who lived on Burgundy between St. Peter and Toulouse. Evans was charged with "grossly insulting, abusing, and threatening" a white woman in violation of the Black Code, which mandated that free colored persons "should not imagine themselves equal to whites; on the contrary, they are to defer to whites on every occasion and treat them with respect." Evans was arraigned and, despite her plea of not guilty, she was sentenced to one week's imprisonment and ordered to pay court costs. On January 11, 1858 Marie furnished $200 security for Elizabeth Martel, known as Zulimé, who resided at 340 St. Peter. The charge against Martel was "grossly abusing and insulting" a white woman. The outcome of this case is not included in the documents. In 1860 Marie again furnished $200 security for Ophelia Garcia, corner of St. Peter and Villere, who was arrested for assault and battery against another free woman of color. Garcia was also arraigned and pleaded not guilty, but was convicted and sentenced to pay a fine of thirty dollars or to spend three weeks in the Parish Prison, plus pay court costs.[15] Despite the LWP informants' declarations of faith in the power of Marie Laveau, in the cases of Julia Evans and Ophelia Garcia her much-touted influence over the police and the judiciary system was of no aid to the defendants.

*   *   *

The antebellum era of privilege and prosperity for New Orleans' Creoles of color was coming to an end. Anglo-Americans had become the dominant force in business and politics, and the English language triumphed over the French. Because of immigration from elsewhere in the United States and the influx of Irish, Germans, and other Europeans, by mid-century whites far outnumbered people of African descent. The U.S. Census for 1860 indicates that the city's population consisted of 149,063 whites, 14,484 slaves, and 10,939 free people of color. Almost all of the free nonwhite residents were French-speaking, Roman Catholic, racially mixed Louisiana Creoles.[16]

During the decade before the Civil War, Louisiana lawmakers began rendering life more restrictive for slaves and whittling away the rights of people of African descent who were already free. Communication between the races was restricted because it might "cause unrest among slaves and free people, or cause the latter to forget their place." By 1855 a free person of color could not move about the city without possible interference: As one historian wrote, "At the slightest whim of the most wretched white citizen or some rascally officer, the most respectable among the *gens de couleur* were subjected to arrest, violence, and imprisonment."[17]

The famous Congo Square assemblies gradually declined. The importance of the slaves' market was diminished by the opening of the huge Tremé Market two blocks away from Congo Square and the enlargement of the French Market along the riverfront in the Vieux Carré. A municipal ordinance prohibited outdoor dances, drumming, and the playing of musical instruments without permission from the mayor. The festivities still occurred sporadically through the 1850s, but they were conducted under police supervision, could only take place from May through August between the hours of 4:00 and 6:30 in the afternoon, and could not be "offensive to public decency." Congo Square was planted with dozens of young sycamore trees, which further inhibited the dancers, and finally they ceased to congregate there. By 1860, what had once been the venue for authentic African cultural practices had faded into oblivion.[18]

In 1859 the legislature enacted stringent provisions against the entry of non-native free people of African descent into Louisiana. The *Picayune* and the *Crescent* reported on "the arrests, made daily by the police, of free persons of color, charged with being in the state in contravention of the law." A group of men employed on a steamship attempted to pass themselves off as slaves to avoid being forcibly expelled. Free blacks were paying white men as much as seventy-five dollars to testify to their having been born in Louisiana. As neighboring states passed acts stipulating that "no person of African blood can remain in the state and be free" and that "those who do not leave voluntarily will be sold into slavery," there was nowhere to go except to the northern free states or a foreign country.[19]

As they saw their rights, status, and fortunes slipping away, many of New Orleans' successful free people of color fled to France, Mexico, or Haiti, where they hoped to experience racial equality. On June 23, 1859, the *Daily Picayune* commented on this exodus, saying that two hundred free colored persons, composed of families headed by "able-bodied and intelligent men, all possessing the advantages of education and industrious habits," had left at the invitation of the president of Haiti. There they would "enjoy the consideration and equality of rights" that had been denied them in New Orleans, where they were considered "an undesirable element to be kept among us." On November 11, 1860, the *Picayune's* reporter was less sympathetic to the emigrants: "As for us in New Orleans," he commented grumpily, "we say let them go and God speed them; we can get along well enough with our faithful and contented slaves."[20]

* * *

The city of New Orleans had attained a degree of prosperity unimaginable during its unpropitious beginnings. The Mississippi riverfront was crowded with steamboats and sailing ships, and dockworkers busily loaded products for export—wheat, corn, lard, pork, furs and hides, whiskey, hemp, and lead from the Midwest, and bales of cotton, hogsheads of sugar, and tobacco from the South. The dingy old Place d'Armes got a face-lift when St. Louis Cathedral was renovated and its plain facade replaced by three soaring Gothic towers, the shacks along St. Ann and St. Peter streets were replaced by the magnificent brick Pontalba Buildings, and the bare earth of the ancient parade ground metamorphosed into a landscaped Jackson Square.

Despite this progress, New Orleans was still an unhygienic and violent place. Every summer the newspapers published harangues about the filthy condition of the streets, with their rotting garbage and dead animals. Livestock roamed

Above: 22. Shipping and warehouses on the New Orleans waterfront. Illustration by J. Barclay in the German-American journal *Die Illustrirte Welt*, n.d. (Author's collection.)

Left: 23. St. Louis Cathedral, flanked by the *Presbytère* on the right with Jackson Square in the foreground. The Cabildo, a building identical to the *Presbytère*, is to the left of the cathedral. Illustration from an unidentified publication, n.d. (Author's collection.)

at will, and residents were menaced by rabid dogs. A six-foot alligator was captured at the corner of Camp and Canal by "a darky with the well-known marks of the Congo tribe on his cheeks." The bodies of unwanted babies were discovered in privies, in parks, and on the riverbank. Children were run over by horse carts and drays. Corpses were fished out of the canal, the bayou, the river, and the lake. An inordinate number of deceased persons, when examined by the coroner, were pronounced dead from "apoplexy due to intemperance." Wife-beating was rife. There were frequent reports of a "melee" or an "affray," usually the result of intoxication. Cuttings, shootings, and assaults were commonplace; people were reported to have gone at each other with brickbats or a "billet of wood." An astonishing number of these rowdies were women. One female assaulted another with a curling tong, one used a saucepan, one beat her neighbor with a clothes pole, and one slit another woman's nose with a knife. A number of "frail ones" (prostitutes) were arrested for "scandalous lewdness and keeping a disorderly house." Lawbreakers and disturbers of the peace were sent to the city's insane asylum, the workhouse, or the Parish Prison, as deemed appropriate by the court. The occasional hanging at the Parish Prison received considerable attention from the press.[21]

*   *   *

The Civil War was approaching, but New Orleans' ruling class was living in a dream world. On the day after Thanksgiving, 1859, the *Daily Picayune* announced that "Everything around us speaks of promise and happy security." In January 1861, the *Picayune* editorialized that "A warlike spirit seems to pervade the community. . . . Military men are in their element, whilst the timid are moaning over the expected loss of their worldly chattels. . . . Real estate owners are not at all disposed to sacrifice their property, and slaveholders have no fears—negroes are selling at advanced prices. Fashionable ladies dress as splendidly as ever; fast gentlemen go to the races . . . and imbibe champagne as readily as of old. . . . There is no sign that New Orleans is disposed to lose her title of the greatest city in the South." A few days later, the *Picayune* announced that the free men of color "have expressed their readiness to form a battalion for the defense of the State, whenever they may by required by the Governor. . . . Not only the colored population of New Orleans, but the slaves of Louisiana will stand by us in the moment of danger."[22] On January 26, 1861, delegates to Louisiana's state convention voted to secede from the United States.

While Louisiana's troops were occupied elsewhere, Admiral Farragut's fleet took New Orleans without a fight on April 24, 1862. The city was occupied for the duration of the war by Union troops under the command of Major General Benjamin Butler, whose harsh regime earned him the nickname "The Beast." The mayor and other city officials were imprisoned, newspapers hostile to the North were seized, merchants who refused to sell to the occupation forces had their stock confiscated, and any female who insulted the Union soldiers was to be arrested "as a woman of the town plying her vocation." Business ground to a halt as production ceased and banks failed. Thousands of slaves on the surrounding cotton and sugar plantations simply left their work and headed for New Orleans.[23]

The Civil War officially ended in 1865, and President Lincoln's Emancipation Proclamation was made law by the ratification of the thirteenth amendment to the Constitution, permanently abolishing slavery in the United States. The "promise and happy security" that characterized the "greatest city in the South" at the end of the antebellum period was gone. Even though New Orleans had not been physically demolished, the war left a city in disarray, peopled by the bereaved, the maimed, the ruined, and the bewildered. The abolition of slavery affected every aspect of business, agriculture, and domestic life, as former masters had to learn to function without slave labor. The carefully constructed three-tiered order of whites, free people of color, and slaves had been knocked to smithereens, and people of every color and station scrambled frantically to find their proper "place" in the new society.

Part II

Voudou

The preceding chapters have been concerned with Marie Laveau's personal history, viewed against the backdrop of colonial and antebellum New Orleans. But Marie was far more than an ordinary citizen of the Crescent City. According to all accounts, from sometime in the 1820s until the early 1870s she was also Queen of the Voudous.

In every French, Spanish, and Portuguese slave-owning colony of the Caribbean and South America, there evolved some synthesis of African traditional beliefs with Roman Catholicism, creating new and vibrant forms of worship. New Orleans Voudou, like Haitian Vodou, Cuban Santería, and Brazilian Candomblé, was an organized religion with a complex theology, a pantheon of deities and spirits, a priesthood, and a congregation of believers. New Orleans Voudou is the only Afro-Catholic religion to emerge in North America. While a vast scholarly literature exists for other African-based New World religions, discussion of New Orleans Voudou has been left, until recently, to newspaper reporters and the writers of local color, popular history, and fiction. It is from these sources, and the Louisiana Writers' Project interviews, that we must piece together some idea of the religion practiced by Marie Laveau and her followers in nineteenth-century New Orleans.

African Antecedents of New Orleans Voudou

We know from a few eighteenth-century accounts that African religious and magical traditions arrived in Louisiana along with the first slaves. Le Page du Pratz noted in his 1758 *Histoire de la Louisiane* that the Africans would "sometimes get together to the number of three or four hundred, and make a kind of Sabbath." In his chapter on the treatment of newly enslaved people, Le Page advised that "they are very superstitious and attached . . . to little toys that they call *gris-gris*. It would be improper to take [the gris-gris] from them . . . for they would believe themselves undone if they were stripped of these trinkets." Court records from New Orleans' Spanish Judicial Archives document a 1773 case in which several slaves, including a recently arrived Mandinga man, were tried for conspiring to kill their master and the slave overseer by means of gris-gris.[1]

In New Orleans, gris-gris has come to mean any assemblage of magical substances employed by believers to attain control over others, success, protection, revenge, or luck. The word is derived from *gregries* (also spelled *gregory* or *ger-regerys*) in the Mende language of the Senegambian peoples who were enslaved in colonial Louisiana.[2] British Royal Navy surgeon John Atkins, writing in 1735 about his experiences on the coast of Sierra Leone, said that the local religion consisted of the "veneration of gregries: everyone keeps in his house, in his canoe, or about his person something [such as] a bundle of peculiar little sticks or bones . . . that he highly reverences and that he imagines can . . . defend him from miscarriage." The slave trader Nicholas Owen noted in 1755 that in Sierra Leone the native people "have great leather bags [that] contain their witches or idols, which they carry about upon all occasions, thinking thereby to preserve themselves from shot, knives, poison, or other accidents of life. These go by the name of gregory bags and . . . are the chief of their worship upon all occasions." Another slave trader, John Matthews, gave a description of gregries in his 1788 *Voyage to the river Sierra-Leone*: "These are made of goatskin . . . into various shapes and sizes, from the bigness of a shilling to the size and form of a sheep's heart, and stuffed with some kind of powder, and bits of paper on which are written in Arabic sentences from the Alcoran [Koran]. . . . They wear [the gregries] tied round their necks, waist, legs, and arms, and in such numbers that when a man is properly equipped for the field, the very weight of them with his gun is an exceeding heavy burden."[3]

* * *

The Afro-Catholic religions that evolved in the New World colonies are derived from the Fon and Yoruba people of West Africa and the Kongo of Central Africa, who were enslaved in great numbers in Louisiana, Saint Domingue, Cuba, and Brazil. All of these African nations recognized a supreme creator and believed in the existence of spiritual entities who acted as intermediaries between human beings and the highest god. These minor deities controlled human creativity, sexuality and reproduction, warfare, commerce, agriculture, disease, healing, and death. In the Fon religion they were called *vodu*—hence the name Voudou. Among the Yoruba, similar deities were called *orisha*. The Kongo called them *minkisi* (the singular is *nkisi*), which were personified by human figures carved from wood and embellished with beads, cloth, animal skins, shells, mirrors, and raffia.

Like the Senegambians with their gregries, the Fon, Yoruba, and Kongo also believed in the efficacy of magical amulets that were worn on the body, hung up in the house, buried in the yard, or placed in the garden to protect the owner and his goods. The Fon called these objects *gbo*; the Yoruba believed that plants, animals, and minerals had their own life force and spiritual power; and the Kongo used the word *minkisi* to refer to small charm assemblages as well as the large wooden figures that represented the deities.[4]

* * *

In 1777 the merchants and planters who served as regidores of the Cabildo under the Spanish administration drew up proposed revisions to the laws governing slaves and free people of color. As in the French Code Noir and the original Spanish Codigo Negro, the first set of articles dealt with religion. But concern had shifted from "heretical" Protestants and Jews to the expurgation of the "superstitious or foreign" rites of Africans imported in the newly reopened slave trade. Although this new black code, called the *Loi Municipale* (municipal law), was never actually ratified, it demonstrates that New Orleanians felt threatened by the religion of the slaves.[5]

The Influence of Haitian Vodou

According to Lyle Saxon's *Fabulous New Orleans*, "the first [official] reference to black magic" in Louisiana is found in a "musty document on file at the Cabildo." Here, wrote Saxon, in a 1782 discussion of imports and exports to the Spanish colony under Governor Bernardo Gálvez, "one is startled to find a terse sentence prohibiting further importation of slaves from Martinique, 'as these negroes are too much given to voodooism and make the lives of the citizens unsafe.'" This statement has been repeated as fact by many subsequent writers, but no such document exists in the Acts and Deliberations of the Cabildo for 1782. Saxon may have been inspired by the 1885 *Historical Sketch Book and Guide to New Orleans and Environs*, which includes the comment that "importation of the San Domingo negroes was forbidden by special edict, [their] being too well acquainted with Voudouism and poisons."[6]

Whether or not this story is true, Louisiana's colonial administrators indeed had cause to fear the Saint Domingue slaves. According to every standard history, the Haitian Revolution began on August 22, 1791, with a Vodou ceremony at Bois-Caiman, near Cap Français (now Cap Haitien). The service was led by a priest named Boukman; a black pig was sacrificed, and the worshipers swore a blood oath to overthrow the French. A few days later, rebel slaves began to burn the sugar plantations and kill the whites. It was said that they fought with such courage and ferocity owing to the belief that their deities made them invulnerable.[7]

New Orleans Voudou is said by both scholars and popular-history writers to have emerged as an organized religion with the arrival of the Saint Domingue refugees during the early years of the nineteenth century. Two-thirds of these newcomers were Africans or people of African descent and an undetermined number were devotees of Vodou. The historian Gwendolyn Midlo Hall conjectured that Fon and Yoruba slaves from the Bight of Benin "probably account for the emergence of voodoo" during Louisiana's colonial period, and that the existing religion "was reinforced by the massive immigration of Haitians in 1809." Zora Neale Hurston wrote in "Hoodoo in America" that "thousands of mulattos and blacks [from Saint Domingue] took refuge in Louisiana . . . bringing with them African rituals long since lost to their continental brothers." Asbury, in *The French Quarter*, asserted that "with this influx began the development of Voodooism in . . . Louisiana." In *Voodoo in New Orleans* Tallant wrote that "Old Negroes passed on a few of the superstitions, remembered a few of the types of *gris-gris* known to their Congo ancestors, but . . . there was only an occasional Voodoo gathering in New Orleans until the arrival of the Santo Domingo Negroes."[8]

* * *

In Haitian Vodou the highest god, equivalent to the Judeo-Christian God the Father, is called *Bondyé* (the good lord) or *Gran Mèt* (the great master). A pantheon of deities called *loa* or *lwa* (the preferred Kreyòl spelling) mediates between human beings and God. Each is identified with one or more of the Roman Catholic saints. Within the Vodou temple are altars dedicated to the lwa, on which are displayed statues and pictures of their corresponding saints, sacred stones, and offerings of flowers, fruit, cooked foods, liquor, candles, tobacco products, perfume, and other symbolic objects.

Large ceremonies, in which the whole congregation participates, are presided over by an initiated *houngan* (priest) or *mambo* (priestess). Worshipers are usually dressed in white. The ceremony begins with ritual salutations between the priests and their attendants. A sword and flags are carried in a procession around the temple. Libations are poured on the earth. Symbols called *vèvè* are drawn on the ground to summon the spirits. There are songs and Roman Catholic prayers. An animal is sacrificed. The lwa communicate with members of the Vodou congregation through spirit possession, during which the deity "mounts" the body of a worshiper and speaks through the possessed *serviteur*. The ceremony is followed by a communal feast.

Vodou priests and priestesses also give consultations, perform healing ceremonies, and formulate charms for individual clients in order to resolve difficulties with relationships, money, employment, or health. These charms, known as *pwen* (a point of concentrated power), resemble the gregries of the Senegambians, the gbo of the Fon, and the minkisi of the Kongo.[9]

Voudou in Antebellum New Orleans

During the first decades of the nineteenth century, Anglo-American authorities in New Orleans had a profound fear of Voudou. They were well aware of the perceived role of this religion in the Haitian Revolution, and they saw Voudou as a potential breeding ground for slave rebellion and a threat to public safety. They also considered this "savage" African practice to be an offense against Christian morality—a horrifying brew of sorcery, devil worship, interracial fraternization, and sexual license. Nevertheless, some people of European descent accepted Voudou as a religion and participated in its ceremonies.

What has entered Voudou lore as the account of an early nineteenth-century New Orleans Voudou service was actually lifted verbatim from a 1797 history of colonial Saint Domingue, Medric Louis Moreau de Saint-Méry's *Description Topographique, Physic, Civile, et Historique de la Partie Francaise de l'Isle Saint-Domingue*. Moreau described a ritual performed by the enslaved Aradas (a people culturally related to the Fon from the Bight of Benin) in which their serpent deity was represented by a snake in a cage adorned with little bells. A "king" and "queen," possessed by the lwa, counseled and instructed the assembled community; a goat was sacrificed; new initiates were received and given a protective charm, and the ceremony ended with drumming and dancing. Like subsequent writers on the African-based religions, Moreau felt compelled to describe this as a sexual orgy.[10]

In 1883 Moreau de Saint-Méry's Vodou narrative reappeared in a travel memoir called *Souvenirs d'Amérique et de France par une Créole*, written in French and published anonymously by the Saint Domingue immigrant Hélène d'Aquin Allain. An English translation of Moreau's account was repeated in George Washington Cable's 1886 "Creole Slave Songs." While Allain and Cable credited Moreau as the source, later writers did not. This description—complete with queen, snake, gris-gris, bloody animal sacrifice, and sexual debauchery—has been endlessly paraphrased and repeated. Over time it has become conflated with stories of Marie Laveau's ceremonies, and the portrayal of the Voudou priestess was attached to Marie herself.[11]

* * *

Marie Laveau is reported to have embarked upon her Voudou career sometime in the 1820s. In some versions of the story, we hear that she was the protégée, and later the rival, of the earlier queens Sanité Dédé and Marie Saloppé. Dédé and Saloppé may have been actual people, but neither could be located in the archival record.

The early nineteenth-century priestess Sanité Dédé was said to be a black street vendor of the fried, sweetened rice balls called *cala*. She was first mentioned in Marie B. Williams' "A Night with the Voudous," published in the *Appleton's Journal* of March 27, 1875. This account was presented as the narrative of "Professor D—— of New Orleans." "Professor D——" might have been Alexander Dimitry (1805–1883). In "Creole Slave Songs," Cable wrote that, according to the "learned Creole scholar" the late Alexander Dimitry, the invocation "Aïe! Aïe! Voudou Maignan" was sometimes heard at Voudou ceremonies. As we will see below, this phrase is also found in Williams' article.

In "A Night with the Voudous," "Professor D——" related how in 1822, as a young teenager, he was taken to a meeting in an abandoned brickyard on the Eve of St. John. By the light of bonfires and torches, the youth could see about sixty people dressed in white, "males and females, old and young, negroes and negresses, handsome mulatresses and quadroons, and half a dozen white men and two white women." Sanité Dédé was the presiding priestess. He described a makeshift altar, in the center of which was a cypress sapling surmounted by "a black doll with a dress variegated by cabalistic signs and emblems, and a necklace of the vertebrae of snakes around her neck." The altar was flanked by a pair of stuffed cats. An old black man named Zozo sat astride a "cylinder made of thin cypress staves hooped with brass and headed by a sheepskin," identical to the one described by Benjamin Latrobe in 1819. With two sticks Zozo "droned away a monotonous ra-ta-ta," others beat an accompaniment with "sheep shank bones and the leg bones of a buzzard or turkey," and "a young negro vigorously twirled a long calabash . . . filled with pebbles."

Four initiates were being received that night. Sanité Dédé "made cabalistic signs over them and sprinkled them vigorously with some liquid from a calabash in her hand." The drummer Zozo "drew forth an immense black snake, which he brandished wildly aloft. . . . He talked and whispered to it . . . [and] passed the snake over the heads and around the necks of the initiates, repeating

24. *Ein Göttenfest in New-Orleans*. Illustration from the German-American journal *Die Illustrirte Welt*, n.d. (ca. 1880), p. 229. Certain details identify this engraving as an illustration for Marie B. Williams' "A Night with the Voudous," which was presumably translated into German and reprinted in this issue. Note the "black doll," the stuffed cats, and old Zozo with his snake; the young narrator appears in the upper left corner, behind a pile of bricks. (Author's collection.)

. . . the words . . . Voudou Magnian." Then, twirling the snake around his head, he cast it into the blazing fire. "Such a yell arose no words can describe. The rude instruments took up their discords. . . . A tall, lithe black woman . . . began to sway . . . [and] gradually the undulating motion was imparted to her body from the ankles to the hips. Then she tore the white handkerchief from her forehead. . . . This was a signal for the whole assembly to . . . enter the dance."

The narrator then lapsed into the sensationalism that was typical of white reporters' depictions of Voudou: "Under the passion of the hour, the women tore off their garments, and entirely nude, went on dancing. . . . The orgies became frightful. . . . I had grown sick from heat [and] from an indescribable horror that took possession of me. With one bound I was out of the shed, and with all speed traversed the yard. . . . If ever I have realized a sense of the real and visible presence of his majesty, the devil, it was that night among his Voudou-worshipers."[12]

We hear no more of Sanité Dédé until 1936, when Herbert Asbury, in *The French Quarter*, declared that Marie Laveau "became a member of the Voo-doo cult about the time her husband died, and usurped Sanité Dédé's place as Queen half a dozen years later." In *Voodoo in New Orleans*, Robert Tallant wrote that in the 1820s "the queen was Sanité Dédé, and Marie Saloppé was coming into power. . . . It was from her that the great Laveau received her train-ing."[13]

Unlike Sanité Dédé, a possibly fictitious character from the nineteenth-century literature, the name of Marie Saloppé derives from the Louisiana Writers' Project interviews. Tallant was inspired by the narrative of LWP in-formant Alexander Augustin: "Marie Saloppé, a colored woman, lived on St. Philip Street. She preceded Marie Laveau in the art of Voudouism. She was equally well known by the older Creoles of that epoch. . . . So great was the faith of some in Marie Saloppé, that after her death, many went to her grave to pray for certain graces. Some hid coins under a little mound of earth and on top of this . . . placed a candle."[14]

Other tellers of the Laveau Legend say that Marie was raised in the Voudou tradition from birth, her mother and grandmother having been priestesses. This idea first surfaced in the *Picayune's Guide to New Orleans* for 1900, which declared that "Her mother before her was the Voudou Queen, and so was her grandmother." The story was repeated in a 1924 *City Item* Sunday magazine article titled "The Snake Dance," where it was reported that Marie Laveau's "mother and grandmother had been voodoo queens, having held their orgies at Congo Square." Zora Neale Hurston, in *Mules and Men*, also declared that Marie's "mama and grandma before her" were priestesses of Voudou.[15]

25. *A Voudoo Woman.*
Illustration by "A. K." for
Charles Dudley Warner's
"New Orleans," *Harper's
New Monthly Magazine,*
January 1887, p. 199.
(Author's collection.)

Robert Tallant combined the themes of Voudou apprenticeship and heritage in his novel *The Voodoo Queen.* Here Marie, who has been trained under Sanité Dédé, is designated as the new queen by Marie Saloppé. When she resists, Saloppé announces that her birthright demands it: "Your mamma was one of us . . . I came with her [and her mother] on the sailing ship [from Saint Domingue]. Your grandmother was a queen on the island, a great woman. That is why you have been chosen."[16]

Following Tallant's lead, in her 1977 novel *Marie Laveau,* Francine Prose portrays Marie Saloppé as Marie Laveau's first teacher. Prose makes Marie the granddaughter of the Saint Domingue refugee Madame Henriette and the Vodou priest Makandal. (Makandal, an actual historic figure, was burnt at the stake in 1757 for leading an attempted slave insurrection that preceded the Haitian Revolution by almost thirty years.) In Jewell Parker Rhodes' 1993 *Voodoo Dreams,* Marie is said to be descended from Voudou priestesses, all of whom are named Marie Laveau. Her African-born great-grandmother, the slave of "Monsieur Laveau," is a priestess of Dambala. After her mother is killed by a mob for conducting a Voudou ceremony in front of St. Louis Cathedral, Marie is raised by her grandmother, who rejects Voudou to embrace Catholicism. Rhodes makes Marie Laveau the pupil of the African conjurer Doctor John, eliminating the characters of Sanité Dédé and Marie Saloppé.[17]

In reality, we have no idea how Marie Laveau came to be a Voudou priestess. In the early years of the nineteenth century there were many among New Orleans' slaves and free blacks who had come from Senegambia, the Bight of Benin, and Central Africa. These community elders and their Louisiana-born descendants probably retained elements of their traditional religions, in which women took responsibility for initiating their daughters. Marie Laveau's mother and grandmother could have served the Voudou spirits in addition to God the Father, Jesus, and the saints of the Roman Catholic faith. Any or all of these neighbors and kinswomen might have trained the young Marie in the religion of her ancestors.

Persecution of Voudou in the 1850s

Most of our knowledge of New Orleans Voudou during the decades before the Civil War comes from newspaper coverage of Voudou-related arrests. The earliest such article, titled "Idolatry and Quackery," appeared in the *Louisiana Gazette* of August 16, 1820. Here we learn that a white man and several free people of color and slaves had been brought before the mayor for holding illegal nighttime meetings. The *Gazette* reported that for some time a house in the Faubourg Tremé, the neighborhood behind the Vieux Carré, had been "used as a temple for certain occult practices and the idolatrous worship of an African deity called *Vaudoo*. It is said that many slaves and some free people repaired there of nights to practice superstitious, idolatrous rites, to dance, carouse, &c." Among the ritual objects seized by the police was the "image of a woman, whose lower extremities resemble a snake."[18]

After the appearance of the *Louisiana Gazette* article, New Orleans' newspapers were silent on the subject of Voudou for several decades. This does not mean that the religion was inactive, only that local news was generally not reported. While early papers like the *Gazette*, the *Louisiana Courier*, and the *Bee* did publish occasional short editorials on events of community interest, daily local news columns, called "City Intelligence" or "The City," only evolved in the late 1840s. These columns provide a fascinating picture of life in New Orleans; their anonymous writers commented on politics, business, and society, but the greatest space was devoted to complaints, scandals, and crimes. Only then did Voudou become a frequent topic. Prior to the advent of the local news columns, there is absolutely no record of Marie Laveau's activities as a Voudou priestess. We can only speculate, from later newspaper accounts and from the recollections of the LWP informants, that she gradually developed a following and began to hold weekly ceremonies at her home on St. Ann Street, provide consultations and gris-gris for clients, and participate in and then lead the annual St. John's Eve celebrations at Lake Pontchartrain.

As the debate over slavery escalated and the United States began its inexorable progress toward civil war, the fears of white New Orleanians increased. Attempted slave insurrections in Louisiana and elsewhere in the South, plus agitation by northern abolitionists, made authorities nervous about any mixed gathering of slaves, free people of color, and whites. Voudou seemed like a particularly dangerous activity. Each of New Orleans' three municipalities had its own police force and an elected magistrate called a recorder, who handled minor infractions like vagrancy, larceny, drunkenness, assault and battery, prostitution, and unlawful assembly—the charge under which Voudou devotees were usually arrested. The accused were remanded to recorder's court and might be held in the local watch house (jail) until arraignment. These places, according to one newspaper article, "abounded with villainous smells, filth, and fetid atmosphere." The recorder passed sentence, assigning fines or time in the workhouse or the Parish Prison for free people, flogging for slaves, and sending more serious cases to criminal court.[19]

During the summer of 1850 the Third Municipality Guards, charged with policing the Faubourg Marigny and the less populated areas near Lake Pontchartrain, regularly raided Voudou ceremonies and arrested the participants for unlawful assembly. Detainees were brought before Recorder John Seuzeneau, known as "Awful John," who presided over the "old, rickety, worm-eaten, rat-infested, and mildewed" courtroom on the corner of Dauphine and Elysian Fields.[20] The Third Municipality Guards' report shows that on June 27, 1850, a group of women were arrested by Captain Mazerat "for being in contravention of the law, being slaves, free colored persons, and white persons assembled and dancing Voudou all together in St. Bernard Street near the woods at eight o'clock p.m." About a hundred women were reported to have been present when the police arrived, but only two white women, fifteen free women of color, and one slave were apprehended. As we will learn, there is some indication that Marie Laveau was present, but the woman designated as the leader of the Voudou society was a free negress named Betsy Toledano.[21]

The arrests were reported in the *Picayune*, the *Crescent*, the *True Delta*, and the *Bee* on June 29, 1850. The *Picayune* stated that the women had been "in the habit of frequenting a house back in the woods near St. Bernard's Canal, where they go through a great variety of superstitious rites in a . . . meager . . . style of dress." Of particular interest is the "large quantity of nonsensical paraphernalia" confiscated by the guardsmen. These "banners, wands, [and] enchanted rods" resemble the flags and sword carried in procession at the beginning of a Haitian Vodou ceremony. As the *Picayune* reported, the case aroused much curiosity, and "Two or three thousand people assembled at the Recorder's office to regale themselves with the sight of these wonderful things and still more wonderful women, who had been engaged in this indecent humbuggery." The *Daily Crescent* gave additional details. After being surprised in their "voluptuous dance" by Captain Mazarat and his officers, the women "rushed for the doors and windows, and bore down all opposition to their flight. Houses were filled with the dismayed fugitives, alleys held others, the canal received a few, and all but an unfortunate squad of eighteen escaped the quick arm of the police. These ran into a yard where a company of racquette players were engaged at this favorite game, and like quails in the net the fluttering birds found themselves suddenly surrounded on every side." After letting the women spend a miserable night in the watch house, Recorder Seuzeneau fined them ten dollars each and released them.[22]

The article in the *Daily True Delta*, "A Motley Gathering—Superstition and Licentiousness," made a connection between Voudou and prostitution. Although the priestess in this case was Betsy Toledano, not Marie Laveau, this could be the source of later characterizations of Marie as a "procuress" who lured respectable women into harlotry. According to the *True Delta*, Betsy Toledano "pretends to possess supernatural powers, and thoughtless women are induced to visit her and participate in the ceremonies she directs, by promises of having their wishes gratified. . . . [Toledano] is one of the most noted procuresses in the city, and like the whole tribe of fortune tellers and practicers of witchcraft, assumes supernatural knowledge and powers to bring within her toils the unsophisticated of her sex and conduct them to speedy ruin."[23]

On July 2, 1850, there was another Voudou raid. We learn from an entry in the Third Municipality Guards' Book that a group of women was arrested "at Milneburg [on Lake Pontchartrain] in a house of ill fame [for] being in contravention of ordinances prohibiting slaves, free people of color, and white persons assembling together." Among those arrested were the free woman of color Sanité Couvreure and three of her slaves. It was to Couvreure that Marie

Laveau had sold the slave Juliette in 1848, and interestingly, one of the women accompanying Couvreure on the night of the arrest was called "Julia."[24] The coverage in the *Daily Crescent* of July 4, 1850, referred to the arrest as "Another Voudou Affair": "It appears that the votaries of these attractive rites have sought refuge in some premises at the Lake, where they have been carrying on their mysterious proceedings since the dispersion of the high priestess [Betsy Toledano] a few days since [from the house on the St. Bernard Canal]. Last evening, we hear, they were again pounced on in their new location."[25]

The ramifications of the Voudou arrests were felt throughout the summer of 1850. The *Daily Delta* reported that on July 14, 1850, the Voudou women took the officers of the Third Municipality Guards to civil court. Led by Betsy Toledano, they claimed they had been illegally arrested while in the performance of religious ceremonies, falsely imprisoned, improperly fined, and subject to assaults, batteries, and general ill-treatment.[26] The July 24 trial was anticlimactic. A *True Delta* article titled "Voudou Humbug" stated that, to the disappointment of the "considerable crowd" gathered in the courtroom, "the question involved was simply the right of the police to arrest the persons composing a mixed assemblage of blacks and whites that were taken roystering in a bath house at the Lake."[27]

On July 30, Betsy Toledano and her followers were arrested at Toledano's home on Bienville Street in the Vieux Carré. The charge, as usual, was unlawful assembly of free people and slaves. This event was reported by the *Louisiana Courier*, the *Picayune,* and the *Crescent*. In "The Rites of Voudou," the *Crescent* described "the rude chapel [with] walls hung round with colored prints of the saints," and an altar on which were found "bowls . . . containing stones varying from the size of gravel to the largest pavers," and "goblets and vases filled with unknown liquids." Betsy Toledano again defended her right to practice the religion of "the mother-land" learned from her African grandmother.[28]

* * *

Marie Laveau's name never appeared in the roster of those arrested during the summer of 1850. She did, however, figure as a complainant against the overly zealous Third Municipality Guards. On July 2, 1850, Marie Laveau and another free woman of color, Rosine Dominique, accused one of the watchmen of harassing their coreligionists during the June 27 raid and confiscating a wooden statue to which Marie laid claim.[29] The *Picayune* reported that "Marie Laveau, otherwise Widow Paris, f.w.c., the head of the Voudou women, yesterday appeared before Recorder Seuzeneau and charged Watchman Abréo of the Third

Municipality Guards with having by fraud come into possession of a statue of a virgin worth fifty dollars."[30] The fact that she was referred to as the "head of the Voudou women" seems to indicate that, although Betsy Toledano acted as both scapegoat and spokeswoman, Marie Laveau was actually the reigning queen.

On August 10 the case of Marie's wooden statue came to trial, drawing a large crowd of "Africa's daughters of every age, of every shape, and of every . . . color, from bright yellow to sooty black." The article in the *Daily Delta*, titled "The Virgin of the Voudous," refers to this artifact as "a quaintly carved figure resembling something between a centaur and an Egyptian mummy." This brings to mind the image of a "woman with the lower extremities of a snake" described in the 1820 *Louisiana Gazette* article and the "black doll" said to have been present on Sanité Dédé's altar. All are reminiscent of the large, carved figural images called nkisi by the Kongo people.

The police retained possession of the wooden statue until it was decided that it would be "restored to those who worshiped at its shrine" for payment of $8.50 in court costs. Curiously, the statue was not returned to Marie Laveau: "A young quadroon was the first to present . . . the ransom. . . . [Then] another, and another, and still another of the colored sisterhood came, presented the stipulated sum—aye, its double—and claimed the Voudou Virgin." In the end, the "the holder of the virgin," meaning the first to pay, was pronounced to have the right to keep it. In quoting the newspapers' coverage of this episode, Robert Tallant conjectured that the "young quadroon" who rescued the statue from the courtroom was Marie Laveau's daughter, "Marie II."[31]

The "Voudou Virgin" case, coupled with the name of Rosine Dominique, Marie Laveau's cocomplainant against Watchman Abréo of the Third Municipality Guards, was probably the inspiration for the tale of the rival priestess, Rosalie, who allegedly tried to usurp Marie's leadership. This was first introduced in *The French Quarter*, where Herbert Asbury wrote that Marie Laveau "dominated Voodooism in New Orleans for at least forty years, and only once [in 1850] was her supremacy even threatened." Rosalie, a quadroon, imported from Africa a large doll "painted in brilliant colors and bedecked in beads and gaudy ribbons." This object was "so obviously a source of magic" that Rosalie began to attract a considerable following. Marie Laveau "met the situation in a characteristically masterful manner. She simply walked into Rosalie's house one day . . . and walked out with the doll. Rosalie had her arrested, but the Voodoo queen presented such a . . . carefully prepared array of proof that the court decided she was the rightful owner and awarded [the doll] to her."[32]

Robert Tallant repeated the "Rosalie" episode in *Voodoo in New Orleans* and *The Voodoo Queen*, and it has become a standard element of the Laveau Legend. In Daniel Du Plantis' 1998 play *Gris-Gris*, Marie Laveau's rival becomes a comic character called Madame Claude, who wheels the coveted African statue through the streets in a baby carriage and is thoroughly terrorized by the rightful Queen of the Voudous. In Wendy Mae Chambers' as-yet-unproduced musical, "Voodoo on the Bayou," Rosalie and Marie Laveau struggle for ownership of the "African Miracle Doll."[33]

* * *

Harassment of the Voudou community continued sporadically throughout the 1850s, as the Civil War approached and racial tensions increased. City authorities feared any gathering of people of African descent, whether religious or secular, that might undermine white control. New laws limiting the assembly of people of color were used to break up church services, Masonic lodge meetings, spiritualist séances, political convocations, and overly exuberant social occasions, as well as Voudou ceremonies. Ordinance no. 3847 was passed by the City Council on April 7, 1858, in response to the "great and constantly growing evil [that] now exists . . . in contravention of the law and the well-being of . . . the South and the safety of the institution of slavery, by the numerous assemblages of persons of color." The new ordinance required that Christian worship must be conducted under the supervision of a white minister and that written permission from the mayor must be obtained for any meeting held by people of African descent.[34]

In the summer of 1859 we once again hear of Marie Laveau. On July 12 the *Picayune*, the *True Delta*, and the *Crescent* reported that a free woman of color called Marie "Clarisse" Laveau had been summoned before the recorder's court of the Third District (formerly the Third Municipality). According to the *Crescent*, "the notorious hag who reigns over the ignorant and superstitious as the Queen of the Voudous was complained of by her neighbor, Bernardo Rodriguez, residing on Love Street between Union and Bagatelle." Marie Laveau and her daughter Marie Heloïse Euchariste Glapion indeed owned a building at 207 Love Street between Union and Bagatelle. The Marie "Clarisse" Laveau referred to by the newspapers could have been either the mother, Marie Catherine, or the daughter, Marie Euchariste. The city directory for 1859 indicates that the site was occupied by Melas Wilder's Grocery and Coal Yard, but this does not preclude the possibility that it was used for nighttime Voudou services. The neighbor charged that "Marie and her wenches were continuously disturbing his peace and that of the neighborhood with their fighting and obscenity and infernal singing and yelling." This, said the *Crescent*, exemplified "the hellish observance of the mysterious rites of Voudou . . . one of the worst forms of African paganism. . . . A description of the orgies would never do to put in respectable print." The newspapers reported that "Her majesty, Queen Marie, was duly sent after." There was no further coverage of the incident, and the outcome is unknown.[35]

Voudou in the Later Nineteenth Century

Although none of the Louisiana Writers' Project informants were old enough to remember Voudou as it was practiced in the years before the Civil War, their interviews provide significant details from the 1870s and 1880s. These narratives were given to LWP fieldworkers by elderly community members as descriptions of Marie Laveau's religious services. The original Voudou Queen —the Widow Paris—was supposedly incapacitated by age and infirmity during most of the 1870s and is known to have died in 1881. Much of what was recounted by the LWP informants took place at the Laveau-Glapion residence or at the homes of other Voudou serviteurs. While some of the interviewees seem to be describing the Widow Paris, most probably did not see her as the officiating priestess. Many spoke of a younger woman, known to them as "Marie Laveau," who lived in the cottage on St. Ann Street and would likely have been continuing the traditions established by the first Marie. The LWP interviews offer numerous descriptions of Voudou practices, and these oral histories concur with nineteenth-century literary and journalistic accounts of New Orleans Voudou.

Frequent visitors to the Laveau-Glapion home talked of rooms filled with altars, candles, and images of the saints, a fact also mentioned in the *Picayune's Guide to New Orleans* for 1887 and 1900. Such displays are also found in Haitian Voudou temples. In these accounts the blending of Voudou, European magic, and folk Catholicism is apparent.

Marie Dédé was born in 1866 and grew up in the St. Ann Street neighborhood. As a child she was constantly in and out of the Laveau-Glapion cottage to play with Marie Laveau's grandchildren—her best friend, "Memie," was the daughter of Philomène Glapion Legendre. Mrs. Dédé recalled that the children would peep into the front room, which was used for services: "[Marie Laveau] had so many candles burning . . . I don't see how that house never caught on fire. . . . She had all kinds of saints' pictures and flowers on the altar." In this room Marie also "had a big [statue of] St. Anthony . . . and she

26. *A Voodoo Dance.* Note the "feast spread for the spirits" on a white cloth and the presence of African-style drums and a stringed instrument. Illustration by Edward W. Kemble for George Washington Cable's "Creole Slave Songs," *The Century Magazine*, April 1886, p. 816. (Author's collection.)

would turn him upside down on his head in her yard when she had 'work' to perform." Then, recounted Mrs. Dédé, "Memie would come get me and say ... 'Come see my grandma got St. Anthony on his head' and [Marie Laveau] ... would put us [children] out and lock the gate." Charles Raphael, born in 1868, also described the altar in Marie Laveau's front room, which was intended for "good luck charms, money-making charms, husband-holding charms. On this altar she had a statue of St. Peter and St. Marron, a colored saint."[36]

New Orleans Voudou serviteurs as well as traditional Catholics enlist St. Anthony of Padua to find lost articles and bring back strayed lovers. Inverting the figure of the saint to arouse the spirit and request his aid is an example of "reversal of the normal order," a practice found in European and African-American magic. St. Marron, a folk saint unique to New Orleans, was the patron of runaway slaves; the name derives from the French word *marron*, meaning a runaway. He was usually represented by an image of St. Anthony; apparently this saint not only found lost people, he aided those who "got lost" on purpose. St. Peter is believed to open the door to the spirit world, guard the home against intruders, invite customers into one's place of business, and remove barriers to success.[37]

According to the LWP informants, Marie Laveau also practiced less beneficent magic. Charles Raphael told interviewers that in the back room of her house, Marie "had an altar for bad work ... [where] she prepared charms to kill, to drive away, to break up love affairs, and to spread confusion. It was surmounted by statues of a bear, a lion, a tiger, and a wolf." A similar description was given by Raymond Rivaros, born in 1873: "Her altar was in the last room of the house on St. Ann Street. I'm positive she had no saints on that altar. It took the width of the room, and had large plaster statues of a bear, a lion, and a tiger, paper flowers, and candles."[38]

*   *   *

Some of the Louisiana Writers' Project interviewees had attended Marie Laveau's weekly services. These were small, private ceremonies of the sort described in newspaper reports of police raids in the 1850s and 1860s. The informants referred to such meetings as *parterres* or *layouts*, derived from the practice of arranging an offering of herbs, food, liquor, flowers, candles, and coins on a white cloth on the ground or the floor. This is also characteristic of Haitian Vodou ceremonies. The congregation was racially mixed, and a core group of serviteurs, called "co-workers," was always present. The music at the weekly ceremonies was provided by a chorus of young singers and an old man who played the accordion.

Oscar "Nom" Felix was born in 1868 and grew up on Dumaine Street between Burgundy and Dauphine, just two blocks from the Laveau-Glapion home. Mr. Felix explained how he came to sing at the weekly ceremonies: "My cousin . . . was one of Marie Laveau's co-workers . . . he got me to come and sing with them when I was a little boy. I [did that] until she died—that was in 1884. I was about sixteen years old then." Asked about the ceremonies, Oscar Felix related that "They were held in different places . . . at the homes of Marie Laveau's co-workers . . . at the house where Helen Thomas lived . . . on St. Philip between Derbigny and Roman, at Joe Goodness's on Villere between Dumaine and St. Ann, and at Joseph Millon's place on Ursulines between Tonti and Rocheblave."[39] All of these addresses are located in the Faubourg Tremé, across Rampart Street from the Vieux Carré.

Charles Raphael, also a singer at the weekly services in the early 1880s, had grown up in the Faubourg Tremé around the corner from the home of Mama Antoine, another Laveau "co-worker." Every Monday, said Mr. Raphael, the woman he called Marie Laveau would "come to do her work" at Mama Antoine's on Dumaine, between Derbigny and Roman, also in the Faubourg Tremé. "A feast was spread for the spirits on a white tablecloth laid on the floor. Certain foods were always present . . . congri [rice and peas], apples, oranges, and red peppers. Candles were lighted and placed in the four corners of the room. The colors depended on the cause for which the ceremony was given.

They were usually red, blue, green, or brown . . . never white. A Negro named Zizi played the accordion for the singers."[40]

Raymond Rivaros said that the services were held on Friday nights. "The color of Marie Laveau's dress depended on the work she was doing; brown was for bad work, white and blue for good work. Her co-workers wore the same color dress. . . . They were all barefoot. Zizi played . . . the accordion. . . . There was a big chair, like they use in church for the bishop, and Marie sat in it at the opening of the meeting. Then she would tell the people to ask for what they want, sprinkle them with rum, and start the dances. . . . I have seen those men turn the women over like a top. They had large handkerchiefs that they would put around the women's waist, and would they shake! There were more white people at the meetings than colored. The meeting lasted from seven to nine o'clock and they would have things to eat and drink."[41]

* * *

The Louisiana Writers' Project interviews also provide information on Marie Laveau's contemporary, the healer and spiritualist Doctor Jim Alexander. Doctor Jim, whose legal name was Charles Lafontaine, was born about 1836 in Hancock County on the Mississippi Gulf Coast, and died in New Orleans on August 18, 1890. His home and temple were located at 319 Orleans, corner of Johnson, in the Faubourg Tremé.[42] Doctor Jim was described by LWP informant Nathan Hobley as "fine looking, very straight, about three-quarters Indian and the other colored. He was powerful in physique and would . . . take a person who needed treatment onto his back, dance the bamboula and sing, and finally put the person down . . . cured." Theresa Kavanaugh added that he "used to dance with fire on his head, and red hot coals and reptiles writhing all over his body."[43]

A June 25, 1887, *Harper's Weekly* article by Charles Dudley Warner, titled "A Voudoo Dance," described a ceremony conducted by an unidentified practitioner. Certain details—the location of the service, the description of the "doctor," and the fiery curative dance—concur with the remembrances of Louisiana Writers' Project interviewees, suggesting that the healing ritual attended by Warner was conducted by Doctor Jim Alexander.

According to Warner, the ceremony took place at "a small frame house in a street just beyond Congo Square"—Doctor Alexander's building at 319 Orleans fits that description. Warner described "the doctor" as "a good-looking mulatto of middle age." The interracial congregation consisted of "coal-black . . . porters and stevedores, fat cooks, slender chamber-maids . . . yellow girls and

27. Illustration by John Durkin for Charles Dudley Warner's "A Voudoo Dance," *Harper's Weekly Magazine*, June 25, 1887. The priest is probably Doctor Jim Alexander. (Author's collection.)

comely quadroons . . . and among them . . . several white people." In the large front room was an altar with a statue of the Virgin Mary, flanked by candles, plates of fruit, dishes of sugar, powdered orris root, and bottles of brandy.

As the meeting became more emotional, the doctor "seized a bottle of brandy, dashed some of the liquid on the floor . . . as a libation . . . and then began . . . a slow measured dance . . . with more movement of the hips than the feet, backward and forward, round and round, but accelerating his movement as the time of the song quickened and the excitement rose in the room." He ignited brandy in a basin, "snatched up apples, grapes, bananas, oranges, deluged them with burning brandy, and tossed them about the room to the eager and excited crowdfigure. . . . His hands were aflame, his clothes seemed to be on fire . . . the floor was covered with the debris of the sacrifice, all more or less in flame. The wild dancer was dancing in fire!" As believers came forward and knelt for "treatment," the priest "scooped the [flaming] liquid from the bowl . . . and with his hands vigorously scrubbed their faces and heads. While the victim was still sputtering and choking he seized him by the right hand, lifted him up, spun him round half a dozen times, and then sent him whirling." This resembles the spiritual cleansings performed during a Haitian ceremony.

Warner, rather than ending the article with the usual description of "sexual orgies," simply stated that "the singing ceased, the doctor's wife passed the hat for contributions, and the ceremony . . . was over." Nevertheless he clearly found the proceedings exotic, adding that "Nothing indecent occurred in word or gesture, but it was so wild and bizarre that one might easily imagine he was in Africa or in hell.[44]

Henry Castellanos, in *New Orleans As It Was*, named Doctor Jim Alexander as the successor of Marie Laveau. In *Mules and Men*, Zora Neale Hurston cast him as Marie's mentor: "Alexander, the great two-headed doctor felt the power in [Marie Laveau] and so he tell her she must come to study with him." Robert Tallant devoted a chapter to Doctor Jim in *Voodoo in New Orleans*, asserting that he was "the most important man in the life of Marie II," and "with his arrival in New Orleans Marie faced the first real challenge to her omnipotence.[45]

* * *

If the emergence of New Orleans Voudou indeed coincided with the arrival of the Saint Domingue immigrants, the lwa of Haitian Vodou would presumably have been served and honored during the Marie Laveau era. But we hear almost nothing of the Vodou deities—in fact the term *lwa* was never used. Instead, reference was made to the *spirits*. Some of the most beloved members of the Haitian Vodou pantheon, such as Ezili-Freda (mistress of love and femininity), Ezili Dantò (the protective mother), Ogou (the warrior), Agwé (master of the ocean), and Gédé/Baron Samedi (lord of the cemetery), are conspicuously absent.

Some of the LWP interviewees spoke of Papa Limba or La Bas, Daniel Blanc, and Yon Sue. Josephine McDuffy, born in 1853, told her interviewer that "Papa Limba was supposed to be St. Peter." Mary Washington, born in 1863, said she was trained in the arts of Voudou by Marie Laveau. She remembered a song that was sung at the weekly ceremonies: "St. Peter, St. Peter open the door; I am callin' you, come to me; St. Peter, St. Peter open the door." Mrs. Washington explained that "St. Peter was called La Bas, St. Michael was Daniel Blanc, and Yon Sue was St. Anthony." She also mentioned a spirit called Onzancaire.[46]

We also hear of these Voudou spirits in two turn-of-the-century novels, both of which incorporate Voudou themes. In George Washington Cable's *The Grandissimes* (1880), the Voudou priestess Palmyre la Philosophe (said to have been modeled after Marie Laveau) invokes Agoussou, Assonquer, and Danny for love and luck, and Papa Lébat is called upon to make the way clear. In Helen Pitkin's *An Angel by Brevet* (1904), the Voudou priestess Ma'm Peggy calls upon Papa Liba to "open the door," is possessed by Blanc Dani, and uses a statue of St. Joseph, whom she calls Vériquite, in a ritual to bring about a marriage. The old sorcerer Wangateur Pastonair conjures up Vert Agoussou, Dambarra Soutons, and Zombi.[47]

The New Orleans spirits Papa Limba, La Bas, Lébat, and Liba are analogous with the Haitian deity Papa Legba. The song offered by LWP informant Mary Washington, "St. Peter, St. Peter, open the door," resembles the song for Legba by which all Vodou ceremonies are opened: "l'uvri bayé pu mwé pu mwé pasé" [remove the barrier for me, so that I may pass through].[48] Daniel Blanc, Blanc Dani, Danny, and Dambarra are probably manifestations of the Haitian serpent deity Dambala. Vériquite might be Ayizan Velekete, ruler of the marketplace and guardian of priestesses. Yon Sue and Vert Agoussou could be Agassu, known in Africa and Haiti as the founder of the Dahomean royal dynasty. Onzancaire/Assonquer is not a name familiar in Haitian Vodou.

The Laveau Legend has much to say about a serpent deity personified by Marie Laveau's gigantic snake called "Grand Zombi." This idea first appeared in the *Picayune's Guide to New Orleans* for 1900 with the publication of the Creole song "Eh yo ye, Mamzelle Marie, li konin bien li Grand Zombi," which speaks of Marie Laveau's intimate acquaintance with the Grand Zombi. In *Mules and Men*, Zora Neale Hurston identified Grand Zombi as a rattlesnake

Table 3. Deities in Africa, Haiti, and New Orleans

Africa *vodu*	Haitian Vodou *lwa*	New Orleans Voudou *spirits*
Mawu-Lisa supreme deity	**Bondyé** (Good Lord) **Gran Mèt** (great master)	**God**
Elegba messenger of the gods, trickster	**Legba** (St. Peter) guardian of the crossroads and keeper of the gate to the spirit world; an old man with a crutch	**Limba, La Bas, Liba, Lébat** (St. Peter) guardian of the crossroads and keeper of the gate to the spirit world
Dan the sacred python, the rainbow serpent, creator of the world	**Dambala** (St. Patrick or Moses) wisdom, gentleness, and creativity; the rainbow serpent	**Blanc Dani, Danny, Daniel Blanc, Dambarra Soutons** (St. Michael) luck and love
Gu spirit of iron and warfare; patron of blacksmiths	**Ogou Feray** (St. James the Great or St. Michael the Archangel) warrior spirit; patron of blacksmiths and soldiers, iron weapons, tools, and machinery; a revolutionary general	no counterpart
Hu master of the ocean	**Agwé** (St. Ulrich) master of the ocean, along with his wife, the mermaid Lasirén; a tough old soldier	no counterpart
no counterpart	**Ezili Freda** (Mater Dolorosa) femininity, love, and beauty; a gorgeous mulatto courtesan **Ezili Dantò** (Mater Salvatoris or Our Lady of Mt. Carmel) hard-working black peasant woman who is a fiercely protective mother	no direct counterpart The Blessed Mother Mary is universally venerated, and Our Lady of Prompt Succor protects against hurricanes
no direct counterpart	**Gédé/Baron Samedi** (St. Gerome) death, the cemetery, sex, and regeneration; trickster; wears formal attire, sunglasses, and smokes cigars	The African American men who mask as skeletons on Mardi Gras day may be inspired by Gédé

continued

Agasu founder of the Dahomean royal dynasty	Agassu founder of the Dahomean royal dynasty	Yon Sue (St. Anthony), Vert Agoussou to defeat enemies
no counterpart	Ayizan Verikete patroness of the temple and the marketplace, presides over initiations	Vériquite (St. Joseph) to bring about a marriage
no counterpart	no counterpart	Onzancaire, Assonquer for good fortune
Nzambi Mpungu (Kongo supreme deity)	no counterpart among the lwa; in Haiti a zombi is a person whose soul has been stolen by sorcery	Grand Zombi spirit who speaks through the snake

that appeared in Marie's bedroom and called her to become a Voudou priestess; it lived atop her altar and slithered off into the woods when she died. The magical snake appears in all three of the Marie Laveau novels. Robert Tallant, in *The Voodoo Queen*, described it as a water moccasin named "Vodu" who lives in an alabaster box and is a preeminent fixture in Marie's ceremonies. In Francine Prose's *Marie Laveau* the snake is called "Mojo Hand," a talking cobra with a ruby in its head, who becomes Marie's trusted advisor. In Jewel Parker Rhodes' *Voodoo Dreams* it is a python, the embodiment of Dambala, given to Marie by Doctor John as a prop for their staged Voudou performances. The snake also turns up in Stephen Hank's film *The Widow Paris* and in Wendy Mae Chambers' "Voodoo on the Bayou."[49]

The notion of Marie Laveau's snake is supported by some of the LWP interviews and refuted by others. Raymond Rivaros told of Marie's dancing in Congo Square with a "black serpent." Josephine Jones remembered visiting the house on St. Ann Street, where she saw "all kinds of snakes, black cats, spiders, and pigeons that [Marie] would use for charms. She had a snake called Zombi the Snake God, and this god [could] bring sickness or health, good or bad fortune, and love or death." Informants Charles Raphael and Cecile Hunt, on the other hand, contended that Marie Laveau never kept snakes in her home or used them in her Voudou ceremonies.[50]

There is no Haitian Vodou lwa called Grand Zombi. The name may refer to Nzambi Mpungu, the supreme being of the Kongo people, or it may be the invention of journalists inspired by "zombie tales" of Haiti's infamous living dead, combined with Moreau de Saint-Méry's endlessly repeated description of a snake-worshiping ceremony in colonial Saint Domingue.

Gris-Gris

In addition to holding regular services for her followers, Marie Laveau is also said to have given private consultations and made and sold gris-gris. In "Hoodoo in America" and later in *Mules and Men*, Zora Neale Hurston published a series of gris-gris formulae and rituals called the "Marie Leveau [*sic*] routines," supposedly taught to her by Marie's grandnephew "Samuel Thompson"/"Luke Turner." While these may indeed represent Voudou tradition, the "routines" in "Hoodoo in America" and *Mules and Men* appear to be copied verbatim from a little booklet called *The Life and Works of Marie Laveau*—even some misspelled words are reproduced. *The Life and Works of Marie Laveau* (not to be confused with Raul Canizares' 2001 work of the same title) is undated and claims no author. Certain stylistic elements indicate that it was issued in the 1920s by New Orleans' famous "hoodoo drugstore," the Cracker Jack on South Rampart Street, as a device for marketing their stock of roots and herbs, animal parts, minerals, candles, powders, oils, and perfumes.[51] In an October 15, 1928, letter to Langston Hughes, Hurston thanked him for directing her to "the drugstore on Rampart."[52]

Louisiana Writers' Project informants Laura Hopkins, Joe Landry, and John Slater claimed to know something of Marie Laveau's magical practices. Mrs. Hopkins, born in 1878, declared herself to have been a Laveau trainee, but she was too young to have studied with the original Voudou Queen. The birth dates of Landry and Slater are unknown. These narrators told of rituals to attract and control a lover, bring about a marriage, improve business, and win in court, as well as those for negative purposes, including separation of couples, revenge, and death. Marie Laveau's gris-gris, analogous to charm assemblages used in Africa and Haiti, were said to be made from roots and herbs, hot peppers, sugar, salt, flavorings, animal parts and by-products, graveyard dirt, gun powder, pins and needles, nails, dolls, candles, incense, holy water, and images of the saints. After the magical "work" had been accomplished, it was necessary to "pay off" with an offering of food, liquor, flowers, or coins—fifteen cents was the usual fee.[53]

The interview with Laveau disciple Mary Washington, born in 1863, supports the claim by tellers of the Laveau Legend that Marie's magic was based at least in part on trickery. "[She] had a way with white people. . . . She would get a gal [for a married man] and tell his wife about it. . . . Then she would show the wife how to get her husband back—that would cost plenty of money. . . . She would . . . tell the man that his wife was about to find out . . . and he had better stop it. . . . In cases like that all she had to do was fool the people." Mrs. Washington spoke of Marie Laveau's black assistant, who would "get up early in the morning and kill the snakes, chickens, alligators and other animals and fix the dusts." He would "go to people's homes and learn their business . . . [and] put cow heads and black cats . . . on their doorsteps." They would "get scared and come running to Marie Laveau. She would tell them they were hoodooed, and charge them big money for a cure. . . . She [already] knew all about their affairs."[54]

*   *   *

From the published sources and oral histories quoted above, we have learned that nineteenth-century New Orleans Voudou was primarily a religion of women, dominated by priestesses who served a racially diverse, mostly female congregation. Voudou temples, in which the rooms were filled with spectacular altars, were located in private homes such as that of Betsy Toledano and Marie Laveau. Services consisted of Roman Catholic prayers, chanting, dancing, and spirit possession, followed by a communal feast. The descriptions of altars and ceremonies in New Orleans greatly resemble the practices of Haitian Vodou. The complex spiritual pantheon of the Haitian religion is absent from New Orleans Voudou, although Legba, Dambala, and a few of the other lwa appear to have survived.

The religion that evolved in nineteenth-century New Orleans and was embraced by Marie Laveau and her Voudou society combined traditions introduced by the first Senegambian, Fon, Yoruba, and Kongo slaves with Haitian Vodou, European magic, and folk Catholicism. It also absorbed the beliefs of blacks imported from Maryland, Virginia, and the Carolinas during the slave trade of the 1830s–1850s. These "American Negroes" were English-speaking, at least nominally Protestant, and practiced a heavily Kongo-influenced kind of hoodoo, conjure, or rootwork. New Orleans Voudou is therefore not identical to Haitian Vodou, but represents a unique North American blend of African and European religious and magical traditions.

St. John's Eve

Until the end of the nineteenth century, June 23, the Eve of the Feast of St. John the Baptist, was celebrated with bonfires, nighttime picnics, singing, dancing, and ritual bathing on the shore of Lake Pontchartrain. The observance of St. John's Eve, which occurs two days after the summer solstice (known in Europe as Midsummer's Eve) was probably introduced into Louisiana by French and Spanish colonists, who would have been continuing a European tradition with both pagan and Christian roots.

Before the Christianization of Western Europe, religious festivals followed the agricultural and pastoral calendar and marked the summer and winter solstices. At these crucial times of the year, the human world and the spirit world were believed to intersect. Men and women responded by lighting bonfires to attract good spirits and drive away bad ones, protect livestock and people from disease, and ensure a successful harvest. Believers also immersed themselves in sacred springs, streams, and lakes that were supposed to be endowed with magical and medicinal virtues. Roman Catholic holy days were grafted onto Celtic and Germanic days of pagan religious observance. Lingering elements of these ancient rituals survived in New Orleans, where the St. John's Eve celebrations continued the tradition of kindling midsummer bonfires and bathing in a sacred body of water.[1]

At some undetermined time, St. John's Eve was adopted by people of African descent and became the most important celebration of the Voudou liturgical calendar. The custom might have been brought to Louisiana by Voudou devotees from Saint Domingue. There, the feast of St. John the Baptist, a patron of Freemasonry who is treated as a minor lwa, is observed with bonfires and ceremonies by both Freemasons and Vodou societies.[2]

In May of 1831, the Frenchman Pierre Forest arrived in New Orleans for a stay of several weeks. Among the many curiosities he described was that of blacks dancing on a "huge green field," called "the camp," on the shore of Lake Pontchartrain. Forest did not give a date for this observation, and one wonders if what he saw was a St. John's Eve ceremony. "The negroes," wrote Forest, "are gathered together in a large number of distinct groups; each has its own flag floating atop a very tall mast. . . . [They] dance with extraordinary speed and agility. . . . They make their music by beating and rolling their sticks on their drums."[3]

Like the earlier Congo Square dances, the St. John's Eve ceremonies—supposedly led by Marie Laveau—became one of the "sights to see" in New Orleans. By the 1870s thousands of outsiders were traveling to the lake to be titillated and amused by the spectacle. As expressed by Louisiana Writers' Project employee Catherine Dillon in her "Voodoo" manuscript, those invited to the "lakeshore festivities" included "reporters, police officials, 'swells' of the sporting population, and the [racially] mixed politicians of the time—for Madame Laveau catered to the Knights of the Carpetbag." Here Dillon was making fun of Louisiana's post–Civil War Reconstruction government, which granted people of African descent the right to vote and hold office.[4]

During most of the nineteenth century the shore of Lake Pontchartrain was uninhabited, and a dense swamp of cypress and scrub palmetto extended from the "back-of-town" to the lake. Fort San Juan, later known as "Spanish Fort," had been erected by the Spanish administration just above the mouth of Bayou St. John to protect New Orleans from invasion via Lake Pontchartrain. Lakeside resorts eventually developed at Spanish Fort, Milneburg, and West End, located approximately a mile and a half apart. Nineteenth-century photographs of West End and Spanish Fort show hotels resplendent with cupolas, galleries, and "gingerbread," with piers and pavilions extending over the water. Both had theaters, restaurants, beer gardens, casinos, dance halls, and

28. Bayou St. John at Spanish Fort, by an unknown photographer, 1895. From John Ficklen, *Art Work of New Orleans*, W. H. Parish Publishing Co. (The Historic New Orleans Collection, Williams Research Center, accession no. 1979.313.7.2 ii.)

29. Pavilions at Spanish Fort. Photograph by Georges François Mugnier, ca. 1900. (Collection of the Louisiana State Museum, accession no. 9813.629.1.)

30. *Pleasure Resorts at West End*, by an unknown photographer, 1892. (The Historic New Orleans Collection, Williams Research Center, accession no. 1970.29.67.)

bathhouses. Milneburg was more modest, with places of entertainment that attracted a less "refined" clientele, and summer cottages and fishing shacks built over the lake and connected by wooden docks.[5]

Revelers who made the seven-mile trip to the lake had several means of public transit. The Pontchartrain Railroad, known as the "Smokey Mary," departed from the foot of Elysian Fields Avenue in the Faubourg Marigny and traveled to Milneburg. The New Orleans and Spanish Fort Railroad began at Canal and Basin streets and ran through City Park to Spanish Fort. Railway authorities anticipated such large crowds on St. John's Eve that they added extra cars and instituted late night trips to the lakeshore. Celebrants could also reach Lake Pontchartrain via the Carondelet Canal, which connected with Bayou St. John and terminated at Spanish Fort. Private conveyances took the oyster-shell road that began at Esplanade Avenue and ran along Bayou St. John.[6]

It should not be assumed that observing or participating in the Voudou ceremonies was the only motivation for going to Lake Pontchartrain on St. John's Eve. This was a festive time for citizens of all sorts and colors. Lakeside residents lit bonfires and set up coffee and gumbo stands for the visitors. New Orleanians made excursions to the lake for picnics, dances, and fireworks, and availed themselves of the area's many restaurants and taverns. The Feast of St. John the Baptist was also important for Freemasons, both black and white, who honored their patron saint with a church service and parade followed by an outdoor feast and pyrotechnic display at Lake Pontchartrain.[7]

By the later nineteenth century St. John's Eve was being celebrated in the downtown neighborhood along the Mississippi River now known as the Bywater. According to a *Daily States* article of June 24, 1887, "St. John's Eve was observed most magnificently . . . by residents of the Ninth Ward. . . . Bonfires were lit on Poland, Hancock, and Delery streets and on the levee."[8]

*   *   *

Although the Voudou community presumably had celebrated St. John's Eve at Lake Pontchartrain for decades, there are no published descriptions of the event from the antebellum period or the Civil War years, when Marie Laveau was still the reigning queen. It is indeed strange that in the 1850s, when the "City Intelligence" columns missed no chance to report on Voudou-related arrests, we find not a word about St. John's Eve. But during the Reconstruction era between 1863 and 1877, and continuing into the Jim Crow years of the 1880s and 1890s, the conservative, white-owned New Orleans newspapers, particularly the *Picayune* and the *Times* (which merged with the *Democrat* in

1881), made every effort to ridicule people of African descent. Voudou was exploited as proof that blacks were ignorant, superstitious, and unworthy of full citizenship.[9] Much of the journalistic obsession with Voudou centered around the St. John's Eve ceremonies. These "orgy stories" tell us more about mainstream attitudes toward race than about Voudou, but they occasionally contain descriptions that, although imperfectly understood by their writers, are surprisingly accurate.

The first newspaper account of the St. John's Eve celebration appeared on July 5, 1869, when the local news column of the *Commercial Bulletin* reported that "June is the time devoted by the voodoo worshipers to the celebration of their most sacred and therefore most revolting rites. Midnight dances, bathing and eating, together with other less innocent pleasures, make the early summer a time of unrestrained orgies for the blacks." Here we find another of the rare appearances of the name Marie Laveau, and this only to announce her retirement: "This season is marked by the coronation of a new voodoo queen in the place of the celebrated Marie Laveau, who has held her office for a quarter of a century and is now superannuated in her seventieth year." Taking a poke at the newly freed slaves, the writer quipped that now "a more youthful hand puts up love philters and makes fetishes for the intelligent freedmen, who elect governors and members of Congress out of their own number."[10]

The *Daily Picayune* announced the upcoming St. John's Eve event in the summer of 1870. The writer obviously had never attended a ceremony, and allowed his overheated imagination free reign: "Today . . . the Voudou worshipers will commence their fetish rites. Annually the believers in this strange superstition indulge in orgies that are attended with singing and dancing and sacrifices which sometimes include human victims. It is a strange and savage religion, shrouded from light, as are the worst passions and most dreadful crimes. . . . Its influences permeate a large class of the colored population, and many white people are subject to its delusions." A few days later the *Times* reported that "Marie Lavou [*sic*], Eliza Nicaux, and Euphrasie" had been seen at the lake in all their "queenly glories."[11]

A journalist from the *Times* described the St. John's Eve ceremony of 1872 in an article titled "The Vous Dous Incantation." It is unlikely that the seemingly robust woman referred to as "Marie Laveau" was the aged Widow Paris—might the reporter have seen "Marie II"? The festival took place near the mouth of Bayou St. John, where the *Times* man observed a racially mixed congregation of about two hundred. Soon another hundred people arrived in a lugger, followed by a skiff carrying "the Voudou Queen, Marie Lavaux [*sic*]. She was hailed with hurrahs." Marie reportedly led the congregation in a Creole song, "Mamzelle Marie chauffez ça" (make it hot); a fire was built for which every participant furnished a piece of wood, making a wish as they threw it on; and over the fire was placed a boiling cauldron into which was put salt, black pepper, a black snake cut into three pieces, a cat, a black rooster, and some colored powders. The writer noted that the contents of the cauldron were not eaten, but were saved "for next year." At midnight everyone undressed and plunged into the lake. Afterwards there was singing and dancing followed by a feast of gumbo and jambalaya. At the end, "all joined hands around the Queen. She preached a sermon, at the close of which all knelt down to pray and receive her benediction. There was a chorus of 'C'est l'amour, oui Maman, c'est l'amour' (it's love, yes Mama, it's love), during which day began to break. Then the Queen said, 'Here is day, we must welcome it with song, and all go home.'"[12]

In 1873 the *Daily Picayune* published an account of the "annual Voudou festival along the borders of Bayou St. John and the Old Lake [between Spanish Fort and Milneburg], at which was practiced all the horrid fetish of African heathenism." According to this article, the lakeshore was lined with bonfires, and around these "the worshipers of the demon assembled in groups, some large and some small, dancing and singing a weird lay in no known language, ancient or modern." This time Marie Laveau was absent: "The old Voudou queen . . . to the regret of her subjects, was unable to attend on account of illness, and her mantle of authority was worn by Mamma Caroline, who is spoken of as the ancient queen's successor. . . . Mamma Caroline held court in a nude state in an old house on the banks of the bayou."[13]

In 1874 both the *Republican* and the *Times* received invitations to "the grand celebration of the Voudou festival" from someone named Zelima, who claimed to be Marie Laveau's secretary. The reporter for the *Republican* "kept away and saved his time and temper," but the *Times* man dutifully trekked out to the lake and was disappointed to find, instead of the famous queen Marie Laveau, "a greasy-looking, middle-aged negress, black as uncleansed sin" presiding over a rather unexceptional dance party. "The fact is," admitted the reporter, "the Voudous are no more, and their mysterious ceremonies . . . have degenerated into a time of unrestrained license for the negroes, when they can get drunk and indulge in their idiotic pranks without fear of interference from the police." A representative of the *Picayune* was also dispatched to the lake, where he found nothing but a large crowd of disgruntled "Voudou hunters," and pronounced the "revels" to be "nonsense—a played-out hoax."[14]

In 1875 the St. John's Eve ceremonies were covered by virtually every newspaper in town—the *Bee*, the *Commercial Bulletin*, the *Picayune*, and the *Times*. The *Times* article, titled "Fetish Worship—St. John's Eve at Milneburg—A Voudou's Incantation—Midnight Scenes and Orgies," described a semicommercial event held at the end of the Milneburg wharf. This reporter, despite his condescending attitude, produced an exceptionally detailed and believable account.

At midnight, wrote the *Times* man, "Every hotel and restaurant [in Milneburg] was brilliantly illuminated, and a crowd of several hundred lingered upon the shell walks of its main thoroughfare." Many of his party "had witnessed the ceremony repeatedly and spoke knowingly of Marie Laveau and the wonders of her incantations." But some of their number were "visiting the scene for the first time and gazed at the glowing fires stretched along the shore as far as the eye could reach with a look of incredulity."

As the hour grew later, a racially diverse crowd of about fifty men and women "made their way out the long wharf, and about half way to the T-head turned into a bridge-like walk, which leads to a white frame building, resting upon piles, perhaps about two hundred feet distant." Two policemen, called "Metropolitans," guarded the entrance to the barroom and collected the admission fees. There the reporter witnessed "a score of 'frail ones' [prostitutes] with members of the sporting fraternity, and men ranked among the young and giddy, swirling in the mazes of a waltz. . . . A majority of the female participants were white, with reputations, candor compels us to admit, not altogether stainless."

The presiding queen was Madame Frazie, "a large, corpulent woman, black as the ace of spades." The reporter described the ceremony, which resembles the smaller, private meetings recounted in the preceding chapter: "Stretched on the floor in the middle of the room was a sheet, the corners of which were ornamented by bouquets in china vases. At each side and between the bouquets stood a lighted candle, and in the center a great nougat pyramid. The lateral intervals were further furnished with plates containing cake and bonbons, and bottles of wine, whiskey, brandy, vinegar, and water." Three men and three women "moved to and fro in a monotonous, swaying dance . . . accompanying themselves [with] an unintelligible chant, as dreary as their motions. . . . [Then] the chant changed to a discord more rapid and grotesque. . . . The group seemed suddenly to become excited, their contortions increased, they clung to each other in a state of semi-frenzy, and one woman, reeling over apparently in an epileptic fit, fell to the floor."

One of the men, according to the *Times*, seized a bottle of wine from off the white sheet and "distributed it plentifully over the room, sprinkling it upon the company." The description that follows is reminiscent of the Louisiana Writers' Project interviews regarding Doctor Jim Alexander's services, and one wonders if it was he who assisted Madame Frazie at the 1875 event on the Milneburg wharf. "He closed his eyes, protruded his head, and, hissing like a snake, moved about [like] a madman," suggesting that he was possessed by Dambala, the serpent deity. "Circling the entire apartment, he seized each spectator by two hands, and giving them a nervous shake, dropped them to clasp those of another.... Swallowing a mouthful of liquid from one of the bottles, he squirted it over the victim's entire face and body." Some of the participants were "taken bodily upon the back of the operator and borne around the room." The *Times* reporter commented that "the work was still in enthusiastic progress" when he left at 3:30 in the morning.[15]

Marie Laveau was last reported to have appeared at the St. John's Eve ceremonies in 1872. Newspaper men nevertheless continued to make the trip to Lake Pontchartrain on the night of June 23, always hoping to see the Queen of the Voudous and always disappointed. Her death in 1881 coincided with a decline in public observance of the Feast of St. John. The Roman Catholic holy day sacred to the Creoles was being replaced by that uniquely American midsummer commemoration, the Fourth of July. The newspapers announced events like the "Twelfth Annual Fourth of July Festival, Grand Pyrotechnical Exhibition, and Ball, to be given by the Clerk's Benevolent Association at the Fairgrounds."[16] The lack of public involvement did not, however, put an end to the yearly St. John's Eve "orgy stories."

On June 24, 1884, the *Times-Democrat* printed an article titled "A Voudou Dance—Revival on the Lake Shore of Voudou Mysteries—How the Eve of St. John was Celebrated Last Night by the Queen and Her Adherents." It was included the following year in the *Historical Sketch Book and Guide to New Orleans* under the title "St. John's Eve—Voudouism." This piece, which has been attributed to Lafcadio Hearn, provides some interesting details of that night's events: "At intervals of scarcely more than three hundred yards, groups of men and women could be seen standing around blazing pine-knot fires, their dark or copper-colored faces weirdly gilded by the red flame and their black forms, thus illumined, appearing gigantic and supernatural against the opaque background of the lake and sky. Negresses [dispensed] gumbo and coffee [from] small tables." Hearing "the faintest sound as of a drum beaten rhythmically . . . and a chorus of voices," the reporter and his party proceeded to a location about three-quarters of a mile below Milneburg, where they came upon a "house of two rooms . . . with a wide gallery." Here they found about twenty-five black men and women engaged in a Voudou ceremony.

The traditional offerings had been placed on "a small tablecloth [in the center of the floor], at the corners of which two tallow candles burned. . . . As a center-piece . . . there was a shallow Indian basket filled with . . . *herbes*. Around the basket were diminutive piles of white beans and corn, and just outside of these a number of small bones, whether human or not could not be told. Some curiously wrought bunches of feathers were the next ornamentations near the edge of the cloth, and outside of all several saucers with small cakes in them."

One old fellow took up a two-stringed fiddle with a long neck and a body covered with snake skin, and two youths beside him began to beat on small gourd drums. A tall, sinewy, fierce-looking black man stepped out onto the floor and gave an impressive performance of the song, "Mallé marché su piquan d'oré" (I will walk upon the golden thorn). Then commenced "the regular Voudou dance with all its twistings and contortions. Two of the women fell exhausted to the floor in a frenzy and frothing at the mouth, and . . . [a] young man was carried out of the room unconscious."

In this 1884 article, Malvina Latour was designated as the successor to Marie Laveau, a statement repeated two years later by George Washington Cable in "Creole Slave Songs." Latour was described as "a bright [light-complexioned] café au lait woman of about forty-eight [born about 1836], who sat in one corner of the room looking on the scene before her with an air of dignity. . . . She was of extremely handsome figure . . . neatly attired in a blue calico with white dots . . . and on her head a brilliant tignon was gracefully tied. On inquiry it was learned that her name was Malvina Latour, and that she was the queen."[17]

Malvina Latour appears nowhere in the New Orleans city directories, municipal and archdiocesan records, or the census. Through a curious intermingling of sources, her identity has become conflated with that of an earlier priestess known as "Madame Lott." In "Voudouism Rampant in Louisiana," a *New Orleans Times* article of July 17, 1870, Madame Lott was said to have lifted an evil spell from the Reverend Mr. Turner, the "learned, eloquent, and gifted divine—the dignified and dusky-hued chaplain" of the racially mixed Louisiana legislature during Reconstruction. The article, obviously intended to discredit black legislators by associating them with Voudou, designated Madame Lott as the sister of state representative Harry Lott. She was described as being dressed in "fantastic and costly attire," but "dreadfully marked by small-pox, and of a color two or three shades deeper than Egyptian darkness," making her "ugly enough to scare the devil out of his own dominions." This story reappeared in James William Buel's *Metropolitan Life Unveiled* (1882), where Buel announced that "the present Voudou queen in New Orleans is a full-blooded black, and is a sister to Harry Lott, former member of the Louisiana Legislature from Rapides Parish.[18]

It was Herbert Asbury, in *The French Quarter*, who creatively combined Madame Lott with Malvina Latour, describing Latour as "a mulatto, *café au lait* in color, whose brother became a member of the notorious 'black and tan' legislature that misgoverned Louisiana for several years during Reconstruction times. She was about thirty years old when she received the scepter of New Orleans Voodooism from the trembling hands of Marie Laveau, and is said to have been very handsome, with a fine, fully developed figure." Asbury repeated the story of the "pious Negro clergyman, the Reverend Mr. Turner, who was chaplain of the Louisiana Legislature." In the presence of a large crowd, wrote Asbury, Malvina Latour rubbed the afflicted minister's hands and chest with "a pungent oil, meanwhile chanting a Voodoo exorcism . . . whereupon the Reverend Turner retched violently, his mouth opened, and out popped a black mouse."[19]

* * *

By the later nineteenth-century New Orleans had entered the infamous era of Jim Crow segregation, and city administrators had become absolutely intolerant of Voudou. Increasing harassment by the authorities and disapproval on the part of the Christian churches forced Voudou, as an organized religion, to go into hiding. Interestingly, the practice was never actually declared illegal. During the antebellum period Voudou ceremonies had been broken up by the police and participants arrested, jailed, fined, or flogged for violating the regulation against unlawful assembly of slaves and free persons. After the abolition of slavery, "unlawful assembly" could no longer be used as an excuse for the repression of Voudou. Newly instituted rules accomplished the same purpose. An 1879 city ordinance forbade loitering, disorderly conduct, and "exposing the body" in public places, while another, passed in 1881, required permission for any sort of meetings, including religious gatherings and the formation of processions in the public squares of the city. In 1887 a state law forbade practicing medicine for pay without a license, which subjected traditional healers to prosecution. In 1897 the New Orleans City Council passed an ordinance against fortune-telling.[20]

The real St. John's Eve ceremonies having been nearly persecuted out of existence, some enterprising individuals staged commercial reenactments. The *Daily States* of June 23, 1887, announced that a "Congo-Creole African Dance" would be held at the Cosmopolitan Pavilion at West End. The next day the *Times-Democrat* reported that this affair, although "creditably conducted," was a "disappointment to the audience," and that to those who had seen the St. John's Eve ceremonies in the days of Marie Laveau, "the whole business was merely a well-rehearsed stage performance." Instead of genuine African dance, the crowd "witnessed a series of breakdowns and double-shuffles." Nevertheless the music, provided by the "jawbone of an ass . . . a half whiskey barrel . . . and a cracker box," and the costumes of the dancers, with "straps trimmed with tin tubes fastened around their knees," sounds reasonably authentic. At midnight men appeared in the water between the pavilion and the levee, and "as they sang . . . they discharged roman candles and skyrockets, producing a pleasing and pretty effect."[21]

By the 1890s the reports that invariably appeared in the New Orleans newspapers around the time of St. John's Eve had plummeted to the depths of sensationalism and racism. These extravagant yarns, often run as filler when there was no actual news, included imaginative depictions of frenzied dancing, bloody animal (or human) sacrifice, drunkenness, nudity, and interracial fornication. On June 24, 1896, the *Times-Democrat* published a lengthy rant titled "Dance of the Voodoos—Outlandish Celebration of St. John's Eve," in which the "Voodoo King," a "huge Negro clad in a breechcloth strung with alligator teeth, with a necklace of bones around his neck and shells in his ears," boiled and ate a black cat while "impassioned black savages danced as naked as islanders to the beating of ox skulls and tom-toms, the weird crooning of the hags, and the sharp ejaculations of bucks and wenches."[22]

In contrast to these anti-Voudou sentiments, New Orleans newspapers occasionally printed sentimental reminiscences about Voudou as it was practiced in the happier days before the Civil War. A *Daily Picayune* article of June 22, 1890, titled "Voudouism—A Chapter of Old New Orleans History—How St. John's Eve Was Celebrated Fifty Years Ago" described an unidentified Voudou queen who, emerging from a lakeside cabin, presided over the St. John's Eve ceremonies of the 1840s. This regal personage certainly fits the description of Marie Laveau: "She was tall, beautiful, and commanding in appearance; old age had not yet set its seal upon her, and one could easily imagine the magnetic sway which her powerful mind held for so many years over the members of her order." The queen "bowed before the serpent god, and tapping three times upon the ground, summoned the powers of darkness to her assistance.... Then [she] rose and recited in a slow, impressive manner the Apostle's Creed and Hail Mary," to which the Voudou serviteurs "responded devoutly."[23]

* * *

The Louisiana Writers' Project interviews provide an interesting counterpoint to the journalistic accounts quoted above. Over the years, according to these elderly New Orleanians, the St. John's Eve celebrations were held by different parties at different venues. We hear that the assemblies sometimes took place on the lakeshore, sometimes on a pavilion or a barge on the lake, and sometimes at a lakeside cabin. Most of these events occurred in the 1880s, although a few of the older informants may have attended ceremonies in the middle or late 1870s. The "Marie Laveau" of whom they spoke could not have been the Widow Paris, who is reported to have retired sometime between 1869 and 1872 and is known to have died in 1881. Like those who recalled the weekly Voudou services of the 1870s and 1880s, they must have seen the second Marie Laveau. By the later nineteenth century the St. John's Eve observances had undoubtedly become more popular spectacle than religious observance, but we can nevertheless conjecture that the ceremonies described by members of the Voudou congregation resembled those of the original Voudou Queen.

Two of the LWP informants, although they did not actually attend the ceremonies, shared recollections of the lakeshore scene that coincide with newspaper reports of the 1870s and 1880s. Mathilda Mendoza, a resident of Spanish Fort born in 1864, described the bonfires created by her family and neighbors: "We save the tar barrels to set in the edge of the water to make fires . . . and [on St. John's Eve] we burn [them] all along the lake and bayou because it's good luck—we shoot off the gun—it's just like the first of the year." Henrietta Nichols, born in 1862, had lived all of her life in Milneburg. She related that on St. John's Eve "there was fires burning all along the lake—that was the hoodoo people; you could hear them singing for miles." She and her young friends spied on the festivities from beneath one of the pavilions: "We'd get in a boat and go under it; you'd have to stoop way down low, not to bump your head. We could hear them dancin' but we couldn't see nothin'. They'd charge a dollar to go in.... My uncle used to take the tickets." This sounds like the celebration of 1875, which, according to the *Times*, was held on the Milneburg wharf, with two policemen guarding the entrance and collecting admission.[24]

Oscar Felix provided a detailed description of the St. John's Eve celebrations, which were held outdoors on the lakeshore, near Milneburg. An altar surmounted by a big cross held candles, offerings, and pictures of St. Peter and St. John. According to Mr. Felix, "They celebrated St. John's Day because they wanted to be like him. He was a great man and always did what was right." The service began with Roman Catholic prayers. "Everybody would kneel before the altar and rap on the ground three times, one—two—three . . . in the name of the Father, Son, and Holy Ghost. After that we would sing in Creole . . . the leader would begin with praise to St. John. [It] was just like a mass in a regular church." Unlike most of the other interviewees, Mr. Felix made no mention of bathing in the lake.

Following the religious portion of the ceremony, said Oscar Felix, the participants would dance: "One man would have two women on each side of him and they would put metal rings on their knees that would jingle and rattle. He would first turn one [woman] around and then he would turn the other . . . then he would dance with one and then the other." After the dance, "everybody would bow down on their knees . . . and say the 'Our Father.' Of course we all would stay afterwards and eat and drink and have a good time. There was chicken . . . cakes, and liquor . . . also red beans and rice to eat."[25]

An old gentleman who would only give his name as "Pops" was approached on the street by an LWP fieldworker. After protesting vigorously that he was "no hoodoo" and wasn't going to tell "nothin'," Pops admitted that he was "a young rascal back in them days," and warmed up enough to share a substantial amount of information. He remembered the St. John's Eve ceremonies, which he said were held on a barge on Lake Pontchartrain around 1875, when he was sixteen. "There was all kinds of saint statues on the barge and a altar fixed up with flowers and things. . . . There was plenty of food . . . cake . . . champagne and liquor . . . [Marie Laveau] sure did spend a lot of money. . . . It was just like Mardi Gras for the people. She was dressed in a long purple dress with some kind of rope around her waist. She wore low shoes with no strings. The women co-workers wore purple dresses too, and the men wore white and purple and carried lighted candles. They all danced some kind of a hula dance. . . . Boy, that was a mess! . . . 'Fore the thing broke up she would disappear. [They say] she walked across the water."[26]

Charles Raphael had also been a participant in the St. John's Eve ceremonies. He recalled that the dances were held on a barge on the lake. "Seven or eight bottles were placed in a large circle . . . the dancers threading their way between them. Little pots of fire were placed here and there on the barge.... The dancers balanced candles on their heads... rum and champagne were served at these functions.... The men would put a big handkerchief around the women's thighs and they would make them shake. I used to sing... and call the ones that was to dance in the middle of the floor." This dance was called "fe chauffe." Like the song "Mamzelle Marie chauffez ça," the name derives from *faire chauffer*, meaning "make it hot" or "heat it up." According to Mr. Raphael, the dancing resembled that of the "bands of Negroes who dress in Indian Chief costumes on Mardi Gras and dance on the Claiborne Avenue neutral ground."[27] This statement provides an interesting link between the dances performed at the St. John's Eve ceremonies and the practices of today's black "Mardi Gras Indian" gangs. The "Indians" first appeared during Carnival around 1885.[28]

William Moore, born in 1864, began frequenting the St. John's Eve ceremonies in 1883: "When we got [to the lakeshore], there was an altar under one of those big trees. Everybody ... had to bring a piece of cake and place it on this altar. Then they would disrobe until they had on only one piece, and lay face down on the ground in a circle." The woman Mr. Moore called Marie Laveau "came out with a thin, thin gown on.... She would start to singing and dancing very slow-like, getting faster all the time ... she could bend her body into all kinds of knots and do everything with it ... she danced so long... until she either went into a trance or was completely exhausted ... they had to bring her to with water.... Yes sir, I knew all those [Voudou] people, and I didn't go just once, I went many times."[29]

Raymond Rivaros told his interviewer that "they had such a crowd out there [at the lake] that you could hardly see." A feast was set outdoors on long tables: "They would serve wine, champagne, anisette and had all kinds of things to eat—pork, rice and peas, chicken, fruits, candies, fancy cakes." The dance itself was held on a barge on the lake. "Marie Laveau wore a long, loose cotton dress with a belt. The women with her wore short dresses and the men wore pants and no shirts. All of them ... were barefoot. [Marie] would line the people up and pick the dancers, calling them by name. The music was from a drum and an accordion. Quart bottles were put on the barge.... The men and women would dance in and out of the bottles and jump over them ... drink liquor, jump from the barge and cut the water with scissors, knives, and hatchets. ... I'm telling you, things would get hot before the dances were over ... they would last way into the night."[30]

Joseph Alfred, born about 1855, and Eugene Fritz, birth date unknown, were interviewed together at the Thomy Lafon Old Folks Home. Like Raymond Rivaros, the two men said they witnessed a St. John's Eve celebration on a barge. "The dancers would put a big Chinese handkerchief behind their necks. They would march out to the center of the floor . . . stomp their feet . . . shake down and then shake up . . . their bodies looked like a turning top . . . [there were] white and colored. . . . [The women] wore all different color [dresses]. They was [cut] low in the front and back and only reached the knees [and] there was nothing underneath. . . . The men wore short pants and summer shirts with wide sleeves, and leather belts three inches wide. [They] danced until they went wild. . . . Marie Laveau stood in the middle and gave directions like a drum major. She started all the movements, kept the time, and danced along with everybody. . . . The people got so hot they would jump off the barge . . . skiffs and boats would pick them up."[31]

The fisherman John Smith, a lifelong resident of Spanish Fort, was one of the few white people interviewed by the Louisiana Writers' Project. He refers to events that happened between about 1882 and 1884. The functions that Mr. Smith attended took place at a lakeside cabin. "On that night the lake was hummin' with people. There were special trains out here on St. John's Eve. Milk wagons, carriages, and all kind of things was lined for miles on the lake, but they couldn't see nothin'. A lot of people came out here to bathe. All the bath houses were rented and they stayed until about four in the morning. . . . Marie Laveau had all the sports and newspaper men to come out. . . . [She] died when I was about sixteen [1884]. No one came to her place after she died and there was no more dances. . . . The police stopped all that."[32]

*   *   *

St. John's Eve provided a gold mine of colorful material for twentieth-century writers. In *Voodoo in New Orleans*, Robert Tallant appropriated bits and pieces of the Louisiana Writers' Project interviews to concoct his own version of the St. John's Eve ceremonies, replete with "snake worship," the "roaring bonfire," the "steaming cauldron," the "breast torn from a living chicken," drunken, naked "Voodoos" who danced with "spasmodic jerking and trembling" until they "fell to the ground unconscious" or, with "wild screams of frenzy," ran out into the lake. These spectacles were presided over by Marie Laveau: "This was the Marie Laveau who consorted with the crocodiles, the Marie Laveau who talked with Lucifer." Adhering to the formula employed by all writers of this genre, Tallant tells us that "The white visitors would usually depart as the climax of sexual orgy began."[33] Similar depictions of the St. John's Eve ceremonies have been incorporated into almost every literary and theatrical treatment of Marie Laveau.

Voudou and Prostitution

For many of those who traveled to the lakeshore on the night of June 23, St. John's Eve was simply an opportunity for men of the "sporting fraternity" to pick up women of easy virtue. A Louisiana historian noted that during the St. John's Eve celebrations some "entrepreneurial Voodoos profited from curious spectators . . . charging admission to old shanties where [mulatto girls] served as dancers and harlots."[34] This reflects the common perception that Voudou, with its "orgiastic" rites, was synonymous with prostitution, and that women of color, by their nature sexually promiscuous, were dangerous both to easily seduced males and to naive females. Marie Laveau was characterized by her detractors as a "procuress."

The comments of Louisiana Writers' Project informants Mary Washington and Marie Brown lend some support to these tales. According to Mrs. Washington, who was one of Marie Laveau's followers, "[She] had all kinds of ways to make money. If a fellow wanted a quadroon gal, she would get one for him." Marie Brown, who never had a good word to say about the Voudou Queen, exclaimed: "Marie Laveau—that she-devil, that hell-cat! Of course I remember her. . . . She was always enticin' young girls to come to her house and meet mens." But Raymond Rivaros dismissed this rumor: "People all say she had a sporting house but I don't know anything about that."[35]

Published accounts made frequent reference to a lakeside cabin, known as the White House or Maison Blanche, that supposedly belonged to Marie Laveau. While Marie and her followers may have had the use of such a place, a search of the Conveyance Office Index to Purchasers and Vendors and the Notarial Archives provides no evidence that any member of the Laveau-Glapion family owned property on Lake Pontchartrain. In some versions of the Laveau Legend, the Maison Blanche was used for Voudou ceremonies. In others, this retreat was said to be a house of assignation, where Marie furnished young women of color for white men.

The first printed reference to Marie Laveau's cabin on Lake Pontchartrain comes from a *Times* article of June 26, 1872, which described a St. John's Eve trip to the "White House," located "a mile and a half from Milneburg." There the reporter and his friends found a "ball" attended by numerous women of "the African demi-monde," but "the mystic Marie Leveaux [*sic*]," was not present. In 1895 Henry Castellanos noted, in *New Orleans As It Was*, that "[Marie Laveau's] secret enclaves were usually held in a retired spot upon the lake shore known as the *figueirs*—once a big orchard, beyond which she had constructed a frame cabin that she used as a summer resort."[36]

In the twentieth century Herbert Asbury resurrected the idea of the White House or Maison Blanche when he wrote, in *The French Quarter*, that "As a lucrative side-line [to Voudou] Marie Laveau acted as procuress for white gentlemen, furnishing quadroon and octoroon girls for their pleasure . . . at her shanty on Lake Pontchartrain." Catherine Dillon mentioned this lakeside bagnio in her "Voodoo" manuscript, attributing its operation to the second Marie Laveau. According to Tallant's *Voodoo in New Orleans*, Marie "built a house near Milneburg and . . . there, for a fee, she would arrange appointments for white men with mulatto or quadroon girls." While the original Marie Laveau supposedly initiated this practice, Tallant declared that it was "carried to its epitome of notoriety by Marie II." Helen Holdredge, creator of *Mammy Pleasant*, the fictionalized biography of the California abolitionist Mary Ellen Pleasant, maintained that Marie Laveau's ceremonies "appealed to white men who sought adventures of an erotic nature. Out on the shore of Lake Pontchartrain . . . [she] had built a cabin known as the 'Maison Blanche.' It was a house of assignation where Negro girls were supplied for an evening to white men . . . [at] prohibitive cost. It was not alone the revenues from the 'Maison Blanche' that made Marie wealthy; men had to pay her to have . . . their adventures hushed up." Jonathan Cott, author of *Wandering Ghost: The Odyssey of Lafcadio Hearn*, has transformed the lakeside cabin into "a famous, lavishly appointed bordello, the Maison Blanche," of which Marie Laveau was the proprietress.[37]

The Maison Blanche is also mentioned in the Louisiana Writers' Project interviews. Most of the informants seem to be referring to events of the 1880s, in the time of "Marie II." John Smith told his interviewer that around 1882 the woman he called Marie Laveau maintained "a nicely painted little white cabin where she had her dances. It was between the London Canal and Milneburg." As Smith remembered, "It was just one large room about twenty by thirty. . . . My people used to fuss at me for goin' to that place, but I wouldn't stay away." There the Voudou Queen held all-night parties for the "white sports." "Sometimes you couldn't get near the place for all the carriages and wagons . . . she charged them a dollar-fifty to get in . . . she only had women workin' with her, and they was sure good lookin' octoroons. She would bring nine girls with her.

... The girls that danced just wore a band tied around their hips and a brassiere. They were almost naked and they would dance and shake.... Marie Laveau was out to make money."[38]

Like John Smith, Joseph Alfred and Eugene Fritz indicated that some form of prostitution was taking place at Marie Laveau's cabin, described as "a hut by the lake at Milneburg" where Marie held parties for white men and mulatto women. "People used to come down here from the North to go to [her] dances and get her to work hoodoo for them."[39]

In Herbert Asbury's *The French Quarter* we discover yet another variation on the supposed connection between Marie Laveau, Voudou, and prostitution. While discussing the notorious nineteenth-century brothel-keepers of Basin Street, Asbury devoted several pages to a madam named Fanny Sweet. In addition to being a procuress, this "bad-tempered harridan" was said to have been a thief, a Confederate spy, a murderer, and a Voudou devotee. "She attended many of the secret meetings of the cult, bought great quantities of charms, love-potions, and amulets from Marie Laveau . . . and was among those arrested when police broke up a Voodoo orgy late in 1860."[40]

As the source for this tale Asbury cited an article from the *Daily True Delta* of December 8, 1861. The *True Delta* of that date did, in fact, devote most of the front page to a piece titled "A Modern Lucretia Borgia—The Last Adventure of Fanny Sweet—An Extraordinary Conspiracy." Here we read that "Mrs. Sweet . . . had a strange infatuation with Voudouism, as practiced by the cunning and superstitious negroes of New Orleans, and used to expend considerable sums [on talismans and love charms] with the old black humbugs who live in the back part of town. . . . A police officer who was present at the breaking up of a Voudou dance . . . assures us that [Fanny Sweet] was one of the parties caught." Although the *True Delta* article contains not one word about Marie Laveau, this story has become part of the Laveau Legend. It resurfaced in Al Rose's 1974 *Storyville, New Orleans: An Authentic, Illustrated Account of the Notorious Red-Light District*, where Rose wrote that "Fanny Sweet . . . was guided by the ubiquitous 'queen of the voodoos,' Marie Laveau."[41]

Doctor John

A major player in the Laveau Legend is Jean Montanée, a.k.a. Doctor John, an African-born conjurer, fortune-teller, and herbal healer. The writers of fiction and popular history have characterized Doctor John as Marie Laveau's mentor, her lover, and her professional rival.

With some exceptions, nineteenth-century newspaper reporters spoke of Marie Laveau with a degree of respect and even awe. In contrast, Doctor John was ridiculed as a charlatan. We first hear of him in the *Daily Picayune* of August 18, 1859, where he was referred to as "Jean Montanée, an African negro of the purest black, who is by trade a doctor, by reputation a performer of miracles." His face was said to "bear the distinctive marks of his tribe."[1] Such ritual scars were called "country marks," and indicated the ethnicity of persons born in Africa.

On October 21, 1860, Doctor John made the news for defrauding a white man, Samuel Wilson, the owner of a stable on the corner of Chippewa and St. Andrew streets in the uptown wharf district. Wilson believed his stable had been cursed, and according to the *Daily Delta*, "Bricks [were thrown] . . . windows smashed, doors banged, housetops thumped, and coal cellars disturbed by unwholesome sounds. . . . A very serious air prevailed and *voudou* was proclaimed to be the alpha and omega of the affair." Wilson sent for "Doctor John of Bayou Road," who offered "about two columns of nonsensical advice equal to the first-class literary twaddle of self-styled pen-scratchers" and collected a fee of sixty-two dollars. The result, however, was not a cessation of the disturbances, but the destruction of Samuel Wilson's stable by fire. Wilson's slaves were charged with arson. Recorder Adams of the Fourth District Court discharged Doctor John from custody after ordering him to refund the fee to his disgruntled client.[2]

On Christmas Eve, 1866, a reporter for the *Daily Crescent* visited the conjurer, here called "Devil John," at his home on Bayou Road. Jean Montanée was described as "eminently respectable" in appearance, his clothes Parisian in style, with ebony skin embellished by "tattoo marks," and eyes that held a "certain cat-like watchfulness of expression." Before the Civil War, according to the

31. A man with ritual scars, or "country marks," indicative of his African ethnicity; Doctor John, a native Bambara, would have had such scars. Illustration by Edward W. Kemble for George Washington Cable's "Creole Slave Songs," *The Century Magazine*, April 1886, p. 813. (Author's collection.)

Crescent, Doctor John had "accumulated a respectable fortune," but owing to "mismanagement and troubles with his wives . . . his property had mostly disappeared." The reporter had come to have his fortune told, and this the doctor did by means of "a handful of shells" that he "held at some distance above the table and let fall. It was by marking the arrangement which these took . . . that a glimpse into the future was obtained."[3] This fortune-telling technique bears a striking resemblance to the *caracoles*, or cowrie shell divination, performed by the Santería priesthood of Cuba. For each question asked, sixteen shells are thrown; 256 configurations of the shells, falling with either their "mouth" side or their back side up, are possible. Each configuration represents a body of proverbs, myths, and recommended sacrifices, which must be interpreted by the priest.

On February 26, 1871, Jean Montanée was in trouble for attempting to cheat a wealthy white widow. The *Commercial Bulletin* reported that the lady was "embarrassed by a disagreeable wine mark on her face." She visited "Voudou John, whose wonderful powers are by a silly few considered great," and received a promise that he could make the blemish disappear. The widow left a valuable gold watch as payment. Weeks went by without the slightest fading of the wine mark, and the client demanded the return of her watch. When Doctor John refused, she returned with a policeman: "With the first saucy word that come from John's big mouth, a human body was lifted in the air, and on returning to mother earth John suddenly remembered that he had pawned the watch . . . and lost the ticket. . . . If the watch is not returned John will have an opportunity to voudou himself out of jail." When more time passed and he had still not produced the widow's property, "that celebrated colored personage, Voudou John" was arrested and called to account for himself in recorder's court.[4] Apparently the conjuror wriggled out of this scrape, since it received no further mention in the press.

The *Daily States* of December 9, 1881, carried the story of Doctor John's intervention in the case of a white man who had deserted his wife and children. Subtitled "A Black Villain's Deep Schemes for Making Money," the article tells of the downfall of a "genial, kind-hearted, and confiding" grocer, whose "fancied friends" had defaulted on loans he made to them, leaving the merchant at the mercy of his creditors. Totally dispirited, he sank into alcoholism, while his wife heroically raised the children and rebuilt the grocery business. For the "good of his family" the man left New Orleans for Galveston. His wife nevertheless wanted him back. At the suggestion of a black servant who was a devotee of Doctor John, the deserted spouse visited the African conjuror. For a down payment of sixty dollars, plus additional sums paid during the course of the work, Doctor John gave the grocer's wife two shells, one to wear in her hair and one to tie in her stocking. Six months later the man returned to his family, but not, sniffed the *Daily States*, thanks to the magic of Doctor John.[5]

Doctor John died at the age of seventy on August 23, 1885. In contrast to the extensive coverage of Marie Laveau's death and funeral in 1881, New Orleans newspapers were silent about the passing of this well-known practitioner. Only the *Daily States* printed a notice in the weekly Board of Health listing of births, marriages, and deaths, where the Voudou doctor was referred to as "John Montagnee."

Although Doctor John's death was ignored in his adopted home town, the event received coverage a few months later in a national publication. Lafcadio Hearn's remembrance, "The Last of the Voudoos," was published in the November 7, 1885, issue of *Harper's Weekly*. This piece confirms the 1866 *Daily*

Crescent description and is considered to be the definitive article on Doctor John. There is no mention of a relationship, friendly or not, between Jean Montanée and Marie Laveau.

Hearn, referring to Doctor John as "the most extraordinary African character that ever obtained celebrity" in New Orleans, declared that Montanée died at the age of nearly one hundred years. "He was a native of Senegal, and claimed to have been a [Bambara] prince's son, in proof of which he was wont to call attention to a number of parallel scars on his cheeks, extending in curves from the edge of either temple to the corner of the lips. . . . He was of middle height, very strongly built, with broad shoulders, well-developed muscles, and inky black skin, retreating forehead, small bright eyes, a very flat nose, and a woolly beard. . . . He had a resolute voice and a very authoritative manner."

Hearn goes on to relate that at an early age Jean Montanée was taken from Africa by slavers and sold in Cuba, where he became a chef. He was eventually granted his freedom, worked as a ship's cook on Spanish vessels, and "voyaged considerably in both hemispheres." Tiring of the sea, he left his ship in New Orleans and became a dock worker, where he "wielded a peculiar occult influence over the negroes. . . . Soon it was rumored that he was a seer of no small powers." Montanée became so successful as a fortune-teller that "thousands of colored people flocked to him for predictions and counsel, and even white people . . . paid him to prophesy for them."

With the money accumulated from this practice, wrote Hearn, Jean Montanée purchased property on Bayou Road, extending from Prieur Street as far as Roman, where he built a house. In addition to telling fortunes, he practiced herbal medicine and "arts still more mysterious." His "reputation became so great that he was able to demand and obtain immense fees. People of both races and both sexes thronged to see him . . . and well-dressed women, closely veiled, often knocked at his door." Patrons paid for herbal remedies, nostrums to make the hair grow, charms for love and revenge, counsel in family problems, and advice on which number to play in the Havana Lottery. In his "office" Doctor John kept "a picture of the Virgin Mary, an elephant's tusk, some shells that he said were African . . . which enabled him to read the future, and a pack of cards in each of which a small hole had been burned. About his person he always carried two small bones wrapped around with a black string."

His clients "poured money into his hands so generously" that he became worth at least $50,000. He had a carriage and horses, dressed elegantly, and ate and drank only the best. "He had at least fifteen wives . . . [obtained] by right of slave purchase . . . who bore him children in great multitude. Finally, he managed to woo and win a white woman of the lowest class."

In his later years, Hearn tells us, Doctor John lost his money and property through gambling, bad investments, and debts. "After he had learned to write his name, he was innocent enough one day to place his signature . . . at the bottom of a piece of paper, and, lo! his real estate passed from his possession in some horribly mysterious manner. . . . He bought other property . . . a grocery, a shoemaker's shop, and other establishments into which he put several thousand dollars as the silent partner of people who cheated him. . . . He invested desperately in lottery tickets. . . . After a score of seizures . . . and evictions, he was at last obliged to seek hospitality from some of his numerous children." Doctor John's death "occurred at the house of his daughter by the white wife, an intelligent mulatto with many children of her own."[6]

Other writers added to the tale of Doctor John without implying any association between Jean Montanée and Marie Laveau. In *New Orleans As It Was*, Henry Castellanos devoted several paragraphs to the legendary conjurer, who "exercised the functions of Voudou royalty for upwards of forty years." Doctor John, wrote Castellanos, "lived out on the Bayou Road near its intersection with Esplanade. He was a negro of the purest African type. His ebony face was horribly tattooed, in conformity with the usages of the Congo tribe. He was glib of tongue, neat in his apparel, always wore a frilled shirt front and claimed miraculous powers for the cure of diseases. His . . . office was packed with all sorts of herbs, lizards, toads, and phials of strange compounds. Thousands visited him. As an Indian doctor [an herbal healer], he was a great success." Castellanos spoke of Doctor John's many white clients: "One would stand aghast were he to be told the names of the high city dames, who were wont to drive in their own carriages, with thickly veiled faces, to this sooty black Cagliostro's abode to consult him upon domestic affairs. As he was well informed of many family secrets through the connivance of the hundreds of negro servants attached to the cause of Voudouism, his powers of vatication cease to be a subject of wonder."[7]

Herbert Asbury, in *The French Quarter*, introduced a new element to the story of Doctor John, saying that the "huge coal-black Negro with a tattooed face . . . numbered among his clients the . . . slave Pauline." Here Asbury referred to a case from the 1840s, involving Pauline, the slave concubine of a white man named Peter Rebennack. While Rebennack was absent from the family home at 52 Bayou Road, Pauline imprisoned his wife and children in a closet, starved and beat them, and for this was sentenced to be hanged at the Parish Prison on March 28, 1846. Asbury may have extracted the story of Pauline from Castellanos' *New Orleans As It Was*, which includes a chapter on her execution. While Castellanos did not suggest a connection between Pauline and Doctor John, Asbury invented one, having Pauline buy a gris-gris from Doctor John with which to attract and control her owner. The story is repeated in Tallant's *The Voodoo Queen*. The present-day New Orleans musician Mac Rebennack wrote in his autobiography, *Under a Hoodoo Moon*, that his adoption of the stage name Doctor John was partially based on this tale: "Doctor John and one Pauline Rebennack were busted in the 1840s for having a voodoo operation. . . . There's a strong chance that Pauline was one of my relatives, so I feel more than an incidental sympathy for the man whose name I took . . . in 1967."[8]

It was Robert Tallant, in *Voodoo in New Orleans*, who first inferred that Doctor John had been one of Marie Laveau's mentors, and in his 1956 novel *The Voodoo Queen*, he laid the groundwork for the alleged rivalry between the two. Here the original Doctor John dies in 1837, but years later a second Doctor John appears to challenge Marie's authority. Tallant described "Doctor John II" as a man whose "coal black face was tattooed . . . on the cheeks and forehead with symbols and snake-like patterns in bright reds and blues that twisted and writhed from his temples to the corners of his mouth." On his forehead was tattooed a third eye "heavily outlined in black [with] a yellow and black pupil." This Doctor John is found later with his throat cut on Marie Laveau's St. John's Eve altar at Lake Pontchartrain. Although, according to *The Voodoo Queen*, the conjurer was actually killed by two of his women, Marie is accused of the murder. She is exonerated by her daughter Marie Philomène, who brings the real culprits to justice.[9]

Later twentieth-century novelists, composers, and filmmakers have had a creative field day with the supposed relationship between Marie Laveau and Doctor John. The two have become archetypes of good and evil. Most have portrayed Marie as the priestess of a valid African-based religion, a healer and worker of beneficent magic who is charitable, maternal, and beautiful. Doctor John is usually characterized as an iniquitous sorcerer exploiting Voudou to gain money and power, and sometimes as an outright pretender. He is manipulative and cruel, but sexually compelling despite his physical ugliness.

Francine Prose's 1977 fantasy novel *Marie Laveau* depicted Doctor John as "a seven-foot black giant . . . thin, broad-shouldered, with long arms and legs in shabby but still-beautiful black evening clothes . . . [and] a black top hat with a snakeskin band. Around his neck hung dozens of cords and chains, bones, rotten teeth, dried snake heads, cowrie shells, and skulls." His face was heavily tattooed with the figure of a snake and a leopard, and he wore dark smoked spectacles. This terrifying personage, who resembles Baron Samedi (the lord of the cemetery in Haitian Vodou), arrives on Marie Laveau's doorstep to announce that she has been chosen as Queen of the Voudous. She rebuffs him, but after her husband disappears, Marie seeks Doctor John's help. "You'll survive without Jacques Paris," he tells her, promising "power, magic, roots, herbs, names, numbers, snakes, hoodoo" in return for the secrets of her hairdressing clients. "Hairdressers and priests and doctors and Jesus Christ himself are all the same. . . . They all hear the secrets and get the power. They're blackmailers—every damn one." Eventually, realizing that Doctor John has nothing more to teach her, Marie starts her own business and takes over his clientele, usurps his leadership of the Congo Square dances, and finally defeats him in a phantasmagoric duel between master magicians.[10]

In Jewell Parker Rhodes' novel *Voodoo Dreams*, Marie is the third in a line of Voudou priestesses named Marie Laveau. Doctor John has been involved with all of them, retaining his youth and vigor by drinking a daily potion of seaweed, coconut oil, graveyard dust, and cat's blood. When Marie grows to lovely young womanhood, the old conjurer returns to make her his sex slave.

Rhodes portrays Doctor John as a fraud, totally lacking in faith or spiritual power. To him Voudou is nothing but a lucrative sideshow performance, and Marie is his star attraction. Even when her genuine gifts become evident, Marie is unable to disentangle herself from the sadistic doctor. She gives birth to his child, the fourth Marie Laveau, and it is only after she perceives that Doctor John will sexually abuse his daughter as he has abused her that Marie determines to kill him. She hands him her giant python, symbol of the rainbow serpent Dambala, and watches as it crushes him to death. Free at last, she assumes her true position as Queen of the Voudous.[11]

The African American novelist Ishmael Reed took the opposite view in *The Last Days of Louisiana Red*, written in 1974 during the Black Power Movement. In Reed's work Marie Laveau represents the power-hungry, manipulative, African American woman who loves to see a black man fail. Her brand of negative Voudou is referred to as "Louisiana Red": "toad's eyes, putting snakes in people, excrement, hostility, evilness, attitude, negroes stabbing negroes—crabs in a barrel . . . each crab trying to keep the other one from reaching the top." Ishmael Reed's Doctor John, on the other hand, represents masculinity, decency, and genuine African spiritual power.[12]

* * *

The supposed battle for supremacy between Marie Laveau and Doctor John especially lends itself to stage and screen performances. In 1983 John Joseph Carbon composed the libretto and musical score for a "Voodoo opera," titled "Marie Laveau," as his Ph.D. dissertation. In his introduction, Carbon wrote that he had "tried to elicit some sympathy for Marie . . . but inevitably she is portrayed as out of balance due to power mania." The opera tells the story of the competition between Marie Laveau and Doctor John. Marie, in an attempt to destroy Doctor John, her rival and former lover, exploits Euphrasine, a young white woman, to seduce and murder him. The plot backfires when, under the power of the conjurer, Euphrasine kills Marie instead, and Doctor John proclaims her the new Voudou Queen.[13]

In Wendy Mae Chambers' musical, "Voodoo on the Bayou," Doctor John is portrayed as a money-grubbing humbug. Marie dances in Congo Square with her snake Dambala, asking for divine power, courage, generosity, purpose, humility, and love. Doctor John is more interested in the commercial possibilities, offering to be Marie's agent: "Oh Dambala, it's true, you'll make us a dollah, or two."[14]

Stephen Hank's 1991 film, *The Widow Paris*, is roughly based on Tallant's *The Voodoo Queen* and Prose's *Marie Laveau*. Rather than dealing with the competition between Marie Laveau and Doctor John, the theme of this film is the contest for the soul of Marie Laveau, played out between the Roman Catholic priest, Père Antoine, and the priest of Voudou, Doctor John.[15]

* * *

Interestingly, Doctor John is barely mentioned in the Louisiana Writers' Project interviews. Either the informants who shared their recollections of Marie Laveau considered him to be of little importance or the LWP fieldworkers failed to ask the right questions. Former Laveau disciple Mary Washington commented scornfully that "Doctor John wasn't nothing but an ignorant country nigger who faked fortune telling. He died in the crazy house." Nathan Hobley offered nothing more than a recollection of Doctor John as "an old Negro named Jean Bayou" who was "the uncle or some relation of Marie Laveau and was the head of a band of Voudous."[16]

* * *

While the later tales of a love-hate relationship between Jean Montanée and Marie Laveau are probably fantasies, the archival evidence shows that at least some of Lafcadio Hearn's 1885 *Harper's Weekly* story, "The Last of the Voudoos,"

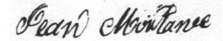

32. Signature of Jean Montanée (Doctor John), Acts of Octave de Armas, January 15, 1847. (Courtesy of the Notarial Archives Research Center, New Orleans, Louisiana.)

is true. A search of the Conveyance Office Index to Vendors and Purchasers shows that Jean Montanée was actively buying and selling land and slaves from 1845 through the 1860s. The earliest of these transactions were signed with an X, but, just as Hearn tells us, Jean Montanée eventually learned to write his name. In 1847 he began to sign in a labored scrawl, and his penmanship improved over the years. His real estate acquisitions included lots in the Faubourg Tremé in the neighborhood of Derbigny, Roman, Prieur, St. Ann, Dumaine, St. Philip, Ursulines, Governor Nicholls, and Bayou Road, and further out on Tonti, Rocheblave, and Dorgenois. He also ventured into the New Faubourg Marigny at the corner of Annette and Urquhart and at Havana and Virtue, where he picked off lots for as little as sixty dollars.[17]

On February 5, 1847, Montanée bought from the free woman of color Nancy St. Martin a house at 406 Annette. This transaction was revoked six months later, when St. Martin petitioned the Second District Court for recovery of her property. In her statement she maintained that she was an "ignorant and illiterate woman," and that she was "prevailed upon by Jean Montanée, with whom she lived in concubinage, to make him a donation [in the form of a simulated sale] of the above property, under the promise that she would continue to be in possession thereof... and that he would... support her... in case of sickness, old age, or infirmity." The sale was declared null and void, and Montanée was ordered to pay Nancy St. Martin seven dollars a month rent from the time of the sale "until she regains possession of the property," plus $300 damages and court costs.[18]

In support of Lafcadio Hearn's statement that Doctor John invested in "a grocery, a shoemaker's shop, and other establishments into which he put several thousand dollars as the silent partner of people who cheated him," we find that on December 29, 1849, Jean Montanée bought a café and grocery store on Bayou Road between Johnson and Prieur for $750, payable in installments. A year later he sold it for $175.[19] This could be one of those transactions in which Doctor John was induced to sign a document and saw his property "pass from his possession in some horribly mysterious manner." On October 22, 1861, three of his lots in the downtown neighborhood of St. Roch and Roman were sold at a sheriff's auction in settlement of a judgment against him. On January 6, 1866, two more lots in the Faubourg Tremé were also sold at a sheriff's auction in settlement of a suit.[20] These might be representative of the "score of seizures" referred to by Lafcadio Hearn.

Between 1850 and 1880 Jean Montanée (also spelled Montanet and Montaine) was enumerated in the U.S. Census and listed in the New Orleans city directories. Both sources verify some of the data reported in Hearn's "Last of the Voudoos." Montanée was always identified in the census as a native of Africa. In 1850 he was listed as the owner of a coffeehouse, with real estate valued at $4,000. In 1860 his occupation was recorded as "physician," although the census enumerator could not resist inserting "quack" in parentheses. His real estate was valued at $12,000 and his personal property at $500, comparable to the holdings of many well-to-do white New Orleanians. In 1870 he was still listed as a physician; the value of his real estate had dropped to $1,500, and his personal property was worth only $250. This not only represented a decline in Montanée's fortunes, but an overall decrease in property values between 1860 and 1870 as a result of the Civil War. The 1880 census, in which the value of real estate and personal property was no longer recorded, called Montanée an "Indian doctor."[21] The city directories listed Jean Montanée at various address in the neighborhood of Bayou Road, Barracks, Roman, and Prieur. He was usually designated as a physician, although in 1866 (confirming Lafcadio Hearn's assertion that Doctor John "invested in a shoemaker's shop") he was listed as the proprietor of a shoe store.

What of Hearn's statement that Doctor John had, among his concubines, "a white woman of the lowest class" and "at least fifteen wives . . . [obtained] by right of slave purchase . . . who bore him children in great multitude"? The archival record tells us nothing of the white consort, but we learn that between 1847 and 1860 Jean Montanée bought seven female slaves. In 1847 he paid $265 for Hyacinthe, age fifty-five, and $300 for Charlotte, age forty-two. Montanée kept Hyacinthe for a little over three years and sold her for $625, making a profit of $360.[22] In 1849 he purchased twenty-five-year-old Mathilde for $600, sold her for $625 in 1850, and bought her back for the same price a year later. Montanée may have been using Mathilde as collateral in a credit transaction; upon repayment of the debt he would have regained ownership of the slave.[23] He bought twelve-year-old Martha for $650 in 1850. In 1852 he picked up two slaves at bargain prices—$100 for twenty-year-old Mary and $150 for Diana, age thirty-four.[24] In 1853 he paid $1,200 for twenty-three-year-old Minnie and her two young children.[25] Diana and Minnie were mulattos; the other women were classified as black.

It should be noted that Doctor John also purchased male slaves. He acquired William for $300 in 1848 and sold him after one year for only $100. In 1857 he bought a blind slave named Henry Davis for $50, but in 1860 he sold this man, now described as being blind in one eye, for $600. In 1849 he liberated the forty-four-year old "native of Guinea," Jean Bermudez. Jean was purchased with a *charge d'affranchissment* (promise of freedom), which has the same meaning as *statu liber*.[26]

According to the 1860 census, the woman designated as Jean Montanée's wife was a Maryland-born black female named Mathilde. Might this have been the slave Mathilde he purchased in 1849? Seven black children, ranging in age from fourteen to three years, were listed in the census. With the exception of four-year-old "Jno." and three-year-old Alfred, their names are illegible. A child named John "Montannet" was born on Bayou Road November 3, 1856, and was designated on his birth certificate as the legitimate son of Jean Montannet and Mathilde Griffin, a native of Baltimore. Birth certificates also exist for Edouard "Montanet," born October 13, 1872, and Joseph "Montaney," born May 30, 1880; both were the sons of John Montanet/Montaney and Marie Populus.[27] In 1870 the black woman listed in the census as Montanée's wife was named Armantine, a native of Louisiana. There were three teenaged children—Catherine, Martin, and Alice, and an infant named Arthemise. Martin and Arthemise were black, and Catherine and Alice were mulattos. In 1880 Armantine was still the "lady of the house," and there were five sons and daughters ranging in age from twenty-one to a one-year-old toddler— Marie, Arthemise, Edward, Oscar, and Philogene, all of whom were classified as black. Eight-year-old Edward, born in 1872, may be the Edouard Montanet mentioned above.

Jean Montanée's death in August of 1885 was reported to the Board of Health by Alicia J. Montanée. Might this have been the mulatto daughter named Alice listed in the 1870 census, and was she the issue of Doctor John's white concubine, characterized by Lafcadio Hearn as "an intelligent mulatto with many children of her own," in whose home the old conjurer was said to have ended his days in poverty? According to his death certificate, "John Montanée, a native of Africa, aged seventy years, departed this life 23 August, 1885, at no. 89 North Villere Street [between Conti and St. Louis], cause of death Bright's disease." Alicia Montanée was never listed in the city directory, and the occupants of 89 North Villere could not be identified.[28]

Doctor John's burial place is unknown. The name of Jean Montanée never appears in the sacramental registers of the Roman Catholic church, indicating that he was not a practicing Catholic. Although he may have been forcibly converted to Catholicism at the time of his enslavement in Cuba, he probably remained faithful to his traditional African beliefs without embracing Christianity in any form. We will therefore find him in neither the Catholic nor the Protestant cemeteries of New Orleans. If he indeed died penniless, he was probably interred in an unmarked grave in Holt Cemetery, the city's graveyard for the indigent.

Part III

Prison Ministry

The Laveau Legend tells us that, in her later years, Marie abdicated leadership of the Voudou community and devoted her time to charitable works. Even before her "retirement" in the early 1870s, Marie Laveau is said to have taken a special interest in the inmates of New Orleans' infamous Parish Prison. This grim edifice was located behind Congo Square and the Tremé Market between Marais, Tremé, Orleans, and St. Ann streets, a short walk from the Laveau-Glapion home.

According to the frequently repeated story, Marie almost saved Jean Adam and Antoine Delisle from the gallows in 1852; comforted James Mullen, Heinrich Haas, Peter Smith, and Joseph Lindsay in 1859 as they awaited execution; mercifully dispatched Antoine Cambre with a bowl of poisoned gumbo in his prison cell in 1860; and won a stay of execution for John Bazar in 1870. All of these men were convicted murderers. Although newspaper reports of 1852, 1859, 1860, and 1870 never referred to Marie Laveau's involvement, such tales were disseminated via Henry Castellanos' *New Orleans As It Was*, Herbert Asbury's *The French Quarter*, and Robert Tallant's *Voodoo in New Orleans* and *The Voodoo Queen*. The Louisiana Writers' Project interviews are silent on this topic. While some informants spoke of Marie as a charitable woman, they never mentioned her attentions to prisoners.

In *New Orleans As It Was* (1895), Henry Castellanos included a chapter on "The Old Parish Prison" in which he gave a detailed description of the hanging of Jean Adam and Antoine Delisle. Adam and Delisle were a pair of house painters who robbed the home of their clients, Monsieur and Madame Chevillon. Caught in the act by the Chevillon's slave woman, they cut her throat and fled with the stolen goods. The two were apprehended and sentenced to hang. According to Castellanos, the execution took place on "a pleasant summer day, with no disturbance in the atmosphere," but just as the hangman released the trap door to plunge the condemned men to their deaths, "a sheet of lightning—so blinding, so dazzling, so stunning as to partake of the unnatural—illuminated the scene and rent the skies in twain.... Simultaneously . . . a torrent of rain descended from the heavens." Owing to the imperfectly tied nooses, the two men fell to the pavement below, where they lay injured and stunned. Following orders from the governor, they were hauled back to

33. The Parish Prison. Illustration by Edward W. Kemble for George Washington Cable's "The Dance in Place Congo," *The Century Magazine*, February 1886, p. 528. (Author's collection.)

the gallows and hanged again. Castellanos described the scene in grisly detail: "Their veins swelled and distended, and . . . ejected copious streams of blood over their light-colored clothes . . . [which] imparted to them a crimson hue. . . . From this heart-sickening spectacle men averted their eyes in disgust and women fainted. . . . This horrid execution shocked the conscience of the community . . . and public hanging became henceforth a thing of the past." There was no allusion to Marie Laveau.[1]

We hear nothing about Marie's prison work from G. William Nott, Lyle Saxon, Zora Neale Hurston, or other writers of the 1920s and early 1930s, but Herbert Asbury, in *The French Quarter*, expounded at length upon the subject. While Castellanos did not credit Marie Laveau with any involvement in the Adam and Delisle case, Asbury said she spent the morning of the execution praying with the two prisoners before an altar she had erected in their cell and that they ate a bowl of her gumbo. He then repeated the story of the terrifying thunderstorm and the bungled execution, adding that "many of [Marie Laveau's] followers were convinced that she had invoked the fury of the elements to prove that Adam and Delisle were not guilty."[2]

Robert Tallant, in *Voodoo in New Orleans* and *The Voodoo Queen*, added other details. Regarding the hanging of Adam and Delisle, Tallant described the sudden storm on this "bright and sunny day," and the thundercloud, "like a black cape," that suddenly appeared above the gallows: "There was a dull roar of wind and the trees in the vicinity swayed and groaned." Children began to cry. A woman in the crowd screamed that it was "like the crucifixion" and promptly fainted. The hanging nevertheless proceeded, and "as the executioner sprung the trap . . . rain came down in torrents and the dark sky was shattered by lightning." After the execution, wrote Tallant, the sun reappeared in the cloudless blue sky, and "a tall woman in a tignon" moved away from the remaining spectators, who whispered "There goes Marie Laveau."

Tallant quoted an unidentified (and probably fictitious) newspaper account of the next day as saying that "Thousands among the citizens of this city give credit to Marie Laveau, the Voodoo high priestess, for the storm that interrupted the execution of Delisle and Adam . . . and because of this case the Louisiana Legislature met and forever outlawed public hangings."[3] In later versions of the story, Marie is credited with having influenced this decision on the part of the lawmakers.

The Adam and Delisle incident is absent from Francine Prose's novel, *Marie Laveau*. In Jewel Parker Rhodes' *Voodoo Dreams* the prisoners are not Adam and Delisle—two white men convicted of killing a slave, but Lee and Cholly —two slaves convicted of killing a white man. Rhodes describes how Marie, calling upon Dambala and the African ancestors, causes the ropes to break and the first attempt at execution to fail. Wendy Mae Chambers' musical, "Voodoo on the Bayou," harks back to *The French Quarter* and *Voodoo in New Orleans*. When lightning, thunder, and rain deluge the crowd in front of the Parish Prison and the condemned men slip through the nooses, Marie is given credit, and the chorus sings "Marie Laveau invoked the fury of the elements—it's divine intervention in the form of a storm."[4]

A somewhat different story emerges from actual newspaper accounts of the hanging of Jean Adam and Antoine Delisle on July 2, 1852. Although executions usually received abundant press coverage, this event slipped by almost unnoticed. On that date New Orleans was observing a day of mourning for the popular Kentucky statesman, Henry Clay, who had died on June 29, and it was this event that filled the columns of the newspapers. The *Commercial Bulletin* devoted a long article to the memorial ceremonies for Clay, describing "the heavy booming of the minute guns, accompanied by the dismal tolling of bells from numerous points of our great metropolis." The weather was not sunny, as described by Castellanos, Asbury, and Tallant, but was consistently gloomy and wet: "Nature herself sympathized in the universal sorrow. Clouds obscured the sun, the tears of heaven descended frequently in rain drops, and the deep reverberations of the artillery of the upper sphere often mingled with the solemn roar of the funeral guns."[5]

The next morning's *Picayune* described the execution of Adam and Delisle on that rainy day: "The two poor wretches, whose forfeit lives the angry law required, were subjected to an exposure and a long torment that are inexpressibly shocking. The ill-adjusted ropes gave way, both men were precipitated to the ground, wounded and bruised, and then, after due process had been taken to bring them back to sensibility, the whole dreadful ceremonial was repeated, the pallid criminals again led up, and on the second trial duly stifled according to law before the gaping multitude." The hanging was similarly described by the *Commercial Bulletin* and the *Crescent*.[6]

In none of these accounts was there one word about Marie Laveau and the devotions at her altar. Nor do we hear about a terrifying storm that descended out of a brilliant blue sky just as the cathedral bells struck noon and the execution was about to take place, and cleared the minute the prisoners were hanged. It is true that, after the Adam and Delisle debacle, executions were no longer open to the general populace. But despite protests by the newspapers that public executions were "only a spectacle for the gratification of a morbid appetite for excitement," the accounts that follow demonstrate that hangings, now held within the prison walls, were still attended by a large number of spectators to whom passes had been issued by the sheriff.

*　*　*

In *The French Quarter*, Herbert Asbury also described Marie Laveau's ministrations to the convicted murderer James Mullen. She supposedly "brought a coffin into [Mullen's] cell and helped him decorate it . . . with religious mottoes and pictures of angels and saints, all enclosed in a border of metallic fringe. . . . Mullen slept in the coffin, using for a pillow a dress which had been worn by his three-year-old daughter." Tallant, in *Voodoo in New Orleans*, elaborated that "in 1859 Marie achieved notoriety when she brought James Mullen his coffin. They worked together day after day, decorating the coffin inside and out with religious pictures. At night Mullen slept in the casket, using the dress of his three-year-old daughter as a pillow, and every day Marie prayed with him, until he was hanged."[7]

According to the *True Delta* and the *Picayune*, Mullen was convicted of stabbing James Maglone in a saloon in April 1859. Mullen and Maglone had been together in California during the Gold Rush, where Mullen was employed by Maglone as a bartender at his boarding house. The *True Delta* explained that "an animosity between these men had long existed. . . . The feud grew and thrived until Mullen ended it in a way that may be considered retributatively just. . . . He was found guilty and sentenced to death. There was no appeal taken to the Supreme Court . . . but yet the convict did not anticipate being executed, forming a hope that the notoriously bad character of the man he killed would save him from the gallows."

Mullen was reported by the newspapers to have been in good spirits owing to his "constant communication with a clergyman," Father Dufaut, the Jesuit priest who usually fulfilled the office of "comforting criminals at their last hour, and reconciling them with a merciful Deity, before whose awful tribunal they are to appear." Regarding the coffin that, according to Asbury and Tallant, Mullen decorated with the help of the Voudou priestess, the *True Delta* said only that "For the last two days he has had his coffin—which was purchased for him by an acquaintance—in his cell, sleeping in it at night, or in the day when he felt so inclined. The pillow was formed of a child's dress, his own child, about three or four years old, the only person belonging or related to him in New Orleans."

The *Picayune* described the hanging, which took place on July 30, 1859: "At eleven o'clock, Mullen appeared on the platform, walking erect, with a firm step and placid countenance, and took his seat beneath the fatal noose. The hangman, disguised and masked as usual, made the necessary dreadful preparations, and the deputy sheriff read aloud the sentence. The priest then exhorted the prisoner." Just at this moment, from the insane asylum adjacent to the Parish Prison, "arose a wild, unearthly song. What were the words slowly chanted by the unfortunate madman, we could not distinguish, but there was something awful in the contrast between those joyous sounds and the mournful, sad scene we beheld." Mullen "recited a short prayer, spoke a few words of thanks to the officers, and all was over. The crowd slowly dispersed, leaving the body of the unfortunate man dangling at the end of the rope."[8]

* * *

Regarding the 1859 triple execution of Heinrich Haas, Peter Smith, and Joseph Lindsay, Asbury wrote in *The French Quarter* that "Marie Laveau erected her altar in Haas's cell [and] prayed before it with the three men. . . . With her assistance [Haas] decorated his cell with religious subjects. Using lead pencil, indigo, and tobacco juice, he drew eleven pictures on the walls . . . and on the ceiling a larger one, depicting the Host with angels praying beside it." Tallant paraphrased Asbury, writing that "The Voodoo queen worked with a trio of murderers, Heinrich Haas, Peter Smith and Joseph Lindsay. Haas seems to have received most of her attention and with her assistance he decorated the walls and ceilings [of his cell] with pictures of a religious nature." Marie is supposed to have walked with the men to the gallows.[9]

We learn from the New Orleans newspapers that, although their crimes
were unrelated, the convicted murderers Haas, Smith, and Lindsay were dispatched in a triple execution for the convenience of prison officials. Haas had
shot his wife for suspected infidelity, Smith had stabbed a man in the course of
a barroom argument, and Lindsay had stabbed the mate of the *Martha Rideout*
during a shipboard quarrel. The date of their execution was set for March 19,
1859. Both the *Picayune* and the *True Delta* gave extensive coverage to the event.
In an article that was obviously the source for Asbury's description, the *True
Delta* reported that Heinrich Haas decorated his place of imprisonment with
religious pictures: "Around his cell were eleven scriptural pictures inscribed
on the walls. He made them eighteen inches long by a foot in breadth, and
used pencil, indigo, ink, and tobacco juice to color his conceptions. They were
all rough, as might be imagined, but several of them displayed many [of the]
qualities of an artist. He had also, with much trouble and excellent effect, inscribed on the ceiling a representation of the Host, with angels praying beside
it."[10]

The *Picayune* described the exectution: "This morning, Heinrich Haas,
Joseph Lindsay, and Peter Smith, all three convicted of murder, suffered the
penalty of death by hanging. At an early hour a large crowd besieged the gates
of the Parish Prison, eagerly seeking to obtain a sight of the terrible spectacle.
This morbid craving was not, however, satisfied, and none could obtain admittance without an order from the Sheriff. About one hundred and fifty persons,
including policemen, officials, &c., were let into the inner yard, where the gallows had been erected."

Again we hear that it was Father Dufaut, not Marie Laveau, who acted as
spiritual counselor for the prisoners, celebrated mass in their cells, and accompanied them during their last moments. "Shortly after ten o'clock the three
condemned men appeared, escorted by the Reverend Father Dufaut, his assistant, and officers of the prison. [The prisoners] were dressed in white shirts and
pants, the head covered with a white night cap, and their hands tied behind
their backs; each wore a crucifix suspended by a black ribbon around his neck.
Their countenances were calm, even smiling. They took their seat on the fatal
bench, and the hangman, a negro, disguised with a loose black domino and a
mask, fixed the rope around their necks."

The deputy sheriff read the death warrant with "a voice choked by emotion,"
and each man addressed his final communication to the crowd, acknowledging

his crime and asking for God's forgiveness. Heinrich Haas, "his features lit with a spiritual enthusiasm, . . . spoke long and feelingly, and after bidding farewell to the people, began chanting a German hymn with much power. While he . . . sang, his two companions seemed to find new courage in his . . . words and preserved a perfect composure." Father Dufaut said a farewell to each man and presented the crucifix, which they "kissed repeatedly." Lindsay "burst out in an act of contrition, repeated by the two others, and was kissed on the cheek by Father Dufaut, who recited aloud an exhortation and gave his blessing to the three doomed men. . . . The hangman appeared, drew the cap over their faces, bid them goodbye, and disappeared into the cell behind. Suddenly the trap door fell from beneath their feet, and three souls were sent into eternity."[11]

*   *   *

It is with the case of Antoine Cambre, allegedly the beneficiary of Marie Laveau's poisoned gumbo, that Henry Castellanos elaborated on the legend that Marie had ministered to condemned prisoners and was sometimes able to save them from the gallows. In *New Orleans As It Was*, Castellanos reported that Cambre was a bouncer hired to "regulate the tough and dangerous element" who frequented the Louisiana Ballroom on Esplanade Avenue. This establishment was described as "one of the numerous dens of iniquity which once infested the Third Municipality [the suburbs below the Vieux Carré], where debauchery, gambling, and intoxication held high carnival." Cambre also "made frequent abuse" of the liquor that was "never stinted there." Leaving his job in a drunken stupor one morning before dawn, Cambre became embroiled in a quarrel with a lamplighter and shot him dead.

Cambre was arrested and sentenced to hang, and it is here that Marie Laveau enters Castellanos' version of the story. According to "an old and faithful officer of the Parish Prison," Marie, said to have been a friend of Cambre's, was selected to build the altar in his cell. She is supposed to have offered to prepare his last meal, "a *gombo filé* such as you have never eaten in your whole life." Cambre accepted, and a few hours later was found dead in his cell. The autopsy, declared Castellanos, confirmed that he had been poisoned.[12]

Herbert Asbury and Robert Tallant adhered closely to Castellanos' telling of the Antoine Cambre episode. Cambre does not figure in the novels of Francine Prose or Jewel Parker Rhodes. Daniel Du Plantis, in his 1998 play *Gris-Gris*, has conflated Antoine Cambre with James Mullen and Heinrich Haas. Marie Laveau visits Cambre in his cell at the Parish Prison, where, like Mullen, he sleeps in his coffin with the dress of his little daughter, draws sacred pictures on the walls of his cell like Haas, and ultimately succumbs to Marie's fatal gumbo.[13]

We learn from newspaper accounts of the time that Antoine Cambre was a violent man. A few months before the murder of the lamplighter, he fatally shot a man at the Louisiana Ballroom and was acquitted on grounds of self-defense.[14]

It was just before Christmas of 1859 that Cambre killed the lamplighter George Frey, a German immigrant, in the downtown neighborhood along the Mississippi River now known as the Bywater. At six o'clock on the morning of December 22, reported the *Daily Picayune*, a blacksmith, arriving at his shop on Louisa Street between Dauphine and Royal, had just gone across to the coffeehouse when he heard shots fired and a man swearing, followed by "a deep groan." The blacksmith and his assistants discovered the body of the lamplighter lying on the floor. They pursued the murderer, who "suddenly turned upon them with his pistol and ordered them to stand back at their peril." Cambre was subsequently arrested.

Antoine Cambre was tried before Judge Hunt in First District Court on June 11, 1860. The all-day trial revealed that Cambre's initial quarrel had been with another German lamplighter, Henry Kathoffer, whom he had encountered early that morning on Louisa Street. Cambre, who was drunk, assaulted Kathoffer over some imagined insult and Kathoffer struck him with his lamplighter's ladder and fled. When George Frey happened along a little later, Cambre mistook him for Kathoffer and shot him. After deliberating for less than an hour, the jury returned "the awful verdict—guilty of murder."[15] Cambre was a member of the notoriously anti-immigrant Know-Nothing or Native American Party, and one wonders if this might have prompted his attack on the German lamplighters.[16]

Sentencing took place before Judge Hunt on July 2, 1860. The judge was utterly unsympathetic, lecturing Cambre on his wasted and dissolute life. Instead of pursuing the "good trade of a carpenter" for which he had been trained, "a love of ease and of false excitement" had prompted him to become "the police officer of a lewd ball-room." To this occupation, scolded Judge Hunt, his "downfall could be traced." The judge then reviewed the case, concluding that Cambre's having "shot Frey and not Kathoffer does not alter the nature of the act. [His] intention was malicious, and unlawful killing . . . [with] malice aforethought is murder, though the party killed was mistaken for another person." He read the sentence: "You, Antoine Cambre, are hereby sentenced to suffer death; and it is ordered that this punishment be inflicted by hanging you by the neck until you be dead; and that this sentence be executed by the Sheriff of the Parish of Orleans, within the walls of the Parish Prison, on such day and at such hour as the Governor of the State of Louisiana in his warrant shall direct. . . . May God Almighty, of His infinite goodness, have mercy upon your soul." The counsel for the defense moved for an appeal to the Supreme Court, and Cambre, looking "calm and collected," was returned to the Parish Prison.[17]

A month later, on the afternoon of August 8, 1860, Antoine Cambre died in his cell. The rumor that Cambre had swallowed poison rather than face the gallows spread rapidly throughout the community. The coroner, however, reported that Cambre had died of "pernicious fever," a vague term that could mean any number of diseases to which New Orleanians regularly fell victim during the summer.

After following Cambre's case from its beginning, the reporter for the *Picayune* was apparently asleep on the job when the climax occurred, and no word of Cambre's dramatic end appeared in the "City" column. The *Delta* and the *Crescent*, however, carried long articles about the incident. The *Delta* provided information about the cause and manner of Cambre's death. Upon hearing the fast-circulating tale that Cambre had deliberately ingested poison or been poisoned by one of his confidants, the *Delta*'s reporter hastened to the Parish Prison and found a group of officials clustered around the body, which was "still warm, his limbs still pliable . . . the face was almost saffron in color, and his neck and ears were discolored a sort of blue black." Questioning those present, the reporter learned that Cambre had "died as if insane, wandering in his speech, suffering in his body, and exhibiting in his manner a fearful picture of a condemned man's last moments." The *Crescent* reported that, owing to rumors that Cambre had died under mysterious circumstances, the coroner's inquest was "held in such a manner as to leave no ground for the weak inventions and cowardly calumnies which a certain class of people delight to circulate in regard to deaths in the Parish Prison." The prison physician testified that Cambre was "growing thin . . . complained of diarrhea and pain in the bowels . . . and had a high fever with chills. . . . He was so weak I had to assist him to get up."[18] City officials were particularly defensive about the charge that Cambre had taken poison. About six weeks earlier Cambre's cell mate, the murderer Eugene Pepe, had committed suicide by swallowing strychnine that he had hidden in his shoe.[19]

A recent addition to the Laveau Legend suggests that Marie Laveau staged Antoine Cambre's death by means of the "zombie poison," tetrodotoxin, a substance derived from the marine puffer fish.[20] The symptoms of tetrodotoxin poisoning are "malaise, pallor, dizziness, paresthesias [tingling] of the extremities . . . developing into severe numbness of the entire body . . . hypersalivation, profuse sweating, subnormal temperatures, decreased blood pressure, a rapid, weak pulse, vomiting and diarrhea . . . respiratory distress . . . [while] the lips, extremities, and body become intensely cyanotic [blue] . . . and in the end, the muscles . . . become paralyzed and the patient is unable to move . . . and may become comatose." Recovery from a nonlethal dose would occur within about twenty-four hours.[21] Some of Cambre's symptoms, notably diarrhea and the bluish discoloration of his neck and ears, do fit this profile, but he is said to have had a high fever, not the subnormal temperature characteristic of tetrodotoxin poisoning. There is still the possibility that Antoine Cambre succumbed to some more conventional poison, provided by persons unknown, and that the coroner, the physician, and the prison officials faked the evidence in order to conceal the truth.

Both the *Delta* and the *Crescent* mentioned a woman who was permitted to come and nurse Cambre in his cell, leading some to conclude that this benefactress was Marie Laveau. The *Daily Delta*, however, makes clear that she was Cambre's domestic partner, described as "a young colored woman of agile form, with a decayed beauty . . . now prematurely gone . . . [and] bearing the grief-worn marks of a life that has had its cup of sorrow full and often overflowing. She had been the object of his indiscreet love and passion, and mid all his wayward progress in a lost life she alone was found by his side in sorrow's hour . . . she saw him in the last moments of pain and life, and held his stalwart frame in the agonies of death."[22]

Cambre's body was claimed by his family and friends for entombment in St. Louis Cemetery No. 1. The burial record reiterates the coroner's report that Cambre was "found dead in the Parish Prison of pernicious fever."[23]

*   *   *

John Bazar was supposedly the next beneficiary of Marie Laveau's prison ministry. According to Asbury's *The French Quarter*, Bazar was a wronged husband who returned from a period of work in Texas to find his wife cohabiting with another man, Joseph Cobez, whom he beat to death with a stone. On the morning of his execution, wrote Asbury, Bazar "prayed with Marie Laveau in the prison chapel, which she had decorated, and was then led to the gallows." In the nick of time, "a messenger galloped into the courtyard with a reprieve from Governor H. C. Warmouth." This story was reiterated by Tallant, who commented in *Voodoo in New Orleans* that "Marie Laveau appears to have done her work well."[24] Asbury's and Tallant's version of the crime of John Bazar turns out to be completely false. In reality, it was Cobez who was the wronged husband and Bazar who was his wife's lover. Asbury obviously invented this tale in order to portray the murderer in a more sympathetic light and justify Marie Laveau's concern.

The *Daily Picayune* of May 28, 1870, tells the true story: Joseph Cobez never left New Orleans to work in Texas. He did, however, become aware that his wife was spending an unseemly amount of time with a younger man, John Bazar, to the detriment of her home and family. Cobez "remonstrated" with her, but "his entreaties were unheeded, and the intimacy which at first was stolen and secret became open and avowed. His wife plainly intimated to him that she wished no more to do with him . . . and that she preferred the protection of Bazar, illicit and illegal though it was, to his own." The couple quarreled frequently. Cobez eventually left his home on Craps Street (now Burgundy) in the Faubourg Marigny and went to stay with his daughter, who lived a few blocks away on St. Anthony Street.

Madame Cobez related this to her lover, John Bazar, saying that she "wished [Cobez] were dead, and that some one would kill him. . . . Bazar construed this as a direct appeal. He hated Joseph Cobez with the bitterness of rivalry; he had dishonored the man, and the wish to kill him was but one step further on the road to depraved wishes and illicit love." Bazar, enlisting the aid of his friend William Pratts, armed himself with a knife and hastened to the home of Cobez's daughter to carry out his "fell design." In the *Picayune*'s account, Bazar "dealt the first blow, full at his victim's heart. It missed its aim but inflicted a dreadful wound nevertheless. The old man sprung from the bed and confronted the assailants. The struggle now became desperate." Pratts panicked and fled the scene, while Bazar stayed behind to finish his "fatal work."

Despite Bazar's heinous crime, according to the *Picayune*, "a sentiment of pity rapidly formed in the public mind, and petitions were set on foot to procure his reprieve from the Governor." Preparations for the execution nevertheless went forward. At an early hour crowds began to assemble around the Parish Prison, and "from Congo Square to Tremé Market, Orleans street was literally thronged with a mass of human beings, some laughing and jesting, some solemn and quiet." As usual, the execution became an occasion for commerce: "The ice cream vendor plied his avocation, and the hawker of patent medicines cried from the street corners his panacea for headaches, swelled limbs, carbuncles and sores. It did not seem to matter to them that . . . the old prison walls contained within their iron recesses the preparations for a tragedy.

... The very entrance of the grave—the agonies of death and human despair—are nothing if they are not the means by which money can be made."

Upstairs in the condemned cell sat John Bazar, surrounded by "anxious men and women, who strove hard to fit his soul for eternity." Bazar spent his days "in prayer and earnest supplication, kneeling at the foot of the crucifix, with the image of the Madonna before him. One of the rooms of his cell has been fitted up as a chapel, and an altar placed there, lighted with burning candles. Flowers have been strewed around it, and the pale faces of the Sisters of Charity were added to the solemn holiness of the place."

The efforts of those opposed to the hanging of John Bazar finally prevailed. An hour before the scheduled execution the governor forwarded a reprieve. The *Picayune* moralized that "This will no doubt act as a final relief from the death penalty. The sentiment of the community is too clearly manifested against these executions to permit it to go forward. Almost universally, it is alluded to as a barbarous custom, justified by no precept of religion and inimical to an enlightened Christian civilization. It is probable the next Legislature will repeal the law that provides for it, and imprisonment for life will be substituted in its stead."[25]

*   *   *

The Louisiana legislature did not, in fact, abolish capital punishment, and in 1871 two more convicted murderers, Pedro Abriel and Vincent Bayonne, were sentenced to die on the gallows. Abriel and Bayonne, both Spaniards, had been hired for "the pitiful sum of twelve dollars" to murder another Spaniard named Ambrose. On May 28, 1869, the three men were seen together "going from one drinking saloon to the other, and appearing at intervals at most of the dance houses on Gallatin and Barracks streets." Having gotten Ambrose thoroughly intoxicated, Abriel and Bayonne headed for the levee where they stabbed the drunken man and threw him into the Mississippi River. They were apprehended, tried, and sentenced to death. Throughout these proceedings they maintained that it was not they, but another man, who had killed Ambrose.

At last we find journalistic evidence of Marie Laveau's prison ministry. On May 10, 1871, the *Daily Picayune* published "The Condemned—The Decorations of the Altar," a highly sympathetic account of Marie Laveau's attentions to Abriel and Bayonne. "For more than twenty years," said the *Picayune*, "whenever a human being has suffered the final penalty in the Parish Prison, an old colored woman has come to his cell and prepared an altar for him. This woman is Marie Lavan [*sic*], better known as the Priestess of the Voudous." Curiously, the case of Abriel and Bayonne did not enter into the telling of the Laveau Legend by Castellanos or Asbury, and Tallant quoted the *Picayune* article only as "proof that [Marie's] prison work was continuing," without elaborating on the story.[26]

The altar erected by Marie Laveau for Abriel and Bayonne consisted of a structure about three feet square surmounted by "three pyramidal boxes, rising to an apex, on which is placed a small figure of the Virgin. . . . The veil of the Virgin is beautifully wrought and ornamented with flowers in silver filigree." The altar was draped in white and decorated with vases of pink and white camellias. In the center was a Spanish prayerbook, and behind it "two angels with wings outspread." Before the altar hung a "curtain of white muslin, deeply fringed in silver lace." Bible verses "in the Spanish tongue, and framed in gold," decorated the walls of the cell. The two convicted men devoted all their time to prayer: "They seem to entertain little hope of pardon, and are fitting themselves for the awful change they are soon destined to experience. It is a sad spectacle, and no heart is so indurated as to contemplate it with indifference."[27]

On May 14, the day after the execution of Abriel and Bayonne, the *Daily Picayune* ran another piece, "The Execution—Infliction of the Death Penalty —Murder Atoned," which provides an insightful description of the carnival atmosphere that prevailed in the streets that morning, compared to the solemn mood within the prison. The sheriff had issued several hundred of the sought-after permits to view the hanging. The prison yard was "crowded with spectators, and long before the time of execution Orleans street was filled with a dense mass of humanity of every shade and color, and every class and condition. Hucksters were vending their wares, and the speculator seized upon the occasion to turn a profitable bargain." Within the prison walls, however, "everything was still as death. Scarcely a whisper could be heard in the eager, breathless crowd that surged along the prison yard." The inmates had been locked in their cells, and "by every possible contrivance were endeavoring to catch a glimpse of what was going on. Pieces of glass, attached to long wooden handles, were inserted between the bars of the cell and extended over the galleries. The reflection of the tragedy upon this glass gave the inmates a view of the execution."

From an early hour in the morning, Abriel and Bayonne had been "earnestly engaged in prayer, and the ministers of their religion had attended them since the previous day. They were humble and contrite in their penitence, and confessed their belief that their sins had been pardoned." The death warrant was read, and the executioner, "clad in black and his face masked, put the rope around their necks." The condemned men addressed the crowd, "proclaiming their innocence and saying that they forgot all wrongs against them. . . . The priest said a prayer; they kissed the crucifix, and the caps were drawn over their heads. A moment later the fatal stroke was given, and the souls passed from earth." The *Picayune's* article once again ended by saying that "all good people wish that this may be the last example of the death penalty."[28]

* * *

If the 1871 *Daily Picayune* article is to be believed, the "Priestess of the Voudous" came regularly to the Parish Prison from about 1850 into the 1870s to prepare altars for the unfortunate men awaiting execution. Her concern for prisoners was reiterated in the newspaper articles that followed her death. The 1881 *Daily Picayune* obituary insisted that Marie Laveau was not only charitable, she was also pious and "took delight in strengthening the allegiance of souls to the church. She would sit with the condemned in their last moments and endeavor to turn their thoughts to Jesus. Whenever a prisoner excited her pity, Marie would labor incessantly to obtain his pardon, or at least a commutation of sentence, and she generally succeeded." The *Daily City Item* proclaimed that if she "could be induced to exercise her influence to save the life of a condemned prisoner she rarely failed; nor were the fruits of her interference ever regretted. No shrewder judge of character could have been found, and when Marie interceded there was generally good ground for mercy." The *New York Times* obituary also reported that she "would often visit the cells of the condemned . . . her coming was considered a blessing by the prisoners." An 1886 *Daily Picayune* article declared that "[Marie Laveau's] heart prompted her to visit the Parish Prison whenever its walls held any unfortunates condemned to death. She labored earnestly for the salvation of the souls of poor sinners such as those, built altars beside which she could pray with them, and went to them often in the last days of their miserable life."[29] It is entirely possible that she attended the prisoners Jean Adam, Antoine Delisle, James Mullen, Heinrich Haas, Peter Smith, Joseph Lindsay, Antoine Cambre, and John Bazar, but the fact was not recorded in the New Orleans newspapers.

Marie Laveau did not, however, bring about the abolition of public hanging. While hangings were no longer open to the general populace after 1850, New Orleanians still fought for the coveted passes that allowed them to witness an execution, and these spectacles continued into the twentieth century.

Final Years

The process of reintegrating Louisiana into the Union, known as Reconstruction, lasted from 1863 until 1877. People of color at first made substantial progress toward gaining their civil rights. The enlightened provisions of the Louisiana constitution of 1868 stipulated that "any conveyance of a public character, and all places of business, or of public resort . . . shall be opened to the patronage of all persons, without distinction or discrimination on account of race." It provided for the establishment of at least one free public school in each parish, which children six to eighteen years of age would be eligible to attend regardless of race or previous condition of servitude. In 1870 the Louisiana Civil Code legalized interracial marriages, and couples who had lived together for years and raised large families took this opportunity to marry and legitimize their children.

The federal Reconstruction Act granted the right to vote, serve on juries, and hold public office to all African American males. Black men were selected for the positions of state treasurer and lieutenant governor, and for a few weeks a man of color served as interim governor. The Louisiana House of Representatives of 1868–1870 included 35 blacks out of a total of 101 members, and the Louisiana Senate had 7 black members out of a total of 36. In New Orleans, many men of color were appointed to positions in city government.[1]

Panicked whites, both Creoles and Americans, characterized these developments as "Negro rule," and only the presence of federal troops could enforce the laws granting full citizenship to people of African descent. The ensuing racist backlash engendered the rise of white supremacist organizations, such as the Knights of the White Camellia, the White League, and the Ku Klux Klan, which specialized in lynching, cross-burning, and other forms of intimidation. Their objective was to "maintain white supremacy, observe a marked difference between the races, and prevent political power from falling into the hands of the inferior race." In 1874 over eight thousand members of the White League clashed with six hundred New Orleans policemen and three thousand black militiamen in what became known as the Battle of Liberty Place.[2]

Bigotry even began to appear at Marie Laveau's home parish, St. Louis Cathedral, once noted by travelers for its racially and ethnically mixed congregation. Sister Mary Bernard Deggs, in her history of the Sisters of the Holy Family, lamented that white and colored had formerly been "like one and the same family, going to the same church, sitting in the same pews, and many of them sleeping in the same bed." After the changes wrought by the Civil War and Reconstruction, parishioners of African descent were made to feel unwelcome at St. Louis Cathedral and other Catholic churches in the city. People of color were no longer allowed to join religious societies, sing in the choir, or serve as acolytes. Many left the Roman Catholic faith and turned for their communal and spiritual needs to all-black Baptist, Methodist, and African Methodist Episcopal congregations. Others rejected organized religion and joined Masonic lodges and Spiritualist societies.[3]

Family Matters

Marie Laveau had undergone a devastating emotional and financial crisis when Christophe Glapion died intestate and insolvent in the summer of 1855. The hardships of the Civil War, following so closely on the loss of her domestic partner, compounded her problems. As the optimism of Reconstruction faded, the social and material condition of the Laveau-Glapion family worsened considerably, and it is in this changed environment that Marie Laveau lived her final years.

By the 1870s Marie had grown old and frail. On June 24, 1875, a *Picayune* reporter called at the cottage on St. Ann Street seeking material for the customary St. John's Eve story. There he found "Marie Lafont [*sic*], the Ancient Queen," whom he described as "once a tall, powerful woman ... now bent with age and infirmity. Her complexion was a dark bronze and her hair grizzled black, while her trembling hand was supported by a crooked stick." When asked about her religious practices, she replied that she no longer served the Voudou spirits, but was now "a believer in the holy faith."[4] In reality, she had always been a practicing Catholic.

A few of the most senior among the Louisiana Writers' Project interviewees recalled the elderly Widow Paris. These women had grown up in Marie's Vieux Carré neighborhood and were adults or teenagers by the time she died in 1881. Some found her to be a rather frightening personage. Marguerite Gitson, born in 1854, told her interviewer: "I lived right across the street from Marie Laveau on St. Ann. She was large and kept herself always neat and nice. She was old. Her hair was white like mine is now." Anita Fonvergne was born in 1860. She also lived on St. Ann Street as a child and saw the aged Widow Paris, whom she described as "so old she could hardly walk." Mrs. Fonvergne remembered being taken to St. Louis Cemetery No. 1 by her mother: "We saw an old, shriveled-up lady . . . sittin' by a tomb. My mamma said 'That's Marie Laveau, the Voodoo woman.' They say she was pretty when she was young, but because of the work she did, when she got old she was dried up and looked like a witch." Alice Zeno, born in 1867, remembered seeing Marie Laveau in the mid-1870s: "I was selling pralines . . . on St. Ann between Burgundy and Rampart, when this old woman that looked just like a ghost saw me and said '*allez petite*' (go away, little one)." She was "tall . . . with snow white hair—her face was all wrinkled. She wore a white mother hubbard [a loose-fitting summer dress] and carried a palmetto fan." Rose Legendre, born around 1868 in Tampico, Mexico, was the widow of Marie Laveau's grandson, Blaire Legendre. Mrs. Legendre had visited the Laveau-Glapion home as a child and recalled her husband's grandmother: "She was a very old, old woman, all wrinkled with white hair. Blaire was a little boy and she would say 'Give me a stick till I hit him,' and she would shake her cane at him. I was scared to go there."[5]

* * *

During these final years Marie Laveau continued to share her home with various family members. Adelai Aldina, Marie, and Victor Pierre Crocker, the children of Marie's older daughter Heloïse with the free man of color Pierre Crocker, were raised in the Laveau-Glapion household. Aldina and Marie were enumerated in the census of 1860, after which Marie Crocker vanished from the archival record. The 1870 census shows twenty-five-year-old Aldina and nineteen-year-old John (Victor Pierre) "Croquoir" residing in the household of the Widow Paris.[6] Victor Pierre, calling himself John or Peter Crocker, was listed in the city directories as a barber, sometimes living at 152 St. Ann, sometimes elsewhere. Adelai Aldina died in 1871. Her death certificate records that she expired at 152 St. Ann from an "abscess of the liver." Evidently she was presumed to be Marie Laveau's daughter. The Burial Book for St. Louis Cemetery No. 1 records the interment of "A. Aldina Croker, daughter of Marie Laveau or Madame Parise," in the Widow Paris tomb on September 10, 1871.[7]

Also enumerated in the 1870 census and city directories as a resident of 152 St. Ann was Christophe Glapion's second cousin, the free man of color Alexis Celestin Glapion. Alexis Celestin was the son of Celestin Glapion, a skilled carpenter and furniture maker, who was the offspring of Christophe's grandfather, the Chevalier Christophe de Glapion, with his slave concubine Lizette. In 1786, following the death of the Chevalier de Glapion, Lizette and her mulatto children were freed.[8] Since Marie Laveau and Christophe Glapion had no surviving sons to carry on the Glapion name, the many African American Glapions now living in New Orleans may be descended from this other branch of the family.

In addition, the Laveau-Glapion household included Marie Laveau's younger daughter Philomène and her children. Sometime in the mid-1850s Philomène had entered a long-term relationship with a white man, Emile Alexandre Legendre. Alexandre Legendre arrived in New Orleans in the early nineteenth century with his parents, Louis George Legendre and Jeanne Aimeé Lepetre, his older brother George Legendre, and his cousin Henry Legendre. The Legendre family was among the many Saint Domingue immigrants who made their way to Louisiana by way of other Caribbean Islands; Alexandre was born in 1804 on the Dutch island of Curaçao. After 1822, Alexandre, George, and Henry Legendre were regularly listed in the New Orleans city directories as merchants, commission brokers, or attorneys, and they appear frequently in the Conveyance Office Index to Purchasers and Vendors.

Philomène not only chose a much older partner—Legendre was thirty-two years her senior—she also chose a married man. In 1830, Emile Alexandre Legendre wed Marie Louise Françoise Judith Toutant Beauregard of St. Bernard Parish, with whom he had four children. Judith, referred to in legal documents as Judith Toutant, was the older sister of the famed Confederate general Pierre Gustav Toutant Beauregard.[9] During the 1830s Alexandre Legendre, occasionally in partnership with one Henry Lawrence, engaged in buying commercial property and buildings in New Orleans' central business district, in the uptown residential suburbs, in the warehouse district, and in the downtown Faubourg Clouet.[10] The "Panic of 1837" put an end to these financial speculations, as it did to those of many New Orleanians. By late 1837 Legendre and his business partner had declared bankruptcy, and their property was being sold to satisfy their creditors.[11] Alexandre's wife Judith subsequently filed for a separation of property. Represented by her father, she began to sell off land and slaves acquired in her dowry or as later donations from her parents.[12] Sometime between 1850 and 1860 Judith Toutant Legendre left Louisiana for New York City, where she established a permanent residence.[13]

Philomène Glapion and Emile Alexandre Legendre remained a couple until Legendre's death in 1872. The birth certificates of their seven children show that all had the surname Legendre and were classified as "colored," the "natural issue of Emile Legendre with Philomène Glapion." Marie Fidelia Alexandre was born November 17, 1857; Alexandre Glapion was born May 8th, 1859; and Marie Noëmie Marguerite, known as Memie, was born on October 10, 1862.

An infant, Eugenie, died on January 29, 1866. Arthur Blaire, who became the husband of LWP informant Rose Legendre, was born on October 18, 1868. Twin boys named Joseph Etienne St. Marc and Charles St. Marc were born February 10, 1870. Joseph Etienne expired the next day, and Charles died five months later.[14] There are no baptismal entries for any of the Legendre children in the registers of St. Louis Cathedral or any of the other downtown churches that Philomène might have attended. According to LWP informants Rose Legendre and Marie Dédé, "Madame Legendre" was a member of the Church of St. Anthony of Padua (now Our Lady of Guadalaupe). Mrs. Dédé explained that Philomène was embarrassed by the attention she experienced at St. Louis Cathedral, where strangers would stare and whisper "Look—that's Marie Laveau's daughter." [15] The 1856–1873 baptismal records for St. Anthony's are missing.

Philomène (minus her children) was enumerated in her mother's household in the 1860 census. The census for 1870 shows that Alexander "Lejendre," white, age sixty-six, was sharing a home with "Philomina" Legendre, age twenty-nine, and their children Fidelia, age eleven; (Alexandre) Glapion, age ten; and Noëmie, age nine. Philomène and the children were designated as mulattos. Blaire, who would have been almost two years old, was not listed.[16] Both the census and the city directories indicate that Alexandre Legendre was a bookkeeper for the Merchants' Mutual Insurance Company. Alexandre, Philomène, and their children occupied a house at 362 Dauphine Street in the Faubourg Marigny. The infant Eugenie and the twins, Joseph and Charles, died there. The attractive two-bay, side-gabled Creole cottage, now 1820 Dauphine, still stands across the street from the corner store formerly owned by Charles Laveaux. I found no record of Alexandre Legendre having bought this property and presume that he and Philomène were renters.

Alexandre Legendre, described on his death certificate as a sixty-seven-year-old white male, died suddenly on July 26, 1872. The cause of death was erysipelas, an infectious disease caused by the streptococcus virus. A funeral announcement appeared in the New Orleans *Bee*: "Died yesterday evening at eight o'clock, A. Legendre. His friends and acquaintances are requested to assist with his funeral, which will begin on Saturday at four o'clock in the afternoon. The funeral procession will depart from the mortuary parlor at number 382 Love Street between St. Anthony and Columbus."[17]

One is always curious about the social interactions (or lack thereof) between a man's white and colored families on the occasion of his funeral. Christophe Glapion's final rites were held at the Laveau-Glapion cottage, and he was in-

34. Creole cottage at 1820 Dauphine Street (formerly 362 Dauphine) in the Faubourg Marigny. This was the home of Philomène Glapion and Alexandre Legendre from sometime in the 1860s until Legendre's death in 1872. (Photograph by author, November 15, 2004.)

terred in the Widow Paris tomb in St. Louis Cemetery No. 1. Emile Alexandre Legendre's funeral procession, rather than departing from the home he shared with Philomène Glapion on Dauphine Street, left from the undertaker's establishment. He was not placed in the Widow Paris tomb along with the children he fathered with Philomène (Eugenie, Joseph, and Charles), but was buried in St. Louis Cemetery No. 3. In the eyes of the law, Alexandre Legendre was still married to Judith Toutant Beauregard. Apparently his funeral arrangements were taken in charge by his white kinspeople, and Philomène and their surviving children, Fidelia, Alexandre, Noëmie, and Blaire, were excluded.[18]

No will or succession could be located for Alexandre Legendre, indicating that he possessed nothing of value to bequeath to his wife Judith, to Philomène, or to his legitimate or natural offspring.

Having lost her home on Dauphine Street, Philomène returned with her children to Marie Laveau's cottage. Philomène was only thirty-six when Alexandre Legendre died. By all accounts she was a great beauty, yet she settled gracefully into "widowhood" and spent the rest of her life in the little house on St. Ann Street. She regularly appeared in the city directories as "Mrs.

Table 4. Residents of the Laveau-Glapion household as enumerated in the U.S. Census, with name and occupation as listed in the city directories

Census and city directory

1850	1860	1870	1880
Widow Paris, age 45; Mrs. Laveau Paris 179 St. Ann	**Widow Paris**, age 60; Mrs. Laveau Paris 152 St. Ann	**Mary Paris**, age 65; Mrs. Marie Laveau 152 St. Ann	**Marie Glapion**, age 95; Mary Glapion 152 St. Ann
C. Glapion, age 63; Christophe Glapion 179 St. Ann			
Heloïse Glapion, age 21			
Henieta (Crocker), age 1	**Amazone Crocker**, age 9	**Alina Croquoir**, age 25	
Malvina (Crocker), age 4	**Alzonia Crocker**, age 12	**John Croquoir**, age 19; Peter Crocker, barber 152 St. Ann	
Philomène Glapion, age 13	**Philomène Glapion**, age 23		**Philomène Legendre**, age 39; Philomène Legendre 152 St. Ann
			Fidelia Legendre, age 18
			Alexandre Legendre, age 19; Alexandre Legendre, laborer 152 St. Ann
			Noëmie Legendre, age 16
		Celestin Glapillon, age 37; Alexis Celestin Glapion, painter 152 St. Ann	
		Honesta Glapillon, age 30	

Philomène Legendre" or the "Widow of Emile Alexandre Legendre," and she was always referred to as "Madame Legendre" by newspaper reporters.

On May 13, 1876, Philomène bought the family home for $2,000 from the widow of Philippe Ross, the friend who had rescued it from the sheriff's auction following Christophe Glapion's death in 1855. At that time she donated legal use of the property to her mother.[19] In the 1880 census, Philomène and her children, Alexandre, Fidelia, and Noëmie Legendre, were enumerated in the household of Marie (Laveau) Glapion at 152 St. Ann. Blaire, who would have been twelve years old, was still not listed.[20]

The archival records relating to the Laveau-Glapion family coincide with the statements of several of the Louisiana Writers' Project informants who remembered the occupants of the St. Ann Street cottage during the 1870s and 1880s. Marie Dédé, a frequent visitor, related that "[Marie Laveau] had two daughters and a son, and their names was Madame Le Jeanne [Legendre], the oldest; Adonisha, the second; and John Laveau." Mrs. Dédé, understandably confused by these relationships, assumed that "Adonisha" and John were Philomène's younger siblings. In actuality they would have been Heloïse's children, Adelai Aldina and Victor Pierre (John) Crocker. Marie Dédé went on to say that Madame "Le Jeanne" had three children, Fidelia; Noëmie, nicknamed Memie; and Alexandre, who was called by his middle name, Glapion. "They were the ones I used to go play with at Marie Laveau's. . . . Memie was fine, she wanted to be colored and went to all the places with us, but not Fidelia. Fidelia was as white as they make 'em. She had blue eyes and everything." Octavia Fontenette, born in 1854 and raised on St. Ann Street, also said she had been a playmate of Marie Laveau's grandchildren, who she called Fidelia, Memie, and "Joe." Mary Washington related that Philomène's daughters Fidelia and Memie "was good lookin' girls. I think one of them passed for white. Her son [Alexandre] was brown-skinned."[21]

* * *

Marie Laveau's financial situation worsened during her later years. Christophe Glapion, shortly before he died, had been denied the forty acres of bounty land to which he was entitled as a veteran of the War of 1812–1815 because the military authorities in Washington found no record of his service. In 1874 Marie made another attempt to acquire Glapion's bounty land, as well as the pension of eight dollars per month due to the widows of veterans. The documents relating to this application contain several startling statements. Marie exaggerated her age, once stating that she was eighty-one years old and another time that she was eighty-six, when she was actually about seventy-three. She claimed to have been married to Christophe Glapion on June 13, 1813, by Père Antoine, "there being no legal barrier to the marriage," and produced two witnesses who claimed to have been present at the ceremony. Had Marie given her true age, simple arithmetic would have revealed that she was only twelve years old at the time of her alleged wedding, of which there is no record in the sacramental registers. This was obviously a strategy to hoodwink the Pension Office and establish her legal marriage to Glapion prior to his military service in order to collect his benefits.

After two years of delay, Marie's petitions for Glapion's bounty land and pension were rejected. On April 9, 1877, A. W. Fisher, special agent for the Pension Office, sent an exasperated report to the commissioner of pensions, stating that "There is no record of the company in which service is alleged and the claimant is unable to furnish any additional evidence as to service. The witnesses to whom she referred . . . did not know the claimant or her husband until a number of years after the war, and yet her attorney makes them testify to being present at claimant's marriage in 1813." For the entertainment of his superior in Washington, Special Agent Fisher added a choice bit of gossip: "I am informed that in her day, claimant was 'Queen of the Voudous.'" This is the only official document in which Marie Laveau's status as a Voudou priestess was acknowledged.[22]

Death of the Queen

A persistent element of the Laveau Legend claims that, toward the end of her life, Marie Laveau nearly drowned when she was swept into Lake Pontchartrain by a storm. In her unpublished "Voodoo" manuscript, Catherine Dillon quoted a 1920 newspaper article in which the narrator, who claimed to have been acquainted with Marie Laveau, presented this recollection without specifying the date or the occasion: "All the voodoo meetings took place out in a small shack, known as the Maison Blanche, on the shore of Lake Pontchartrain. Marie was caught out there during the storm and when the rescuing party got to her, she was found seated on an old stump half dead. The negroes always said that she had died during the storm and had come to life when it was over."[23]

G. William Nott repeated this tale in his 1922 *Times-Picayune* Sunday magazine article, "Marie Laveau, Long High Priestess of Voudouism in New Orleans." According to Nott, a hurricane passed over the city in 1884: "Marie Laveau was then living in a shanty on Lake Pontchartrain. The force of the wind was so great that her cabin was wrenched from its foundations and hurled into the angry waters. Obliged to seek shelter on the roof, there she remained for several hours, discouraging the attempts of her would-be rescuers and telling them 'Mo oulé mourri dan lac lá' (I want to die in the lake). She was finally prevailed upon to accept assistance, and none too soon, for the cabin . . . was completely shattered by the waves a few moments later."[24]

Zora Neale Hurston, in "Hoodoo in America," embellished Nott's version of the near-drowning incident: "[Marie Laveau] resisted rescue, saying that she wished to die there in the lake. . . . She was always the magnificent savage, and she perhaps felt that, being old, her end was near. She preferred to exit with nature itself playing its most magnificent music, rather than die rotting in bed. She was forcibly rescued, but it is said that neither wind, water, nor thunder ceased until she had set foot on land."[25]

In 1936 Herbert Asbury retold the story in *The French Quarter*: Marie's "flimsy shanty" was swept into Lake Pontchartrain by a hurricane; she protested that the Voudou gods wanted her to die in the lake, and was only pulled from the water against her will.[26]

Almost every person interviewed by Louisiana Writers' Project fieldworkers had some version of the near-drowning episode. Some seem to be referring to the Widow Paris, while others are apparently speaking of her successor, "Marie II." Most believed that Marie Laveau was rescued, although a few, none of whom knew her personally, said that she actually drowned. Marie Dédé believed the accident had occurred on St. John's Eve in the mid-1870s. "Everybody thought [Marie Laveau] was drowned but they found her floating on the water and they . . . brought her on the shore and rolled her to bring her through. . . . She lived for about seven years after that . . . she died of old age at her house in 1881." In Oscar Felix's narrative, Marie was in a boat by herself when the storm came up on St. John's Eve and blew the boat out into the lake, where she was rescued by some of her followers. "She wasn't drowned in no storm; she died [later on] from sickness." Mary Washington told her interviewer that it was she who found Marie after her misadventure. Three days after the St. John's Eve celebration she discovered a woman lying in one of the creeks near the lake. She took her home, gave her coffee, and rubbed her with oil, and was astonished to learn that her guest was the Voudou Queen. Mrs. Washington indicated that this brush with death prompted Marie Laveau's retirement: "She promised God to give up the hoodoo work if he would save her. She did a little good work [after that] but nothing bad."[27]

Another LWP informant, Marie Martin, believed it was a priestess named

Angèlie Levasseur who drowned in the St. John's Eve storm. Mrs. Martin told her interviewer that Levasseur "was celebrating the St. John's feast out at Milneburg, when suddenly a storm came up. Her cabin was swept away. Angèlie was carried by the wind and was caught on the limb of a tree where she remained suspended for two or three days, to be finally discovered, dead, by some huntsmen."[28]

* * *

If anyone drowned in Lake Pontchartrain, it was definitely not the Widow Paris. As official records and the New Orleans newspapers attest, and as several of the Louisiana Writers' Project informants correctly remembered, the original Marie Laveau died at home from the complications of old age in the summer of 1881. New Orleans was experiencing what the newspapers described as "the hottest spell for half a century." In June, the *City Item* reported that "The heat yesterday and last evening was excessive. Unrelieved by a breath of air, it prostrated the vital energies of man and beast and made comfort impossible." At least eight men and women of every age and race, visitors and natives alike, collapsed on the street and died from sunstroke.[29]

On June 15, surrounded by her family and her community, the Queen of the Voudous passed into the spirit world. Members of the household would have set about the duties traditionally associated with death, stopping all the clocks in the house, covering the mirrors, draping the front door with black crepe, and putting on dark-colored mourning attire. Augustin Lamothe, a boarder in the Laveau-Glapion home, dutifully reported the event to the Board of Health. According to her death certificate, "Marie Glapion born Laveau (colored) aged ninety-eight years, departed this life yesterday, 15 June 1881." The official cause of death was given as "diarrhea."[30] Marie Laveau had probably succumbed to weakness and dehydration, exacerbated by old age and the intense heat, from one of the intestinal maladies that constantly plagued New Orleanians.

The body of the family matriarch would have been lovingly washed and dressed. Surrounded by candles, flowers, and religious images, she was laid out in the front room of her home so that relatives, friends, and followers could say their goodbyes and offer prayers for her soul. As the *Daily Picayune* reported, "Those whom she had befriended crowded into the little room where she was exposed, in order to obtain a last look at the features, smiling even in death, of her who had been so kind to them."

Marie's daughter Philomène made funeral arrangements with the undertaking establishment of Alcée Labat and Joseph Ray, just around the corner on

North Rampart Street.[31] Embalming was not customary in nineteenth-century New Orleans, and the dead were interred as quickly as possible. Marie Laveau's funeral was scheduled for five o'clock of the evening following her death. The public would have been alerted by black-edged notices posted throughout the city and at St. Louis Cathedral. The ceremony was conducted by Father Hyacinth Mignot, marking the end of a life in which participation in the rituals of the Roman Catholic faith was central.

Despite the poverty and decrepitude of her final years, Marie Laveau was famous, and most of New Orleans turned out for her funeral. Such services usually took place at the home of the deceased, although the rites for such a well-known personage may have been held at the cathedral. Afterwards her coffin would have been placed on a hearse drawn by horses, draped and plumed with black, to make the short journey to the family tomb in St. Louis Cemetery No. 1. According to the *Picayune,* "Her remains were followed to the grave by a large concourse of people, the most prominent and the most humble joining in paying their last respects to the dead."[32]

Several of the Louisiana Writers' Project interviewees spoke of the racially and economically diverse crowd of devotees and curiosity seekers who attended the last rites of the Voudou Queen. Rose Legendre described the funeral as "an elaborate affair, attended by numerous white people, not a small percentage of whom were members of the topmost crust of society." Marie Dédé reported that "there were so many people that you could not get three blocks from her house," and Laura Hopkins said that Marie Laveau "had a big funeral; people stood in line with their hats off and their heads bowed."[33]

Alexander Augustin declared that Marie's funeral was organized by one of the burial societies to which she belonged—*Les Dames Amies Sacrées* (Ladies' Sacred Friends), *Les Dames aux Tignons* (Ladies with Tignons), and *Les Dames de la Poussinière* (Ladies of the Chicken Coop). Such societies were popular with New Orleanians of African descent. In return for a small monthly fee, members were assured of a dignified and sometimes lavish funeral. Society members, attired in matching outfits, always marched in the funeral procession. Mr. Augustine reported that both Les Dames aux Tignons and Les Dames de la Poussinière dressed in black skirts and a white shirtwaist for funerals, the former wearing blue silk scarves and the latter wearing black hats.[34]

The St. Louis Cemetery No. 1 ownership record for the Widow Paris tomb includes the notation that "Dame Christophe Glapion" was interred in the middle vault. By using this name, Philomène sustained the fiction that her mother was a respectable married lady and that she herself was a legitimate daughter. The age of the deceased was written in numerals as *98*, corrected as *78* inserted in parentheses above.[35]

* * *

Although the archival record states unequivocally that Marie Laveau's remains were laid to rest in her family tomb in St. Louis Cemetery No. 1, the Louisiana Writers' Project narrators held divergent opinions regarding her burial place. Most agreed that she was interred in the Widow Paris tomb, but some advocated a wall vault, known as the "Wishing Vault," in St. Louis Cemetery No. 2.[36]

Both the Widow Paris tomb and the Wishing Vault were the site of rituals intended to honor the Voudou Queen and solicit her aid. In New Orleans it was (and still is) customary to leave offerings of food, liquor, money, flowers, and candles on the tombs of persons believed to possess great spiritual power. Believers also draw cross marks, an African tradition symbolizing a point of concentrated power where the world of the living meets the world of the spirits. Identical rituals are observed in Haitian Vodou, where the drawing of a cross mark is called *kwasiyen* (to sign with a cross) and is used to establish contact with the lwa and the dead.[37] LWP informants remembered seeing offerings and cross marks at the Widow Paris tomb in St. Louis Cemetery No. 1 and at the Wishing Vault in St. Louis Cemetery No. 2.

Ayola Cruz, sexton of St. Louis Cemetery No. 1 since the early 1920s, told his interviewers that people of all colors "come almost daily to make offerings to Marie's spirit. They make crosses with red brick, charcoal, and sharp rocks." Mr. Cruz, acting under the orders of archdiocesan authorities, immediately removed the markings, but, as an LWP fieldworker noted, "close observation discloses scratched crosses under the fresh whitewash." Some of the visitors, according to Ayola Cruz, left cooked foods, cakes, bread, flowers, apples, oranges, bananas, pineapples, or money. "Devotees knock three times on the marble slab . . . and put their ears to a crack, listening for an answer from the Voodoo Queen. Many of them pray, and, until a recent rule prohibited it, they used to burn tapers." Mr. Cruz insisted that "the real and only" Marie Laveau was interred in the Widow Paris tomb.[38]

Raymond Rivaros, former sexton at the St. Louis Cemeteries, agreed: "Marie Laveau is buried . . . in St. Louis No. 1 . . . but the [cross] marks are washed off as soon as [the people] put them on. . . . When I worked [at St. Louis no. 2] . . . a white lady would come every first Friday and bury two dollars [in the wall vault said to be the burial place of Marie Laveau]. As soon as she left I'd dig it out." Anita Fonvergne told her interviewer, "Some people say that Marie Laveau is buried in the St. Louis cemetery on Claiborne Avenue [No. 2], but that's wrong. Her tomb is right in the old cemetery on Basin [No. 1]. I've heard that Marie Laveau used to go to this tomb in St. Louis 2 to do her bad works . . . and that's where people get the idea she's buried in the Claiborne cemetery. I don't know whose tomb that was . . . I guess it was some woman like herself." Oscar Felix said that "Most people will tell you she was buried in St. Louis 2. You will even see them go to the tomb and make the sign of the cross on the tombstone there, but that's not her grave. She was buried in St. Louis 1."[39]

Other informants supported the Wishing Vault in St. Louis Cemetery No. 2 as the final resting place of the Voudou Queen. Aileen Eugene said that "For years after [Marie Laveau] died people used to go put silver money on her grave in the Saint Louis Cemetery on Claiborne Avenue [No. 2] . . . in the rear wall on Iberville Street on the left side. . . . People [still] goes there to make a cross . . . with brick and ask for a favor. . . . The tomb is covered with crosses . . . [They] puts their hand on her grave and makes a wish and their wish is granted." According to John Slater, "a Puerto Rican woman comes here [to St. Louis No. 2] every first Monday and Friday of the month [with] paper flowers. People bury money, always three 'nocks' [three nickles—the traditional payment to the spirits]. We sometimes find three black candles, and notes, and other stuff."[40]

The belief that the Wishing Vault holds the remains of the second Marie Laveau was seemingly confirmed in 1980 as a result of the "Black History Tour of St. Louis Cemetery No. 2," sponsored by the New Orleans NAACP. While the tour brochure says only that a Madame Charles Laveau was buried in the Iberville Street wall of vaults on October 6, 1890, a February 12, 1980, article in the *States-Item* unabashedly declared that this person was "Marie II." This "fact" was repeated in a *Times-Picayune* article of June 24, 1984.[41] In reality, the "Madame Laveau" in question was the widow of Marie Laveau's half-brother Laurent Charles Laveaux and was therefore the sister-in-law of the Widow Paris. She is not interred in the Wishing Vault, but in a nearby vault in the same wall.[42]

Many of the LWP informants believed that Marie Laveau—either the first or the second—had originally been buried in the wall vault in St. Louis Cemetery No. 2, but that her remains had been moved to the Girod Street Protestant Cemetery, near the site of the present-day Louisiana Superdome. Sophie Rey remembered going to St. Louis Cemetery No. 2 "to wish at [Marie Laveau's] grave. On Wednesday and Friday you couldn't hardly get near for the crowd. They put a dollar-fifteen-cents through the iron slats . . . bottles of wine,

35. The Widow Paris tomb in St. Louis Cemetery No. 1. Note the X marks and the offerings of flowers and Mardi Gras beads. (Photograph by author, April 5, 1996.)

preserves, pralines, most everything, and they burned candles. . . . Then they moved her away [to Girod Street Cemetery]. . . . Some said her family didn't want so much attention paid to her. They didn't like it and they got mad when she was called a Voudou." Theresa Kavanaugh said that "People commenced a-flocking to her tomb [in St. Louis Cemetery No. 2] by the Claiborne Street wall. . . . After a while, when they broke her tomb to divide the wall for an of-fice they found a lot of money and jewelry inside where a hole had been made. They moved her bones to that uptown cemetery on Girod Street." This was confirmed by Marie Brown, who told her interviewer, "At first she was in St. Louis No. 2, but when they wanted that space . . . for an office, they moved her to Girod Cemetery.[43]

36. The "Wishing Vault" in St. Louis Cemetery No. 2. (Photograph by author, All Saints Day, 1998.)

Inquiries at the Office of the Superintendent of St. Louis Cemeteries revealed that the row of vaults torn down to construct an office was not on Iberville Street, the location of the Wishing Vault, but on Claiborne Avenue, where some wall vaults were demolished because they were dangerously deteriorated. The bodies from these vaults were indeed transferred to Girod Street Cemetery. There are no records of ownership for the Wishing Vault, officially designated as square three, St. James aisle, row twenty-five, range three. The entry simply states that "this vault is full."[44]

Today the Widow Paris tomb in St. Louis Cemetery No. 1 receives thousands of visitors—one tour guide estimated the number at 250,000 people per year.[45] The tomb has become what folklorists call a "legend-trip" site, where both tourists and residents leave offerings and make cross marks. Some take bits of soft brick from adjacent tombs with which to draw their Xs, and others use ballpoint ink, indelible markers, or lipstick. These practices have led to the disintegration of surrounding tombs and have damaged the marble tablet of the Widow Paris tomb. In 2005 a coalition of cemetery preservationists, tour guides, and the archdiocesan cemetery authority posted signs stating that "desecration" of the tomb is unlawful and that violators will face fines and possible jail sentences.[46]

Few tourists venture into St. Louis Cemetery No. 2, adjacent to a notoriously dangerous housing project, because visitors have been robbed and even killed there. The Wishing Vault is nevertheless being used as a ritual site by devotees, who leave flowers, notes, personal photographs, money, candles, rosaries, and religions images, and draw cross marks. On All Saints' Day (when police protection is offered to those who want to visit their family tombs) I observed an African American lady, accompanied by her grandchildren, adding her offering to the display. Her account was almost identical to those of the Louisiana Writers' Project interviewees: "Yes, this is where the *real* Marie Laveau is buried. You know they moved her from over in St. Louis no. 1. The local people come here to honor her."

Descendants

Reconstruction in Louisiana was ultimately a failure, and the rights gained by people of African descent were followed by ever more repressive Jim Crow segregation and racism in the 1880s and 1890s. New Orleans was transformed from a tripartite society of white, colored, and black to a rigidly segregated society of white and black. The Louisiana Legislative Code of 1890 classified persons with "any appreciable amount" of African ancestry as Negro, obliterating the distinction between the unsophisticated and uneducated black freedmen and the people of mixed race who had been free for generations. Creole neighborhoods that had once been racially integrated became all black. In 1893 the New Orleans City Council renamed the venue formerly known as Congo Square for the Confederate general P.G.T. Beauregard, and it, like many other public places, was thereafter reserved for white use. Interracial marriages, after being legal for twenty-four years, were again outlawed in 1894. Concubinage between "a person of the Caucasian race and a person of the Negro race" was made a felony. Schools that had been open to all races became segregated, and after 1898 public schooling for children of color was limited to the first five grades. Discriminatory tactics served to disenfranchise voters of African descent.[1]

Of most lasting significance was the Separate Car Act of 1890, which required railway companies to provide separate coaches for white and black passengers. The *Comité de Citoyens* (Citizens' Committee), composed of prominent Creoles of color, determined to challenge this law. Homer Plessy, a man of predominantly European ancestry, was chosen as the defendant in their test case. In June 1892, Plessy boarded the "white car" of the East Louisiana Railway in New Orleans, bound for the nearby town of Covington, and was arrested when he identified himself as colored and refused to move to the car for black riders. His conviction was upheld by Judge Ferguson of the Louisiana Supreme Court on the grounds that, because the East Louisiana Railway operated only within the state, it was not subject to the fourteenth amendment to the constitution. The *Plessy v. Ferguson* case eventually made its way to the U.S. Supreme Court, where its defeat in 1896 resulted in the odious doctrine of "separate but equal." Within a few years, white supremacy and segregation were complete,

Table 5. Descendants of Marie Laveau and Christophe Glapion

Sixth Generation—Grandchildren

Natural Children of Heloïse Glapion and Pierre Crocker (broker, builder, architect)
Joseph Eugene Crocker
  quadroon; born 1844, died 1845
Esmeralda Crocker
  quadroon; born ?, died 1850
Adelai Aldina Crocker (also called Malvina or Alzonia)
  quadroon; born 1847, died 1871
Marie Crocker (also called Henrietta or Amazone)
  quadroon; born 1850, died after 1860
Victor Pierre Crocker (also called John or Peter)
  (barber) quadroon; born 1853, died after 1887

Natural Children of Philomène Glapion and Emile Alexandre Legendre (insurance clerk)
Marie Fidelia Legendre
  octoroon; born 1857, died in St. Louis 1898
Alexandre Glapion Legendre
  (street peddler) octoroon; born 1859, died 1903
Noëmie Marguerite Legendre
  octoroon; born 1862, died after 1897
Eugenie Legendre
  octoroon; died in infancy 1866
Arthur Blaire Legendre
  (house painter) octoroon; born 1868, died 1932
Charles St. Marc Legendre and Etienne St. Marc Legendre
  octoroons; died in infancy 1870

Seventh Generation—Great-Grandchildren

Legitimate Children of Fidelia Legendre and Julius Westenberg (waiter) (married November 17, 1890)
Julius Westenberg Jr.
  (newspaper circulator) classified as white; born St. Louis 1890, died ?
Anna Westenberg
  classified as white; born St. Louis 1892, died ?
Clara Westenberg
  classified as white; born St. Louis, died in infancy in New Orleans April 5, 1897

Legitimate Son of Alexandre Glapion Legendre and Mathilde Lachapelle (married June 24, 1885)
Blaire Manuel Legendre
  (carpet cleaner) classified as Negro; born July 16, 1887, died after 1956

Natural Children of Alexandre Glapion Legendre and Ernestine L'lado
Arthur Legendre
  classified as white; born October 21, 1885, died ?

continued

Table 5—*Continued*

Ernest Alexandre Legendre
 (shoe repair) classified as white; born November 16, 1887, died 1948
Amelie Legendre
 classified as mulatto; born January 27, 1890, died 1896
Pierre Legendre
 classified as mulatto; born January 7, 1892, died ?
Pauline Legendre
 classified as mulatto; born October 1, 1894, died ?

Legitimate Son of Noëmie Legendre and John Benjamin Santenac (clerk) (married October 16, 1880)
Benjamin Alexandre Santenac
 classified as mulatto; born January 17, 1881, died ?

Legitimate Son of Blaire Legendre and Rose Camille (no marriage record in Orleans Parish)
Cyril John Legendre
 (house painter) classified as Negro; born April 12, 1902, died in Los Angeles 1965

Eighth Generation—Great-Great-Grandchildren

Legitimate Children of Anna Westenberg and Frank Schmidt (executive of iron foundry)
Frank Schmidt Jr.
 classified as white; born St. Louis 1915, died ?
Virginia Schmidt
 classified as white; born St. Louis 1923, died ?

Legitimate Children of Blair Manuel Legendre and Carmen Madere (married December 27, 1915)
Rodney Legendre
 (baker) classified as Negro; born July 27, 1920, died in Los Angeles 1996
Mabel Legendre
 (maid) classified as Negro; born 1923, died after 1949
Leonard Legendre
 (driver) classified as Negro; born May 1, 1924, died 1992

Legitimate Children of Ernest Legendre and Violet Caubert (married April 30, 1910)
Theodore Legendre
 (watch repair) classified as white; born January 1, 1911, died 1978
Ethel Legendre (Karl)
 (grocery clerk) classified as white; born 1913, died Bay St. Louis, Mississippi, 2005
Thomas Legendre
 (meat cutter) classified as white; born December 13, 1913, died Bay St. Louis, Mississippi, 1989

Note: Birth and death dates, racial classifications, and occupations are derived from sacramental records, birth, marriage, and death certificates, the census, city directories, the Social Security death index, and newspaper obituaries. All births, marriages, and deaths occurred in Orleans Parish unless otherwise noted.

with separate—and certainly unequal—churches, cemeteries, schools, libraries, hospitals, prisons, restaurants, train cars, waiting rooms, toilets, and drinking fountains for whites and blacks.[2]

Light-complexioned men and women of mixed race had been relatively comfortable within the earlier antebellum Afro-Creole community. But the humiliating circumstances of the Jim Crow era provoked some of Marie Laveau's descendants to leave New Orleans and begin new lives as white people. Others stayed in the Crescent City and were absorbed into the African American community. Unlike their well-to-do free colored forbears, all of whom were merchants, landlords, and professionals, these men and women were employed as laborers and servants and were renters rather than homeowners. Even the branch of the family who remained in New Orleans and identified themselves as Caucasian did not occupy high-status positions.[3]

* * *

After the death of Marie Laveau, her daughter Marie Philomène Glapion (Madame Legendre), continued to live in the Laveau-Glapion home with her extended family. Her adult daughters and sons, Fidelia, Alexandre, Noëmie, and Blaire Legendre, and her nephew Victor Pierre Crocker, along with their spouses and children, moved in and out of the cottage on St. Ann Street. In 1886 a *Daily Picayune* reporter found Philomène with her two daughters and a daughter-in-law, one of whom had "a chubby child across her lap." He noted that "every one of the group was comely," especially Madame Legendre, who "although her heavy mass of hair is turning as white as that of her mother, still shows the signs of beauty that she inherited. Tall, majestic, graceful, the eye still flashing fire, and with firm step notwithstanding months of illness, she rules her household, even if she has not the tact of Marie Laveau to extend her realm and number her subjects by the hundreds."[4]

Philomène's financial situation was becoming critical. The surrounding neighborhood had always consisted of modest cottages occupied by a racially mixed Creole population. While not as grand as the streets nearer to the cathedral and Jackson Square, the area was certainly no slum. But by the 1880s this part of the Vieux Carré was on its way downhill. In 1885 the newspapers reported crime, prostitution, and drug use in the "filthy pest houses" clustered together on Dauphine, Burgundy, Bienville, Conti, St. Louis, and Toulouse streets, just a few blocks above St. Ann. There, women "of the lowest order" lured male customers into their rooms, where they would "seize a man bodily and rob him of what he has in his pockets." At least three Chinese-owned opium dens operated in this locality. A reporter for the *Daily States* observed men and women of apparent respectability reclining on platforms covered with pillows and smoking long bamboo pipes tipped with ivory.[5] Such activities undoubtedly contributed to a devaluation of the Laveau-Glapion property.

To make ends meet, Philomène was renting out rooms in the outbuildings behind the old Creole cottage. The 1880 census reveals that, in addition to family members, a number of other people were living at 152 St. Ann, and the city directories list various boarders residing there throughout the 1880s and 1890s.[6] On two occasions, in 1886 and 1889, the State of Louisiana impounded the family residence for unpaid taxes, and Philomène's daughter Fidelia had to redeem it for the amount overdue. In 1889 Philomène was driven by necessity to mortgage the house to the Eureka Homestead Association for $510 cash, paying an exorbitant interest rate when she reclaimed it six months later for $1,000.[7]

Philomène's younger daughter, Noëmie (Memie) Legendre, was the first to wed. In 1880 she married a clerk named John Benjamin Santenac, and four months later she gave birth to a child named Benjamin Alexander Santenac. Benjamin was classified on his birth certificate as "colored." By 1890, Memie and her husband had separated, and she was once again living at 152 St. Ann where she was listed in the city directory as "Mrs. Naomi Santenac."[8]

In 1885 Alexandre Glapion Legendre, by trade a seller of wild game, married Mathilde Lachapelle. The couple had a son named Blaire Manuel Legendre, born in 1887, who was also classified as "colored." Alexandre, like his sister Memie, eventually left his wife and returned to the Laveau-Glapion cottage; Mathilde Legendre was later listed in the city directory as the "Widow of Alexandre."[9] Louisiana Writers' Project informant Marie Dédé, apparently not aware of Alexandre's marriage, said that her former playmate never took a legitimate partner "but he had children with Ernestine L'lado." The archival record confirms that between 1885 and 1894 five children were born to Alexandre Legendre and Ernestine L'lado—Arthur, Ernest, Amelie, Pierre, and Pauline Legendre. All, according to their birth certificates, came into the world at 152 St. Ann Street, and all were classified as "colored." Later records identified Arthur and Ernest as white.[10]

Victor Pierre Crocker, a barber by profession, had grown up in the Laveau-Glapion household. In 1887 he married a young widow named Catherine Teche, and there is no further record of Victor Pierre and his wife.[11] They may have left New Orleans in search of a better life.

Arthur Blaire Legendre, employed as a cooper and later as a house painter, married Rose Camille, a native of Tampico, Mexico. They had one son, Cyril John Legendre. I found no marriage record in Orleans Parish for Blaire and Rose, and no birth certificate or baptismal record for Cyril. Although Blaire was a witness at the weddings of family members in 1885 and 1890, he was not listed in the New Orleans city directory until 1902 and was first enumerated in the U.S. census for New Orleans in 1910. At that time Blaire was identified as a mulatto and Rose and Cyril were identified as white.[12]

Philomène's older daughter Fidelia was the last to marry. Marie Dédé, the LWP informant most knowledgeable about the Laveau-Glapion family, related that Fidelia, who had blue eyes and fair skin, "married a white man and went to New York." In 1890, at the rather late age of thirty-three, Fidelia indeed married Julius Westenberg, a native of Germany. This interracial marriage would have been legal at the time. Fidelia and her husband departed New Orleans, not for New York as Marie Dédé recollected, but for St. Louis. Julius Westenberg was listed in the St. Louis city directory as a waiter. Their children, Julius Jr., Anna, and Clara, were born in St. Louis between 1890 and 1896. All members of the family were identified in official documents as white.[13]

In 1897 Fidelia Legendre and her husband and children returned to New Orleans from St. Louis, no doubt owing to the illness of Fidelia's mother Philomène. It was a tragic visit. On April 5 their daughter Clara died of cholera at the Laveau-Glapion cottage. An infant named Mary Legendre, probably one of Alexandre's children, died there on April 16, 1897.[14] Marie Philomène Glapion Legendre died two months later. According to her death certificate, "Philomène Legendre (colored) age 62 years, died June 11, 1897 . . . at 1020 St. Ann Street [formerly 152 St. Ann]. . . . Cause of death acute bronchitis."[15]

Philomène was interred in the Widow Paris tomb in St. Louis Cemetery No. 1 along with her parents, several brothers and a sister, three of her children, and other relatives. The inscription reads:

> Famille Vve. Paris
> née Laveau
> Ci-Git
> Marie Philomé Glapion
> décédée le 11 Juin 1897
> Agée de Soixante-deux ans
> Elle fut bonne mère, bonne amie, et
> regrettée par tous ceux qui l'ont connue
> Passant priez pour elle.

(Family of the Widow Paris, born Laveau. Here lies Marie Philomé Glapion, died June 11, 1897, aged sixty-two years. She was a good mother, a good friend, and regretted by all who knew her. Passerby pray for her.)

On September 24, 1897, Philomène's daughter Noëmie Legendre Santenac sold the family home to Clement Dabezies for $1,000.[16] The property had belonged to Marie Laveau's ancestors since 1798 and had sheltered her grandmother, her mother, Marie and her partner Christophe Glapion, their children, grandchildren, and great-grandchildren. With this sale the old St. Ann Street cottage passed out of the Laveau-Glapion family.

* * *

Marie Laveau's descendants began to disperse. After the death of Philomène and the sale of the Laveau-Glapion cottage, Fidelia Legendre Westenberg returned with her German-born husband to St. Louis, where she died of "posterior spinal sclerosis" on December 29, 1898. The death certificate contains some interesting discrepancies and omissions. She was designated as white, her age was declared to be thirty-three when she was actually forty-one, and her date and place of birth and the names and birthplaces of her parents were left blank. Fidelia's identity as an Afro-Creole of Louisiana was apparently being kept secret. The widowed Julius Westenberg continued to live with his daughter Anna, her husband Frank Schmidt, and their children. This branch of the Laveau-Glapion family was absorbed into St. Louis's white German-American community.[17]

An interview with Rose Legendre, the widow of Philomène's son Blaire, led Louisiana Writers' Project fieldworkers to believe that Noëmie Legendre Santenac had also left New Orleans, remarried, and crossed the color line. During the interview, Mrs. Legendre mentioned that her husband's sister Memie had "married a man named Jolly . . . [and] moved to Louisville, Kentucky." When the interviewers attempted to learn more about Memie, Rose and her son Cyril became evasive. Based on photographs of Memie's children, who appeared to be Caucasian, the fieldworkers concluded that Memie was "married to a white man and is passing for white."[18] City directories and census records for Louisville failed to turn up anyone who might be Noëmie Legendre, and she and her descendants vanish from the record.

Alexandre Glapion Legendre remained in New Orleans, where he continued his employment as a game dealer and died of "abscess of the lungs" (probably tuberculosis) on January 7, 1903.[19] His legitimate son, Blaire Manuel Legendre, worked in later years as a carpet cleaner. Of the children that Alexandre fathered with Ernestine L'lado, all but Ernest Legendre, who was employed at a shoe repair shop, disappear from the archival record.

Blaire Legendre, still pursuing the trade of house painter, lived in New Orleans until his death in 1932. His son Cyril, also a painter, left New Orleans for Los Angeles, one of many people of African descent who moved to that city in the 1930s–1950s in search of economic opportunity and racial equality. He died of "consumption" in 1965 and was designated on his death certificate as a Negro.[20]

* * *

The Laveau-Glapion cottage was demolished in 1903. As Helen Pitkin tartly declared in the foreword to *An Angel by Brevet*, "Marie La Veau, long the Voudou Queen, is dead, her hovel in St. Ann Street with its superb votive offerings . . . razed in the new progress. . . . New Orleans is yearning upward . . . but for many years to come the traditions of the Congo . . . will cling to her still, until, mayhap, her noisome marshes are converted into foundations for skyscrapers."[21]

An early twentieth-century double shotgun house—numbers 1020 and 1022—now occupies the place where six generations of Marie Laveau's family once resided. Catherine Dillon conjectured, in her "Voodoo" manuscript, that Marie's cottage still exists, and that the new house was simply added onto the front.[22] It was common practice for an early twentieth-century double shotgun house to be constructed in front of an older Creole cottage that was set further back on the lot, but high fences and adjacent buildings make this impossible to verify in the case of the Laveau-Glapion home.

The site is pointed out as the home of Marie Laveau by tour guides on their way to St. Louis Cemetery No. 1 and Congo Square. Some make it clear that this is not the original house and others do not. On a Spring day I encountered a mule-drawn tourist buggy rounding the corner of St. Ann and Burgundy, and overheard the driver, smartly arrayed in tails and a top hat, announce to his incredulous passengers that "in this cottage lived Marie Laveau, who ruled New Orleans as Queen of the Voudous for a *hundred and forty years*!"

The Second Marie Laveau

According to every present-day teller of the legend, as the original Marie Laveau became incapacitated by old age, she was gradually and secretly replaced by her daughter, "Marie II," creating the illusion that one woman of imperishable beauty reigned as Queen of the Voudous until the turn of the twentieth century. Was there, in fact, a second Marie Laveau who impersonated the Widow Paris as she grew older and succeeded her in the later nineteenth century, or is this simply the invention of popular historians and local-color scribes?

All of the nineteenth-century writers on Voudou recognized the Widow Paris as the one and only Marie Laveau. In the summer of 1869 a local newspaper proclaimed her retirement, saying that the St. John's Eve celebration of that year was "marked by the coronation" of a new queen. In 1870 Marie Laveau, along with Eliza Nicaux and Euphrasie, was said to have been present at the St. John's Eve celebration. In 1872 a journalist—perhaps mistakenly—identified the leader of the St. John's Eve ceremony as Marie Laveau.[1] There were no further reports of public appearances by the Voudou Queen.

The newspapers subsequently named various women as the "ancient queen's" successor. In 1873 it was Mama Caroline. In 1875 the place of honor was occupied by Madame Frazie, possibly the same "Euphrasie" mentioned in 1870. In 1884 Malvina Latour was acknowledged as the queen.[2] Ten years later Henry Castellanos cited Doctor Jim Alexander and the faith healer Don Pedro the Prince of Darkness: "A fellow by the name of Doctor Alexander succeeded [Marie Laveau] in her profession of dupery. . . . [Another] prince of the occult science, styling himself Don Pedro, is now the recognized head of the sect." The *Picayune's Guide to New Orleans* for 1897 and 1900 designated a man called the "Congre Noir" as the leader of the Voudou congregation.[3]

When the Widow Paris died in 1881, her obituaries mentioned one surviving daughter, Marie Philomène Glapion, called Madame Legendre. Nobody, neither Cable, Hearn, Castellanos, nor any of the anonymous newspaper reporters of the 1880s and 1890s, ever suggested that this daughter became the new Voudou Queen. Nevertheless, seeds were sown in the nineteenth century from which the legend of the second Marie Laveau might have germinated.

In addition to commenting on local news in his *Daily City Item* column, Lafcadio Hearn sometimes wrote strange little stories that he labeled "fantastics." One of these, titled "El Vomito" (Yellow Fever), concerns a mother and daughter who have poisoned their Cuban tenant, causing symptoms resembling the dreaded disease. "El Vomito" was cited by Louisiana Writers' Project researcher Marcus Christian as a portrayal of Marie Laveau and her daughter.[4] Hearn describes the mother as a "small and almost grotesque personage, with a somewhat medieval face, oaken colored and long and full of Gothic angularity; only her eyes were young, full of vivacity and keen comprehension." She was a "professed sorceress who told the fortunes of veiled women by the light of a lamp burning before a skull." The daughter was "tall and slight and dark; a skin with the tint of Mexican gold; hair dead black and heavy with snaky ripples that made one think of Medusa; eyes large and of almost sinister brilliancy, heavily shadowed and steady as a falcon's. . . . On her face reigned the motionless beauty of bronze—never a smile or frown." The murder of the tenant presumably gives the two women access to his money, a practice by which they have enriched themselves in the past.[5]

Tales of the Voudou Queen's being succeeded by her daughter might also have been fueled by George Washington Cable's 1886 *Century Magazine* piece, "Creole Slave Songs," in which he said that Marie Laveau was cared for by her only surviving daughter. The accompanying illustration by Edward W. Kemble depicts Marie, the very personification of a sorceress with her snaky white locks, sitting in a rough wooden rocker. A middle-aged woman, presumably Philomène, stands beside her in front of a stone fireplace. This engraving, captioned "The Laveaus, Mother and Daughter," was reproduced in an 1890 *Daily Picayune* article and subsequently reappeared in later publications.[6]

* * *

The notion of a second Marie Laveau surfaced only in the early twentieth century. An article in the November 7, 1915, *New Orleans American* by journalist G. William Nott set the stage for the idea of a younger Marie, characterized by Nott as "a dangerous woman, wicked in the truest sense of the word." Nott was the first to delve into what he called the "musty records" of St. Louis Cathedral, where he found the baptism of Marie Héloïse Glapion, born February 2, 1827, to Marie Laveau and Christophe Glapion. "Being an illegitimate child [she] took her mother's name, Laveau. . . . With the passing of years [her] fame as a dabbler in black magic began to spread." In his 1922 *Times-Picayune* article, "Marie Laveau, Long High Priestess of Voudouism in New Orleans,"

37. Marie Laveau and
her daughter at the
Laveau-Glapion cot-
tage on St. Ann Street.
Illustration by Edward
W. Kemble for George
Washington Cable's
"Creole Slave Songs,"
The Century Magazine,
April 1886, p. 819.
(Author's collection.)

Nott claimed that it was this Marie, not the Widow Paris, who became the Voudou Queen.[7]

In Lyle Saxon's *Fabulous New Orleans* (1928) we first encounter the theory that there were two Marie Laveaus. Both Nott and Saxon cited the February 2, 1827, birth date, but Nott made Marie Heloïse Glapion the *only* Marie Laveau. According to Saxon, however, the Widow Paris was the original "Queen of the Voodoos." She was succeeded by her daughter, also named Marie Laveau, who "as a very young woman [was] known to the police as a worker of black magic. She became officially known as the Voodoo Queen and even today her name is used to frighten children."[8] Zora Neale Hurston, in her 1931 article "Hoodoo in America" and later in *Mules and Men*, hypothesized that there were three

Voudou queens named Marie Laveau: "The first is said to have been a small black Congo woman. The daughter was a mulatto of very handsome body and face. The granddaughter was an octoroon of great beauty." Hurston asserted that "according to the birth records in the St. Louis Cathedral" the third and greatest queen was born February 2, 1827, "the natural daughter of Marie Leveau [*sic*] and Christophe Glapion."[9]

In *The French Quarter* (1936), Herbert Asbury alluded to a daughter named Marie Glapion. Here he confused Marie's older daughter, Marie Heloïse, with her younger daughter, Marie Philomène: "She had a daughter in February 1827—whether by Paris or by Glapion is unknown—who was named Marie and who subsequently married a man named Legendre." Asbury did not infer that this daughter succeeded the original Marie Laveau as Queen of the Voudous.[10]

*   *   *

The twentieth-century belief that the aged Widow Paris was replaced by her daughter could easily be dismissed as journalistic and literary fantasy were it not for the Louisiana Writers' Project interviews, which would be used by Catherine Dillon and Robert Tallant to further the notion of a second Marie Laveau.

We have seen that Marguerite Gitson, Anita Fonvergne, and Alice Zeno, all of whom had lived in the St. Ann Street neighborhood during the 1870s, characterized Marie Laveau as a "wrinkled, shriveled-up lady" with snow-white hair, who "looked like a witch" and was "so old she could hardly walk." These views are consistent with published descriptions of the time. A *Daily Picayune* reporter who saw the Widow Paris in 1875 described her as "bent with age and infirmity." The *Daily States* man who visited on New Year's Eve of 1879 portrayed the ancient Voudou Queen as "pale of face, with grayish-white hair frowzled around her high temples." George Washington Cable wrote in "Creole Slave Songs" that, on his visit to Marie Laveau just before her death, he found her "quaking with feebleness . . . her body bowed, and her wild, gray witch's tresses hanging about her shriveled, yellow neck."[11]

But the "Marie Laveau" known to most of the LWP narrators as a neighbor and spiritual leader was a tall, handsome, energetic middle-aged woman of predominantly European ancestry—she had light skin, Caucasian features, and long, wavy black hair. Everyone commented on her majestic stride, saying that she "walked like she owned the city." She dressed nicely, but not fashionably, wearing the long skirt, over-blouse, and low shoes typical of working women of the nineteenth century. Her only indulgence was her jewelry, upon which many of the interviewees commented. All agreed that this Marie Laveau resided in the Laveau-Glapion cottage on St. Ann Street between Rampart and Burgundy, and that she went about the neighborhood, received clients and held Voudou services at her home and elsewhere in the Creole suburbs, and led the St. John's Eve celebrations at Lake Pontchartrain in the 1870s, 1880s, and even into the 1890s.

Nathan Hobley was born in 1858, the son of plantation slaves who had purchased their freedom before the Civil War. Although Mr. Hobley was old enough to have known the first Marie Laveau, he moved to New Orleans only in 1880, just before the Widow Paris died. The woman he remembered must therefore have been "Marie II": "She attired herself in the simple style of the old Creole Negroes . . . a dress of guinea-blue calico, skirt made very full, a kerchief 'round her neck and a tignon; large hoop earrings of gold, some beads and a brooch. She walked on the streets as unconcerned as any washerwoman, smiling and speaking to those she met. . . . People would stand aside and whisper, 'Here comes Marie Laveau,' and wait until she passed."[12]

According to Charles Raphael, who was born around 1868 and sang at the second Marie Laveau's services in the 1880s, "She was a tall, good-looking woman . . . she might have been mistaken for a South American. She had fine features and straight black hair. . . . She was about fifty or sixty at the time. . . . Marie Laveau was fond of jewelry . . . and wore diamond rings and earrings, a handsome brooch, a diamond horseshoe, and a plain gold bracelet."[13]

John Smith, who had attended the St. John's Eve ceremonies in the early 1880s, was also born in 1868. The younger woman he remembered definitely would have been "Marie II": "When I knew Marie Laveau she was a good-looking woman, about forty-five or fifty. She made plenty of money. She was a neat dresser, always attired in a long blue or white dress. She had fine jewelry and wore it all the time—large diamond earrings, diamond pin, and rings. Her hair was black and it was sort of combed with curls, sometimes she would wear a ribbon bow on the side."[14]

Raymond Rivaros was born about 1873. The Marie Laveau he described could not have been the Widow Paris: "I remember Marie Laveau very well. When I knew her, which was about forty-five years ago [1895] she was a woman of about fifty. She was nice looking, had fine features, and pretty black hair, which she wore hanging when she conducted her services."[15]

James Santana, birth date unknown, had been acquainted with Marie Laveau as a friend and religious leader. He recalled that she was "well-built and could have passed for white. . . . She held her head high and walked straight and proud. She walked on the street every day and had nice ways for everybody. She wore a madras [tignon] on her head."[16]

Josephine Harrison, whose birth date is also unknown, grew up on Chartres Street, a few blocks away from Marie Laveau's house. She told her interviewer that Marie Laveau "always wore a tignon and her dress was like the Creoles wore then. It was a skirt and a long loose shirt like, tied round the waist with strings. . . . Around her neck she wore a kerchief. . . . She was friendly with everybody, white and colored, and she walked very proud like a society lady."[17]

*   *   *

Louisiana Writers' Project employee Catherine Dillon, creator of the unpublished "Voodoo" manuscript, coined the names "Marie I" and "Marie II." Like Lyle Saxon, Dillon assumed that this second Marie Laveau was a daughter of the first. Dillon conjectured that Malvina Latour, the dignified, middle-aged "bright *café au lait* woman . . . of extremely handsome figure" who appeared at the St. John's Eve celebration of 1884, was in fact Marie Laveau's daughter, "Marie II."[18]

Catherine Dillon would have had access to the birth records for both of the Laveau-Glapion daughters, Marie Heloïse Euchariste and Marie Philomène. Dillon was also aware of the affidavits stating that Eloise Euchariste Glapion had died in 1862, but she did not equate Eloise with Heloïse, and wrote as though Eloise Euchariste were yet another of Marie Laveau's daughters. In speaking of "Marie II," Dillon's attention was usually fastened on Heloïse because of her February 2, 1827, birth date. But when Philomène reclaimed the St. Ann Street cottage in 1876 and gave the legal use of it to her mother, Dillon, referring to G. William Nott's article in which Marie was alleged to have acquired her house from a grateful client, remarked that the family home was "not given to Marie Laveau by any man who she had aided, but by her own daughter, who later became her successor."[19]

In *Voodoo in New Orleans*, Robert Tallant elaborated on Catherine Dillon's "Marie I/Marie II" theory: "There is evidence that a dynasty was established in an attempt to pass the rule of the cult from mother to daughter. It seems also to have been a deliberate attempt to found a legend of immortality." Following her "retirement," Tallant tells us, the Widow Paris "entered her home on St. Ann Street and she did not leave it until her death six years later." This marked the emergence of "Marie II," a younger woman who "walked the streets of New Orleans and lived in the St. Ann Street cottage." Sometimes "a passerby told of

having seen a withered crone with yellow skin and wisps of white hair showing from beneath a dingy *tignon* and announced he had seen 'Marie Laveau's
mother.' The neighborhood and the generations were changing, and though
people were well aware of the existence of Marie Laveau, they were forgetting
the Widow Paris."[20]

There were some who disagreed with this hypothesis. LWP researcher Marcus Christian, in the "Voodooism and Mumbo-Jumbo" chapter of his unpublished black history of Louisiana, dismissed the idea of a second Marie Laveau:
"As to the succession of one voodoo practitioner by another, the same conditions seem to have prevailed [in the nineteenth century] that are found . . . today. There were some leaders, some followers, and many contemporaries." Although Zora Neale Hurston herself had earlier advanced the theory that there
were three Marie Laveaus, in her review of *Voodoo in New Orleans*, she fumed
that Tallant's chapters on "the spurious Marie Leveau II [are] both worthless
and wasted, for numerous women sprang up after Marie Leveau to attempt to
profit by her reputation."[21]

Like Catherine Dillon, Tallant would have had access to archival records regarding Marie Heloïse and Marie Philomène. He should have been aware that
Heloïse died in 1862. He also should have known that Philomène Glapion and
Madame Legendre were the same person, yet he referred to the rigidly proper
Madame Legendre as though she were someone else entirely. For narrative purposes Tallant conflated Heloïse and Philomène into one woman called "Marie Glapion," giving her Heloïse's 1827 birth date and Philomène's death date
of 1897. Of the Voudou Queen's successor, Tallant wrote: "This other Marie
[Glapion] was born on February 2, 1827, to Marie I and Christophe Glapion.
Nothing is known of her early life. She was one of the many Glapion children
inhabiting the St. Ann Street cottage, and why or when her mother chose her
for the role she was to play—or whether she chose it for herself—remains a
mystery." Citing the June 11, 1897, inscription on the Widow Paris tomb for the
"good mother and good friend" Marie Philomène Glapion, Tallant maintained
that this is the resting place of the second Marie: "A great many Voodoos accept this vault as the burial place of the Marie Laveau they remember. . . . Most
of them know nothing of [the Widow Paris] and are seeking favors of Marie
II."[22]

To bolster the theory of a second Marie Laveau, Tallant concocted several
bogus "interviews" that have no prototype in the LWP files. According to
Tallant, "Gerald July, a mulatto porter in a New Orleans office building," was
certain there were two women, mother and daughter, called Marie Laveau:

"The mother had about fifteen children and one of them, named Marie, took her place as hoodoo queen. She was a terrible woman—worse than the first." To "Tony Miller," supposedly an "inmate in a home for aged colored people," is attributed the statement that "The daughter lived her mother again." To an elderly white woman, "Miss Annie Ferguson," Tallant assigns the comment, referring to "Marie II," that "Lots of people told me her real name was Marie Glapion and that she had taken her mother's name because her mother had been a famous Voodoo queen." To explain the disappearance of this daughter from the Laveau-Glapion household, Tallant invented an interview with "an old colored woman" called "Virgie Wilson": "Marie Glapion was an outcast from her family. You see, that Madame Legendre, her sister, was so stuck up that she done denied her. She . . . didn't have nobody there but her and her two daughters. They wanted to pass for white."[23]

Some tellers of the Laveau Legend say that "Marie II," assumed to be Marie Heloïse Glapion, left the family home on St. Ann Street and moved into the lakeside cabin known as the Maison Blanche. Catherine Dillon conjectured that Heloïse "lived in the wooden shack near Milneburg" where she gave "soirees to which only white men were admitted." This, wrote Dillon, explains why "many who remember the Voodoo queen from the St. Ann Street cottage recall only the older woman," while those who witnessed the events at the Maison Blanche "remember the younger Marie Laveau." In *Voodoo in New Orleans*, Robert Tallant asserted that "Marie II lived in the Maison Blanche for some years and most of her livelihood was earned by acting as a procuress for white men who wanted . . . quadroon girls."[24]

According to *Voodoo in New Orleans*, "Marie II" subsequently returned to the city and opened a hairdressing establishment. Tallant's inspiration comes from earlier sources. G. William Nott's 1915 *New Orleans American* article espoused the notion that Marie Laveau's daughter—presumably Heloïse—became a hairdresser like her mother, providing her services in a house "a little below the enclosed square in the rear of the St. Louis Cathedral, a block or two nearer Esplanade Avenue. In this old house, years and years ago, Marie Laveau had a rear room where she had her hairdressing parlor and where her aristocratic patrons visited her to obtain charms and advice. . . . Society dames were not infrequent callers [and] she waxed rich at the expense of a gullible public." In 1938 the *Roosevelt Review*, a monthly magazine published by the Roosevelt Hotel for the edification of its guests, featured William McFadden Duffy's article, "Voodoo Queen." Duffy located the alleged hairdressing parlor in the rear room of "an old house with arched windows" at 810 Royal Street between St. Ann and Dumaine. "Many aristocratic ladies, using hairdressing as an excuse, came to Marie to seek advice about private matters and to obtain charms."[25] In actuality, "society dames" and "aristocratic ladies" never went out to have their hair dressed, but were attended in their own homes by a private coiffeuse.

Robert Tallant embellished these stories by Nott and Duffy with more of his invented "interviews." He allegedly learned from an unidentified informant that the woman he called Marie II "opened some sort of hairdressing establishment, the location of which is designated as having been on Royal Street down toward Esplanade." Tallant attributes to "Edna Martin" the statement that "[Marie II] was livin' on Bourbon Street around 1888. She told fortunes and messed wit' a lot of hoodoo stuff." The house was specified to be "the first one in the block from Toulouse Street . . . now a bar. She had living quarters above the downstairs place of business and here she told fortunes and sold gris-gris."[26]

Alternatively, we hear from Ina Fandrich (*Mysterious Voodoo Queen*) that in the 1850s the second Marie Laveau, identified as Marie Heloïse Euchariste Glapion, moved into the house on Love Street donated to her by her mother in 1832, and there she "conducted her own Voodoo business." We do know from newspaper reports of July 12, 1859, that a "regular Voudou concern" was operating in the block of Love Street where Marie Laveau owned property, and that a "notorious hag" called "Marie Clarisse Laveau" was summoned before the recorder's court to account for the "infernal singing and yelling" that so disturbed the neighbors.[27] Heloïse Glapion was never listed in the city directory, and there is no proof that she resided at 207 Love.

* * *

Marie Laveau has been the subject of literary, theatrical, and musical works in which her daughter "Marie II" sometimes plays a prominent role and is sometimes omitted from the plot altogether.

In Robert Tallant's *The Voodoo Queen* it is Philomène, the last of Marie and Christophe's "fifteen children," who succeeds her mother as Queen of the Voudous. Even as a small girl, she plays at making gris-gris, "wrapping shells and bits of dirt in pieces of cloth." Conflict arises when Philomène begs to enter "the work." Marie objects, desiring for her daughter "a husband and children and a home," a "better life" than that of a Voudou priestess. Eventually Philomène leaves the family home to establish her own hairdressing business and Voudou practice on Bourbon Street. She is bitterly disappointed when Marie bypasses her and chooses Malvina Latour to assist on St. John's Eve. On the night of the ceremony, Doctor John is found with his throat cut on Marie's altar at Lake Pontchartrain. Marie is accused of the murder and is saved by Philomène, who identifies the killers to the authorities, finally proving to her mother that she is her true successor.[28]

In Francine Prose's *Marie Laveau*, Marie has only one child, called Ti-Marie, born on February 2, 1827. Marie assumes that this girl, who greatly resembles her, will be her Voudou successor, but Ti-Marie has other ideas. She prefers church, the smell of incense, the taste of communion wafers; she cuts up holy cards and makes paper dolls of the saints; she asks to be enrolled in the Ursuline nuns' school. As she grows up, she wishes only for "a normal life—a good man, a child, mass every morning." It is only with reluctance that she helps Marie with her work. During the annual St. John's Eve Voudou ceremony, Marie and Christophe, along with many of the worshipers, are drowned by a storm on Lake Pontchartrain. Three days later, Ti-Marie appears in public dressed in her mother's customary attire, and Marie's followers believe the Voudou Queen has risen from the dead. Ti-Marie is visited by Jesus, who tells her to continue the magic and healing in his name. She devotes more time to church, to charity, to nursing, to her prison ministry; she speaks more of Jesus and the saints than of the lwa. She ages rapidly—she indeed becomes her mother—and dies on June 15, 1881.[29]

In Jewel Parker Rhodes' *Voodoo Dreams*, Marie's daughter, the fourth to bear the name Marie Laveau, is the result of her sexual and psychological domination by Doctor John. This girl plays no further part in the story, and we learn in the final pages that Marie and her child have been estranged for years.[30]

The plot of Daniel Du Plantis' 1998 play, *Gris-Gris*, revolves around the conflict between "Old Marie," portrayed as an aging dissembler whose "supernatural" powers depend upon the faith of her followers, and her sprightly daughter "Young Marie." Young Marie has no interest in becoming her mother's successor and yearns to flee New Orleans with her white lover. In Wendy Mae Chambers' musical, "Voodoo on the Bayou," the denizens of New Orleans are confused by simultaneous sightings of Marie Laveau and her look-alike daughter: "It sounds like hooey / that something's screwy / that you're a dimwit and I'm a dunce / how could it be that we see Marie / in two places at once?"[31] "Marie II" does not appear as a character in John Carbon's 1983 opera, "Marie Laveau," or in *The Widow Paris*, the 1991 film by Stephen Hank.

* * *

In furthering the legend of the omnipresence and longevity of the Voudou Queen, the creators of fictional, theatrical, and musical works have relied on Saxon's *Fabulous New Orleans*, Asbury's *The French Quarter*, Hurston's *Mules and Men*, and Tallant's *Voodoo in New Orleans*. All have assumed that the Widow Paris was succeeded by the daughter who was born in 1827. Present-day Laveau scholars have had access to the archival record and the files of the Louisiana Writers' Project, but these authors have also concluded that it was Marie Heloïse Euchariste Glapion, born in 1827, who became the second Marie Laveau.

In addition to Marie Heloïse, there are other women who might have assumed leadership of the Voudou congregation in the 1870s–1890s. Let us now look closely at some other possibilities, including Marie Laveau's half-sister, her daughters, and her granddaughters.

* * *

Marie had a younger half-sister, Marie Dolores Laveaux, born January 3, 1804, the legitimate daughter of Charles Laveaux and his wife Françoise Dupart. Marie Dolores married a free man of color named François Auguste with whom she had seven children. Owing to her husband's abusiveness, she eventually obtained a separation of bed and board that granted the return of her personal property, half of the couple's community property, alimony, and child support.[32] Marie Dolores died in Paris on June 22, 1839, at the age of thirty-five. Four months later her body was returned for burial in New Orleans.[33] While Marie Dolores Laveaux could have been a Voudou serviteur, her death in 1839 precludes the possibility of her being her sister's successor.

* * *

Marie Laveau's daughter, Marie Heloïse Euchariste Glapion, born February 2, 1827, is the woman most often identified as "Marie II." She would have been fifty-four when her mother died in 1881 and certainly could have exercised control over the Voudou community until the end of the nineteenth century.

But what of the November 28, 1881, petition of Heloïse's son, Victor Pierre Crocker, to the Civil District Court for possession of her estate? This document states clearly that Eloise Euchariste Glapion "departed life" in 1862. Victor Pierre was only seven years old when his mother died. It was not uncommon for an heir to wait many years before undertaking the legal procedure of opening a succession. Victor Pierre did so only when he wanted to sell the property at 207 Love Street. He was granted ownership one day after filing his petition, and two months later, on January 17, 1882, he sold the lot and house for $450 cash.[34]

Laveau scholar Ina Fandrich did not have access to the full text of Victor Pierre Crocker's petition when she wrote her 1994 dissertation. She was at that time persuaded that Heloïse Glapion had passed away in 1881, a few months after her mother. Based on new evidence available in the original document, Fandrich conceded in her 2005 *Mysterious Voodoo Queen* that Heloïse had died in 1862 and that those who claimed to have attended Marie Laveau's rituals during the later nineteenth century must have seen some other priestess. Fandrich nevertheless continued to name Heloïse as the "second Marie Laveau," stating that when the Widow Paris "retired from her leadership role . . . her [eldest] daughter took over her position as the reigning Queen of the Voodoos. . . . Though being two historical persons, the mythical Marie Laveaux with her legendary power is one figure."[35]

Martha Ward speculated, in her 2004 Laveau biography *Voodoo Queen*, that Heloïse Glapion died sometime after 1874. Ward believes that Victor Pierre Crocker, Philomène Glapion Legendre, and the other witnesses, owing to some agenda of their own, falsely testified to the 1862 death date to cover up "a disappearance or a disgrace. . . . Maybe the circumstances of her demise were so traumatic that family members managed to conceal them—she went crazy and her family locked her away somewhere, she committed suicide, or she moved away, as so many Creoles of color did."[36]

Because Victor Pierre Crocker's 1881 petition does leave some room for doubt, I sought for more concrete verification of Heloïse's death. I looked under any of her possible names—Marie, Heloïse, Eloise, and Euchariste— Glapion, Laveau, and Crocker, and, given the possibility that the family might have remembered the date incorrectly, I searched the years 1860–1880. There was no death certificate in the files of the Louisiana Division of Archives. The newspapers published no funeral notice. I searched the burial records for New Orleans cemeteries, but she was not there. I found nothing in the Charity Hospital Record of Bodies Deceased or the Coroner's Record of Inquests and Views.

While it is possible that Victor Pierre Crocker and the other witnesses gave false testimony before the Civil District Court, it seems more likely that Heloïse actually died in June of 1862. In a time when most people expired at home, it was up to family and friends to report the death to the Board of

Health and the responsibility of the clergy to enter the burial into the cemetery register. Even under normal circumstances many deaths went unrecorded. The summer of 1862 was anything but normal. The nation was embroiled in civil war; New Orleans had fallen to Admiral Farragut that April, and Major General Butler's troops had arrived to occupy the city on the first of May. It comes as no surprise that municipal and church record-keeping were in disarray and that Marie Heloïse Euchariste Glapion's death simply "fell through the cracks." The woman alleged to be "Marie II" does, as Robert Tallant wrote in *Voodoo in New Orleans*, "seem to dissolve slowly into a state of non-existence, as if she had been a ghost or a mirage."[37]

* * *

Could Marie Philomène Glapion, known as Madame Legendre, have been the second Marie Laveau? She indeed fits the description—she is the appropriate age, her beauty and stature are said to have resembled her mother's, and she lived in the Laveau-Glapion home from the 1870s until her death in 1897. On the other hand, both written and oral evidence argue against her having been a Voudou priestess.

Marie Philomène, reacting to the Jim Crow–era conviction that Voudou exemplified the ignorance and superstition of people of African descent, rejected the religion of her ancestors. By the mid-1880s, the St. Ann Street cottage had become a tourist destination, cited in guidebooks like the *Historical Sketch Book* and the *Picayune's Guide to New Orleans*, and the household was besieged by visitors and reporters. Strangers were guaranteed an outburst of indignation from Madame Legendre at the mere suggestion that her mother had been Queen of the Voudous.

Philomène's aversion to Voudou is illustrated by a *Daily Picayune* article of April 11, 1886. The reporter described his visit to Madame Legendre, during which he read to her from Cable's recently published "Creole Slave Songs." Madame Legendre was furious: "What for they say that about [my mother] when she is dead? . . . A great many people could not now hold up their heads so high if she had not been good. What did she know about a snake in a box? Nobody ever see her dance like that paper say. She worshiped God and said her prayers. I did that too until I was too sick, and now I pray at home. It is all a lie from beginning to end."[38]

In the 1890 *Daily Picayune* article "Voudooism—A Chapter of Old New Orleans History" we hear that "Marie Laveau died about nine years ago, a devout Christian and Catholic," and that her surviving daughter "stoutly denies that her mother was ever a Voudoo queen, or had the least connection with the mystic order." Philomène was characterized as a pious woman who "attends mass regularly every morning, and is devoted to orphan children, many of whom she has raised at her own expense. Her reverence for the memory of her mother is beautiful to witness, and she keeps in each chamber of the old home an altar to her memory, upon which lighted candles are continually burning for the repose of her soul."

The *Picayune* also praised Philomène's personal attractiveness. She was, enthused the reporter, "a splendid specimen of womanhood. Her eyes are large, dark, and dreamy, and when lit up by excitement shine with a wonderful light; a mass of snow-white hair crowns her head and she is queenly and majestic in her bearing; she is very gracious to visitors and never tires of speaking of the virtues of her departed mother. She says that she possesses the noblest blood of France in her veins, and from her . . . refinement of manner there is no reason to doubt it." The piece ends by declaring that Madame Legendre "never had any connection" with Voudou, and that she maintained her mother's old home "for the sake of a happy and memorable past."[39]

But by 1900 the *Picayune's Guide to New Orleans* was hinting that Philomène was indeed a Voudou serviteur. Despite the fact that the Laveau-Glapion family had sold the St. Ann Street cottage and moved away after Philomène's death, the *Picayune's Guide* directed visitors to "the ancient home of the famous Voudou queen Marie Laveau" and gave the impression that Marie's daughter was still living there: "There are those who say that the sacred serpent is still guarded as in days of yore in this old house, and that the numerous little children, which [Marie Laveau's daughter] is raising as orphans, are destined to supply the Voudou ranks. Who can tell? To all outward appearances she is good and pious and devoted to the service of God. But somehow the whole place, with its lights, its altars, its relics and superstitious memories, is so full of weird mystery that you are glad to emerge from it into the glorious sunlight."[40]

In a 1937 *Louisiana Historical Quarterly* article, "Old New Orleans Houses," John Kendall also described the "large and dreamy eyes" of Marie Laveau's daughter, but, not satisfied with this complimentary portrayal, went on to say that "they shone with a strange light—a light almost of madness." Then, like the *Picayune's Guide*, Kendall cast doubt on Philomène's apparent rectitude: "Some irreverent persons said that this was merely a 'blind' and a cover for the traffic in spells and charms which daughter no less than mother carried on with much profit."[41]

It is unlikely that Marie Philomène Glapion Legendre was leading a clandestine existence as successor to the Queen of the Voudous. The Louisiana Writers' Project informants distinguished between the proper Catholic matron Madame Legendre and the Voudou priestess they knew as Marie Laveau. They also affirmed that Philomène had no involvement with Voudou. Alice Zeno and Anita Fonvergne both grew up on St. Ann Street and knew the Widow Paris as a neighbor. According to Mrs. Zeno, "[Marie Laveau's] daughter Philomène lived in the house and I know she was no Voodoo. . . . She was a very good and pious woman, always praying for her mother's soul." Anita Fonvergne told her interviewer that "I never heard of any of her daughters doing any kind of 'work,' and [the Widow Paris] is the only Marie Laveau I ever saw." The statement of Martha Grey does imply that Philomène, who "had a heart of gold," dabbled in beneficent magic: "Mrs. Legendre was a sister of Marie Laveau. . . . Her specialty was making novenas for those in trouble, like the spiritualists do today. She had an altar with red lamps."[42]

*   *   *

In addition to Marie Heloïse and Marie Philomène, there are other even less probable candidates. Might Marie Laveau have been succeeded by one of her two older daughters, the issue of her relationship with Jacques Paris? Felicité Paris was born about 1817, before Marie's marriage to Jacques, but was not baptized until 1824. She was designated in the sacramental register as the daughter of "the late Jacques Paris and [Marie] Catherine Lilavoix." Marie Angèlie Paris was born in 1822 and baptized a few months later as the legitimate daughter of Jacques Paris and Marie Laveau. In 1832 Marie Laveau declared herself to be "the childless widow of Jacques Paris," leading one to conclude that both girls died young. But assuming that they *did* outlive their mother, Felicité would have been sixty-four years old and Marie Angèlie fifty-nine when Marie Laveau died in 1881. Either of them would have been the age of the woman described by the LWP interviewees as "Marie Laveau."

We should also consider Marie Laveau's granddaughters. Heloïse had two surviving daughters who were fathered by Pierre Crocker. Both were raised in the Laveau-Glapion household. The eldest, Adelai Aldina Crocker, was born in 1847 and died at the age of twenty-five on September 10, 1871. In addition to the fact that Adelai Aldina is too young to have been the middle-aged priestess described in the LWP interviews, her early death rules her out as the "Marie II" of the 1870s–1890s. The other daughter, Marie Crocker (named for her godmother, Marie Laveau), was born in 1850. She disappears from the archival record after 1860. Assuming she was still alive, this Marie would have been thirty-one when the Widow Paris died in 1881, while the second Marie Laveau was described as being in her fifties or sixties. Philomène's daughters, Fidelia and Noëmie Legendre, were even younger, and are therefore not a possibility.

*   *   *

If "Marie II" indeed existed, and the Louisiana Writers' Project interviews would seem to indicate that she did, she was probably not a daughter or granddaughter of the Widow Paris. Although writers of popular history as well as serious scholars cite Marie Heloïse Euchariste Glapion as the second Marie Laveau, I do not share this opinion. The record of Heloïse's death in 1862 seems reasonably convincing despite the lack of corroborating evidence. Having pondered this question for years, I can only conjecture that the second Marie Laveau, successor to the Queen of the Voudous, must have been some other woman who, although unidentified and undocumented in the archival record, lived in the famous cottage on St. Ann Street during the later decades of the nineteenth century.

Conclusion

As with all legendary villains, heroes, and saints, we have created an imagined Marie Laveau in fulfillment of our own fears and desires. Over the years, from the 1850s until the present, the Laveau Legend has evolved and transmuted with each generation. Influenced by the social and political milieu of the time, attitudes toward Voudou have run the gamut of fear, condemnation, derision, exploitation, tolerance, interest, and reverence. Perceptions of Marie Laveau have cycled from saintly provider to she-devil to mother goddess.

True believers will be more interested in this make-believe Voudou Queen than in the considerably less flamboyant woman revealed in the preceding chapters. Newspaper reporters, popular historians, novelists, tour guides, and the operators of Web sites will continue to tell their personal version of the Laveau Legend. The purpose of this book, however, is to separate legend from reality. I have dissected the newspaper articles, popular histories, and fiction of the nineteenth and twentieth centuries; analyzed the narratives of Louisiana Writers' Project interviewees who lived during Marie Laveau's own lifetime; and ferreted out the dry facts of Marie's life as a citizen of New Orleans from the archival record.

Some elements of the Laveau Legend can be debunked as pure fantasy, some cannot be verified or refuted, and some are true. Additional information has also come to light, backed by solid evidence from the sacramental registers of the Roman Catholic church; notarial records of property transactions, wills, and successions; civil certificates of births, marriages, and deaths; city directories; and the census.

Marie Laveau's foremothers did not come from Saint Domingue as the legend relates, and we have no idea whether any of them were Voudou serviteurs. Her maternal great-grandmother, Marguerite, was the slave of the white New Orleans Creole Henry Roche *dit* Belaire. Her grandmother, Catherine, grew up enslaved in the Roche household. After passing through the hands of two subsequent owners, Catherine was sold to the free woman of color Françoise Pomet, from whom she purchased her freedom in 1795. Following her liberation, Catherine adopted the surname Henry. She was listed in the city directories as a marchande, and notarial documents show that she bought a lot on St. Ann Street and erected the cottage that became famous as the home of Marie Laveau. Marie's mother, also named Marguerite, was born a slave in the home of Henry Roche. She was manumitted from slavery by a second owner in 1790. Marguerite later became the concubine of the Frenchman Henri D'Arcantel and took his surname. Sacramental and notarial records show that she had four children with D'Arcantel and that in his will of 1817 he left a bequest to Marguerite and their two surviving offspring.

Contrary to the legend, Marie Laveau was not the daughter of a wealthy white planter. Despite her mother's long-term relationship with Henri D'Arcantel, the future Voudou Queen was fathered by Charles Laveaux, a well-to-do free man of color. A quantity of evidence indicates that Marie Laveau was born in 1801, but we cannot say with certainty that the 1801 baptismal record for the free mulatto girl named Marie is hers. She was likely raised in the home of her grandmother on St. Ann Street, but this cannot be proven.

The legend of Marie Laveau's marriage to the carpenter Jacques Paris, a free quadroon from Saint Domingue, is supported by archival evidence. The wedding was indeed solemnized at St. Louis Cathedral by Père Antoine on August 4, 1819. Marie and Jacques did not remain childless, as we have been led to believe, but were the parents of two daughters named Felicité and Marie Angèlie Paris. As the legend maintains, Marie's husband vanished a few years after their marriage, and she was thereafter referred to in official documents as "the widow of Jacques Paris." Whether Paris died or simply deserted his wife remains unknown.

Marie subsequently formed a conjugal relationship with Christophe Duminy de Glapion. Glapion was not, as is widely believed, a free man of color from Saint Domingue. He was a white native of Louisiana and the descendant of a noble French family, making legal marriage between Marie and Christophe impossible because of Louisiana's antimiscegenation laws. The legend correctly depicts Glapion as a veteran of the Battle of New Orleans. He was not, however, a captain in the colored battalion of Men of Santo Domingo, but a private in the all-white Cavellier's Second Regiment of Louisiana Militia.

The legendary fifteen children born to Marie and her domestic partner is an exaggeration. The baptisms and funerals of three daughters and four sons are recorded in the sacramental registers of St. Louis Cathedral. Of these seven children, only Marie Heloïse Euchariste and Marie Philomène survived to adulthood.

The notion that Marie Laveau learned the secrets of elite families through her profession as a hairdresser cannot be proved or disproved. City directory and census listings never specified Marie's occupation, but it is entirely possible that she, like many free woman of color, pursued this career.

Marie did not, as the legend says, acquire her home on St. Ann Street by means of a Voudou spell. Christophe Glapion bought the cottage in 1832 from the succession of Marie's maternal grandmother. While Marie is usually depicted as rich and powerful, this is not borne out by the archival record. With the exception of a lot given to her by her father at the time of her marriage to Jacques Paris, she owned no real estate. There is no indication that she exercised unprecedented influence over police and city officials. After Glapion's death in 1855, the family home was seized for debt and sold at auction, and Marie and her daughters and grandchildren were only allowed to remain in residence through the kindness of the new owner. In 1874 she was forced by poverty to use subterfuge in an attempt to secure Glapion's military pension and bounty land.

Marie Laveau died in 1881. She was not ninety-eight years old, as the legend tells us, but was a few months short of her eightieth birthday. Cemetery records prove that she was interred in the "Widow Paris" tomb in St. Louis Cemetery No. 1. The legend that her remains rest in the "Wishing Vault" in St. Louis Cemetery No. 2 is unfounded. Her older daughter, Marie Heloïse, is stated to have died in 1862, although the lack of a death record casts some uncertainty on this date. Her younger daughter, Marie Philomène, died in 1897. It is unlikely that either of these women became the successor to the Voudou Queen known as "Marie II."

Unfortunately, there exists no verifiable record of Marie Laveau's role as a Voudou priestess, and it has been necessary to reconstruct this essential aspect of her story from newspaper accounts and the Louisiana Writers' Project narratives. During the 1830s and 1840s, when Marie would have been coming into power, her name never appeared in the New Orleans newspapers. She was mentioned once as the "head of the Voudou women" in 1850, and in 1859 she was accused of maintaining a "noisy and disorderly" Voudou meeting place in the Faubourg Marigny. Ten years later, one newspaper announced her retirement. Although journalistic coverage of Voudou was frequent during the 1870s, reporters who sought Marie Laveau at the St. John's Eve observances on Lake Pontchartrain were usually disappointed. The LWP interviews do provide credible descriptions of Voudou ceremonies, but most of the informants were too young to have remembered the original Marie Laveau and are presumably speaking of "Marie II."

The true character of Marie Laveau likewise remains elusive—was she the healer and philanthropist portrayed by the 1881 obituaries, the cunning fraud and procuress described by Henry Castellanos, the sexually alluring sorceress depicted by earlier twentieth-century writers, or the feminist religious leader and antislavery activist conceived of by recent scholars?

The numerous factual inaccuracies in the 1881 obituaries and remembrances could easily lead one to dismiss them altogether. But unless the reporters for three New Orleans newspapers and the *New York Times* were being fed dis-information by Marie Philomène—or were indulging in unwarranted flights of imagination—why should we not believe that Marie Laveau was kind and charitable? It is entirely plausible that she possessed knowledge of herbal medi-cine and used it to nurse the victims of yellow fever and cholera. Archival docu-ments prove that between 1850 and 1860 Marie posted bond for several free women of color accused of minor crimes, and that in 1852 she sponsored the education of an orphaned boy referred to as her protégée. If the *Daily Picayune* of 1871 is to be believed, she did minister to condemned men at the Parish Prison. In newspaper interviews from 1886 and 1890 Marie Philomène praised her mother's goodness, claiming that Marie Laveau devoted her entire life to aiding the poor, the homeless, and the orphaned.

Kindness and charity, however, are not synonymous with public activism, and if Marie Laveau was indeed a leader of New Orleans' people of African descent, her role was performed behind the scenes. Neither the archival re-cord nor the newspapers document such acts of leadership, in contrast with the accomplishments of the African-born former slave Marie Justine Cou-vent, who endowed the Catholic Institution for Indigent Orphans; the Afro-Creole philanthropist Thomy Lafon; the free woman of color Henriette Del-ille, foundress of the Sisters of the Holy Family; or even the Voudou priestess Betsy Toledano, who during the summer of 1850, when police repeatedly raid-ed Voudou ceremonies and arrested the participants, went to court to protest the persecution of those engaged in valid religious observances.

The claim by present-day scholars that Marie Laveau was a vigorous oppo-nent of slavery, racism, and segregation has no basis in fact. Notarial documents show that she and Christophe Glapion behaved like many New Orleanians of the antebellum period and that together they bought and sold eight slaves and freed none of them. Two of these slaves were designated as *statu liber*, but in each case this promise of freedom was not conferred by Marie or Christophe but by the slave's former owner. We cannot know if Marie treated her slaves with indulgence or severity, and we have no inkling of her position on the "race question" before, during, or after the Civil War—whether she supported or op-posed secession from the Union and was appalled or gratified when slavery was abolished. The 1881 *Daily Picayune* obituary includes the curious statement that "during the late rebellion she proved her loyalty to the South . . . and fully dispensed help to those who suffered in defense of the lost cause."

Our present understanding of the Voudou religion enables us to see no conflict between the Marie Laveau who appears in the sacramental registers of St. Louis Cathedral as bride, mother, and godmother and was buried with the full rites of the Roman Catholic Church and the Marie Laveau who was Queen of the Voudous. Her fame endures as her legend continues to evolve. Now, in the twenty-first century, those who are devoted to Marie Laveau as a spiritual leader accord her the honor of a Voudou deity.

What we can piece together from the published sources and oral histories is a silhouette of Marie Laveau, her mere outline, lacking all the detail and color of a real portrait. Tantalizingly incomplete, she is perhaps even more magnetic than she would be if fully known. Her enigma tempts us to shape her to our will, and her image has evolved over time in response to the shifting prejudices, fantasies, and desires of those who look for her. As a mirror, Marie tells us more about the era from which she is observed than she does about herself. She remains untouched and unknown, secure in her enduring aura of mystery.[1]

Appendix

The Louisiana Writers' Project Informants

Between 1936 and 1941, LWP fieldworkers interviewed seventy elderly New Orleanians on the topics of Marie Laveau and Voudou. The forty-seven informants listed below provided the most complete and believable accounts. Although some of these individuals are not quoted directly, their statements nevertheless influenced the writing of this book. Space considerations and the flow of the narrative necessitated omission of much of the rich detail and range of topics contained in the LWP interviews. Those wishing to read the interviews in their entirety may order copies from the Cammie G. Henry Research Center at the Northwestern State University Library in Natchitoches, Louisiana.

*   *   *

Alfred, Joseph. Age 85, born ca. 1855
Address at time of interview: Thomy Lafon Old Folks Home, 1125 North Tonti. Interviewed by Robert McKinney, n.d. Relationship with Marie Laveau: neighbor. Witnessed a St. John's Eve celebration but did not participate. Provided information on personal appearance, clients, services, St. John's Eve. Parts of this interview are attributed to Howard LeBreton in *Voodoo in New Orleans*, 27–28.

*   *   *

Augustin, Alexander. Age ?, born ?
Address at time of interview: Sere Street, near Gibson. Interviewed by Henriette Michinard, May 16, 1940; June 1940; July 1940; August 2, 9, 15, and 22, 1940. Relationship with Marie Laveau: friend, co-worker. Provided information on Marie Sallopé, Doctor Jim Alexander, Maison Blanche, funeral, tomb. Parts of this interview are attributed to "August Augustine" in *Voodoo in New Orleans*, 126.

*   *   *

Brown, Marie. Age ?, born ?
Address at time of interview: 1012 St. Philip. Interviewed by Zoe Posey, December 13, 1939 and April 14, 1941. Relationship with Marie Laveau: neighbor

—grew up on St. Philip Street between Rampart and Burgundy. Provided information on personal appearance, family, Congo Square, prostitution, near-drowning incident, funeral, tomb. Parts of this interview are attributed to "Adele Brown" in *Voodoo in New Orleans*, 95–97, 139–40, where she is also quoted under her own name, 139–40.

* * *

Butler, Mary Louise. Age ?, born ?
Address at time of interview: Avery Island. Interviewed by Catherine Dillon, November 27, 1939. Relationship with Marie Laveau: none. Provided information on near-drowning incident, tomb. Parts of this interview are attributed to "Doris Gibson" in *Voodoo in New Orleans*, 123–24.

* * *

Camille, Harrison. Age ?, born ?
Address at time of interview: Spanish Fort. Interviewed by Maude Wallace, January 9 and 11, 1940. Relationship with Marie Laveau: none. Provided information on personal appearance, St. John's Eve, near-drowning incident.

* * *

Cruz, Ayola. Age ?, born ?
Address at time of interview: 718 Esplanade; sexton of St. Louis Cemetery No. 1. Interviewed by Maude Wallace, March 15, 1940, and by Hazel Breaux and Jacques Villere, n.d. Relationship with Marie Laveau: none. Provided information on tomb.

* * *

Dauphine, Mrs. Age ?, born ?
Address at time of interview: 2304 London Avenue. No interviewer (possibly Henriette Michinard), n.d. Relationship with Marie Laveau: none. Provided information on family, charitable works, Congo Square, near-drowning incident.

* * *

Dédé, Marie. Age 74, born 1866
Address at time of interview: 2618 Banks Street. Interviewed by Robert McKinney, n.d. Relationship with Marie Laveau: neighbor, family friend—grew up on St. Peter near Rampart. Provided information on personal appearance, family, house, Choctaw women, gris-gris, services, Doctor Jim Alexander, St.

John's Eve, near-drowning incident, funeral, tomb. Parts of this interview are attributed to "Annie Ferguson," "Mrs. Dixon," and "Jennie Collins" in *Voodoo in New Orleans*, 90, 103–4, 105.

* * *

Delavigne, Mimi. Age ?, born ?
Address at time of interview: unrecorded. Interviewed by Henriette Michinard, December 13, 1939. Relationship with Marie Laveau: neighbor—grew up corner St. Peter and Rampart. Provided information on gris-gris, services. Parts of this interview are attributed to "an anonymous white woman" and parts to "Annie Ferguson" in *Voodoo in New Orleans*, 62–63, 89–90.

* * *

Eugene, Aileen. Age ?, born ?
Address at time of interview: 1919 North Prieur/1805 London Avenue. No interviewer, n.d. Relationship with Marie Laveau: none. Provided information on tomb.

* * *

Felix, Oscar. Age 72, born 1868
Address at time of interview: 1220 South Prieur. Interviewed by Hazel Breaux and Robert McKinney, October 22 and December 5 and 9, 1936, others n.d.; interviewed by Edmund Burke, March 14, 1940. Relationship with Marie Laveau: neighbor, friend—grew up on Dumaine Street between Burgundy and Dauphine, sang for Marie Laveau's services from the mid-1870s until 1884. Provided information on personal appearance, house, services, Congo Square, St. John's Eve, near-drowning incident, funeral, tomb. Parts of this interview are attributed to "Joe Goodness" in *Voodoo in New Orleans*, 16–18.

* * *

Fontenette, Octavia. Age 86, born 1854
Address at time of interview: 4615 Camp Street. Interviewed by Edmund Burke, March 11, 1940. Relationship with Marie Laveau: neighbor, family friend—grew up on St. Ann Street. Provided information on personal appearance, family.

* * *

Fonvergne, Anita. Age 79, born 1860
Address at time of interview: 1612 St. Philip. Interviewed by Hazel Breaux,

April 13 and 17, 1939. Relationship with Marie Laveau: neighbor—grew up on St. Ann Street. Provided information on personal appearance, house.

* * *

Fritz, Eugene. Age ?, born ?
Address at time of interview: Thomy Lafon Old Folks Home, 1125 North Tonit. Interviewed by Robert McKinney, n.d. Relationship with Marie Laveau: none. Witnessed a St. John's Eve celebration but did not participate. Provided information on Congo Square, St. John's Eve, prostitution. Parts of this interview are attributed to "Tom Bragg" in *Voodoo in New Orleans*, 57.

* * *

Gitson, Marguerite. Age 87, born 1854
Address at time of interview: 1128 Burgundy. Interviewed by Zoe Posey, February 20, 1941. Relationship with Marie Laveau: neighbor—grew up on St. Ann Street. Provided information on personal appearance.

* * *

Gray, Martha. Age ?, born ?
Address at time of interview: unrecorded. Interviewed by Henriette Michinard, n.d. Relationship with Marie Laveau: neighbor—grew up on St. Ann near Roman. Provided information on family.

* * *

Harrison, Josephine. Age ?, born ?
Address at time of interview: 1500 Peoples Avenue. Interviewed by Zoe Posey, July 14, 1939. Relationship with Marie Laveau: neighbor. Provided information on personal appearance, family, tomb. Parts of this interview are attributed to "Jimmie St. Clare" in *Voodoo in New Orleans*, 129–30.

* * *

Hobley, Nathan. Age 82, born 1858
Address at time of interview: 2831 St. Philip. Interviewed by Zoe Posey, October 25, 1940, and January and April 4, 1941. Relationship with Marie Laveau: friend. Provided information on personal appearance, financial situation, grisgris, Doctor John, Doctor Jim Alexander, death, funeral, tomb. Tallant used Hobley's own name in *Voodoo in New Orleans*, 108–12, and also attributed parts of this interview to "Nathan Barnes," 35–36, and to "Clare Scott," 138.

* * *

Hopkins, Laura. Age 62, born 1878
Address at time of interview: 1508 North Roman. Interviewed by Maude Wallace, February 9, 16, and 21, March 4 and 7, and April 1940; Henriette Michinard, April, 1940; Robert McKinney, n.d. Relationship with Marie Laveau: neighbor, friend, pupil—grew up on Burgundy Street between Orleans and St. Ann. Provided information on house, gris-gris, co-workers, St. John's Eve, near-drowning incident, funeral, tomb. Tallant calls Laura Hopkins by her nickname, "Lala," in *Voodoo in New Orleans* and attributes parts of this interview to "Clare Scott," 136–38.

* * *

Hunt, Cecile. Age 74, born 1866
Address at time of interview: Jackson and Dryades. Interviewed by Zoe Posey, November 6, 1940. Relationship with Marie Laveau: neighbor. Provided information on gris-gris, co-workers.

* * *

Jefferson, Alberta. Age 68, born 1869
Address at time of interview: 2406 St. Louis. Interviewed by Hazel Breaux and Robert McKinney, April 27, 1937. Relationship with Marie Laveau: neighbor—grew up around the corner from Marie Laveau; family opposed to her being interviewed. Provided information on personal appearance.

* * *

Johnson, St. Ann. Age 75, born 1865
Address at time of interview: Pailet Lane. Interviewed by Maude Wallace, February 8, 1940. Relationship with Marie Laveau: neighbor. Provided information on snakes.

* * *

Jones, Josephine. Age ?, born ?
Address at time of interview: 1716 St. Philip. Interviewed by Robert McKinney, n.d. Relationship with Marie Laveau: none. Provided information on gris-gris.

* * *

Justine, Marie. Age ?, born ?
No interviewer, n.d.; quoted in Dillon, "Voodoo/Marie the Mysterious," section 7, p. 14, LWP folder 317. Relationship with Marie Laveau: none. Provided information on clients.

* * *

Kavanaugh, Theresa. Age 80, born ca. 1860
Address at time of interview: 1137 North Villere. Interviewed by Zoe Posey, n.d. Relationship with Marie Laveau: none. Provided information on personal appearance, hairdresser story, Congo Square, Doctor Jim Alexander, tomb.

* * *

Labat, Emile. Age ?, born ?
Address at time of interview: 1615 St. Philip. Interviewed by Zoe Posey, December 5, 1940. Relationship with Marie Laveau: undertaker. Provided information on funeral, tomb.

* * *

Landry, Joe. Age ?, born ?
Address at time of interview: 1509 St. Ann. Interviewed by Zoe Posey, July 18, 1939. Relationship with Marie Laveau: neighbor—grew up on St. Ann Street between Villere and Robertson. Provided information on gris-gris, co-workers.

* * *

Laveaux, Louis. Age 67, born 1872
Address at time of interview: 331 North Derbigny. Interviewed by Zoe Posey, August 15, 1939. Relationship with Marie Laveau: grandnephew; his grandfather was Marie's half brother, Laurent Charles Laveaux. Provided information on family. Parts of this interview are attributed to "Octave Labeau" in *Voodoo in New Orleans*, 135.

* * *

Legendre, Rose. Age: 72, born: ca. 1868
Address at time of interview: 1619 North Laharpe/2716 Havana. Interviewed by Hazel Breaux and Jacques Villere, n.d.; interviewed by Maude Wallace, March 20, 1940. Relationship with Marie Laveau: widow of grandson, Blaire Legendre. Provided information on personal appearance, family.

* * *

Martin, Marie. Age 76, born 1864
Address at time of interview: London Avenue. Interviewed by Henriette
Michinard, August 19, 1940. Relationship with Marie Laveau: none. Provided
information on near-drowning incident.

* * *

Maury, Cecilia. Age 85, born 1855
Address at time of interview: 2426 Havana Street. Interviewed by Henriette
Michinard, August 1940. Relationship with Marie Laveau: none. Owned a
cabin on Lake Pontchartrain between Spanish Fort and Milneburg. Provide
information on near-drowning incident.

* * *

McDuffy, Josephine. Age 87, born 1853
Address at time of interview: unrecorded. Interviewed by Henriette Michi-
nard, 1940. Relationship with Marie Laveau: none. Provided information on
St. John's Eve. Parts of this interview are attributed to "Josephine Green" in
Voodoo in New Orleans, 57–58.

* * *

Mendoza, Mathilda. Age 76, born 1864
Address at time of interview: Spanish Fort. Interviewed by Maude Wallace,
January 11 and 17, 1940. Relationship with Marie Laveau: none. Provided in-
formation on St. John's Eve. Parts of this interview are attributed to "Mattie
O'Hara" in *Voodoo in New Orleans,* 82–83.

* * *

Moore, William. Age 76, born 1864
Address at time of interview: 2019 Lapeyrouse. Interviewed by Edmund
Burke, March 1, 1940. Relationship with Marie Laveau: friend, participated in
St. John's Eve celebrations. Provided information on St. John's Eve.

* * *

Morris, Joseph. Age 72, born 1868
Address at time of interview: 803 North Claiborne. Interviewed by Edmund
Burke, March 26, 1940. Relationship with Marie Laveau: neighbor—grew up

on St. Ann between Marais and Villere. Provided information on personal appearance, family, Congo Square.

* * *

Nelson, George. Age ?, born ?
Address at time of interview: 4032 Flood Street. No interviewer, n.d. Relationship with Marie Laveau: none. Provided information on gris-gris, charitable works.

* * *

Nichols, Henrietta. Age 78, born 1862
Address at time of interview: Milneberg. No interviewer, March 19, 1940. Relationship with Marie Laveau: none. Provided information on St. John's Eve.

* * *

"Pops." Age 81, born ca. 1859
Address at time of interview: 4804 Calliope. Interviewed by Robert McKinney, n.d. Relationship with Marie Laveau: attended St. John's Eve celebrations. Provided information on St. John's Eve. Parts of this interview are attributed to Howard LeBreton in *Voodoo in New Orleans*, 27.

* * *

Raphael, Charles. Age 72, born ca. 1868
Address at time of interview: Derbigny between Dumaine and St. Philip. Interviewed by Hazel Breaux and Jacques Villere, n.d. Relationship with Marie Laveau: neighbor, friend—grew up in the house he now occupies; sang for Marie Laveau's services in early 1880s. Provided information on personal appearance, family, gris-gris, services, co-workers, Doctor Jim Alexander, St. John's Eve, tomb. Parts of this interview are attributed to "Gerald July," "Tony Miller," and "Raoul Desfrene" in *Voodoo in New Orleans*, 61, 76, 77–79.

* * *

Rey, Sophie. Age ?, born ?
Address at time of interview: unrecorded. Interviewed by Zoe Posey, December 13, 1939. Relationship with Marie Laveau: none. Provided information on tomb.

* * *

Richard, Mary. Age: 72, born: 1869
Address at time of interview: 1013 Royal. Interviewed by Zoe Posey, April 25, 1941. Relationship with Marie Laveau: family friend. Provided information on personal appearance, house, family, clients, gris-gris, near-drowning incident. Parts of this interview are attributed to "Myrtle Rose White" in *Voodoo in New Orleans*, 123.

* * *

Rivaros, Raymond. Age 64, born ca. 1873
Address at time of interview: Thomy Lafon Old Folks Home, 1125 North Tonti. Interviewed by Hazel Breaux, n.d. Relationship with Marie Laveau: friend. Former sexton at St. Louis Cemetery No. 2. Provided information on personal appearance, gris-gris, altars, services, Congo Square, St. John's Eve, prostitution, tomb.

* * *

Santana, James. Age ?, born ?
Address at time of interview: 5300 Peoples Avenue. Interviewed by Zoe Posey, July 10, 1939. Relationship with Marie Laveau: friend. Provided information on personal appearance, house, gris-gris, co-workers, St. John's Eve, tomb.

* * *

Slater, John. Age ?, born ?
Address at time of interview: 916 Marais Street. Interviewed by Cecile Wright, n.d. Relationship with Marie Laveau: none. Provided information on gris-gris, co-workers, tomb. Parts of this interview are attributed to "Octave Labeau" in *Voodoo in New Orleans*, 135.

* * *

Smith, John. Age 72, born ca. 1868
Address at time of interview: Spanish Fort. Interviewed by Hazel Breaux, n.d. Relationship with Marie Laveau: friend—attended celebrations at Maison Blanche. Provided information on personal appearance, Doctor Jim Alexander, St. John's Eve, Maison Blanche, prostitution. Parts of this interview are attributed to "a white man in downtown New Orleans" and "a restauranteur at a present-day resort near the lake" in *Voodoo in New Orleans*, 85–86.

* * *

Thomas, Virginia. Age ?, born ?
Address at time of interview: 1512 Governor Nicholls Street. Interview by Zoe
Posey, December 19, 1939. Relationship with Marie Laveau: none. Provided
information on tomb.

* * *

Washington, Mary. Age 75, born 1863
Address at time of interview: 1247 North Claiborne. Interviewed by Robert
McKinney, n.d. Relationship with Marie Laveau: neighbor, friend, pupil. Pro-
vided information on personal appearance, hairdresser story, family, house,
Choctaw women, co-workers, gris-gris, Doctor John, Doctor Jim Alexander,
St. John's Eve, prostitution, near-drowning incident. Parts of this interview
are attributed to "Mary Ellis" and "Louise Walters" in *Voodoo in New Orleans*,
103, 124–25.

* * *

Zeno, Alice. Age 73, born 1867
Address at time of interview: 920 North Johnson. Interviewed by Hazel
Breaux, n.d. Relationship with Marie Laveau: neighbor—grew up on St. Ann
Street. Provided information on personal appearance, near-drowning incident.
Parts of this interview are attributed to "Alice Reno" in *Voodoo in New Orleans*,
123.

Notes

ABBREVIATIONS

AA   Archives of the Archdiocese of New Orleans
COB   Conveyance Office Book, Conveyance Office, Civil District Court Build-
          ing, New Orleans
ED   Census Enumeration District
THNOC   The Historic New Orleans Collection, Williams Research Center
LSM/HC   Louisiana State Museum Historical Center, Old Mint Building, New Or-
          leans
LDA   Louisiana Division of Archives, Records Management, and History, Baton
          Rouge
LWP   Louisiana Writers' Project, Cammie G. Henry Research Center, Federal
          Writers' Collection, Watson Memorial Library, Northwestern State Uni-
          versity of Louisiana at Natchitoches
NARC   Notarial Archives Research Center, New Orleans
NARA   National Archives and Records Administration, Washington, D.C.
NOPL   City Archives, Louisiana Division, New Orleans Public Library
SLC   St. Louis Cathedral, New Orleans
S/FPC   Slaves and Free Persons of Color

Translations of French and Spanish documents are by the author unless otherwise noted. All newspapers cited are from New Orleans unless another city is specified.

PROLOGUE: THE "LAVEAU LEGEND" IN PRINT AND PERFORMANCE

1. "Death of Marie Laveau—A Woman with a Wonderful History, Almost a Century Old, Carried to the Tomb Thursday Morning," *Daily Picayune*, June 17, 1881, p.
8, c. 3. "Wayside Notes—The Death of Marie Laveau," *Daily City Item*, June 17, 1881,
p. 1, c. 5. The only surviving copy of the *Daily City Item* for this date is housed in Special Collections, Howard-Tilton Memorial Library, Tulane University; it has not been
microfilmed, but is reprinted in Starr, ed., *Inventing New Orleans*, 70–72, where it is
attributed to Lafcadio Hearn.

2. "Recollections of a Visit on New Years' Eve to Marie Laveau, the Ex-Queen of the
Voudous," *Daily States*, June 17, 1881, p. 3, c. 3.

3. "Marie Lavaux—Death of the Queen of the Voudous Just Before St. John's Eve,"
Democrat, June 17, 1881, p. 8, c. 2.

4. "A Sainted Woman," *Democrat*, June 18, 1881, p. 2, c. 1.

5. "Voudou Vagaries—The Spirit of Marie Laveau to be Propitiated by Midnight
Orgies on the Bayou," *Times*, June 23, 1881, p. 7, c. 4. See also "The Voudous—What a
Times Man Saw Last Night," *Times*, June 24, 1881, p. 7, c. 4.

6. "The Departed Voudou Queen," *Times*, June 24, 1881, p. 3, c. 2; the original interview with "Doctor Bass" could not be found in the *New York Sun* and may have been a fabrication. "Voudouism—Charms of Wonderful Efficacy Compounded of Snakes, Toads, Frogs, Cats' Ears and Lizards' Eyes," *Daily States*, August 26, 1881, p. 4, c. 1–2. This article was supposedly reprinted from the *New York Star*, a newspaper that did not exist.

7. "The Dead Voudou Queen," *New York Times*, June 23, 1881, p. 2, c. 3–4.

8. Jordan and de Caro, "Race, Class, Identity, and Folklore Studies in Louisiana," 38–42.

9. Cable's view on white Creoles who believed in Voudou is from "Creole Slave Songs," 820. The derogatory pamphlet is believed to have been written by the poet/priest Adrien Roquette. For more on Cable, see Tinker, "Cable and the Creoles," *American Literature* 5, 313–26; Turner, *George W. Cable*, 102, 222–23; Tregle, "Creoles and Americans," 174–80.

10. Cable, *The Grandissimes*, 57, 60. In an 1881 letter quoted in Turner's biography (231 n. 9), Cable denied that Marie Laveau was the model for Palmyre.

11. Cable, "Creole Slave Songs," 807–28.

12. Tinker, *Lafcadio Hearn's American Days*, 26–28, 128–32.

13. Murray, *Fantastic Journey*, 307, quoting the *Cincinnati Enquirer*, the *Kansas City Journal*, and the *New York Sun* of July 27, 1906, 4.

14. Kennard, *Lafcadio Hearn*, 85–86.

15. Tinker, *Lafcadio Hearn's American Days*, 132–37; Cott, *Wandering Ghost*, 145–47.

16. Castellanos, "The Voudous: Their History, Mysteries, and Practices," *Times-Democrat*, June 24, 1894, p. 18, c. 3–5; *New Orleans As It Was*, 90–101.

17. *Historical Sketch Book*, 66. According to the introduction, the *Historical Sketch Book* was "edited and compiled by eminent historians, *litterateurs*, and journalists," including Charles Gayarré, Alexander Dimitry, Lafcadio Hearn, and others less well known. *Picayune's Guide to New Orleans* for 1900, 65–67.

18. See Seabrook, *The Magic Island*; Wirkus, *The White King of La Gonave*; Craige, *Black Bagdad* and *Cannibal Cousins*; and Loederer, *Voodoo Fire in Haiti*. For a scholarly account of this period in American history, see Renda, *Taking Haiti*.

19. Nott's *New Orleans American* article of November 7, 1915, is quoted in Catherine Dillon's "Voodoo" manuscript (Chapter 11, "Marie the Mysterious," section 1, p. 3, LWP folder 317), but no copy of the newspaper has been preserved. Nott, "Marie Laveau, Long High Priestess of Voudouism in New Orleans," *Times-Picayune* Sunday magazine, November 19, 1922, p. 2.

20. Saxon, *Fabulous New Orleans*, 243. Information on Lyle Saxon from Jordan and de Caro, "Race, Class, Identity, and Folklore Studies in Louisiana" and from Harvey, *Life and Selected Letters of Lyle Saxon*.

21. Asbury, *The French Quarter*, 254–83. Asbury's four-month stay in New Orleans was described in "Pulp Nonfiction," a December 20, 2002, *Gambit Weekly* article inspired by the release of a motion picture version of *Gangs of New York*.

22. Zora Neale Hurston to Langston Hughes, August 6, 1928, in Kaplan, ed., *Zora Neale Hurston: A Life in Letters*, 124; see also Hurston to Hughes, September 20, 1928 (126), October 15, 1928 (127), November 22, 1928 (131), and December 10, 1929 (155). Hurston's account notebook, May 3, 1930, Alain Locke Papers, box 164–99, folder 8, Moreland-Springarn Research Center, Howard University, Washington, D.C.

23. Hurston, "Hoodoo in America," 320–414; *Mules and Men*, 183–285. The spiritual professionals represented in Hurston's published works may have been a composite of various individuals with whom she studied. She called her mentors by different names in the two published versions of her New Orleans fieldwork, and definitely stated that she "substituted other names for the real ones in *Mules and Men*" (Review of Robert Tallant's *Voodoo in New Orleans*, 436–38).

24. Lyle Saxon sent cartons of LWP files to Melrose Plantation in Natchitoches, Louisiana, where his friend Cammie Henry maintained a haven for writers and artists. The LWP collection remained at Melrose until 1970, when it was donated by Mrs. Henry's descendants to the Watson Memorial Library at Northwestern State University in Natchitoches.

25. Holdredge, *Mammy Pleasant*, 26–29, 72–73, 75, 77–78, 176–77. Compare with Tallant, *Voodoo in New Orleans*, 7–8, 85–86. Also see Reed, *The Last Days of Louisiana Red*, 138, where Reed characterizes "Mammy" Pleasant as a true leader of the African American community and Marie Laveau as a fraud who seeks only personal power.

26. Important scholars like Melville Herskovits, in *The Myth of the Negro Past* (245–51), and Albert Raboteau, in *Slave Religion* (75–80), used secondary sources for their brief discussion of New Orleans Voudou. Raboteau's account of Marie Laveau appears to have come primarily from Tallant's *Voodoo in New Orleans*, and he speaks of "Robert Tallant's informants" as though Tallant had conducted the interviews himself. Similarly, Jessie Gaston Mulira, in her essay, "'The Case of Voodoo in New Orleans," (34–68), has obtained much of her information from Tallant and his confrères and even from Tallant's 1956 novel, *The Voodoo Queen*. Michael A. Gomez, in *Exchanging Our Country Marks* (58), makes the statement that "Marie Laveau . . . disappeared mysteriously in 1822 while at the apex of her influence in New Orleans." Gomez must have confused Marie Laveau with her husband Jacques Paris, said by some to have vanished in 1822. The entry on Marie Laveau in *The Dictionary of Louisiana Biography*, Conrad, ed. (489–90), and the entries on "Haitians in the South," "Voodoo," and "Religion and Women" in *The Encyclopedia of Southern Culture*, Wilson and Ferris, eds. (443, 492, 1563), also rely heavily on Tallant.

27. Rosendale, "Marie Laveau: The Voodoo Queen Repossessed," 157–78; Fandrich, "Mysterious Voodoo Queen Marie Laveaux," Ph.D. dissertation, Temple University, later revised and published as a book of the same title; Sussman, "Conjuring Marie Laveau," Master's thesis, Sarah Lawrence College; Bibbs, *Heritage of Power*; Ward, *Voodoo Queen*; Trevigne, "Prominent People and Places in New Orleans," 175–96.

28. Fandrich, "Mysterious Voodoo Queen," 253, 309 n. 53. In a 2002 interview, Fandrich characterized Marie Laveau as a clairvoyant and an herbal healer who "wielded an enormous amount of power in New Orleans, unheard of for a woman of color during

those times. . . . She gave value to African culture, which I believe is her greatest contribution, [and] she was an activist against a racist system" (William Hageman, "The Death Grip of a Voodoo Queen," *Chicago Tribune*, October 31, 2002, section 5, p. 1 and 9).

29. Bibbs, *Heritage of Power*, 19, 58.

30. Ward, *Voodoo Queen*, introduction.

31. Douglas MacCash, "Midsummer Rite—Voodoo devotees show the tourists how they celebrate a holy day," *Times-Picayune* Living section, E1 and E4, June 30, 1999. Glassman, *Vodou Visions*, 52–53.

CHAPTER 1. THE COLONIAL PAST

1. Robin, *Voyages dans l'interieur de la Louisiane* (translated as *Voyages to Louisiana* by Stuart Landry, 2000), 81–85; Hall, *Africans in Colonial Louisiana*, 2–274; J. Johnson, "Colonial New Orleans: A Fragment of the Eighteenth-Century French Ethos," 12–57; Ingersoll, *Mammon and Manon in Early New Orleans*, 3–65.

2. Letter of Nicolas de la Salle to the Ministry of the Colonies, August 20, 1709, quoted in Hall, *Africans in Colonial Louisiana*, 57 n. 2.

3. Harms, *The Diligent*. Although Harms is describing one specific slaving voyage, that of the ship *Diligent* from the French city of Vannes to the African coast and on to Martinique, his findings can be applied to the French slave trade in general. For trade goods and use of cowrie shells as currency, see 80–82; for a detailed account of the Middle Passage, see 295–329. Also see the eighteenth-century eyewitness reports of Snelgrave, *A New Account of Some Parts of Guinea and the Slave-Trade*, especially 158–60, and Owen, *Journal of a Slave Dealer*.

4. Hall, *Africans in Colonial Louisiana*, 29–95; see especially 35, figure 2, "Slaves Landed in Louisiana by French Slave Trade: Numbers and Origins," and 60, table 2, "French Slave-Trade Ships from Africa to Louisiana." For more on the African slave trade, see Rice, *Rise and Fall of Black Slavery*, 102–52; Thornton, *Africa and Africans in the Making of the Atlantic World*; and Berlin, *Many Thousands Gone*, 17–28, 77–92, 95–105.

5. Cruzat, "Sidelights on Louisiana History—Slave Ordinances," 108–10. For examples of brutal treatment of slaves, see Hall, *Africans in Colonial Louisiana*, 150–55. For a discussion of laws against concubinage between slave and free, black and white, see Spear, "Colonial Intimacies: Legislating Sex in French Louisiana," 91–93.

6. Le Page du Pratz, *Histoire de la Louisiane*, 376–87. Saxon included a chapter on Le Page du Pratz in his book of historical sketches, *Old Louisiana*, 57–76.

7. Will of Catherine Henry, Acts of Octave de Armas, March 19, 1831, vol. 10, p. 359, act 213, NARC; typed translation, Robert Kornfeld, "Marie Laveau" manuscript, 1943, box 13, Lyle Saxon Papers, Special Collections, Howard-Tilton Memorial Library, Tulane University.

8. Henry Roche *dit* Belaire was the son of early French settlers Arnaud Roche *dit* Belaire (or Bellair) and Marianne Marguerite Birot. A marginal note on the 1722 map of *La Nouvelle Orléans* drawn by La Tour de la Blond shows that Arnaud Roche *dit* Belaire

was granted a plot of land at the corner of Chartres and Toulouse. The French census of 1726 lists Arnaud Roche as a "workman by the day" living with his wife and three children (Vieux Carré Survey, square 42, lot 18488, now 601 and 611 Chartres and 607 Toulouse Streets, THNOC). Also see the entries for Arnaud Roche *dit* Bellair from the census of 1721 and 1731 in G. Conrad, *First Families of Louisiana*, vol. 2.

9. Marriage contract of Henry Roche *dit* Belaire and Catherine Laurandine, February 24, 1756. Rather than being filed with other documents for 1756, the contract is attached to the succession of Catalina Laurandine, wife of Enrique Roche, September 11, 1782, document no. 748, file no. 3432, Judicial Records of the Spanish Cabildo, microfilm THNOC (original in box 40, LSM/HC). A summary and translation of this succession (lacking the details of the inventory) is found in the "Index to the Spanish Judicial Archives of Louisiana," *Louisiana Historical Quarterly*, vol. 19, 522–26. A translation of the marriage contract, minus the inventory, is included in Forsyth, *Louisiana Marriage Contracts*, vol. 2, p. 137. The chain of title for the Roche property on Royal Street is found in the Vieux Carré Survey, square 61, lot 18647, now 629 Royal, THNOC.

10. Hall, *Africans in Colonial Louisiana*, 60, table 2, "French Slave-Trade Ships from Africa to Louisiana," gives the names of the ships, year and port of embarkation, and number of slaves landed. For details on the *St. Louis*, see 93–95; for the *St. Ursin*, see 137–42.

11. Le Page du Pratz, *Histoire de la Louisiane*, 382–83. For the preponderance of Wolof women and their exceptional intelligence and beauty, see Hall, "African Women in French and Spanish Louisiana," 248–49.

12. Le Page du Pratz, *Histoire de la Louisiane*, 387.

13. Nolan, *A History of the Archdiocese of New Orleans*, 9–20. Clark and Gould, "The Feminine Face of Afro-Catholicism in New Orleans," 416–18.

14. For more on the conspiracy to overthrow the Spanish government, see French, *Historical Memoirs of Louisiana*, 178–233; Gayarré, *Louisiana: Its History as a French Colony*, 186–208; Cable, *The Creoles of Louisiana*, 52–79; Hanger, *Bounded Lives, Bounded Places*, 7–8.

15. Clarence Bispham, "Fray Antonio de Sedella," 24–37.

16. Hall, *Africans in Colonial Louisiana*, 276–302; Hall, "The Formation of Afro-Creole Culture," 83–85; Leglaunec, "Slave Migrations in Spanish and Early American Louisiana," 185–209, and "A Directory of Ships with Slave Cargoes," 211–30.

17. The authoritative works on free people of color in New Orleans during the Spanish period are Gould, "In Full Enjoyment of Their Liberty," and Hanger, *Bounded Lives, Bounded Places*. See also Baade, "The Law of Slavery in Spanish Luisiana," 43–85; Hall, *Africans in Colonial Louisiana*, 336–37; and J. Johnson, "Colonial New Orleans," 52–54.

18. Transfer of house and shop on Royal Street by Enrique Roche to his son Andre Roche is cited as Acts of Jean Baptiste Garic, February 15, 1770, Vieux Carré Survey, square 61, lot 18647, now 629 Royal. Purchase of property at Bourbon and St. Louis by Roche from the estate of Nicolas Piery is cited as Acts of Almonester y Roxas, January

15, 1781, Vieux Carré Survey, square 71, lot 18701, now 501-507 Bourbon. The Survey notes that both these acts are missing from the Notarial Archives. Will of Catherine Laurandine, wife of Enrique Roche, Acts of Leonardo Mazange, August 26, 1782, vol. 6, p. 742; 1782 inventory attached to succession of Catherine Laurandine, document no. 748, file no. 3432, Judicial Records of the Spanish Cabildo, microfilm THNOC (original in box 40, LSM/HC).

19. Citations for all slave transactions were located through Hall's *Louisiana Slave Database* and *Louisiana Free Database*. Sale of slave Catalina and two-year-old son Josef by Enrique Roche to Bartholemé Magnon, Acts of Raphael Perdomo, September 30, 1784, vol. 4, p. 426 verso, NARC. Henry Roche's daughter Henriette was married to Arnaud Magnon (marriage contract, Acts of Andres Almonester y Roxas, February 10, 1774, no vol., p. 53, NARC).

20. Sale of slave Catalina and son Josef by Bartolomé Magnon to Joseph Viscot (Bizot), Acts of Raphael Perdomo, August 5, 1784, vol. 4, p. 430, NARC. For evidence that Roche and Bizot were neighbors and comrades at arms, see Churchill, *Men Under General Don Bernardo de Galvez*, 95–97; for occupations of Roche and Bizot, see 106. Bizot had a slave concubine, the mulatress Magdelaine, with whom he had four quadroon children. In 1782, before purchasing Catherine, Bizot had freed these children gratis, declaring himself to be motivated by "love and affection." Later, in 1791, he freed their mother Magdelaine. Joseph Bizot, Magdelaine, and their children continued to live together as a family. When Bizot made his will on June 21, 1799, he left his entire estate, including a house on Toulouse Street between Bourbon and Royal, furniture, and four slaves, to Magdelaine Bizot and their natural children. (Emancipation of slaves Clarice, Naneta, Celestine, and Santiago by Joseph Bizot, Acts of Leonardo Mazange, April 20, 1782, p. 406; emancipation of slave Magdelaine by Juan Josef Bizot, Acts of Pedro Pedesclaux, July 27, 1791, p. 494. Will of Juan Josef Bizot, Acts of Pedro Pedesclaux, June 21, 1799, vol. 35, p. 543, NARC. Vieux Carré Survey, square 61, lot 18657, now 119–123 Toulouse, THNOC.)

21. Françoise Pomet was the natural daughter of the white Creole Balthazar Fabre de Mazan, a ringleader in the attempt to overthrow the Spanish government in 1768. She was the domestic partner of Jean Baptiste Pomet, a white Saint Domingue immigrant. She owned several other female slaves and their children (Francisca Pomet, Spanish census of 1791, NOPL; Will of Marie Françoise Mazan *dite* Pomet, Acts of Stephen de Quinones, March 30, 1815, vol. 15, p. 18).

22. Sale of slave Catalina and nursing infant by Josef Visot (Bizot) to Francisca Pomet, Acts of Raphael Perdomo, August 12, 1788, vol. 12, p. 354, NARC.

23. Emancipation of slave Joseph by Juan Joseph Bisot (Bizot), Acts of Carlos Ximines, July 4, 1891, vol. 1, p. 330, NARC. As an adult, Catherine's son Joseph used the surname *Bizou*.

24. Emancipation of slave Catarina by Francisca Pomet, Acts of Carlos Ximines, January 13, 1795, vol. 9, p. 12, NARC.

25. The chain of title for the St. Ann Street cottage comes from the Vieux Carré Survey, THNOC; original acts of sale were located at the Notarial Archives Research

Center. Sale of lot by the Capuchin friars to Hilaire Boutte, Acts of Raphael Perdomo, August 2, 1786 (this document is missing from the acts of Perdomo, but is cited in the subsequent sale); sale of lot by Boutte to Maneta Brion f.w.c., Acts of Pedro Pedesclaux, July 1, 1794, vol. 21, p. 642; sale of lot by Brion to Miguel Meffre, Pedesclaux, August 23, 1796, vol. 28, p. 399; sale of lot by Meffre to Cathalina Pomet (Henry), Pedesclaux, March 23, 1798, vol. 31, pp. 185–86, NARC. By a strange twist of circumstances, Catherine Henry's former owner, Françoise Pomet, became her next-door neighbor when Pomet inherited the property from her sister, Marie Jeanne Mazan (Acts of Stephen de Quinones, October 29, 1811, vol. 13, p. 302).

26. Will of Enrique Roche, Acts of Pedro Pedesclaux, April 26, 1788, vol. 3, p. 567, NARC. Sale of slave Margarita from the succession of Enrique Roche to Francisco Langlois, March 23, 1789, document no. 2062, file no. 2334, p. 30, Judicial Records of the Spanish Cabildo, microfilm THNOC (original in box 53, LSM/HC). Emancipation of slave Margarita by Francisco Langlois, Acts of Pedro Pedesclaux, October 16, 1790, vol. 11 , p. 720, NARC. These three documents were translated by Paula Artal-Isbrand.

27. For plaçage in Louisiana, see Domínguez, *White by Definition*, 23–25; Schafer, *Slavery, the Civil Law, and the Supreme Court of Louisiana*, 180–200; Hanger, "Coping in a Complex World," 218–31; Gould, "A Chaos of Iniquity and Discord," 231–46. Ingersoll, in opposition to these historians, argues in *Mammon and Manon* (336–39) that plaçage was a myth and that interracial couples were uncommon.

28. Don Esteban Miró, *Bando de Buen Gobierno*, Deliberations of the Cabildo, June 1, 1786, vol. 3, no. 1 (1784–1787); Records of the Cabildo Proceedings, English translation, pp. 106–7, microfilm NOPL. For an example of the misinterpretation of this law, see Tallant's *The Voodoo Queen*, 66–67.

29. Tallant, *Voodoo in New Orleans*, 61. Williams, "A Night with the Voudous," *Appleton's Journal*, March 27, 1875, 403–4.

30. Henri D'Arcantel was a native of Thionville in the French province of Lorraine, son of Nicholas D'Arcantel and Marguerite St. Maxent. Information on D'Arcantel's occupation comes from an inventory of the correspondence and documents of the *contraduria* 1765–1794, in the *Papales Procedentes de Cuba* in the *Archivo General de Indias* in Seville, *legajo* 653 (cited in Voorhies, *Some Late Eighteenth-Century Louisianians*, xxxvi).

31. Hy. D'Arcantel and Marguerite, free mulatress, *Recencement du 1795*, household 27, quartier 2, p. 2, islet no. 2, in Gould, "Household Census Databases for New Orleans, Mobile, and Pensacola," *Databases for the Study of Afro-Louisiana History and Genealogy*. The original is found in *legajo* 216, *Papeles Procedentes de la Isla de Cuba*, *Archivo General de Indias*, Seville, Spain.

32. Baptism of Miguel Germelo D'Arcantel, SLC Baptisms of S/FPC, July 30, 1795, vol. 5, p. 218, act 867. The godparents were the white merchant and shipowner Don Miguel Fortier and a white lady, Doña Maria Renata Almada Riviere née Douzan. Funeral of Germano D'Arcantel, SLC Funerals of S/FPC, October 26, 1795, vol. 2, p. 133 verso, act 1004. I found no baptismal records for Marie Louise and Antoine D'Arcantel, but their names appear in other official documents.

33. Baptism of Maria, SLC Baptisms of S/FPC, September 16, 1801, vol. 7, part 1, p. 41 verso, act 320. Marie Laveau used the name *Catherine* when she stood as godmother to her nephew Eugene Foucher in 1820 and at the baptism of her daughter Felicité Paris in 1824. The 1801 birth date is supported by archival evidence. Marie Laveau's 1819 marriage contract characterized her as a minor. The 1833 birth certificate of her son Maurice Christophe (François) states that Marie was thirty-three at the time, and her daughter Philomène's 1836 birth certificate stated that Marie was thirty-five. An article in the *Commercial Bulletin* of 1869 reported her to be seventy years old. LWP employee Catherine Dillon also proposed a birth date of 1801 ("Voodoo," chapter 10, "Marie the Great," p. 3, 45, LWP folder 319). Ina Fandrich, author of *Mysterious Voodoo Queen,* announced her discovery of the 1801 baptismal record in "The Lowdown on Laveau—1801 baptismal certificate holds long-lost truth about legendary voodoo priestess, researcher claims," *Times-Picayune,* February 17, 2002. In a later essay, Fandrich offered further evidence that this is indeed the baptismal record of Marie Laveau, stating that a search of the baptismal records between 1780 and 1810 revealed that only this one described a free colored female infant named Marie, daughter of Marguerite, free mulatress, and goddaughter of Catherine, free negress (Fandrich, "Birth of New Orleans' Voodoo Queen," 306–7).

34. Catherine Dillon's "Voodoo" manuscript states that "It has been said that [Marie Laveau's] father was a prominent planter, who served in one of the early legislatures, but this, according to documentary reports, was not so. The best that can be said of Marie Laveau's father is that he was a comfortably situated free man of color" ("Voodoo," chapter 10, "Marie the Great," p. 2, LWP folder 119). Tallant, *Voodoo in New Orleans,* 53; *Voodoo Queen,* 13–16. Prose, *Marie Laveau,* 15–26; Rhodes, *Voodoo Dreams,* 198, 335.

35. Charles Laveaux is designated in his marriage and death records as the son of Marie Laveaux, free negress. Maria Lavoz, free negress, Spanish census of 1791, p. 10, line 4, NOPL.

36. Louisiana Writers' Project workers were obviously pursuing the connection between the free man of color Charles Laveaux and the white Creole Charles Laveau Trudeau; Catherine Dillon refers to Charles Laveaux in her unpublished "Voodoo" manuscript as "a descendant of the Laveau Trudeau family" ("Voodoo," chapter 10, "Marie the Great." p. 8). Gehman, in her 1994 *Free People of Color of New Orleans* (56), also makes this assertion, but provides no documentation. Fandrich repeats the story in her dissertation on Marie Laveau (244, 304 n. 19), and in her book *Mysterious Voodoo Queen* (155, 291 n. 19), basing this statement on Charles Laveaux's "close association with members of the Trudeau family" without offering any proof of this association. In *Voodoo Queen* (67), Ward shows Charles Laveau Trudeau and Marie Laveaux as the parents of Charles Laveaux in a chart titled "Genealogy of the Widow Paris born Laveau."

37. Marriage of Carlos Trudeau and Charlotte Perrault, January 24, 1780, Nolan, ed., *Sacramental Records,* vol. 3, 290.

38. Governor Claiborne's description of Charles Laveau Trudeau is from a May 20, 1804, letter to President Thomas Jefferson (Carter, ed., *Territorial Papers—Territory of Orleans,* 240).

39. Will of Charles Laveau Trudeau, Acts of Narcisse Broutin, October 26, 1801, vol. 3, p. 330, NARC. Funeral of Carlos Laveau Trudeau, October 6, 1815, SLC Funerals of White Persons, Nolan, ed., *Sacramental Records*, vol. 12, 230. A search of Hall's *Louisiana Slave Database* and *Louisiana Free Database* gave no indication that Laveau Trudeau ever bought, sold, or freed a slave named Marie.

40. Marriage of Charles Labeau and Maria Francisca Dupart, SLC Marriages of S/FPC, August 2, 1802, vol. 1, p. 21, AA.

41. Robin, *Voyages to Louisiana*, 95–96; J. Johnson, "Colonial New Orleans," 12–57.

CHAPTER 2. THE ANTEBELLUM CITY

1. Robin, *Voyages to Louisiana*, 65–66; Laussat, *Memoirs of My Life*, 88–93; Lawrence, "Picture Perfect: The New Orleans of Pierre Clément Laussat, 1803–04," 45; Hirsch and Logsdon, introduction to "The American Challenge," in *Creole New Orleans*, 91.

2. Dargo, *Jefferson's Louisiana*, 25–29, 190 n. 26, quoting from a letter of Joseph Dubreuil de Villars. Governor Claiborne wrote to President Jefferson that, while the Louisianians seemed "attached to the American Government," they were "uninformed, indolent, luxurious—in a word, illy fitted to be useful citizens of a Republic" (Claiborne to Jefferson, January 16, 1804, in Carter, ed., *Territorial Papers—Territory of Orleans*, 161).

3. Dargo, *Jefferson's Louisiana*, 107, 142–44; the quote is from a letter of Thomas Jefferson to John Dickinson, 228 n. 56.

4. The best explanation of the differences between civil law and common law is found in Dargo, *Jefferson's Louisiana*, 12–17. For a discussion of Louisiana's civil laws regarding women's property rights, see Schafer, *Slavery, the Civil Law, and the Supreme Court of Louisiana*, 180–200, and Domínguez, *White by Definition*, 83. For a similar discussion of women's property rights under common law, see Lebsock, *The Free Women of Petersburg*, 23.

5. Lachance, "The 1809 Immigration of Saint-Domingue Refugees to New Orleans," 110–42, 145 (see especially table 1) 247, 251, 262–63; Debien and Le Gardeur, "Saint-Domingue Refugees in Louisiana," 239; Lachance, "The Foreign French," 103–11.

6. Claiborne to Secretary of State Robert Smith, July 29, 1809, and January 1, 1810, *Official Letter Books of W.C.C. Claiborne*, quoted in Lachance, "1809 Immigration," 252–59.

7. Richardson, "The Admission of Louisiana into the Union," 333–52.

8. Funeral of Adelaide D'Arcantel, daughter of Marguerite, age six years, SLC Funerals of S/FPC, August 28, 1815, vol. 6, p. 36, AA.

9. Will of Henri D'Arcantel, Recorder of Wills, Will Books, vol. 3 (1817–1824), pp. 65–66, microfilm NOPL (translation by Christine Barollier). The will was first discovered by Ina Fandrich, although she interpreted it to mean that Henri D'Arcantel was Marguerite's father ("Mysterious Voodoo Queen," 242); Fandrich later changed her opinion, characterizing D'Arcantel as Marguerite's domestic partner (*Mysterious*

Voodoo Queen, 153–54). Martha Ward, on the other hand, retained the idea that D'Arcantel was Marguerite's father (*Voodoo Queen,* 40).

10. In 1817, when Henri D'Arcantel made his will, a father could leave one-third of his estate to his natural children; after 1825, it was reduced to one-fourth (Kilbourne, "An Overview of the Work of the Territorial Court, 1804–1808," 115; Domínguez, *White by Definition,* 62–63, 79–84; Dargo, *Jefferson's Louisiana,* 12–16, 108, and 219 n. 11).

11. Funeral of Henrique D'Arcantel, Nolan, ed., *Sacramental Records,* vol. 12, 94. D'Arcantel landholdings are shown in the "Plan of the plantation of Mr. Ducourneau in the Quarter of Gentilly with the neighboring plantations of New Orleans," June 26, 1818, accession no.1966.33.16; "City of New Orleans," Francis B. Ogden, January 8, 1829; and Zimpel Map, 1834, THNOC. Inventory of Henry D'Arcantel, April 8, 1818, vol. D (1805–1818), p. 497, microfilm NOPL (translation by Christine Barollier).

12. Following the transfer of the Louisiana Territory to the United States in 1803, the former Spanish governor and other Spanish officials were slow to depart, encouraging the Creoles to believe that the Americans would soon be gone and the Spanish would be back in power. In July 1805, Claiborne received a list of "persons employed in the service of his Catholic Majesty [the King of Spain] who are to remain in this Province in order to settle their business," including "Don Henry Darcancel [*sic*]." In January 1806, under pressure from President Jefferson and Governor Claiborne to leave the Territory, the Spanish intendant, Juan Ventura Morales, protested that "There are many affairs whose conclusion awaits the decision of the . . . tribunal of accounts" and that certain "sums have not been paid, in consequence of the money not being remitted." Claiborne also received a petition from a group of "merchants and inhabitants of New Orleans," saying that the Spanish treasury owed them "considerable sums of money" and that they had been "in daily expectation that the Intendant of his C. M. [his Catholic Majesty] would receive sufficient funds to pay the bills before his departure from this country." The petitioners protested that now that Morales had been ordered to leave before payment was made, they were "exposed to suffer . . . total loss of that property, and some of them the ruin of their fortunes," and asked that some agent be allowed to stay "for the purpose to settling the remaining accounts of the Spanish treasury with the inhabitants of this territory." Thirty-one men signed the petition, but Henri D'Arcantel was not among them. On February 12, 1806, Governor Claiborne issued a letter of safe conduct for "his Excellency, the Marquis de Casa Calvo, together with his family and suite, on their return to the Dominions of his Catholic Majesty" (Andrés Lopez de Armesto to Claiborne, July 30, 1805, 486–87; Morales to Claiborne, January 11, 1806, 564–65; Petition to Claiborne, January, 1806, 578–79; Claiborne to Casa Calvo, February 12, 1806, 665, in *Territorial Papers—Territory of Orleans,* Carter, ed.).

13. Funeral of Margueritte D'Arcantel, SLC Funerals of S/FPC, July 31, 1825, vol. 7, p. 201 verso, act 2905, AA.

14. Baptism of Carlos Labeau, SLC Baptisms of S/FPC, November 20, 1802, vol. 7, part 2, p. 105; funeral of Carlos, age twelve days, SLC Funerals of S/FPC, November 21, 1802, vol. 3, part 2, p. 111 verso, act 1286. Baptism of Marie de los Dolores Labeau, SLC

Baptisms of S/FPC, June 2, 1804, vol. 7, part 3, p. 245, act 1771. Baptism of Lorenzo Labeau, SLC Baptisms of S/FPC, November 30, 1805, vol. 8, part 2, p. 167, act 760, AA.

15. Sale of slave by J. B. Moyorquin to Laveaux, Acts of Narcisse Broutin, March 30, 1807; sale of slaves by Bernard Marigny to Laveaux, Acts of Narcisse Broutin, August 31, 1808; sale of lot by Bernard Marigny to Laveaux and Baptiste Hardy, Acts of Michel de Armas, June 2, 1809; sale of slave by Martin Gordin to Laveaux, Acts of Michel de Armas, October 24, 1810, and sale of lot by the City of New Orleans to Laveaux, Acts of Michel de Armas, October 24, 1810; sale of lot by Laveaux to Michel Sterlin, Acts of Michel de Armas, January 2, 1811; sale of slaves and lot by Laveaux to Joseph Cabaret, Acts of Narcisse Broutin, February 11, 1811; sale of lots by Laveaux to Louis Gallitan, Acts of Narcisse Broutin, February 27, 1811; sale of slaves and lot by Laveaux to Charlotte Leclere, Acts of Narcisse Broutin, February 28, 1811; sale of slave by Laveaux to Charles Forneret, Acts of Michel de Armas, March 1, 1811; sale of slave by Marguerite Contale di Gote f.w.c. to Laveaux, Acts of Michel de Armas, May 23, 1814; sale of slave Bat by Simon Knight to Laveaux, Acts of John Lynd, March 6, 1816; sale of lot by Charles Robert Caune to Laveaux, Acts of Marc Lafitte, July 21, 1818; sale of slave by Laveaux to Antoine Jonau f.m.c., Acts of Felix de Armas, February 20, 1826; sale of lot by Laveaux to Juste Lebeau, Acts of Marc Lafitte, March 18, 1826.

16. Latrobe, *Impressions Respecting New Orleans*, 21–23; 100–102. Latrobe's original journal and sketchbook are now at the Maryland Historical Society in Baltimore.

17. Ibid., 128–31.

18. Alliot, *Historical and Political Reflections on Louisiana*, 81–83. Alliot established a successful medical practice in New Orleans, but within a few months he was deported to France and held in jail for practicing without a license. He blamed his predicament on the jealousy of a rich and influential New Orleans physician. From his jail cell he composed his *Historical and Political Reflections on Louisiana*, sending the manuscript to President Thomas Jefferson.

19. 1805 census figures from Flannery, compiler, *A Directory and Census*. Reinders, "The Free Negro in the New Orleans Economy, 1850–1860," 273–85; Evans, "Free Persons of Color," 35.

20. Baltimore had a population of free people of African descent more than twice the size of that of New Orleans, but they were predominantly uneducated and impoverished laborers, with property holdings worth 5.5 percent that of free nonwhite New Orleanians. The racially mixed free population of Charleston, the only American city with anything resembling New Orleans' free colored community, was a fraction of that of New Orleans. See Berlin, *Many Thousands Gone*, and Hirsch and Logsdon, introduction to "The American Challenge," in *Creole New Orleans*, 100.

21. Hirsch and Logsdon, introduction to "Franco-Africans and African-Americans," in *Creole New Orleans*, 189.

22. The percentage of racially mixed households listed in the 1805 census was calculated by Domínguez in *White by Definition*, 198.

23. For early antebellum travelers' accounts of plaçage, see Alliot, *Historical and Political Reflections on Louisiana*, 85–87, 103, 111; Perrin du Lac, *Voyage dans les Deux Loui-*

sianes, 185, 205; Watson, "Notitia of Incidents at New Orleans in 1804 and 1805," quoted in Holmes, "Do It! Don't Do It!: Spanish Laws on Sex and Marriage," 23; Schultz, *Travels on an Inland Voyage*, vol. 2, 193–94. For an account of plaçage in the mid-nineteenth century, see Olmsted, *Journeys and Explorations in the Cotton Kingdom*, 235–37.

24. For more on the quadroon balls, see Martin, "Plaçage and the Louisiana *Gens de Couleur Libres*," 65. Also see the section on quadroon balls in *Gumbo Ya-Ya*, Saxon, Dreyer, and Tallant, eds., 158–60. Travelers' accounts of quadroon balls are found in Robin, *Voyage to Louisiana*, 56–57, and Schultz, *Travels on an Inland Voyage*, 195.

25. Nolan ed., *Sacramental Records*, vol. 15, xx.

26. Latrobe, *Impressions Respecting New Orleans*, 35, 62, 94.

27. Martineau, *Retrospect of Western Travel*, vol. 1, 259–60.

28. Nolan, *History of the Archdiocese of New Orleans*, 24–33. For a history of the Sisters of the Holy Family, see the account of Sister Mary Bernard Deggs in *No Cross, No Crown: Black Nuns in Nineteenth-Century New Orleans*, Gould and Nolan, eds. Henriette Delille may have been related to Marie Laveau through their descent from Henry Roche *dit* Belaire. Roche was the father of Andre (also called Enrique) Roche with his first wife, and may have been the father of Marguerite Henry (D'Arcantel) with his slave Catherine. Therefore Andre and Marguerite were possible half-siblings. Marguerite was the mother of Marie Laveau with Charles Laveaux. Andre was the father of Maria Josefa Diaz with Henriette Labeau, making Marguerite and Maria Josefa possible first cousins. Maria Josefa was the mother of Henriette Delille, meaning that Henriette Delille and Marie Laveau may have been second cousins.

29. The most complete coverage of the history of Congo Square is found in Jerah Johnson's "New Orleans's Congo Square: An Urban Setting for Early Afro-American Culture Formation." David Estes' earlier article, "Traditional Dances and Processions of Blacks in New Orleans as Witnessed by Antebellum Travelers," includes reports of dances and processions at other venues in addition to descriptions of the Congo Square dances.

30. J. Johnson, "Congo Square," 141–42 n. 36, citing "Police Code, or Collection of the Ordinances of Police Made by the City Council of New Orleans, March 14, 1808," p. 203.

31. The annual arrival of Gaetano Mariantini's Congo Circus is immortalized in Cable's 1886 "Creole Slave Songs" (813), where he quotes the song about "Cap'm Cayetano who comes from Havano with his monkeys and his nags." An addendum to the Louisiana Landmarks Society's publication of *Congo Square in New Orleans* (54) points out that Mariantini died in New Orleans and was buried in St. Louis Cemetery No. 1 on November 3, 1817. His widow subsequently sold the horses, costumes, and equipment.

32. Atkins, *A Voyage to Guinea*, 53.

33. Schultz, *Travels on an Inland Voyage*, 197, quoted in Estes, "Traditional Dances and Processions," 2–3.

34. Latrobe, *Impressions Respecting New Orleans*, 49–51. The three drums, the gourd "banjo," and the holed calabash studded with nails have been identified as being of

Yoruba, Fon, Kongo, and Ashanti origin (Joyce, "Notes on the Drawings of Benjamin Henry Latrobe," in *Congo Square in New Orleans*, 31–32).

35. Paxton, *New Orleans Directory and Register*, 40–41.

36. Creecy, *Scenes in the South*, 20–23, quoted in Estes, "Traditional Dances and Processions," 7–8.

37. For some early descriptions of sanitary conditions in New Orleans, see Alliot, *Historical and Political Reflections on Louisiana*, 71, and Perrin du Lac, *Voyage dans les Deux Louisianes*, 52. Governor Claiborne lost his first wife and infant daughter to yellow fever shortly after arriving in the Territory. He wrote to Jefferson that he was "nearly undone" by the death of his second wife from the same disease, which he blamed on the "filth and putrefaction" that accumulated right outside the doors of the Government House (Governor Claiborne to President Jefferson, December 17, 1809, in *Territorial Papers—Territory of Orleans*, Carter, ed., 859–60).

38. Cable, *Creoles of Louisiana*, 284–308; Clapp, *Autobiographical Sketches*, 115–37; Din and Harkins, *New Orleans Cabildo*, 224–30; Vella, *Intimate Enemies*, 88; Hollandsworth, "Death and Disease Among Union Soldiers in New Orleans During the Civil War." The curators of the New Orleans Pharmacy Museum also provided information on yellow fever and cholera.

39. S. Wilson, "Early History," 3–24; Evans, "Free Persons of Color," 25–36; Tregle, "Creoles and Americans," 154–57.

40. "Plan de Faubourg Marigny conforme du trace fait par Barthelemy Lafon, Geographer et Arpenteur du Comte d'Orleans le 30 de Juin 1807," accession no. 1966.34.5, Plans and Plats of New Orleans Interest, print case 1, THNOC.

41. Funeral of Maria Francisca, wife of Charles Laveaux, SLC Funerals of S/FPC, June 23, 1824, vol. 7, part 2, p. 162 verso, act 2503.

42. Inventory of the Estate of Marie Françoise Fanchon Dupart, Wife of Charles Laveaux, July 27, 1824, typed translation LWP folder 495. In owning fourteen slaves, Charles Laveaux and Françoise Dupart would have been among the larger slaveholders in New Orleans. In 1860, only 128 people owned as many as six slaves, forty owned fifteen slaves, three owned forty, and two owned one hundred slaves (Reinders, *End of an Era*, 28).

CHAPTER 3. DOMESTIC LIFE

1. Marriage contract between Santyaque Paris and Marie Laveaux, July 27, 1819, Acts of Hugues Lavergne, vol. 1, act 5, NARC (there are multiple pagination series in vol. 1, and act 5 begins on the verso of page 2 of a later series, near the back of the book); typed translation LWP folder 319, pp. 4a–6.

2. Marriage of Santiago Paris and Maria Labeau, SLC Marriages of S/FPC, August 4, 1819, vol. 1, p. 59, act 256, AA; typed translation LWP folder 586.

3. Tallant, *Voodoo in New Orleans*, 53; *The Voodoo Queen*, 48.

4. New Orleans city directories, USGenWeb Orleans Parish Archives Index Project, http://www.rootsweb.com/~usgenweb/la/orleans.htm, accessed April 10, 2003.

5. Baptism of Eugene Foucher, SLC Baptisms of S/FPC, July 20, 1820, vol. 16, p. 213, act 1157, AA. On the significance of godparenting, see Clark and Gould, "The Feminine Face of Afro-Catholicism," 424, 429.

6. Charles Laveaux owned property in square 76, lot 18817, presently 914-916-918 Dauphine Street, and in square 85, lot 18835, presently 923-927-929 Dauphine, Vieux Carré Survey, THNOC.

7. Baptism of Marie Angèlie Paris, SLC Baptisms of S/FPC, February 14, 1823, vol. 18, p. 2 verso, act 13; the first letter of the child's name is strangely drawn, and could be an A or a V—her name might have been Vangèlie, a variant of Evangeline. Baptism of Felicité Paris, SLC Baptisms of S/FPC, November 17, 1824, vol. 18, p. 170 verso, act 857, AA. My assumption that Lilavoix is a misspelling of Laveau is based on the fact that the name *Lilavoix* is found nowhere in the archival records of New Orleans.

8. Saxon, *Fabulous New Orleans*, 243; Asbury, *The French Quarter*, 266; Tallant, *Voodoo in New Orleans*, 53; Tallant, *The Voodoo Queen*, 75; Prose, *Marie Laveau*, 107–24; Rhodes, *Voodoo Dreams*, 360–68.

9. Potter, *A Hairdresser's Experience in High Life*, 68.

10. Castellanos, *New Orleans As It Was*, 97; Asbury, *The French Quarter*, 266; Tallant, *Voodoo in New Orleans*, 53; Tallant, *The Voodoo Queen*, 68–70; Prose, *Marie Laveau*, 142–51.

11. Theresa Kavanaugh, interview by Zoe Posey, n.d.; Mary Washington, interview by Robert McKinney, n.d., LWP folder 25.

12. Saxon, *Fabulous New Orleans*, 243; Tallant, *Voodoo in New Orleans*, 55; Tallant, *The Voodoo Queen*, 74, 96; Prose, *Marie Laveau*, 79, 280–305.

13. Arthur, *Old Families of Louisiana*, 68; this information is verified in Nolan, ed., *Sacramental Records*, vol. 2, 137, and vol. 4, 144.

14. Porteous, "Renunciation made by Daniel Fagot . . . to Don Cristoval de Glapion, 1776," 372–82; Din and Harkins, *New Orleans Cabildo*, 111–12. The Chevalier Christophe de Glapion resigned this position in 1778 (Acts and Deliberations of the Cabildo, microfilm NOPL).

15. The children of the Chevalier Christophe de Glapion and Jeanne Antoinette Rivard were Jeanne Antoinette (b. 1758), Jean Baptiste (b. 1759), Renée (b. 1763) and Denis Christophe (b. 1764) (Arthur, *Old Families of Louisiana*, 69). Baptism of Denis Christophe de Glapion, SLC Baptisms of White Persons, January 24, 1765, vol. 2, p. 137, AA.

16. Marriage of Dionisio Cristobal de Glapion and Jeanne Sophie Lalande Ferrier, SLC Marriages of White Persons, January 31, 1785, Nolan, ed., *Sacramental Records*, vol. 4, p. 144. Their children were Jeanne Coulon (b. 1785), Catherine Sophie (b. 1787), Louis Christophe Dominic (b. 1789), Elizabeth Hortense (b. 1791), Elizabeth Heloïse (b. 1792), Jeanne Azelie (unknown), Arthemise (unknown), Felonis (b. 1793), Celeste (b. 1794), Louis (unknown), Françoise (b. 1799), and Etienne (b. 1802). The sacramental registers for St. Charles Borromeo church have been lost, but a certified copy of Christophe Glapion's 1790 baptismal record was deposited by his father with the notary

Felix de Armas (Acts of Felix de Armas, January 3, 1833, vol. 38, act 1, NARC). Also see Robichaux, *German Coast Families*, 71.

17. Muster roll of Captain Barthelemy Favre's (Fabré Daunoy's) Company of Louisiana Militia, bounty land files, War of 1812, NARA. Thanks to Ina Fandrich for directing me to this source.

18. Dillon, "Voodoo," chapter 10, "Marie the Great," p. 6.

19. Gould, "In Full Enjoyment of Their Liberty," 149–54, 220; Bell, *Revolution, Romanticism, and the Afro-Creole Protest Tradition*, 112–14, 134.

20. *Picayune's Guide to New Orleans* for 1897, 32–33, NOPL.

21. "Journal des Seances, Institution Catholique des Orphelines, 47eme Seance du 3 Septembre, 1852," p. 109, AA; thanks to Connie Birabent for calling this entry to my attention. For more on Madame Couvant's school, see Desdunes, *Our People and Our History*, 101–8; Rousseve, *The Negro in Louisiana*, 42–44; Bell, *Revolution, Romanticism, and the Afro-Creole Protest Tradition*, 123–26.

22. Baptism of Marie Heloïse Glapion, SLC Baptisms of S/FPC, August 19, 1828, vol. 21, p. 220, act 1232, AA (the baptism was not entered in the register until February 1829).

23. Baptism of Marie Louise Glapion, SLC Baptisms of S/FPC, September 10, 1829, vol. 22, p. 56, act 317; Funeral of Caroline Laveau Glapion, SLC Funerals of S/FPC, December 9, 1829, vol. 9, part 1, p. 2, act 8, AA.

24. Funeral of Christophe (no surname), natural son of Marie Lavaux, SLC Funerals of S/FPC, May 21, 1831, vol. 9, part 1, p. 129, act 848, AA.

25. Funeral of Jean Baptiste Paris, natural son of Marie Laveau, SLC Funerals of S/FPC, July 12, 1832, vol. 9, part 2, p. 274, act 1730, AA.

26. Birth certificate for Maurice Christophe Clapion [*sic*], natural son of Marie Laveaux Widow Paris and Christophe Dumini Clapion, issued April 3, 1834, vol. 4, p. 55, LDA. Baptism of François Glapion, natural son of Christophe Glapion and Marie Lavon [*sic*], SLC Baptisms of S/FPC, May 13, 1834, vol. 23, part 3, p. 403, act 2715. Funeral of François Glapion, SLC Funerals of S/FPC, May 18, 1834, vol. 10, part 3, p. 301, act 2019, AA; LWP file of tomb inscriptions for St. Louis Cemetery No. 2, LSM/HC; typed copy in LWP folder 24.

27. Baptism of Phélonise Lavan, SLC Baptisms of S/FPC, April 1, 1836, vol. 25, p. 35, act 100; corrected baptism of Philomène Glapion, SLC Baptisms, May 31, 1836, unnumbered volume for 1838, S/FPC, act 363, AA. Birth certificate for Philomène Glapion, June 1, 1836, vol. 4, p. 159, LDA; typed copy in LWP folder 202.

28. Baptism of Archange Edouard (no surname), natural son of Marie, *libre*, SLC Baptisms of S/FPC, May 7, 1839, unnumbered volume for 1838, S/FPC, act 438, AA; death certificate for Archange Glapion, vol. 10, p. 297, microfilm NOPL.

29. "Flagitious Fiction: Cable's Romance About Marie Laveau and the Voudous," *Daily Picayune*, April 11, 1886, p. 3, c. 4.

30. Alberta Jefferson, interview by Hazel Breaux and Robert McKinney, April 27, 1937; Washington/McKinney interview; Joseph Morris, interview by Edmond Burke, March 26, 1940, LWP folder 25.

31. Catlin scholar William Truettner, curator, American Art Museum, Smithsonian Institution, verified that the style of the portrait is typical of Catlin (interview by the author, January 3, 2001).

32. Edward A. Parsons later transferred his collection of eighteenth- and nineteenth-century Louisiana documents to the Center for American History at the University of Texas, Austin, but the portrait is not listed in the catalog. "Cabildo Will Get Catlin Portrait," *Times-Picayune*, August 24, 1933, p. 23, c. 7, photocopy in Marie Laveau accession file, Louisiana State Museum. "Marie Laveau," unpublished paper by Thomas Furlong, December 1947, NOPL.

33. The portrait, identified as "Marie Laveau the Younger" or "Marie Laveau's Daughter," is discussed in Wiesandanger, *Nineteenth-Century Louisiana Painters and Paintings*, 49; and Bundy, *Painting in the South*, 242.

34. Miniature by A. Alaux, accession no. 03038, Louisiana State Museum.

35. "Dr. I. M. Cline Finds Lost Portrait of Marie Laveau," *Daily City Item*, April 18, 1937, photocopy in Marie Laveau accession file, Louisiana State Museum.

36. Huber, *New Orleans: A Pictorial History*, 5; Heard, *French Quarter Manual*, 22, 28–33.

37. Nott, "Marie Laveau, Long High Priestess of Voudouism," *Times-Picayune* Sunday magazine, November 19, 1922, p. 2.

38. Asbury, *The French Quarter*, 267; Tallant, *Voodoo in New Orleans*, 58; Tallant, *The Voodoo Queen*, 84–89; Prose, *Marie Laveau*, 59–61; Rhodes, *Voodoo Dreams*, 116, 133. Variants of the story also appear in Martinez, *Mysterious Marie Laveau Voodoo Queen*, 17–19; Gandolfo, *A Strolling Tour of Voodoo in the Vieux Carré*, 5.

39. Will of Catherine Henry, Acts of Octave de Armas, March 19, 1831, vol. 10, p. 359, NARC; typed translation, Robert Kornfeld, "Marie Laveau" manuscript, 1943, box 13, Lyle Saxon Papers, Special Collections, Howard-Tilton Memorial Library, Tulane University.

40. Funeral of Catherine Henry, SLC Funerals of S/FPC, June 18, 1831, vol. 9, part 1, p. 137, act 709, AA. A receipt filed with Catherine's succession papers shows that the funeral cost $29.50 for the assistance of two priests, two cantors, three choir boys, and one *suisse* (an usher employed by the church to keep order) and for "droits et bénéfices de la fabrique" (a fee to the wardens for use of the church).

41. Succession of Catherine Henry, June 28, 1831, Orleans Parish, Court of Probate, Probate and Succession Records: 1805–1848, 107 H 1831–1832, vol. 4, p. 317, microfilm NOPL.

42. Donation by the Widow Paris to her daughter Epicaris (Euchariste) Glapion, Acts of Louis T. Caire, July 25, 1832, vol. 21A, act 763, NARC; typed translation in Dillon, "Voodoo," chapter 10, "Marie the Great," pp. 11–12. The name *Epicaris* is not a simple misspelling of Euchariste. In Roman history, Epicaris was a freed slave charged with plotting against the emperor Nero in 65 A.D.; she hanged herself while under torture to avoid naming the leader of the conspiracy.

43. *Marie Laveau wife of François Auguste v. Charles Laveau*, suit no. 387; *Laurent Laveau v. Charles Laveau*, suit 392, Court of Probates, microfilm NOPL. Laveaux

claimed that, after payment of his wife's debts and funeral expenses, he was left with only $422.

44. "Procuration par Marie Laveaux Veuve Paris a Charles Laveaux," Acts of Theodore Seghers, vol. 5, act 396, NARC. The amount of the mortgage was not specified. A marginal note states that the transaction was "revoked by an act of December 5, 1832 in this office."

45. Purchase of St. Ann Street cottage by Christophe Glapion from the succession of Catherine Henry, sheriff's auction, September 28, 1832, COB 12, p. 246. The creditor testified that his claim had been satisfied; quittance and discharge by Jean Baptiste Colson to the succession of the late Catherine Henry, Acts of Octave de Armas, October 10, 1832, vol. 16, act 495, NARC.

46. *Charles Laveaux v. his Creditors*, Parish Court, docket no. 6555, microfilm NOPL; meeting of the creditors of Charles Laveaux, Acts of Louis T. Caire, November 15, 1832, vol. 23A, pp. 196–98, act 1054. Sale of store in Faubourg Marigny, corner Histoire and Grands Hommes by "syndic des creaniers" (receiver for the creditors) of Charles Laveaux to Joseph Sauvinet, Acts of Louis T. Caire, January 2, 1833, vol. 25, p. 2, act 2, NARC. Charles Laveaux died on September 27, 1835. His death certificate records that "Charles Laveaux, a native of this city aged sixty years, late a trader," died at his home at 128 Love Street between Bagatelle and Union (Death certificate for Charles Laveaux, September 29, 1835, vol. 4, p. 273, microfilm NOPL; funeral of Charles Laveaux, SLC Funerals of S/FPC, vol. 11, part 1, p. 33, act 156, AA). I found no succession for Charles Laveaux.

47. Quittance and discharge by the heirs of the late Catherine Henry, Acts of Octave de Armas, November 28, 1832, vol. 17, act 547, NARC.

48. Christophe Glapion, purchase of stock and mortgage from Citizens' Bank of Louisiana, Acts of Theodore Seghers, August 11, 1836, vol. 18, act 247, NARC.

49. Sale of lot with buildings by Christophe Glapion to Pierre Charles Marioux, Acts of C. V. Foulon, June 8, 1838, vol. 1, pp. 179–80, act 92; *inter vivos* donation by Marioux to Philomène and Archange Glapion, Acts of Theodore Seghers, September 23, 1839, vol. 33, act 728, NARC. These transactions are outlined in Dillon, "Voodoo," chapter 10, "Marie the Great," pp. 31–32, and typed copies are appended to Robert Kornfeld's "Marie Laveau" manuscript.

50. New Orleans city directories: Pitts and Clark's 1841; Michel and Co. 1842, 1846; Cohen's 1852–1855; Gardner's 1858, 1859, 1861–1869; Graham's 1870; Soard's 1878, 1880, 1881.

51. U.S. Census for New Orleans 1850, Widow Paris, sheet 178, line 3, microfilm NARA. Laveau researchers Ina Fandrich and Martha Ward assert that Christophe Glapion deliberately "passed for colored" in all aspects of his life (Fandrich, "Mysterious Voodoo Queen," 246, and *Mysterious Voodoo Queen*, 157–58; Ward, *Voodoo Queen*, 45–47).

52. Baptism of Pedro Croker, natural son of Celeste Camasac Maldonado and Raphael Bazile Crokère, April 3, 1803, SLC Baptisms of S/FPC, vol. 7, p. 116, AA. For more on Bazile Crokère, see Desdunes, *Our People and Our History*, 77–79. Marriage of Pedro Croker and Rosa Gignac, SLC Marriages of S/FPC, February 17, 1827, vol. 1,

part 2, p. 85, act 411, AA. The children of Pierre Crocker and Rose Gignac were Celeste (b. 1828), Rose (b. 1830, d. 1831), Marie Elizabeth (b. 1831, d. 1832), Henriette (b. 1832, d. 1832), Pierre Jr. (b. 1833), Matilde (b. 1835, d. 1836), Adele (b. 1837), Joseph Erneste (b. 1843, d. 1845), Florentine (b. 1839, d. 1846), and Raphael (b. 1849); information from Baptismal Books, AA; birth and death certificates, LDA. Rose Gignac died on December 21, 1860 (death certificate, vol. 22, p. 119, microfilm NOPL). Pierre Crocker was listed in the city directory from 1832–1858 at 292 St. Philip. There is no death certificate for Pierre Crocker, but his funeral notice appeared in the *Louisiana Courier*, July 10, 1857, p. 2, c. 5. The funeral was held at St. Augustine's Church. Thanks to Barbara Trevigne for directing me to this source.

53. Baptism of Joseph Eugene Crocker, St. Augustine's Church Baptisms of S/FPC, May 18, 1844, vol. 1A, p. 19, act 13, AA. The witnesses who signed with Pierre Crocker were L. P. Sindos and Ulissc Thiac.

54. Baptism of Adelai Glapion, SLC Baptisms of S/FPC, February 3, 1848, vol. 32, part 2, p. 353; baptism of Marie Glapious [*sic*], SLC Baptisms of S/FPC, July 9, 1850, vol. 32, part 3, p. 454, AA.

55. Victor Pierre Crocker's birth date is known from his petition to the Civil District Court, cited below, n. 56. Despite the testimony of witnesses that he was baptized at the Laveau-Glapion home, there is no entry for Victor Pierre in the baptismal registers of St. Louis Cathedral or St. Augustine's Church.

56. Succession of Eloise Euchariste Glapion, November 28, 1881, judgment no. 4597, Civil District Court, Judge F. A. Monroe; the document is missing from the microfilm, but the original, handwritten in English, is at NOPL, and a typed copy is in LWP folder 499. The other witnesses were Evelina Courcelle, Clemence Dauphin, Anthony Prados, and Augustin Lamothe. It was Lamothe, a boarder in the Laveau-Glapion home, who reported Marie Laveau's death to the Board of Health; he was also a witness at the marriage of one of Philomène's daughters.

57. Marie Dédé, interview by Robert McKinney, n.d.; Anita Fonvergne, interview by Hazel Breaux, April 13, 1937; Washington/McKinney interview; Rose Legendre, interview by Maude Wallace, March 20, 1940; James Santana, interview by Zoe Posey, July 10, 1939, LWP folder 25.

58. Dédé/McKinney interview; Washington/McKinney interview; unattributed report, n.d., LWP folder 25. Information about the Choctaw Indians is found in the *Picayune's Guide to New Orleans* for 1903, p. 33.

59. 152 St. Ann, Sanborn Fire Insurance Map, 1885, vol. 2, sheet 44; 1896, vol. 1, sheet 23, microfilm THNOC.

CHAPTER 4. SLAVES

1. "An Act for the Organization of the Territory of Orleans and the Louisiana District," March 26, 1804; Governor Claiborne to President Jefferson, April 15, 1804; Claiborne to Jefferson, November 25, 1804, in Carter, ed., *Territorial Papers—Territory of Orleans*, 209, 222, and 341. Taylor, "The Foreign Slave Trade After 1808," 36–43. Leglaunec, "Slave Migrations in Spanish and Early American Louisiana," 202–9.

2. Claiborne to Jefferson, March 25, 1805; James Brown to Albert Gallatin, secretary of the treasury, in Carter, ed., *Territorial Papers—Territory of Orleans*, 424, 548. For more on the smuggling of Africans into Louisiana, see *State, Snipes, et al. v. Five African Negroes*, September 1817, quoted in Schafer, *Slavery, the Civil Law, and the Supreme Court of Louisiana*, 153–57. For Africans smuggled into Mississippi, see "Africans in Mississippi," *Daily Picayune*, June 27, 1859, p. 4, c. 4. For Africans smuggled into Florida, see "More Africans," *Daily Picayune*, August 2, 1859, p. 5, c. 5, and August 3, 1859, p. 1, c. 5.

3. The advertisements quoted ran in the *Daily Picayune* during 1859. The most complete discussion of the New Orleans slave market is found in W. Johnson, *Soul by Soul*.

4. Potter, *A Hairdresser's Experience*, 172–74.

5. Ibid., 185–87.

6. Index to the Orleans Parish Court Slave Emancipation Petitions for 1814–1843, microfilm NOPL.

7. Roussève, *The Negro in Louisiana*, 30–31; Baade, "Law of Slavery," 74; Gould, "In Full Enjoyment of Their Liberty," 70–129; Schafer, *Slavery, the Civil Law, and the Supreme Court of Louisiana*, 1–10, 180–200.

8. Buckingham, *Slave States*, 307. See also Gould, "In Full Enjoyment of Their Liberty," 72–74; and Bell, "Hermann-Grima House: A Window on Free Black Life and Urban Slavery in Creole New Orleans," 76.

9. Curry, *The Free Black in Urban America*, 44–45, tables C-5–C-8, "Free Black Slaveholding (New Orleans)," 270–71. See also Rankin, "The Politics of Caste," 122; Carter G. Woodson, *Free Negro Owners of Slaves in the United States in 1830*, quoted in Roussève, *The Negro in Louisiana*, 45.

10. Fandrich, "Mysterious Voodoo Queen," 253, 309 n. 53; *Mysterious Voodoo Queen*, 163, 295 n. 56. Bibbs, *Heritage of Power*, 19, 58. Ward, *Voodoo Queen*, 13, 80–88. These researchers were misled by the fact that two of the Laveau-Glapion slaves were *statu libri* rather than "slaves for life." Ward cites an additional *statu liber* slave case, the sale of Alexandrine by Jean Jacques Christophe Paris to Adrien Dumartrait (Acts of Louis T. Caire, May 19, 1838, vol. 65A, acts 407 and 408, NARC), claiming that Christophe Glapion was impersonating Marie Laveau's deceased husband, Jacques Paris. Jean Jacques Christophe Paris was, in fact, a native of France who was employed as a clerk at the Bank of Louisiana and died at his home on Bourbon between St. Ann and Dumaine on August 12, 1843 (vol. 9, p. 508, LDA). Fandrich and Ward cite the interview with the alleged New York Voudou expert, "Doctor Bass" ("The Departed Voudou Queen," *Times*, June 24, 1881; "Voudouism-Charms," *Daily States*, August 26, 1881), as evidence that Marie Laveau helped slaves escape to the North.

11. Sale of slaves Michaux and Catherine by Charles Hardy to Christophe Glapion, May 1, 1810, 212; sale of slave Michaux by Glapion to Jacques Dreux, June 22, 1810, act 313; sale of slave Jacques Congo by Rosette Toultan f.w.c. to Glapion, November 12, 1810; sale of slave Catherine by Glapion to Gertrude Daigle, December 2, 1815, 538 (all Acts of Pedro Pedesclaux, cited in Hall, *Louisiana Slave Database*).

12. Sale of slave Eliza by John Woolfolk to Christophe Dumesnil de Glapion, Acts of Carlisle Pollock, March 14, 1828, vol. 24, p. 178, NARC. Although notarial acts usually

cite the previous act by which the seller acquired the property being sold, this one does not, indicating that Woolfolk did not purchase Eliza in Louisiana. For the practice of selling young, allegedly orphaned, slaves separately from their mothers, see W. Johnson, *Soul by Soul*, 122–23.

13. Sale of slave Molly and her son Richard by Pierre Joseph Tricou to Marie Laveau, Acts of Carlisle Pollock, February 7, 1838, vol. 60, p. 19. On November 5, 1840, Marie sold Molly, Richard, and Louis to Christophe Glapion for $800. Pierre Joseph Tricou was also present, claiming the $400 still owed him from the previous sale of Molly and Richard to Marie Laveau. This was obviously a simulated sale made for the purpose of paying Marie's debt to Tricou, and Molly and her children stayed in the Laveau-Glapion household (Sale of Molly and her sons Richard and Louis by Marie Laveau to Christophe Glapion, Acts of Achille Chiapella, November 5, 1840, vol. 3, p. 633, act 325, NARC).

14. Article 37, Louisiana Civil Code of 1825.

15. Sale of slave Irma by Pierre Oscar Peyroux to Marie, f.w.c., Widow of Santiague Paris, Acts of Louis T. Caire, August 10, 1838, vol. 66A, pp. 235–36, act 594 (569), NARC; translation by Nancy McKeon. The transactions involving Irma are also cited in Fandrich, "Mysterious Voodoo Queen," 309 n. 52; *Mysterious Voodoo Queen*, 295 n. 56; Ward, *Voodoo Queen*, 86–87.

16. Sale of slave Irma by Constance Peyroux to Pierre Oscar Peyroux, Acts of Louis T. Caire, February 13, 1838, vol. 63A, p. 166, act 87 (86); promise of freedom by Pierre O. Peyroux to the slave Irma, Acts of Louis T. Caire, May 19, 1838, vol. 65A, p. 346, act 411, NARC; translations by Nancy McKeon.

17. Article 196 of the Louisiana Civil Code of 1825 states that "The child born of a woman after she has acquired the right of being free at a future time follows the condition of the mother and becomes free at the time fixed for her enfranchisement, even if the mother should die before that time."

18. Sale of slave Irma by Widow L. Paris to Demoiselle C. Peyroux, Acts of Louis T. Caire, October 21, 1839, act 676, NARC. A receipt from the Bureau of Mortgages, also dated October 21, was attached to the act of sale as proof that the Widow Paris had repaid the mortgage of $35.88 from Fernand Durcy resulting from "a judgment rendered by the city court dated February 23, 1833." According to Walter Johnson's *Soul by Soul*, "Slaves were regularly used as collateral in credit transactions; rather than giving an IOU when they borrowed money, many slaveholders simply wrote out a bill of sale for a slave who would actually be transferred only if they failed to pay their debt" (25–26).

19. Funeral of Irma, slave of Constance Peyroux, SLC Funerals of S/FPC, March 22, 1842, vol. 11, part 2 (slaves), p. 312, act 766, AA.

20. Slaves Emancipated by the Council of Municipality No. 1 (May 27, 1846–June, 1850), May 7, 1850, microfilm NOPL.

21. Will of Jeanne Gabrielle Bidonne [*sic*], Widow of Jean Baptiste Montignac, July 19, 1841, filed with Judge Joachim Bermudez, Will Book 6, pp. 356, 361, microfilm NOPL.

22. Sale of slave Juliette by Pierre Allarde (testamentary executor of the Widow Montignac) to Catherine Victoire Racquié, Acts of Paul Bertus, September 21, 1841, vol. 2, act 136. Sale of Juliette by Racquié to Leonard Lévesque, Acts of Paul Bertus, September 5, 1842, vol. 3, act 99. Sale of Juliette by Lévesque to Christophe Glapion, Acts of Jean Agaisse, August 17, 1843, vol. 1, p. 108, act 48. Sale of Juliette by Glapion to Gustave Ducros, Acts of Charles Boudousquié, November 11, 1843, vol. 13A, act 191, NARC.

23. Sale of slave Juliette by Gustave Ducros to Marie Marsoudet, Acts of Charles Boudousquié, June 8, 1846, vol. 21, act 128. Sale of Juliette by Marsoudet to Pierre Monette f.m.c., Acts of Charles Boudousquié, June 20, 1846, vol. 21, act 135. Sale of Juliette by Monette to Marie Laveau, November 15, 1847, Acts of Paul Laresche, act 223, NARC. Sale of Juliette to Laveau also cited in Fandrich, "Mysterious Voodoo Queen," 309 n. 52; *Mysterious Voodoo Queen*, 295 n. 56; Ward, *Voodoo Queen*, 87–88.

24. Sale of slave Juliette by Marie Laveau to Sanité Couvreure f.w.c., Acts of Jean Agaisse, April 27, 1848, vol. 6, pp. 79–80, act 42, NARC. Also cited by Fandrich, *Mysterious Voodoo Queen* 295 n. 56, and Ward, *Voodoo Queen*, 87–88. *State v. Charlotte Miles charged with harboring the runaway slave Nounoun* [Juliette], First District Count, 1848, quoted in Gould, "In Full Enjoyment of Their Liberty," 160.

25. Sale of slave Juliette by Sanité Couvreure to Augustus Reichard, Acts of Jean Agaisse, March 24, 1849, vol. 7, p. 50, act 23, NARC.

26. Manumission of slave Juliette by Augustus Reichard, Acts of Achille Chiapella, May 22, 1852, vol. 27, p. 1153, act 385, NARC.

27. Sale of slave Peter by the Syndics of Pierre Crocker to Arnold Bodin, Acts of Theodore Seghers, March 30, 1843, recorded in COB 34, p. 33; sale of Peter by Bodin to Christophe Glapion, Acts of Joseph Lisbony, April 12, 1848, vol. 3, act 84; sale of Peter by Glapion to Pierre Maurice Mervoyer, Acts of Jean Agaisse, October 24, 1849, vol. 7, p. 220, act 109, NARC. Also cited in Ward, *Voodoo Queen*, 88.

28. Sale of slave Richard by Christophe Glapion to Elihu Creswell, Acts of S. H. Lewis, March 8, 1850; this act should be in vol. 20 of Lewis, but the book is badly deteriorated, the pages are unbound and stored loose in an envelope, and the acts skip from October 2, 1848 to June 14, 1850. It is, however, recorded in COB 51, p. 475. For more on the slave trader Elihu Creswell, see W. Johnson, *Soul by Soul*, 120, 168, and Schafer, *Slavery, the Civil Law, and the Supreme Court of Louisiana*, 178–79.

29. Will of Elihu Creswell, deposited in his box at the Merchants and Traders' Bank, Succession of Elihu Creswell, Fourth District Court Suit Records, June 19, 1851, docket no. 4554, microfilm NOPL.

30. "Intervention of the several slaves named in the will, praying to be emancipated in this State," November 8, 1851, docket no. 2423; "Account of the administration of Lewis E. Simonds, executor of the estate of Elihu Creswell," September 17, 1852, docket no. 3521; *Alfred Hewson v. Mrs. Sarah Creswell* [Elihu Creswell's mother], April, 1855, docket no. 3692; *L. E. Simonds v. Mrs. Sarah Creswell*, May, 1855, docket no. 4033, Fourth District Court, Supreme Court of Louisiana Collection of Legal Archives

(1846–61), Department of Archives and Manuscripts, Earl K. Long Library, University of New Orleans. Thanks to UNO archivist Marie Windell for locating and copying these records.

31. Sale of slaves Molly and Louis to Philippe Ross f.m.c., Acts of A. E. Bienvenu, April 26, 1850, vol. 5, act 63, NARC. The 1860 U.S. Census for New Orleans lists Philippe Ross, age 68, watchmaker, with real estate holdings worth $4,000 and personal property worth $200 (5th Ward, sheet 572, line 36).

32. Sale of slave Eliza by Christophe Glapion to Pierre Monette f.m.c., Acts of A. E. Bienvenu, April 26, 1854, vol. 5, act 62, NARC. It was from Monette that Marie Laveau bought the slave Juliette in 1847.

33. The Emancipation Proclamation of January 1, 1863, freed only those slaves held in bondage in "states and parts of states" that were in rebellion against the Union. Orleans Parish and twelve other rural parishes were specifically exempted because they were occupied by Union troops and therefore not technically "in rebellion." The first article of the Louisiana constitution of 1864 stated that slavery was "forever abolished and prohibited throughout the State" (Taylor, *Louisiana Reconstructed*, 50).

CHAPTER 5. HARD TIMES

1. Bounty land files, War of 1812, no. 332.037, NARA. In French and Spanish documents the letters B and V were used interchangeably, thus the confusion between the names *Fabré* and *Favré*.

2. *Citizens' Bank of Louisiana v. Christophe Glapion*, May 4, 1855, docket no. 10,323, Fifth District Court; Fifth District Court to the Sheriff of the Parish of Orleans, June 4, 1855, order to seize the property of C. Glapion, original documents in NOPL.

3. Sale of lot, 192 Union, by Christophe Glapion to Philippe Ross f.m.c., Acts of A. E. Bienvenu, May 30, 1855, vol. 10, act 1855, NARC.

4. Death certificate for Christophe Glapion, June 26, 1855, vol. 17, p. 42, microfilm NOPL; typed copy in LWP folder 202.

5. Funeral announcement for Christophe Glapion, *Bee*, June 27, 1855, p. 2, c. 5; typed copy in LWP folder 202.

6. The payment to undertaker Pierre Casenave is cited in Glapion's succession: "To P. Casenave for his bill for funeral expenses amount of $150 but is admitted only for $100 considering the small intake left by the deceased" (Succession of Christophe Glapion, February 4, 1856, docket no. 9,168, records of Second District Court 1846–1880, microfilm NOPL; typed translation in LWP folder 511). Interment Payment Records St. Louis Cemetery No. 1, June 27, 1855, vol. 5, part 1, p. 263, no. 737, AA.

7. *Citizens' Bank of Louisiana v. Estate of Christophe Glapion*, docket no. 10,323, Fifth District Court, original in NOPL.

8. Purchase of the St. Ann Street property by Pierre Crocker f.m.c., agent for Phillipe Ross f.m.c., from sheriff's auction, July 23, 1855, COB 68, p. 332.

9. Biron claimed that he was owed $25 for representing Glapion in a suit against Phillipe and A. P. Lanaux for default on a promissory note for $150 (*Christophe Glapion v. Philippe Lanaux and A. P. Lanaux*, docket no. 8872, Second District Court, micro-

film NOPL). Information on Pierre Casenave from U.S. Census for New Orleans 1850, 7th Ward, sheet 388, NARA.

10. Succession of Christophe Glapion (full citation in n. 6).

11. Castellanos, *New Orleans As It Was*, 98; Hurston, "Hoodoo in America," 327, *Mules and Men*, 193.

12. Tallant, *Voodoo in New Orleans*, 86–87.

13. Joseph Alfred, interview by Robert McKinney, n.d.; Santana/Posey interview, LWP folder 25. Tallant may have derived the name *Pop Abou* from Robert McKinney's interview with a man called "Pops."

14. Mary Richard, interview by Zoe Posey, April 25, 1941; Nathan Hobley, interview by Zoe Posey, October 25, 1940; Dédé/McKinney interview; Mimi Delavigne, interview by Henriette Michinard, December 13, 1939, LWP folder 25.

15. *State of Louisiana v. Julia Evans f.w.c.*, First District Court, September 4, 1850, docket no. 5410; *State of Louisiana v. Elizabeth Martel f.w.c.*, First District Court, January 11, 1858, docket no. 13416; *State of Louisiana v. Ophelia Garcia f.w.c.*, First District Court, December 3, 1860, docket no. 14840, NOPL. Thanks to Dr. Judith Schafer for calling my attention to these cases.

16. Population data for free people of color in 1860 from Reinders, *End of an Era*, 23.

17. Gould, "In Full Enjoyment of Their Liberty," 156–59; Schafer, *Slavery, the Civil Law, and the Supreme Court of Louisiana*, 6 n. 9, and 180. The quotation is from Roussève, *The Negro in Louisiana*, 47–48.

18. J. Johnson, "New Orleans's Congo Square," 148 n. 47, 151.

19. *Daily Picayune*, September 5, 1859, p. 4, c. 1; December 3, 1859, p. 1, c. 6; "Exclusion of Free Negroes," *Daily Picayune*, January 14, 1860, p. 1, c. 5. "Colored Folks," *Daily Picayune*, September 21, 1860, p. 4, c. 1. "A Rare Smell of Perjury," *Daily Crescent*, September 8, 1859, p. 1, c. 4.

20. Logsdon and Bell, "The Americanization of Black New Orleans," 208–9. "Free Black Emigration," *Daily Picayune*, June 23, 1859, p. 5, c. 5; "Hayti and Emigration Thither," *Daily Picayune*, July 16, 1859, p. 5, c. 2; "Emigration to Hayti," *Daily Picayune*, November 11, 1860, p. 5, c. 2.

21. Information and direct quotes on conditions in the 1850s and early 1860s are from the local news columns of the *Daily Delta*, the *Daily Crescent*, the *Daily Picayune*, the *Daily True Delta*, and the *Louisiana Courier*.

22. *Daily Picayune*, November 25, 1859, p. 2, c. 2; January 10, 1861, p. 5, c. 4; January 12, 1861, p. 5, c. 4. For more on the enlistment of free men of color on the side of the Confederacy, see Schafer, *Becoming Free, Remaining Free*, 163–64.

23. Taylor, *Louisiana Reconstructed*, 1–10.

CHAPTER 6. VOUDOU

1. Le Page du Pratz, *Histoire de la Louisiane*, 377. Porteous, "The Gri-Gri Case," 48–63.

2. For the origin of the word *gris-gris*, see Hall, *Africans in Colonial Louisiana*, 38, 51.

3. Atkins, *A Voyage to Guinea*, 38, 56, 58, 86. Owen, *Journal of a Slave Dealer*, 49–50; I have converted Atkins' and Owen's grammar, phonetic spelling, and erratic punctuation into standard English. Owen's drawing of a priest and a "large gregory bag or witch" is reproduced in plate X, p. 51. John Matthews' description is quoted in a note on p. 113 of Owen's published *Journal*.

4. For more on the Fon religion, see Herskovits, *Dahomey: An Ancient West African Kingdom*, and Blier, "Vodun: West African Roots of Vodou." For the Yoruba religion, see Brandon, *Santería from Africa to the New World* and Thompson, *Flash of the Spirit*. For the Kongo religion, see MacGaffey, *Religion and Society in Central Africa* and "The Eyes of Understanding: Kongo Minkisi."

5. Article 2, "Code Noir ou Loi Municipale," quoted in Ingersoll, "Slave Codes and Judicial Practice in New Orleans," 47–48.

6. Saxon, *Fabulous New Orleans*, 237; *Historical Sketch Book*, 168.

7. Dayan, in *Haiti, History, and the Gods* (29), notes that the first published account of Boukman's Bois-Caiman ceremony appeared in *Histoire de la Révolution de Saint-Domingue*, written in 1814 by Antoine Dalmas, a former French colonist. Thus the legendary origin of the Haitian Revolution is "a [Vodou] service quite possibly imagined" by a white author who sought to "link the first successful slave revolt to a gothic scene of blood drinking and abandon." The ceremony at Bois-Caiman is discussed in C.L.R. James, *The Black Jacobins* (86–88), in Alfred Métraux, *Voodoo in Haiti* (43–47), and in most other texts on Haitian history and Vodou. James cites no source for the story; Métraux cites J. C. Dorsainvil, *Manuel d'histoire d'Haiti*, a school textbook published in 1949 by the Frères de L'Instruction Chrétienne (Brothers of Christian Instruction). For additional information on the role of Vodou in the Haitian Revolution, Métraux cites Colonel Malenfant, *Des colonies et particulièrement celle de Saint-Domingue* (1814), Thomas Madiou, *Histoire d'Haiti* (1847), and Dantes Bellegarde, *Histoire du peuple haitian* (1953).

8. Hall, "The Formation of Afro-Creole Culture," 85–86. See also Gomez, *Exchanging Our Country Marks*, 54–57; Hurston, "Hoodoo in America," 318; Asbury, *The French Quarter*, 254; Tallant, *Voodoo in New Orleans*, 12.

9. The literature on Haitian Vodou is vast, but a good understanding may be gained from Métraux, *Voodoo in Haiti*; Courlander, *The Drum and the Hoe;* Brown, *Mama Lola: A Vodou Priestess in Brooklyn*; Cosentino, *Sacred Arts of Haitian Vodou*; and Glassman, *Vodou Visions*. Also see Long, "African-Based Religions in the Latin-Catholic Colonies," in *Spiritual Merchants*, 17–36. For more on *pwen*, see McAlister, "A Sorcerer's Bottle: The Visual Art of Magic in Haiti," 305–15; Brown, "Serving the Spirits," 213, 220–22; and Thompson, "From the Isle Beneath the Sea: Haiti's Africanizing Vodou Art," 111–18. For more on the connection between the religion in Haiti and New Orleans see Long, "Haitian Vodou and New Orleans Voudou: A Comparison."

10. Spencer, *A Civilization That Perished*, abridged translation of Moreau de Saint-

Méry's *Description Topographique*, 1–7 and 56. Moreau's description of a Vodou ceremony is found in vol. 1 of the original, 45–51.

11. Allain, *Souvenirs d'Amérique*, 130. Cable, "Creole Slave Songs," 818–19. Subsequent versions of Moreau's narrative appear in Castellanos, *New Orleans As It Was*,
91–96; Puckett, *Folk Beliefs of the Southern Negro*, 178–83; LeBlanc, "Beware These
Closing Days of June," *Times-Picayune* Sunday magazine, June 26, 1927, p. 2; Saxon,
Fabulous New Orleans, 240–41; Christian, "A Black History of Louisiana," the chapter
titled "Voodooism and Mumbo-Jumbo," 9–11; Tallant, *Voodoo in New Orleans*, 8. The
source of this description was known by Louisiana Writers' Project workers and was
more recently noted by Bryan in *The Myth of New Orleans in Literature*, 107, and by
Palmié in "Conventionalization, Distortion, and Plagiarism in the Historiography of
Afro-Caribbean Religion in New Orleans."

12. Williams, "A Night with the Voudous," 403–4. Buel, *Metropolitan Life Unveiled*,
518–30; Buel attributed the story to "an old gentleman, once a wealthy planter, living in
Plaquemines Parish, Louisiana, [who] gave me a most realistic description of a Voudou
celebration he attended near New Orleans when he was a boy."

13. Asbury, *The French Quarter*, 266; Tallant, *Voodoo in New Orleans*, 46–47, 53.

14. Alexander Augustin, interview by Henriette Michinard, May 16, 1940, LWP
folder 25. Saloppé was probably not the real name of this Voudou priestess. In French,
salope is a derogatory appellation meaning trashy, dirty slut, or bitch, indicating that she
was considered a woman of bad character.

15. *Picayune's Guide to New Orleans* for 1900, 65; "The Snake Dance," *Daily City Item*
Sunday magazine, March 30, 1924, p. 8, 9, 12; Hurston, *Mules and Men*, 192. Also see
Ward, *Voodoo Queen*, 61.

16. Tallant, *The Voodoo Queen*, 36.

17. Prose, *Marie Laveau*, 13–14, 17; Rhodes, *Voodoo Dreams*, 34, 104–5, 328–42. In
her fictionalized biography of Mary Ellen Pleasant, *Mammy Pleasant*, Holdredge makes
Pleasant, like Marie Laveau, the descendant of "a succession of Voodoo Queens of Santo
Domingo" (8).

18. "Idolatry and Quackery," *Louisiana Gazette*, August 16, 1820, p. 2, c. 3.

19. New Orleans municipal government is discussed in Reinders, *End of an Era*,
51–54, 71. Reinders' quotation on conditions at the municipal watch houses is from the
New Orleans Daily Mirror, September 18, 1858.

20. Reinders, *End of an Era*, 73, quoting the *Daily Crescent* of June 25, 1858, on Recorder Seuzeneau.

21. Third Municipality Guards, Mayor's Book 1838–1850, June 27, 1850, vol. 7, p.
495, microfilm NOPL; cited by Fandrich, "Mysterious Voodoo Queen," 234 n. 33, 496;
Mysterious Voodoo Queen, 137, 287 n. 51. Maps of the period show St. Bernard Avenue
and the St. Bernard Canal beginning at St. Claude Avenue and connecting with Bayou
Gentilly in a wooded area at White Street (S. Pinistri, "New Orleans General Guide and
Land Intelligence," 1841; "Norman's Plan of New Orleans and Environs," 1849, maps
THNOC). Betsy Toledano never appeared in the city directory, but she was enumer-

ated in the 1850 census as a forty-year-old Louisiana-born black female of no stated occupation (U.S. Census for New Orleans 1850, First Municipality [Wards 1–4], sheet 15B, line 29, microfilm NARA).

22. "Great Doings in the Third Municipality," *Daily Picayune*, June 29, 1850, p. 2, c. 6; "A Singular Assemblage," *Bee*, June 29, 1850, p. 1, c. 5; "A Mystery of the Old Third," *Daily Crescent*, June 29, 1850, p. 3, c. 1. The racquette game (similar to lacrosse) was probably between the black teams called the Bayous and the Lavilles, consisting of "eighty and more men on a side, with the players shoeless, stripped to the waist, and wearing red or blue caps" (Reinders, *End of an Era*, 163). The arrests of June 27 were immortalized by Castellanos in *New Orleans As It Was* (99–100) and were further elaborated upon by Asbury in *The French Quarter* (256–57) and by Tallant in *Voodoo in New Orleans* (41–42).

23. "A Motley Gathering—Superstition and Licentiousness, *Daily True Delta*, June 29, 1850, p. 3, c. 1.

24. Third Municipality Guards, Mayor's Book 1838–1850, July 2, 1850, vol. 7, p. 507, microfilm NOPL. The three slaves of Sanité Couvreure were named Hermione, Estella, and Julia; Couvreure had sold Juliette in 1849, so the suggestion that Julia and Juliette were the same person is only speculative.

25. "Another Voudou Affair," *Daily Crescent*, July 4, 1850, p. 2, c. 1.

26. "The Voudous vs Municipality No. Three," *Daily Delta*, July 14, 1850, p. 2, c. 2.

27. "The Voudou Humbug," *Daily True Delta*, July 25, 1850, p. 3, c. 1. Also see "Voudouism," *Daily Picayune*, July 24, 1850, p. 1, c. 4. The case of the Voudou women was heard before Justice Derbes.

28. "The Rites of Voudou," *Daily Crescent*, July 31, 1850, p. 3, c. 1. See also "The Voudous in the First Municipality," *Louisiana Courier*, July 30, 1850, p. 2, c. 5; "Unlawful Assemblies," *Daily Picayune*, July 31, 1850, p. 2, c. 2; and "More of the Voudous," *Daily Picayune*, July 31, 1850, p. 1, c. 6.

29. Third Municipality Recorder's Office Judicial Record Books, 1840–1852, vol. 3, *State v. Abréo*, July 2, 1850, p. 206. This charge is evidently related to an accusation in the Third Municipality Guards Mayor's Book for June 30, 1850: "Sergeant Pollock reports Watchman Abréo for receiving twenty dollars and keeping half of said sum for his own use and benefit on the 28th instant," vol. 7, p. 502, microfilm NOPL.

30. "Curious Charge of Swindling," *Daily Picayune*, July 3, 1850, p. 2, c. 6; "Recorder Seuzeneau's Court," *Louisiana Courier*, July 3, 1850, p. 1, c. 4; "Obtaining a Statue under False Pretenses," *Daily Delta*, July 3, 1850, p. 3, c. 2.

31. "The Virgin of the Voudous," *Daily Delta*, August 10, 1850, p. 2, c. 2. The case of the "Voudou Virgin" was tried before Justice of the Peace J. L. Winter.

32. Asbury, *The French Quarter*, 265–66.

33. Tallant, *Voodoo in New Orleans*, 68; Tallant, *The Voodoo Queen*, 138–39; Du Plantis, *Gris-Gris*; Chambers, "Voodoo on the Bayou," act 1, scenes 10–12, pp. 34–43.

34. Ordinance no. 3847, April 7, 1858, Mayor Charles Waterman; typed copy in LWP folder 44.

35. "Local Intelligence—Recorder Long's Court," *Daily Crescent*, July 12, 1859, p. 1,

c. 7. "Police Matters—Recorder Long's Court," *Daily True Delta*, July 12, 1859, p. 2, c. 5. "Superstitious," *Daily Picayune*, July 12, 1859, p. 1, c. 7. Thanks to Norm Helmers of the USGenWeb Orleans Parish Archives Index Project for locating the occupant of 207 Love Street in his database. Melas Wilder was listed in the city directory at 207 Love Street from 1857 to 1859.

36. Dédé/McKinney interview; Charles Raphael, interview by Hazel Breaux and Jacques Villere, n.d., LWP folder 25.

37. For reversal of the normal order, see Long, *Spiritual Merchants*, 15; for use of the saints in New Orleans Voudou, see *Spiritual Merchants*, 57.

38. Raphael/Breaux-Villere interview; Raymond Rivaros, interview by Hazel Breaux, n.d., LWP folder 25.

39. Oscar Felix, interview by Edmund Burke, March 14, 1940, LWP folder 25.

40. Raphael/Breaux-Villere interview.

41. Rivaros/Breaux interview.

42. For newspaper coverage of Doctor Alexander see "Trouble Among the Voudous," *Daily Picayune*, August 18, 1871, p. 2, c. 5; "A Voudou Orgie—Sensational Disclosure in the Third District," *Times-Democrat*, May 28, 1889, p. 4, c. 3; "A Voudou Entertainment," *Daily States*, May 29, 1889, p. 2, c. 2; "An Astounding Revelation," *Daily Picayune*, May 30, 1889, p. 4, c. 4; "The Voudou Doctor—Death of a Notorious Negro Who Throve on the Superstitions of His Kind," *Daily Picayune*, August 20, 1890, p. 8, c. 3; "Death of the Voodoo Doctor," *Daily States*, August 20, 1890, p. 5, c. 2.

43. Hobley/Posey interview; Kavanaugh/Posey interview.

44. Warner, "A Voudou Dance," 454–55. Warner (1829–1900) was a colleague of George Washington Cable; their professional association is mentioned in Turner's *George W. Cable*.

45. Castellanos, *New Orleans As It Was*, 99; Hurston, *Mules and Men*, 192; Tallant, *Voodoo in New Orleans*, 108.

46. Josephine McDuffy, interview by Henriette Michinard, 1940, LWP folder 25; Washington/McKinney interview.

47. Cable, *The Grandissimes*, 55, 67, 216, 306, 308; Pitkin, *An Angel by Brevet*, 178–212, 259–88.

48. Song for Legba, Métraux, *Voodoo in Haiti*, 101.

49. *Picayune's Guide to New Orleans* for 1900, 66; Hurston, *Mules and Men*, 192–94; Tallant, *The Voodoo Queen*, 107; Prose, *Marie Laveau*, 189, Rhodes, *Voodoo Dreams*, 204; Hank, *The Widow Paris*; Chambers, "Voodoo on the Bayou," act 1, scene 1, p. 5, scene 3, p. 13.

50. Rivaros/Breaux interview; Josephine Jones, no interviewer, n.d., LWP folder 25. Snakes were also mentioned by St. Ann Johnson, interview by Maude Wallace, February 8, 1940, and Eugene Fritz, interview by Robert McKinney, n.d., LWP folder 25. Dissenting opinions are from Raphael/Breaux-Villere interview; Cecile Hunt, interview by Zoe Posey, November 6, 1940, LWP folder 25.

51. The Cracker Jack, located at 435 South Rampart, was in business from 1897 until 1974, selling "spiritual products" formulated by its proprietor, Dr. George A. Thomas,

and later by his widow, Alice Vibert (Thomas) Karno. In 1927 an unidentified South Rampart Street pharmacist, probably Dr. Thomas, faced mail fraud charges for marketing such merchandise, including the booklet called *The Life and Works of Marie Laveau* ("Federal Agents Expose Business in Goofer Dust," *New Orleans Tribune*, May 14, 1927, p. 1, c. 3). *The Life and Works of Marie Laveau* may have been written by Dr. Thomas or his wife. For more on the Cracker Jack, see Long, *Spiritual Merchants*, 144–48. Martha Ward (*Voodoo Queen*, 27–28) accepts the "Marie Laveau routines" as genuine examples of Marie Laveau's rituals.

52. Zora Neale Hurston to Langston Hughs, October 15, 1928, in *Zora Neale Hurston: A Life in Letters*, Kaplan, ed., 127.

53. Laura Hopkins, interview by Maude Wallace, February 9, 16, and 21, and March 4, 1940, and by Wallace and Henriette Michinard, April, 1940, LWP folder 43; Joe Landry, interview by Zoe Posey, July 18, 1939; John Slater, interview by Cecile Wright, n.d., LWP folder 25.

54. Washington/McKinney interview.

CHAPTER 7. ST. JOHN'S EVE

1. Frazer, *The Golden Bough*, 724. St. John's Eve is still celebrated in France and Spain, in French Quebec, and in the former French and Spanish colonies of Latin America and the Caribbean.

2. Cosentino, *Sacred Arts of Haitian Vodou*, 47–52. Masonic lodges worldwide recognize St. John the Baptist and St. John the Evangelist as their patrons; the feast days of these two saints coincide with the summer and winter solstices (*An Encyclopedia of Freemasonry*, Mackey, ed., 199–202).

3. Joyaux, ed. and trans., "Forest's *Voyage aux États-Unis de l'Amérique en 1831*," 457–72, quoted in Estes, "Traditional Dances and Processions," 8–9.

4. Dillon, "Voodoo," chapter 10, "Marie the Great," p. 21.

5. James P. Baughman, "A Southern Spa: Ante-Bellum Lake Pontchartrain," 5–31. Reinders, in *End of an Era* (2–3), describes the swamp as it appeared in the 1850s.

6. *Historical Sketch Book*, 32.

7. "St. John's Day—Grand Celebration by the Knights Templar of New Orleans," *Daily Picayune*, June 25, 1874, p. 1, c. 5; "St. John's Day Celebrated by Masons with Fitting Ceremony," *Daily Picayune*, June 25, 1890, p. 8, c. 1–2; "A Notable Affair—The Celebration of St. John's Day by the Masons," *Daily States*, June 25, 1890, p. 2, c. 1–4.

8. "St. John's Eve Celebrations," *Daily States*, June 24, 1887, p. 6, c. 4.

9. Touchstone, "Voodoo in New Orleans," 381, 386.

10. "Voodooism," *Commercial Bulletin*, July 5, 1869, p. 1, c. 7.

11. "Fetish Rites," *Daily Picayune*, June 23, 1870, p. 2, c. 5; "The Voudous' Day," *Times*, June 25, 1870, p. 6, c. 2.

12. "The Vous Dous Incantation," *Times*, June 28, 1872, p. 1, c. 6. See also "Making a Night of It—A Search for the Vous Dous Queen—An African Ball," *Times*, June 26, 1872, p. 2, c. 1–2.

13. "St. John's Eve—The Voudous," *Daily Picayune*, June 24, 1873, p. 4, c. 2.

14. "Fate and Mystery," *Republican*, June 21, 1874, p. 5, c. 1; "The Voudou Ceremonies," *Republican*, June 25, 1874, p. 3, c. 1. "Voudou Vagaries—The Worshipers of Obeah Turned Loose," *Times*, June 26, 1874, p. 2, c. 2–4. "Voudou Nonsense—A Plain, Unvarnished Account of the Lake Shore Revels—Full Particulars of the Hell-Broth and Orgies—A Played-Out Hoax," *Daily Picayune*, June 26, 1874, p. 1, c. 5.

15. "Fetish Worship—St. John's Eve at Milneburg—A Voudou's Incantation—Midnight Scenes and Orgies," *Times*, June 25, 1875, p. 2, c. 1 and 2. See also "St. John's Eve—After the Voudous—Some Singular Ceremonies—A Night in Heathenness," *Daily Picayune*, June 25, 1875, p. 2, c. 1.

16. Advertisement for Fourth of July festival, *Daily City Item*, June 23, 1881, p. 4, c. 6.

17. "A Voudou Dance—Revival on the Lake Shore of Voudou Mysteries—How the Eve of St. John was Celebrated Last Night by the Queen and Her Adherents," *Times-Democrat*, June 24, 1884, p. 2, c. 3. A shorter version appeared in the *Historical Sketch Book* of 1885, 239–51, and is reprinted in Starr, ed., *Inventing New Orleans*, 72–76. Starr attributes this piece to Lafcadio Hearn on the basis of Hearn's employment at the *Times-Democrat* from 1882 until 1887. The song "Mallé marché su piquan d'oré" was translated in the *Times-Democrat* article as "I will wander into the desert, I will march through the prairie, I will walk upon the golden thorn. Who is there who can stop me? To change me from this plantation? I have the support of Louisiana. Who is there who can resist me?" A later version, using the phrase "walk on gilded splinters," was published in Herbert Moore's "Voodoo!" in the *Times-Picayune* Sunday magazine of March 16, 1924. These words inspired the 1967 composition "Walk on Gilded Splinters," by New Orleans singer and songwriter Mac Rebennack, recorded on the *Gris-Gris* album by his band Doctor John and the Night Trippers.

18. "Voudouism Rampant in Louisiana," *Times*, July 17, 1870, p. 3, c. 4–5. Buel, *Metropolitan Life Unveiled*, 536–39.

19. Asbury, *The French Quarter*, 276–77. For more on the common belief that loathsome creatures can be introduced into the human body by hoodoo and removed by the same means, see Long, *Spiritual Merchants*, 75, 81.

20. New Orleans city ordinance no. 3046 passed May 7, 1879; New Orleans city ordinance no. 7086 passed May 17, 1881; state law against practicing medicine without a license, Louisiana House of Representatives, 1887; New Orleans city ordinance no. 13,347, passed May 23, 1897; typed copies in LWP folder 44.

21. "St. John's Eve," *Daily States*, June 23, 1887, p. 5, c. 3; "A Cungi Dance," *Times-Democrat*, June 24, 1887, p. 3, c. 3.

22. "Dance of the Voodoos—Outlandish Celebration of St. John's Eve," *Times-Democrat*, June 24, 1896, p. 2, c. 6–7.

23. "Voudouism—A Chapter of Old New Orleans History—How St. John's Eve Was Celebrated Fifty Years Ago," *Daily Picayune*, June 22, 1890, p. 10, c. 1–4. For another such account, see *Picayune's Guide to New Orleans* for 1900, 66.

24. Henrietta Nichols, no interviewer, March 19, 1940; Mathilda Mendoza, interview by Maude Wallace, January 11 and 17, 1940, LWP folder 25.

25. Felix/Burke interview.

26. "Pops," interview by Robert McKinney, n.d., LWP folder 25. The idea that Marie Laveau rose from the depths of the lake and walked on the water turns up in Hurston's *Mules and Men* (193), where it was attributed to Hurston's mentor, "Luke Turner." Jewel Parker Rhodes, no doubt inspired by Hurston, also included the water-walking incident in her novel, *Voodoo Dreams* (305–7).

27. Raphael/Breaux-Villere interview.

28. A report from 1900 described black men masking as Indian warriors on Mardi Gras day, wearing "war paint and feathers, bearing the tomahawk and bow . . . running along the streets in bands from six to twenty and upwards, whooping, leaping, brandishing their weapons, and, anon, stopping in the middle of the street to go through the movements of a mimic war-dance, chanting the while in rhythmic cadence an outlandish jargon of no sensible import to any save themselves" (Rightor, ed., *Standard History of New Orleans*, 631). For more on the "Mardi Gras Indians," see Smith, *Spirit World* and *Mardi Gras Indians*.

29. William Moore, interview by Edmund Burke, March 1, 1940, LWP folder 25.

30. Rivaros/Breaux interview.

31. Alfred/McKinney interview; Fritz/McKinney interview. Joseph Alfred and Eugene Fritz lived at the Thomy Lafon Old Folks Home, a retirement facility for people of color established by the Afro-Creole philanthropist Thomy Lafon and administered by the Sisters of the Holy Family.

32. John Smith, interview by Hazel Breaux, n.d., LWP folder 25.

33. Tallant, *Voodoo in New Orleans*, 65–66.

34. Touchstone, "Voodoo in New Orleans," 380.

35. Washington/McKinney interview; Marie Brown, interview by Zoe Posey, April 14, 1941, LWP folder 25; Rivaros/Breaux interview.

36. "Making a Night of It—A Search for the Vous Dous Queen—An African Ball," *Times*, June 26, 1872, p. 2, c. 1–2. Castellanos, *New Orleans As It Was*, 98.

37. Asbury, *The French Quarter*, 266; Dillon, "Voodoo," chapter 11, "Marie the Mysterious," section 6, p. 1a; Tallant, *Voodoo in New Orleans*, 84–87; Holdredge, *Mammy Pleasant*, 28; Cott, *Wandering Ghost*, 145–47.

38. Smith/Breaux interview. The location cited by John Smith concurs with a 1924 *Daily City Item* Sunday magazine interview with two longtime Milneburg residents, Madame Boudro and Madame Acosta, who reported that Marie Laveau's lakeside cabin was a "hut perched upon high pillars on the [London] canal between Milneburg and Bayou St. John" ("The Snake Dance," March 30, 1924, p. 9).

39. Alfred/McKinney and Fritz/McKinney interviews.

40. Asbury, *The French Quarter*, 378–87.

41. "A Modern Lucretia Borgia—The Last Adventure of Fanny Sweet—An Extraordinary Conspiracy," *Daily True Delta*, December 8, 1861, p. 1, c. 1–5. Rose, *Storyville, New Orleans*, 14.

CHAPTER 8. DOCTOR JOHN

1. "Africa Triumphant," *Daily Picayune* , August 18, 1859, p. 2, c. 5.

2. "Voudouist Disgorged—Credulity and Cunning—Ghosts and Greenhorns, *Daily Delta*, October 21, 1860, p. 8, c. 3.

3. "A Visit to a Professor of the Black Art," *Daily Crescent*, December 24, 1866, p. 2, c. 2.

4. "Voudouing a Wine Mark," *Republican*, February 26, 1871, p. 5, c. 1; "Voudou John Arrested," *Commercial Bulletin*, March 10, 1871, p. 1, c. 7.

5. "Faithful Wife Pays Doctor for the Return of her Husband," *Daily States*, December 9, 1881, p. 1, c. 7.

6. Lafcadio Hearn, "The Last of the Voudoos," *Harper's Weekly*; reprinted in Starr, ed., *Inventing New Orleans*, 77–82.

7. Castellanos, *New Orleans As It Was*, 167–76. In calling Doctor John a "black Cagliostro," Castellanos is alluding to the eighteenth-century adventurer and imposter Count Alessandro Cagliostro.

8. Castellanos, *New Orleans As It Was*, 167–76; Asbury, *The French Quarter*, 257–58; Tallant, *The Voodoo Queen*, 180–82. Rebennack, *Under a Hoodoo Moon*, 141. Rebennack mistakenly attributes the story of Doctor John and Pauline to Lafcadio Hearn instead of Herbert Asbury.

9. Tallant, *Voodoo in New Orleans*, 36; Tallant, *The Voodoo Queen*, 155, 177–80, 302–14.

10. Prose, *Marie Laveau*, 62–73, 135–40, 175, 205–6, 224–26, 236–48.

11. Rhodes, *Voodoo Dreams*, 19–20, 96, 116–17, 334–35, 418–22.

12. Reed, *The Last Days of Louisiana Red*, 136–44.

13. Carbon, "Marie Laveau: A Full-Length Voodoo Opera." The story of Euphrasine comes from Tallant, *Voodoo in New Orleans*, 141–51.

14. Chambers, "Voodoo on the Bayou," act 1, scene 3, pp. 13–15.

15. Hank, *The Widow Paris*. A University of New Orleans production, Hank's film won best Louisiana film in the 1993 New Orleans Film and Video Festival and was selected for a New York screening. More information on Hank's work can be obtained from the University of New Orleans Department of Film, Theater, and Communication Arts.

16. Washington/McKinney interview; Hobley/Posey interview.

17. Sale of two lots facing St. Philip by Constance Landreaux f.w.c. to Jean Montanée for $1,000, Acts of C. F. Foulon, April 3, 1845; sale of lot corner Urquhart and Annette by P. Montruil f.m.c. to Montanée for $200, Acts of Octave de Armas, May 12, 1845; sale of lots 25 and 26 in square bounded by Prieur, Roman, Ursulines, and Hospital by V. Chedville to Montanée for $400, Acts of L. F. Maureau, March 21, 1846; sale of lot facing Bayou Road by Adéle Doriocourt to Montanée for $680, Acts of Antoine Doriocourt, July 27, 1847; sale of lot 10, in square bounded by Dumaine, St. Ann, Prieur, and Roman by J. de Lizardi to Montanée for $400, Acts of Lucien Hermann, September 17, 1847; sale of lot in square bounded by Tonti, Rocheblave, Ursulines, and Hospital by

Municipality no. 1 to Montanée for $83, Acts of Joseph Cuvillier, September 30, 1848; sale of lot in square bounded by London Walk, Force, Liberal, and Havana by F. Jacobs to Montanée for $60, Acts of Antoine Doriocourt, September 30, 1848; sale of three lots in square bounded by Tonti, Havana, Rocheblave, Warsaw, and the St. Bernard Canal Promenade by F. Jacobs to Montanée for $110, Acts of Antoine Doriocourt, January 22, 1849; sale of six lots in square bounded by Macarty property and by Independence, Prosper, and Solidelle by F. Jacobs to Montanée for $60, Acts of Alphonse Barnett, November 28, 1851; sale of lot in square bounded by Bayou Road, Hospital, Prieur, and Roman by Aimée Gautier to Montanée for $1,200, Acts of Antoine Doriocourt, September 9, 1854; sale of lot in square bounded by Prieur, St. Philippe, Johnson, and Dumaine by B. Saloy to Montanée for $525, COB 66, p. 604, January 29, 1859.

18. Sale of lot by Nancy St. Martin to Jean Montanée, Acts of Octave de Armas, February 5, 1847, vol. 40, act 9; cancellation of sale by St. Martin to Montanée, Acts of Octave de Armas, July 19, 1847, vol. 41, act 193, with petition of St. Martin to Second District Court attached, NARC.

19. Sale of café and grocery store by Jacques Augies to Jean Montanée for $750, Acts of Antoine Doriocourt, December 29, 1849, COB 49, p. 242; sale of café and grocery store by Montanée to François Caubére for $175, Acts of Antoine Doriocourt, December 17, 1850, COB 52, p. 302.

20. Sheriff's sale, October 22, 1861, three lots in the square bounded by St. Roch, Prosper, and Roman, judgment in suit of *Henriette Cazas v. Jean Montanée*, Fourth Justice of the Peace, docket no. 24,643, COB 86, p. 210. Sheriff's sale, January 6, 1866, two lots in the square bounded by Hospital, Galvez, Ursulines, and Johnson, judgment in suit of *Pierre Theophile Commagere v. Jean Montanée*, Fifth Justice of the Peace, docket no. 15,263, COB 89, p. 378 and COB 90, p. 375.

21. U.S. Census for New Orleans 1850, John Montanet, Ward 6, sheet 364, line 33. U.S. Census for New Orleans 1860, John Montane, Ward 6, sheet 186, line 21. U.S. Census for New Orleans 1870, John Montaine, Ward 6, sheet 263, line 33. U.S. Census for 1880, Jno. Montanet, ED 46, sheet 90, line 39, NARA.

22. Sale of slave Hyacinth for $275 by Céphine Piseros, Widow of Labranche, to Jean Montanée, Acts of Octave de Armas, May 15, 1847, vol. 40, act 103, NARC; sale of Hyacinth for $625 by Montanée to Louis Carlon, Acts of Antoine Doriocourt, December 17, 1850, COB 52, p. 302. Sale of slave Charlotte for $300 by François Enoul Livaudais to Jean Montanée, Acts of Antoine Doriocourt, August 10, 1847, COB 44, p. 105.

23. Sale of slave Mathilde for $600 by Celeste Daprement, wife of Poré, to Jean Montanée, Acts of Theodore Guyol, March 5, 1849, COB 48, p. 419; sale of Mathilde for $625 by Montanée to Louis Vino, Acts of Antoine Doriocourt, December 16, 1850, COB 54; sale of Mathilde for $625 by Vino to Montanée, Acts of Antoine Doriocourt, July 21, 1851, COB 56, p. 115.

24. Sale of slave Martha for $650 by Hypolite Daunoy to Jean Montanée, Acts of Antoine Doriocourt, April 23, 1850, COB 50, p. 473. Sale of slave Mary for $100 by Lucien Mansion f.m.c. to Jean Montanée, Acts of Antoine Doriocourt, April 27, 1852, COB 55, p. 566. Sale of slave Diana for $150 by Daniel Rèvoille to Jean Montanée, Acts

of Onesiphore Drouet, November 10, 1852, COB 59, p. 226. Montanée gave the seller $25 for Diana, promising to free her upon payment of the full price, but I found no record that he did so.

25. Sale of slave Minnie called Cécelia and her daughter Flora and infant for $1,200 by David R. Godwin to Jean Montanée, Acts of James Graham, June 3, 1853, COB 65, p. 156.

26. Sale of slave William for $300 by Armande Trabuc to Jean Montanée, Acts of Amadée Ducatel, April 6, 1848, COB 44, p. 554; sale of William for $100 by Montanée to Pierre Devergés, Acts of Antoine Doriocourt, March 23, 1849, COB 48, p. 451. Sale of slave Henry Davis for $50 by James Austin to Jean Montanée, May 7, 1857, COB 74, p. 88; sale of Henry Davis for $600 by Montanée to Bertrand Saloy, February 17, 1860, COB 80, p. 619. Emancipation of slave Jean Bermudez, native of Guinea, by Jean Montanée, Acts of Octave de Armas, June 9, 1849, vol. 45, act 184, NARC. The notarial act notes that the slave Jean was purchased from Madame Emma Bermudez on October 16, 1845.

27. Birth certificate for John Montannet, November 3, 1856, vol. 10, p. 891; birth certificate for Edouard Montanet, October 13, 1872, vol. 605, p. 1014; birth certificate for Joseph Montaney, May 30, 1880, vol. 98, p. 635, LDA.

28. Death certificate for John Montanée, August 23, 1885, vol. 87, p. 914, microfilm NOPL. At the time of this writing, a searchable database for the 1885 New Orleans directory has not been compiled by the USGenWeb Orleans Parish Archives Index Project and I am therefore unable to say in whose home Doctor John died.

CHAPTER 9. PRISON MINISTRY

1. Castellanos, *New Orleans As It Was*, 104–10.

2. Asbury, *The French Quarter*, 270–73.

3. Tallant, *Voodoo in New Orleans*, 69–71, and *The Voodoo Queen*, 213–24.

4. Rhodes, *Voodoo Dreams*, 383–91; Chambers, "Voodoo on the Bayou," act 2, scene 2, 4–7.

5. "The Day of Mourning," *Commercial Bulletin*, July 3, 1852, p. 2, c. 1.

6. "The Execution Today," *Daily Picayune*, July 2, 1852, p. 2, c. 5; "Public Execution," *Daily Picayune*, July 3, 1852, p. 2, c. 2; "Execution," *Commercial Bulletin*, July 3, 1852, p. 2, c. 4; "Execution of Adam and Delisle—Horrid Spectacle," *Daily Crescent*, July 3, 1852, p. 2, c. 5.

7. Asbury, *The French Quarter*, 274; Tallant, *Voodoo in New Orleans*, 71–72.

8. "Execution of James Mullen," *Daily True Delta*, July 30, 1859, p. 1, c. 4, 5; "Execution This Morning," *Daily Picayune*, July 30, 1859, p. 5, c. 5.

9. Asbury, *The French Quarter*, 274; Tallant, *Voodoo in New Orleans*, 72.

10. "Murder and Its Punishment—Three Men Executed," *Daily True Delta*, March 19, 1859, p. 2, c. 3, 4, 5.

11. "The Execution," *Daily Picayune*, March 18, 1859, p. 4. c. 1.

12. Castellanos, *New Orleans As It Was*, 104–14.

13. Du Plantis, *Gris-Gris*.

14. "The Louisiana Ball-Room Homicide," *Daily True Delta*, March 16, 1859, p. 1, c. 6.

15. "Mysterious Murder," *Daily Picayune*, December 22, 1859, p. 1, c. 5; "Post Mortem Examination" and "Arrest," *Daily Picayune*, December 23, 1859, p. 6, c. 1; "Inquest of George Frey," *Daily Picayune*, December 24, 1859, p. 2, c. 3. "First District Court—Judge Hunt," *Daily Picayune*, June 12, 1860, p. 4, c. 1–2, and June 14, 1860, p. 2, c. 2.

16. For more on the Know-Nothing, or Native American Party, see Reinders, *End of an Era*, 56–60. Elsewhere in the United States, the Know-Nothings were also anti-Catholic, but this was less true in Louisiana owing to its Roman Catholic Creole population.

17. "First District Court—Judge Hunt," *Daily Picayune*, July 3, 1860, p. 2, c. 1–2.

18. "Another Condemned Prisoner Dead in the Parish Prison," *Daily Delta*, August 8, 1860, p. 2, c. 2–4. "Death of Antoine Cambre," *Daily Crescent,* August 8, 1860, p. 1, c. 3.

19. "Death of Eugene Pepe," *Daily Picayune*, June 21, 1860, p. 1, c. 1.

20. Fandrich, "Mysterious Voodoo Queen," 257; *Mysterious Voodoo Queen*, 166–67, quoting her 1992 interview with Randall Mitchell.

21. Davis, *Passage of Darkness*, 6–8, 154–55, quoting from the medical literature on tetrodotoxin poisoning.

22. "Another Condemned Prisoner Dead in the Parish Prison," *Daily Delta*, August 8, 1860, p. 2, c. 2–4. A search of the usual archival sources failed to uncover the identity of Cambre's domestic partner. Ward, in *Voodoo Queen* (129), theorizes that the woman mentioned by the newspapers was Marie Laveau.

23. Burial of Antoine Cambre, Burial Book, St. Louis Cemetery No. 1 (1859–1864), August 9, 1860, p. 41, AA.

24. Asbury, *The French Quarter*, 274–75; Tallant, *Voodoo in New Orleans*, 72.

25. "The Death Penalty—Reprieve of the Condemned—Scene at the Parish Prison," *Daily Picayune*, May 28, 1870, p. 2, c. 3, 4, 5.

26. Tallant, *Voodoo in New Orleans*, 73. Castellanos included the case of Abriel and Bayonne in his chapter on the "Old Parish Prison" (*New Orleans As It Was*, 118–21), but did not connect it with Marie Laveau.

27. "The Condemned—The Decorations of the Altar," *Daily Picayune*, May 10, 1871, p. 2, c. 6.

28. "The Execution—Infliction of the Death Penalty—Murder Atoned," *Daily Picayune*, May 14, 1871, p. 13, c. 3–7.

29. "Death of Marie Laveau," *Daily Picayune*, June 17, 1881, p. 8, c. 3; "Wayside Notes—The Death of Marie Laveau," *Daily City Item*, June 17, 1881, p. 1, c. 5; "The Dead Voudou Queen," *New York Times*, June 23, 1881, p. 2, c. 3–4; "Flagitious Fiction," *Daily Picayune*, April 11, 1886, p. 3, c. 4.

CHAPTER 10. FINAL YEARS

1. Roussève, *The Negro in Louisiana*, 104–8; Taylor, *Louisiana Reconstructed*, 114–55, 173–74, 279–96, 437; Logsdon and Bell, "The Americanization of Black New Orleans,"

221–61; Tregle, "Creoles and Americans," 171, 250–51. Antoine Dubuclet, Oscar J. Dunn, C. C. Antoine, and P.B.S. Pinchback held the offices of Louisiana state treasurer and lieutenant governor. Pinchback also served for a few weeks as interim governor.

2. Taylor, *Louisiana Reconstructed*, 162, 281–96; Tregle, "Creoles and Americans," 172. The connection between New Orleans' white elite Carnival krewes and white supremacist organizations is explored in Gill, *Lords of Misrule*, 77–143.

3. Deggs, *No Cross, No Crown*, 91–92. Roussève, *The Negro in Louisiana*, 40–42, 108–9; Labbé, *Jim Crow Comes to Church*, 27–41, 50–56, 63–84; Logsdon and Bell, "Americanization of Black New Orleans," 214, 234–35; Bell, *Revolution, Romanticism, and the Afro-Creole Protest Tradition*, 82–85, 186–88, 206–21.

4. "Fetish—Its Worship and Worshipers—Their Customs and Rites—Voudous and Voudouism," *Daily Picayune*, June 24, 1875, p. 1, c. 4–5. Catherine Dillon doubted the validity of this interview, speculating that the reporter had spoken with some other old woman who lived in the Laveau-Glapion household (Dillon, "Voodoo," chapter 10, "Marie the Great," 36).

5. Marguerite Gitson, interview by Zoe Posey, February 20, 1941; Fonvergne/Breaux interview; Alice Zeno, interview by Hazel Breaux, n.d.; Legendre/Wallace interview, LWP folder 25.

6. U.S. Census for New Orleans 1860, Widow Paris, Ward 4, sheet 649, line 24; here Adelai Aldina was listed as "Alzonia" Crocker, age 12, and Marie was listed as "Amazone" Crocker, age 9. U.S. Census for New Orleans 1870, Mary Paris, Ward 5, sheet 149, line 14, NARA.

7. Death certificate for Aldina Croker, vol. 52, p. 245, microfilm NOPL; burial of A. Aldina Croker, Burial Book, St. Louis Cemetery No. 1 (1870–1873), September 9, 1871, p. 245, AA.

8. Emancipation of slave Lizette and her mulatto children Marie and Celestin from the estate of Christophe de Glapion, Hall, *Louisiana Free Database*. Hall commented that "Glapion is possibly the father of Marie and Celestin." A fine armoire, now at the Louisiana State Museum, is signed C. Glapion and is believed to be the work of Celestin Glapion. Celestin "Glapillon," age 37, and his wife Honesta, age 30, were enumerated in the U.S. Census for New Orleans 1870 in the Laveau-Glapion household headed by "Mary Paris." Alexis Celestin Glapion, painter, was listed in the city directory at 152 St. Ann.

9. Judith (born 1813) and her brother Pierre Gustave Toutant Beauregard (born 1818) were the children of Jacques Toutant Beauregard and Judith Hélène de Reggio. Marriage contract of Alexandre Legendre and Marie Judith Toutant, Acts of Felix de Armas, November 1, 1830, vol. 30, act 849; marriage of Alexandre Legendre and Marie Françoise Judith Toutant, SLC Marriages of White Persons, November 1, 1830, vol. 5, act 26. The children of Alexandre Legendre and Judith Toutant were James Arthur, Marie Amanda, Gustave, and Armand. Arthur was born October 22, 1833, and Amanda was born January 11, 1835; both were baptized at Saint Louis Cathedral on January 28, 1835. No baptismal record could be found for Gustave (born ca. 1836) and Armand (birth date unknown). The names of the three sons are listed on a genealogical chart displayed at

the Beauregard-Keyes House in New Orleans, with the additional information that an unnamed daughter (presumably Marie Amanda) married a Mr. Casado from Málaga, Spain.

10. Sale of three lots in the square bounded by Girod, Camp, Lafayette, and St. Charles by James Colles and Benjamin Harrod to Henry Lawrence and Alexandre Legendre, Acts of Louis T. Caire, February 22, 1836, COB 19, p. 66. Sale of two lots in the square bounded by Carondelet, Union, Baronne, and Gravier by Henry William Palfrey to Lawrence and Legendre, Acts of H. B. Cenas, May 13, 1836, COB 19, pp. 434–35. Sale of five lots in Faubourg Lafayette by Richard Bien to Lawrence and Legendre, Acts of W. Y. Lewis, June 15, 1836, COB 19, p. 428. Sale of two lots in the square bounded by Tchoupitoulas, Josephine, St. Thomas, and Robin by Raphael Toledano and George Legendre to Alexandre Legendre, Acts of Carlisle Pollock, July 14, 1836, COB 19, p. 607. Sale of lot in square bounded by Urquhart, Girod, France, and Lesseps by Alexandre Legendre to Achille Rivarde, Acts of G. Legardeur, September 17, 1836, COB 22, p. 148. Sale of three lots in the square bounded by Tchoupitoulas, Josephine, St. Thomas, and Robin by Alexandre Legendre to E. W. Sewell and James Burdon, Acts of W. Y. Lewis, March 9, 1837, COB 22, p. 458. Purchase of two lots corner Louisa and Dauphine by Alexandre Legendre from sheriff's auction, June 9, 1837, COB 24, p. 48. Sale of two lots corner Louisa and Dauphine by Alexandre Legendre to William Collerton, Acts of Carlisle Pollock, September 26, 1837, COB 22, p. 343.

11. Sale of two lots in the square bounded by Carondelet, Union, Baronne, and Gravier by J. M. Lapeyre and J. H. Raboteau, syndics for the creditors of Lawrence and Legendre, to Samuel Chase, Acts of Felix Grima, December 10, 1837, COB 25, p. 629 and 644, NARC.

12. Sale of slaves Irma, Charles, Oscar, and Rosa, the dotal property of Judith Toutant, wife of Legendre, to Felix McManus for $1,500, Acts of Theodore Guyol, October 16, 1852, vol. 24, act 606. Sale of slaves Auguste and Louis, born in the possession of Judith Toutant, wife of Legendre, [children] of the negress slave Seraphine, her dotal property, to Rosa Gomez for $1,000, Acts of Achille Chiapella, April 19, 1854, vol. 35, act 301. Sale of slave Seraphine and her children Victor and Victorine, donated to Madame Legendre by her parents in 1834, to Madame Adolphe Plauche for $1,800, Acts of Octave de Armas, April 20, 1854, vol. 57, act 115. Sale of lot corner Louisa and Greatmen [Dauphine] by Judith Toutant, wife of Legendre to Adolphe and Edmond Goldman for $2,600, Acts of Octave de Armas, January 17, 1856, vol. 35, act 201, NARC. Judith Toutant last appeared in the archival record when she sold two lots in the neighborhood of Montegut, Casacalvo (now Royal), and 1st Street from the succession of her mother Judith de Reggio, Acts of Abel Dreyfus, October 11, 1865, COB 89, p. 253.

13. Frances Parkinson Keyes lived in the Beauregard-Keyes House, in which General P.G.T. Beauregard rented rooms after the Civil War. Her 1962 novel, *Madame Castel's Lodger*, is a fictionalized, but historically accurate, account of the general's later years. Here Keyes wrote that Beauregard's sister Judith, "had gone to New York to educate her children and had steadfastly refused to return to the South; she said quite frankly that she did not want to see its desolation" (14). Keyes' assertion is borne out by census

data. In 1850 Gustave and Arthur Legendre, ages 14 and 16, both natives of Louisiana, were enumerated among the students of a Roman Catholic boys' school at West Farms, Westchester, New York, and Amanda Legendre, age 15, native of Louisiana, was listed at a school in New York City (U.S. Census for Westchester, N.Y., 1850, West Farms, p. 288; U.S. Census for New York City 1850, Ward 18, p. 113). In 1860 Judith Legendre, age 47, Arthur Legendre, age 26, and Gustave Legendre, age 22, all natives of Louisiana, were living in a boarding house in downtown Manhattan (U.S. Census for New York 1860, Ward 18, District 2, p. 267). The absence of a Louisiana death record for Judith Legendre suggests that she never returned to New Orleans.

14. Birth certificate for Fidelia Legendre, vol. 49, p. 746; Alexandre Legendre, vol. 49, p. 747; Noëmie Legendre, vol. 49, p. 746; Blaire Legendre, vol. 49, p. 747; Charles St. Marc and (Joseph) Etienne St. Marc Legendre, vol. 53, p. 289. Death certificate for Eugenie Legendre, vol. 32, p. 289; Charles Legendre, vol. 47, p. 897; Joseph Legendre, vol. 52, p. 245, LDA. The children who died were interred in the Widow Paris tomb and are recorded in the Burial Book for St. Louis Cemetery No. 1 (Burial of Eugenie Legendre, January 30, 1866, Burial Book, St. Louis Cemetery No. 1 (1865–1869), p. 146; burial of Charles (St. Marc) Legendre, May 24, 1870, burial of Joseph (Etienne St. Marc) Legendre, July 12, 1870, Burial Book, St. Louis Cemetery No. 1 (1870–1873), pp. 111, 127; AA). Note that Philomène gave both twins the middle name *St. Marc*, similar to *Semard*, quoted in the 1881 *Picayune* obituary as the surname of Marie Laveau's grandmother, and *San Marre*, one of the surnames used by Marie's mother.

15. Dédé/McKinney interview; Legendre/Breaux-Villere interview.

16. U.S. Census for New Orleans 1860, Widow Paris, Ward 4, sheet 649, line 24. U.S. Census for New Orleans 1870, Alexandre Lejendre, Ward 7, sheet 572, line 39, microfilm NARA.

17. Death certificate for Alexandre Legendre, July 26, 1872, vol. 55, p. 263, microfilm NOPL; funeral announcement, *Bee*, July 27, 1872, p. 2, c. 7.

18. The LWP cemetery file for St. Louis Cemetery No. 3 (LSM/HC) shows the interment of Emile Alexandre Legendre in section B, St. Joseph alley. Alana Mendoza, superintendent of St. Louis Cemeteries was unable to find this burial record.

19. Sale of 152 St. Ann for $2,000 by Eugenie Alsar, Widow of Philippe Ross, to Philomène Glapion, with donation of usufruct by Philomène Glapion to Marie Laveau, May 13, 1876, Acts of Octave de Armas, vol. 97, act 56, NARC.

20. U.S. Census for New Orleans 1880, Marie Glapion, Ward 5, ED 35, sheet 216B, line 45, microfilm NARA.

21. Dédé/McKinney interview; Octavia Fontenette, interview by Edmond Burke, March 11, 1940; Washington/McKinney interview, LWP folder 25.

22. War of 1812, bounty land files, no. 332.037; pension files, no. 11616, NARA. Marie Laveau did successfully apply for Glapion's pension from the state of Louisiana. Her petition to Edmond Meunier, judge of the Third District Court for Orleans Parish, is reproduced in Loomis, *Negro Soldiers, Free Men of Color in the Battle of New Orleans*, 17. Loomis obviously was not aware that Christophe Glapion was white. Thanks to Ina Fandrich for photocopies of this material.

23. Quoted in Dillon, "Voodoo," chapter 11, "Marie the Mysterious," section 7, p. 1, as "A Sketch of Marie Laveau—Medallions and Curios Carved by Descendant of Count De Lesseps Here," *Daily City Item*, December 12, 1920, p. 4, c. 1. The article could not be found as cited.

24. Nott, "Marie Laveau, Long High Priestess of Voudouism," *Times-Picayune* Sunday magazine, November 19, 1922, p. 2.

25. Hurston, "Hoodoo in America," 326.

26. Asbury, *The French Quarter*, 266–67.

27. Dédé/McKinney interview; Felix/Burke interview; Washington/McKinney interview. Versions of the near-drowning incident were also contributed by Cecilia Maury, Alice Zeno, Mrs. Dauphine, Laura Hopkins, Mary Richard, and Marie Brown. Only Harrison Camille (interview by Maude Wallace, January 9 and 11, 1940, LWP folder 25) and Mary Louise Butler (interview by Catherine Dillon, November 27, 1939, LWP folder 25) believed that Marie Laveau actually drowned.

28. Marie Martin, interview by Henriette Michinard, August 19, 1940, quoted in Dillon, "Voodoo," chapter 11, "Marie the Mysterious," section 7, p. 9a. The name *Levasseur* is common in Orleans Parish, but no record of an Angèlie Levasseur could be found.

29. "The Heat's Victims," *Daily City Item*, June 16, 1881, p. 1, c. 7; "The Thermometer," *Times*, June 23, 1881, p. 7, c. 3; "Struck by the Sun," *Times*, June 23, 1881, p. 7, c. 5; "The Slaying Sun," *Times*, June 24, 1881, p. 7, c. 5.

30. Death certificate for Marie Glapion born Laveau, vol. 78, p. 1113, microfilm NOPL. Augustin Lamothe, the man who reported Marie Laveau's death, was listed in the census as a white lawyer residing at 152 St. Ann.

31. LWP informant Emile Labat told interviewer Zoe Posey that his family's undertaking establishment, Labat and Ray at 310 North Rampart, had charge of Marie Laveau's funeral (interview December 5, 1940, LWP folder 25). The ownership records for St. Louis Cemetery No. 1 (book 1, p. 13) indicate that the opening of the family tomb was ordered by Philomène Glapion.

32. "Death of Marie Laveau," *Daily Picayune*, June 17, 1881, p.8, c. 3. Information on nineteenth-century funeral customs from Huber, McDowell, and Christovich, *New Orleans Architecture: The Cemeteries*, 13–14, and from Florence and Florence, *New Orleans Cemeteries*, 32. An example of a funeral notice can be seen in Tinker's *Lafcadio Hearn's American Days*, 43.

33. Legendre/Wallace interview; Dédé/McKinney interview; Hopkins/Wallace interview. Marie Laveau's June 16, 1881, entombment is recorded in the Burial Book for St. Louis Cemetery No. 1 (January 17, 1881–January 8, 1883), p. 467, but I was unable to verify the reports of her grand funeral in the Interment Payment Records. While there are several entries for the week of June 16th, none is for Marie Laveau.

34. Alexander Augustine, interview by Henriette Michinard, August 9, 1940, LWP folder 25. Mr. Augustine was interviewed many times. The August 9 interview contains the information on burial societies.

35. Ownership record for the Widow Paris tomb, number seven, alley two, facing St. Louis Street, New Orleans Archdiocesan Cemeteries office, book 1, p. 13.

36. For more on New Orleans cemeteries, see Wilson and Huber, *The St. Louis Cemeteries of New Orleans*; Florence, *City of the Dead*; and Florence and Florence, *New Orleans Cemeteries*.

37. The definition of *kwasiyen* comes from Haitian Voudou priest Max Beauvoir, personal communication, September 13, 1997. For more on cross marks, see Thompson, *Flash of the Spirit*, 108–15; Ferguson, *Uncommon Ground*, 10, 26; Long, "Voodoo-Related Rituals in New Orleans Cemeteries," 1–14.

38. Ayola Cruz, interview by Maude Wallace, March 15, 1940, interview by Hazel Breaux and Jacques Villere, n.d., attached to Rose Legendre interview, LWP folder 25.

39. Rivaros/Breaux interview; Fonvergne/Breaux interview; Felix/Burke interview.

40. Aileen Eugene, no interviewer, n.d.; Slater/Wright interview.

41. "New Orleans Black History Tour of St. Louis II Cemetery Square 3," compiled by Raphael Cassimere, Jr., Danny Barker, Florence Borders, D. Clive Hardy, Joseph Logsdon, and Charles Rousseve in 1980. Marjorie Roehl, "The Voodoo Queen Sleeps . . . There!" *States-Item*, February 12, 1980, A1, A4; Marjorie Roehl, "Marie Laveau: A Woman of Mystery," *Times-Picayune*, June 24, 1984, section 3, p. 4.

42. Death certificate for Marie Laveau, age 75, October 6, 1890, vol. 97, p. 1202, microfilm NOPL. Burial record of Widow Charles Laveau, Burial Book, St. Louis Cemetery No. 2 (1888–1893), p. 131, AA. The Wishing Vault is in row 25, range 4 (top), and the Widow Laveau's vault is in row 19, range 3 (middle). The Widow Marie Laveaux, age 65 (born ca. 1815), was enumerated in the household of her son, Charles J. Laveaux (U.S. Census for New Orleans 1880, vol. 9, ED 36, sheet 227B, line 41, microfilm NARA). Charles J. Laveaux was the son of Laurent Charles Laveaux.

43. Rey/Posey interview; Kavanaugh/Posey interview; Brown/Posey interview.

44. Alana Mendoza, superintendent of St. Louis Cemeteries, telephone interview by the author, February 17, 2000. LWP fieldworker Zoe Posey had also researched the Wishing Vault. When she questioned the sexton at St. Louis Cemetery No. 2, she was shown the register of vault owners whose family members were removed when an office and tool shed were constructed. Some of the remains were reinterred in St. Louis Cemetery No. 3 and some in Girod Street Cemetery, but there were no names related to Marie Laveau. For information on the Girod Street Cemetery, see John Magill, "Oblivion's Blight: Girod Street Cemetery 1822–1957," exhibition catalog, THNOC, 2001.

45. Chris Grant, office manager for New Orleans Spirit Tours, was quoted in the *New York Times* as saying that Marie Laveau's tomb is "one of the most visited graves in the United States." His company takes about 12,000 people there each year. "Multiply that by a dozen companies, and then at least double that total to include people who go on their own, and you've got a quarter of a million people per year," he said. Grant "estimated that the number of visitors to Laveau's grave had doubled over the last decade" (Steven Kinzer, "Interest Surges in Voodoo and Its Queen," *New York Times*, November 30, 2003, section 1, p. 28, c. 1).

46. Greg LaRose and Richard A. Webster, "New Orleans Wants to Stop Laveau 'Desecration,'" *Times-Picayune*, May 26, 2005, Business Briefcase; Lynne Jensen, "Just Who Was Marie Laveau?" *Times-Picayune*, May 27, 2005, A1, A8; Lynne Jensen, "Voodon't,"

Times-Picayune, May 27, 2005, A1, A8. These articles prompted several letters to the editor of the *Times-Picayune*, some for and some against the new policy. One letter-writer (Your Opinions, June 1, 2005) called it an effort by "a small group of citizens" to "sanitize, whitewash, and neuter the city of New Orleans. . . . Marking Marie Laveau's tomb with an X is an act of faith, not vandalism."

CHAPTER 11. DESCENDANTS

1. Woodward, *The Strange Career of Jim Crow*, 67–71, 209–14. Blessingame, *Black New Orleans*, 206–10; Jones, "Race Relations in Louisiana, 1877–1898," 301–23. In 1970, Act 46 of the Louisiana Legislative Code changed the definition of a Negro from a person having "any appreciable amount" of Negro ancestry to a person having "more than 1/32 Negro blood." Louisiana's laws against interracial marriage and miscegenation remained in effect until 1972. The so-called one drop law was only repealed in 1983. See Domínguez, *White by Definition*, 27–29, 57, and Charles Hargroder, "Repeal of 'Black Blood' Law Awaits Signature of Governor," *Times-Picayune*, June 23, 1983, section 2, p. 2, c. 2–3.

2. Desdunes, *Our People and Our History*, 140–45; Rousseve, *The Negro in Louisiana*, 129–41; Logsdon and Bell, "Americanization of Black New Orleans," 257–58; Bell, *Revolution, Romanticism, and the Afro-Creole Protest Tradition*, 280–82. The definitive work on the *Plessy v. Ferguson* case is Medley, *We as Freemen*. The doctrine of "separate but equal" was finally overturned in 1954 with the *Brown v. Board of Education* decision, but it was still years before any substantive change occurred as a result of the Civil Rights Movement.

3. For more on the situation of the former free people of color during the Jim Crow era, see Toledano and Christovich, *New Orleans Architecture—Faubourg Tremé and the Bayou Road*, 104–5; Tregle, "Creoles and Americans," 183; Rousseve, *The Negro in Louisiana*, 99–100; Anthony, "Lost Boundaries," 295–316.

4. "Flagitious Fiction," *Daily Picayune*, April 11, 1886, p. 3, c. 4.

5. "Dangerous Localities—Where the Female Robbers Reside," *Daily States*, December 7, 1884, p. 8, c. 1; "Into Dreamland—Through the Fumes of Opium," *Daily States*, February 14, 1884, p. 8, c. 3; "Opium Again—Another Joint Raided," *Daily States*, July 25, 1885, p. 5, c. 1.

6. U.S. Census for New Orleans 1880. In addition to family members Marie (Laveau) Glapion and Philomène, Fidelia, Noëmie, and Alexandre Legendre, thirteen adult boarders and three children lived at 152 St. Ann, one of whom was Augustine Lamothe, the man who reported Marie Laveau's death. Some of these people were designated as white, some as mulatto, and some as black. Thanks to Norm Helmers of the USGenWeb Orleans Parish Archives Index Project for providing information from his city directory databases.

7. Sale by State of Louisiana of property belonging to Marie Philomène Glapion for unpaid taxes (1875–1878) to Fidelia Legendre, Acts of Alphonse Rabouin, December 31, 1886, vol. 1, p. 229; sale by State of Louisiana of property belonging to Marie Philomène Glapion for unpaid taxes (1880–1883) to Fidelia Legendre, Acts of M. T.

Ducros, September 9, 1889, vol. 3, p. 700, act 89. Mortgage of lot with buildings to Eureka Homestead Association by Marie Philomène Glapion and Fidelia Legendre, Acts of M. T. Ducros, September 7, 1889, vol. 27, act 293; cancellation of mortgage by Marie Philomène Legendre to Eureka Homestead Society, Acts of M. T. Ducros, February 6, 1890, vol. 29, act 52, NARC.

8. Marriage of Noëmie Marguerite Legendre and John Santenac, SLC Marriages, October 16, 1880, vol. 15, p. 87, AA; marriage certificate, vol. 13, p. 155, microfilm NOPL. The witnesses were Noëmie's brother Alexandre Legendre, her cousin Victor Pierre Crocker, neighbor Henry Heyl, and family friend and boarder Augustin Lamothe. Birth certificate for Benjamin Alexander Saintignac [*sic*], colored, January 17, 1881, vol. 76, p. 965, LDA.

9. Marriage of Alexandre Legendre and Mathilde La Chapelle, SLC Marriages, June 24, 1885, vol. 15, p. 581, AA; marriage certificate, vol. 11, p. 315, microfilm NOPL. One of the witnesses was J. P. Crocker, presumably Alexandre's cousin Victor Pierre, who was calling himself John Peter by then. Birth certificate for Blair Manuel Legendre, colored, July 16, 1887, vol. 85, p. 666, LDA. Until 1889 Alexandre and Mathilde resided uptown at 46 Washington Street, but in the city directory for 1894, Mathilde was listed as the "Widow of Alexander," still at 46 Washington.

10. Dédé/McKinney interview. Birth certificate for Arthur Legendre, October 21, 1885, vol. 83, p. 328; birth certificate for Ernest Alexandre Legendre, November 16, 1887, vol. 86, p. 326; birth certificate for Amelie Legendre, January 27, 1890, vol. 97, p. 100; birth certificate for Pierre Legendre, January 7, 1892, vol. 106, p. 578; birth certificate for Pauline Legendre, October 1, 1894, vol. 106, p. 578, LDA.

11. Marriage of Victor Pierre Crocker and Catherine Teche, Widow of Armand Massel, SLC Marriages, May 5, 1887, vol. 16, p. 193, AA; marriage certificate, vol. 12, p. 512, LDA. One of the witnesses was Blaire Legendre. Victor Pierre was stated to be the son of Perriquite (Pierre?) Crocker and Anne H. D. (Heloïse Duminy?) Glapion.

12. U.S. Census for New Orleans 1910, Blaire Legendre, vol. 43, Ward 6, ED 100, sheet 4A, line 48. Also living in the household were Rose's two sons from a previous marriage, Fernand and Gustave Roussel, who were classified as white.

13. Marriage of Fidelia Legendre and Julius Westenberg, SLC Marriages, November 17, 1890, vol. 16, p. 589, AA; marriage certificate, vol. 14, p. 834, microfilm NOPL. The witnesses were Fidelia's two brothers Alexandre and Blaire, her sister Noëmie (who signed her name "Mrs. John Santenac"), and her mother Philomène Glapion. I was unable to find Missouri birth certificates for Julius, Anna, or Clara.

14. Death certificate for Clara Westenberg, April 5, 1897, vol. 113, p. 549; Clara's race was originally designated as "colored," but this was crossed out and "white" written in. Death certificate for Mary Legendre, designated as colored, April 16, 1897, vol. 113, p. 618, LDA.

15. Death certificate for Philomène Legendre, June 12, 1897, vol. 114, p. 15, microfilm NOPL; typed copy in LWP folder 202.

16. Sale of lot with buildings for $1,000 by Noëmie Legendre, wife of Benjamin Santenac, to Clement Dabezies, Acts of Antoine Doriocourt, September 24, 1897, vol. 54,

act 59, NARC. The Vieux Carré Survey indicates that Dabezies was a major landowner in the late nineteenth century. Prior to this final sale, the house had gone through two other transfers of ownership within the family: sale of lot with buildings for $1,000 by Philomène Legendre, Widow of Emile Alexandre Legendre, to her son-in-law Julius Westenberg of St. Louis, Missouri, Acts of M. T. Ducros, November 20, 1894, vol. 48, act 485; sale of lot with buildings by Marie Philomène Glapion acting as agent for Julius Westenberg to Security Building and Loan Association, Acts of F. Zengel, April 5, 1895, vol. 33, act 4096; sale of lot with buildings for $600 by Security Building and Loan Association to Noëmie Santenac, Acts of F. Zengel, April 5, 1885, vol. 33, act 4097, NARC.

17. Death certificate for Fidelia Westenberg, white, December 29, 1898, at 4233 Labadie, St. Louis, Missouri, vol. 37, p. 155, County Library RDSL 46, Missouri Archive C 10402, SLGS roll 330; certified copy no. 5789, City of St. Louis Bureau of Vital Statistics, Division of Health. U.S. Census for St. Louis 1920, ED 270, sheet 22A, line 20. U.S. Census for St. Louis 1930, ED 96–495, sheet 6A, line 8, microfilm NARA.

18. Legendre/Breaux-Villere interview.

19. Death certificate for Alexander Legendre, January 8, 1903, vol. 128, p. 1184, LDA.

20. U.S. Census for New Orleans 1920, Blaire Legendre, Ward 7, ED 125, sheet 12, line 2. U.S. Census for New Orleans 1930, Blaire Legendre, ED 106, sheet 31B, line 99, microfilm NARA. Rose Legendre told LWP interviewers that her husband died in 1932, but I found no death certificate in Orleans Parish. Death certificate for Cyril John Legendre, October 18, 1965, file no. 65-122655, State of California Department of Health Services. Funeral arrangements by Spalding Mortuary, burial in Holy Cross Cemetery. Elizabeth Mullener, "California Creole," *Times-Picayune* Sunday magazine, May 20, 1984, pp. 9–16, cont. May 28, 1984, pp. 8–18. The section of Los Angeles surrounding Holy Name Roman Catholic church, along Jefferson Boulevard from Arlington Street to Tenth Avenue, was called "Little New Orleans."

21. Pitkin, *An Angel by Brevet*, 6.

22. Dillon, "Voodoo," chapter 11, "Marie the Mysterious," section 9, p. 6.

CHAPTER 12. THE SECOND MARIE LAVEAU

1. "Voodooism," *Commercial Bulletin*, July 5, 1869. "The Voudous' Day," *Times*, June 25, 1870, p. 6, c. 2. "The Vous Dous Incantation," *Times*, June 28, 1872, p. 1, c. 6.

2. Mama Caroline is named in "St. John's Eve—The Voudous," *Daily Picayune*, June 24, 1873, p. 4, c. 2; Madame Frazie in "Fetish Worship," *Times*, June 25, 1875, p. 2, c. 1 and 2; and Malvina Latour in "A Voudou Dance," *Times-Democrat*, June 24, 1884, p. 2, c. 3.

3. Castellanos names Doctor Alexander and Pedro Prince of Darkness as Marie Laveau's successors in *New Orleans As It Was*, 99. For more on "Pedro Prince of Darkness" see "The Trance Cure—Unlicenced Physicians to be Prosecuted by the Board of Health," *Daily Picayune*, April 26, 1894, p. 3, c. 3. Here we learn that the Prince of Darkness, whose name was H. M. Turpia, was not a Voudou priest but a quack doctor

who claimed to cure patients while in a trance. When an inspector from the Board of Health visited Turpia's office on Galvez Street, he found it "draped with black curtains and [decorated with] crucifixes and lighted wax candles to give the place an air of gloom and mystery. In one portion of the room there is a box of [live] snakes." The Prince was charged with practicing medicine without a diploma from an accredited medical school. The "Congre Noir," *Picayune's Guide to New Orleans* for 1897, 32–33; *Picayune's Guide to New Orleans* for 1900, 66.

4. Christian, "A Black History of Louisiana/Voodooism and Mumbo-Jumbo," 44.

5. Lafcadio Hearn, "El Vomito," *Daily City Item*, March 21, 1881, reprinted in *Fantastics and Other Fancies*, 136–42. Hearn wrote to his friend Henry Krehbiel in February 1881, that he was "living in a ruined Creole house [on Bourbon between St. Louis and Toulouse]. A fortune-teller occupies the lower floor. She has a fantastic apartment kept dark all day except for the light of some little tapers burning before two human skulls" (Bisland, *The Life and Letters of Lafcadio Hearn*, 222–23; Tinker, *Lafcadio Hearn's American Days*, 95–96). Catherine Dillon assumed that this fortune-teller was the second Marie Laveau (Dillon, "Voodoo," chapter 11, "Marie the Mysterious," 19).

6. Cable, "Creole Slave Songs," 819. Kemble's illustration was reproduced in "Voudouism—A Chapter of Old New Orleans History—How St. John's Eve Was Celebrated Fifty Years Ago," *Daily Picayune*, June 22, 1890, p. 10, c. 1–4.

7. Though no copy of the newspaper has survived, Nott's November 7, 1915, article from the *New Orleans American* is quoted in Dillon, "Voodoo/Marie the Mysterious," section 1, p. 3, LWP folder 317; Nott, "Marie Laveau, Long High Priestess of Voudouism," *Times-Picayune* Sunday magazine, November 19, 1922, p. 2.

8. Saxon, *Fabulous New Orleans*, 243.

9. Hurston, "Hoodoo in America," 326; Hurston, *Mules and Men*, 192.

10. Asbury, *The French Quarter*, 266, 270.

11. "Fetish—Its Worship and Worshipers," *Daily Picayune*, June 24, 1875, p. 1, c. 4–5; "Recollections of a Visit on New Years' Eve to Marie Laveau, the Ex-Queen of the Voudous," *Daily States*, June 17, 1881, p. 3, c. 3; Cable, "Creole Slave Songs," 817.

12. Hobley/Posey interview.

13. Raphael/Breaux-Villere interview.

14. Smith/Breaux interview.

15. Rivaros/Breaux interview.

16. Santana/Posey interview.

17. Josephine Harrison, interview by Zoe Posey, July 14, 1939.

18. Dillon, "Voodoo," chapter 1, "Famous Wangateurs," 22–26; on page 22 Dillon conjectured that "Malvina Latour . . . seems to have been confused with [Marie Laveau's] daughter." Latour, reported to have been born about 1836, would have been the same age as Marie Philomène Glapion.

19. Dillon, "Voodoo," chapter 10, "Marie the Great," 32, 51. In the purchase of the St. Ann Street cottage, enacted before Notary Octave de Armas, Marie Philomène was referred to as "Miss Marie P. Glapion."

20. Tallant, *Voodoo in New Orleans*, 52, 73–74.

21. Christian, "A Black History of Louisiana/Voodooism and Mumbo-Jumbo," p. 45. Zora Neale Hurston, book review of Robert Tallant's *Voodoo in New Orleans*, 437.

22. Tallant, *Voodoo in New Orleans*, 127.

23. Ibid., "Gerald July," 62; "Tony Miller," 75; "Annie Ferguson," 90; "Vergie Wilson," 121.

24. Dillon, "Voodoo," chapter 6, "St. John's Eve," section 6, p. 1a; Tallant, *Voodoo in New Orleans*, 122.

25. Tallant, *Voodoo in New Orleans*, 77; Nott, *New Orleans American*, November 7, 1915 (see note 7 above); Duffy, "Voodoo Queen," 46. Martha Ward believes that Heloïse, like Eliza Potter, worked as a hairdresser at fine New Orleans hotels such as the St. Charles and the St. Louis (*Voodoo Queen*, 80).

26. Tallant, *Voodoo in New Orleans*, 77, 122. This address at Bourbon and Toulouse coincides with that of the "fortune-teller's house" occupied in 1879–1881 by Lafcadio Hearn (see note 5 above).

27. For newspaper reports of the alleged voudou house on Love Street, see chapter 6, n. 35. Fandrich, "Mysterious Voodoo Queen," 255, 310 n. 60; *Mysterious Voodoo Queen*, 176. In her dissertation, Fandrich used citations for unpaid taxes in 1865 and 1866 as proof that Heloïse Glapion was living at 207 Love Street. Martha Ward used the same citations to confirm that Heloïse did not die in 1862, since "dead people are not required to pay real estate taxes" (Ward, *Voodoo Queen*, 166). These documents prove nothing. They provide neither the full name of the delinquent taxpayer nor the address of the property (Sixth District Court, docket E [January 21, 1864–February 21, 1865], no. 14103, *City of New Orleans v. M. Ann Glapion*; Sixth District Court, docket F [February 21, 1865–November 22, 1866], no. 16067, *City of New Orleans v. E. Glapion*, original in NOPL). Even assuming that Heloïse Glapion is the person cited, she would have remained on the city tax roles because her death was never reported.

28. Tallant, *The Voodoo Queen*, 191, 197–98, 242–56, 262–72, 310–11, 314.

29. Prose, *Marie Laveau*, 305–23, 340–74.

30. Rhodes, *Voodoo Dreams*, 431.

31. Du Plantis, *Gris-Gris*. Chambers, "Voodoo on the Bayou," act 2, scene 4, pp. 14–20.

32. *Marie (Dolores) Laveaux v. François Auguste her husband*, Parish Court, August–October, 1828, docket no. 5041, microfilm NOPL. First will of Marie (Dolores) Charles Laveaux, January 19, 1829, Acts of Louis T. Caire, vol. 6, p. 55, act 56; second will of Marie (Dolores) Laveaux, Acts of Charles Victor Foulon, March 25, 1839, vol. 3, p. 192, act 100, NARC. Marie Dolores Laveaux had one natural son, Laurent, born in 1819 before her marriage to François Auguste. Her legitimate children with François Auguste were Marie Henriette (b. 1820), Eveline (b. 1821), Françoise (b. 1822), Joseph Jean Hermogene (b. 1824), Felix (b. 1826), Louise Augustine (b. 1833), and Marie Hermina (b. 1835). Sacramental records of baptisms and funerals from AA; birth and death certificates from LDA.

33. Marie Dolores' death in Paris and the shipment of her body to New Orleans for

burial is recorded in a marginal note on her baptismal entry in the sacramental registers of St. Louis Cathedral. The record of her first-class funeral is found in the Burial Book, St. Louis Cemetery No. 1, October 29, 1839, pp. 286–87, act 702, AA.

34. Succession of Eloise Euchariste Glapion, Putting in Possession Victor Pierre Duminy Dieudonné de Glapion, November 28, 1881, COB 144, p. 846. The property was described as "a lot of ground and buildings thereon in the Third District of this city, Faubourg Marigny, forming part of lot no. 207, in the square bounded by Love, Craps, Union, and Bagatelle Streets." Sale of property by Victor Pierre Duminy Dieudonné de Glapion to Frederick Dummet, Acts of Charles Rolle, January 17, 1882, vol. 2, act 88. When the street names and house numbers changed in 1860, 207 Love Street between Bagatelle and Union became 430 North Rampart between Bourbon and Union. The Sanborn Fire Insurance Map for 1887 shows the lot occupied by a one-story house and three outbuildings, with a large front yard. When the street names and house numbers changed again in 1894, it became 1930 North Rampart between Truro and Pauger (Sanborn Fire Insurance Map for 1887, vol. 3, sheet 60; Sanborn Fire Insurance Map for 1896, vol. 1, sheet 18, microfilm THNOC). The present house at 1930 North Rampart is an early twentieth-century raised bungalow built much closer to the street.

35. Fandrich, "Mysterious Voodoo Queen," 270–71; *Mysterious Voodoo Queen*, 159, 179, 205.

36. Ward, *Voodoo Queen*, 165.

37. Tallant, *Voodoo in New Orleans*, 122.

38. "Flagitious Fiction," *Daily Picayune*, April 11, 1886, p. 3, c. 4.

39. "Voudooism—A Chapter of Old New Orleans History—How St. John's Eve Was Celebrated Fifty Years Ago," *Daily Picayune*, June 22, 1890, p. 10, c. 1–4.

40. *Picayune's Guide to New Orleans* for 1900, 65–67, THNOC.

41. Kendall, "Old New Orleans Houses and Some of the People Who Lived in Them," 799.

42. Zeno/Breaux interview; Fonvergne/Breaux interview; Martha Gray, interview by Henriette Michinard, n.d., LWP folder 25.

CONCLUSION

1. Thanks to my friend Erin Loftus for helping me articulate my thoughts about Marie Laveau when, at the end of almost ten years of work on this project, I could think no more.

Bibliography

PRIMARY SOURCES

Civil and Ecclesiastical Records

Birth, marriage, and death certificates, Louisiana Division of Archives, Baton Rouge, La.

City Directories: Matthew Flannery, *A Directory and Census Together with Resolutions Authorizing Same* (1805); B. Lafon, *Annuaire Louisianais* (1807, 1809); Whitney, *Directoire de la Nouvelle-Orleans* (1811); John Adem Paxton, *New Orleans Directory and Register* (1822–24); S. E. Percy & Co., *New-Orleans Directory of the City and Suburbs* (1832); Michel & Co., *New Orleans Annual and Commercial Register of the City and Suburbs* (1834, 1841, 1843, 1846); Gibson, *Guide and Directory of the Cities of New Orleans and Lafayette* (1838); Pitts and Clark, *Guide and Directory, New Orleans, Lafayette, and Gretna* (1841, 1842); Cohen, *New Orleans and Lafayette Directory, Including Algiers, Gretna, and McDonoughville* (1849–56); Mygatt, *New Orleans Directory* (1857); Charles Gardner, *New Orleans Directory* (1858–59, 1861–69); Graham's *New Orleans Directory* (1870); Edwards' *New Orleans Directory* (1872–73); Soard's *New Orleans Directory* (1874–1935).

Conveyance Office Index to Purchasers and Vendors and Conveyance Office Books, Civil District Court, New Orleans, La.

Notarial Acts, Notarial Archives Research Center, New Orleans, La.

Sacramental Registers of the Roman Catholic Archdiocese of New Orleans: St. Louis Cathedral and St. Augustin's Church; Burial Records, St. Louis Cemetery No. 1 and No. 2; Funeral Expenses, St. Louis Cathedral, Archdiocesan Archives, New Orleans, La.

Unpublished Documents

Christian, Marcus. "Voodooism Mumbo-Jumbo," from "A Black History of Louisiana." Unpublished manuscript, Louisiana Writers' Project. Archives and Manuscripts Division, Earl K. Long Library, University of New Orleans.

Dillon, Catherine. "Voodoo." Unpublished manuscript, 1940. Louisiana Writers' Project, folders 118, 317, and 319, Federal Writers' Collection, Watson Memorial Library, Cammie G. Henry Research Center, Northwestern State University, Natchitoches, La.

Kornfeld, Robert. "Marie Laveau." Unpublished manuscript, 1943. Box 13, Lyle Saxon Papers. Special Collections, Howard-Tilton Memorial Library, Tulane University, New Orleans, La.

Louisiana Writers' Project. Unpublished interviews and research materials, 1935–1943. Federal Writers' Collection, Watson Memorial Library, Cammie G. Henry Research Center, Northwestern State University, Natchitoches, La.

Records of the Works Projects Administration, Record Group 69. Records of the Federal Writers' Project Relating to Louisiana, 1935–1943, Civil Records. National Archives and Records Service, College Park, Md.

Published Indexes to Civil and Ecclesiastical Records

Bertin, P. M., compiler. *General Index of All Successions Opened in the Parish of Orleans from the Year 1805 to the Year 1846.* New Orleans: Yeomans and Fitch, 1849.

Conrad, Glenn R. *First Families of Louisiana.* Baton Rouge: Claitors, 1970.

———. *The German Coast: Abstracts of the Civil Records of St. Charles and St. John the Baptist Parishes, 1804–1812.* New Orleans: Louisiana Historical Association, 1981.

Forsyth, Alice Daly. *Louisiana Marriage Contracts: Abstracts from Records of the Superior Council of Louisiana, 1728–1769.* Vol. 2. New Orleans: Genealogical Research Society, 1989.

Genealogical Research Society of New Orleans. *Libro Primero de Confirmaciones de esta Parroquia de San Luis de la Neuva Orleans, 1789–1841.* New Orleans: Genealogical Research Society, 1967.

Gould, Virginia. "Household Census Databases for New Orleans, Mobile, and Pensacola." In Hall, *Databases for the Study of Afro-Louisiana History and Genealogy 1699–1860.*

Hall, Gwendolyn Midlo, ed. *Databases for the Study of Afro-Louisiana History and Genealogy 1699–1860.* (Includes *Louisiana Slave Database* and *Louisiana Free Database.*) CD-ROM. Baton Rouge: Louisiana State University Press, 2000.

Hebert, Donald J., ed. *Southwest Louisiana Records: Church and Civil Records of Settlers.* Vol. 1, *1756–1810* and vol. 7, *1861–1865.* Eunice, La.: privately published, 1974.

Maduell, Charles R., Jr., compiler and indexer. *Marriage Contracts, Wills, and Testaments of the Spanish Colonial Period in New Orleans, 1770–1804.* New Orleans: privately published, 1969.

McBee, L. A., compiler. *General Index of All Successions, Emancipations, Interdictions, and Partition Proceedings Opened in the Civil District Court, Parish of Orleans, Louisiana, from August 31, 1894 to January 1, 1902.* New Orleans: L. A. McBee, 1902.

McBee, W. L., compiler. *General Index of All Successions Opened in the Civil District Court, Parish of Orleans, Louisiana, August 1, 1880 to August 31, 1894.* New Orleans: W. L. McBee, 1894.

Murray, Nicholas Russell. *Computer Indexed Marriage Records, Orleans Parish, Louisiana, 1830–1900.* North Salt Lake, Utah: Hunting for Bears, 1980.

Nolan, Charles E., ed. *Sacramental Records of the Roman Catholic Church of the Archdiocese of New Orleans.* Vols. 1–17. New Orleans: Archives of the Archdiocese of New Orleans, 1987–2004.

Porteous, Laura. "Index to the Spanish Judicial Archives of Louisiana." *Louisiana Historical Quarterly* 19, no. 2 (1936), 510–46.

Robichaux, Albert J., Jr. *German Coast Families: European Origins and Settlement in Colonial Louisiana.* Rayne, La.: Hebert Publications, 1997.

Villere, A. J., compiler. *General Index of All Successions Opened in the Parish of Orleans from the Year 1846 to the Month of August, 1880*. New Orleans: E. A. Peyroux, 1880.

Voorhies, Jacqueline K. *Some Late Eighteenth-Century Louisianians, Census Records 1758–1796*. Lafayette, La.: USL History Series, 1973.

Newspaper Articles

Articles for which no author is cited were written by anonymous staff reporters.

L'Abeille de la Nouvelle-Orléans/New Orleans Bee
"A Singular Assemblage," June 29, 1850, p. 1, c. 5.
Funeral announcement for Christophe Glapion, June 27, 1855, p. 2, c. 5.
Funeral announcement for Alexandre Legendre, July 27, 1872, p. 2, c. 7.

Commercial Bulletin
"The Day of Mourning [Henry Clay]," July 3, 1852, p. 2, c. 1.
"Execution," July 3, 1852, p. 2, c. 4.
"Voodooism," July 5, 1869, p. 1, c. 7.
"Voudou John Arrested," March 10, 1871, p. 1, c. 7.

Daily City Item
Hearn, Lafcadio. "El Vomito," March 21, 1881.
"The Heat's Victims," June 16, 1881, p. 1, c. 7.
"Wayside Notes—The Death of Marie Laveau," June 17, 1881, p. 1, c. 5.
Advertisement for Fourth of July festival, June 23, 1881, p. 4, c. 6.
Mejia, Lillian. "The Snake Dance," Sunday magazine, March 30, 1924, p. 8, 9, 12.
"Dr. I. M. Cline Finds Lost Portrait of Marie Laveau," April 18, 1937.

Daily Crescent
"A Mystery of the Old Third," June 29, 1850, p. 3, c. 1.
"Another Voudou Affair," July 4, 1850, p. 2, c. 1.
"The Rites of Voudou," July 31, 1850, p. 3, c. 1.
"Execution of Adam and Delisle—Horrid Spectacle," July 3, 1852, p. 2, c. 5.
"Local Intelligence—Recorder Long's Court," July 12, 1859, p. 1, c. 7.
"A Rare Smell of Perjury," September 8, 1859, p. 1, c. 4.
"Death of Antoine Cambre," August 8, 1860, p. 1, c. 3.
"A Visit to a Professor of the Black Art," December 24, 1866, p. 2, c. 2.

Daily Delta
"Obtaining a Statue under False Pretenses," July 3, 1850, p. 3, c. 2.
"The Voudous vs Municipality No. Three," July 14, 1850, p. 2, c. 2.
"The Virgin of the Voudous," August 10, 1850, p. 2, c. 2.
"Another Condemned Prisoner Dead in the Parish Prison," August 8, 1860, p. 2, c. 2–4.

"Voudouist Disgorged—Credulity and Cunning—Ghosts and Greenhorns," October 21, 1860, p. 8, c. 3.

Daily Picayune
"Great Doings in the Third Municipality," June 29, 1850, p. 2, c. 6.
"Curious Charge of Swindling," July 3, 1850, p. 2, c. 6.
"Voudouism," July 24, 1850, p. 1, c. 4.
"Unlawful Assemblies," July 31, 1850, p. 2, c. 2.
"More of the Voudous," July 31, 1850, p. 1, c. 6.
"The Execution Today," July 2, 1852, p. 2, c. 5.
"Public Execution," July 3, 1852, p. 2, c. 2.
"The Execution," March 18, 1859, p. 4, c. 1.
"Free Black Emigration," June 23, 1859, p. 5, c. 5.
"Africans in Mississippi," June 27, 1859, p. 4, c. 4.
"Superstitious," July 12, 1859, p. 1, c. 7.
"Hayti and Emigration Thither," July 16, 1859, p. 5, c. 2.
"Execution This Morning," July 30, 1859, p. 5, c. 5.
"More Africans, "August 2, 1859, p. 5, c. 5; August 3, 1859, p. 1, c. 5.
"Africa Triumphant," August 18, 1859, p. 2, c. 5.
"Exclusion of Free Negroes," September 5, 1859, p. 4, c. 1; December 3, 1859, p. 1, c. 6; January 14, 1860, p. 1, c. 5.
"Mysterious Murder," December 22, 1859, p. 1, c. 5.
"Post Mortem Examination," and "Arrest," December 23, 1859, p. 6, c. 1.
"Inquest of George Frey," December 24, 1859, p. 2, c. 3.
"First District Court—Judge Hunt," June 12, 1860, p. 4, c. 1–2; June 14, 1860, p. 2, c. 2; July 3, 1860, p. 2, c. 1–2.
"Death of Eugene Pepe," June 21, 1860, p. 1, c. 1.
"Colored Folks," September 21, 1860, p. 4, c. 1.
"Emigration to Hayti," November 11, 1860, p. 5, c. 2.
"The Death Penalty—Reprieve of the Condemned—Scene at the Parish Prison," May 28, 1870, p. 2, c. 3, 4, 5.
"Fetish Rites," June 23, 1870, p. 2, c. 5.
"The Condemned—The Decorations of the Altar," May 10, 1871, p. 2, c. 6.
"The Execution—Infliction of the Death Penalty—Murder Atoned," May 14, 1871, p. 13, c. 3–7.
"Trouble Among the Voudous," August 18, 1871, p. 2, c. 5.
"St. John's Eve—The Voudous," June 24, 1873, p. 4, c. 2.
"St. John's Day—Grand Celebration by the Knights Templar of New Orleans," June 25, 1874, p. 1, c. 5.
"Voudou Nonsense—A Plain, Unvarnished Account of the Lake Shore Revels—Full Particulars of the Hell-Broth and Orgies—A Played-Out Hoax," June 26, 1874, p. 1, c. 5.

"Fetish—Its Worship and Worshipers—Their Customs and Rites—Voudous and Vou-
dousim," June 24, 1875, p. 1, c. 4–5.

"St. John's Eve—After the Voudous—Some Singular Ceremonies—A Night in Heathenness," June 25, 1875, p. 2, c. 1.

"Death of Marie Laveau—A Woman with a Wonderful History, Almost a Century
Old, Carried to the Tomb Thursday Morning," June 17, 1881, p. 8, c. 3.

"Flagitious Fiction: Cable's Romance About Marie Laveau and the Voudous," April 11,
1886, p. 3, c. 4.

"An Astounding Revelation," May 30, 1889, p. 4, c. 4.

"Voudouism—A Chapter of Old New Orleans History—How St. John's Eve Was Celebrated Fifty Years Ago," June 22, 1890, p. 10, c. 1–4.

"St. John's Day Celebrated by Masons with Fitting Ceremony," June 25, 1890, p. 8, c.
1–2.

"The Voudou Doctor—Death of a Notorious Negro Who Throve on the Superstitions
of His Kind," August 20, 1890, p. 8, c. 3.

"The Trance Cure—Unlicenced Physicians to be Prosecuted by the Board of Health,"
April 26, 1894, p. 3, c. 3.

Daily States

"Recollections of a Visit on New Years' Eve to Marie Laveau, the Ex-Queen of the Voudous," June 17, 1881, p. 3, c. 3.

"Voudouism—Charms of Wonderful Efficacy Compounded of Snakes, Toads, Frogs,
Cats' Ears and Lizards' Eyes," August 26, 1881, p. 4, c. 1–2.

"Faithful Wife Pays Doctor for the Return of her Husband," December 9, 1881, p. 1, c.
7.

"Dangerous Localities—Where the Female Robbers Reside," December 7, 1884, p. 8,
c. 1.

"Into Dreamland—Through the Fumes of Opium," February 14, 1884, p. 8, c. 3.

"Opium Again—Another Joint Raided," July 25, 1885, p. 5, c. 1.

"St. John's Eve," June 23, 1887, p. 5, c. 3.

"St. John's Eve Celebrations," June 24, 1887, p. 5, c. 3.

"A Voudou Entertainment," May 29, 1889, p. 2, c. 2.

"A Notable Affair—The Celebration of St. John's Day by the Masons," June 25, 1890,
p. 2, c. 1–4.

"Death of the Voodoo Doctor," August 20, 1890, p. 5, c. 2.

Daily True Delta

"A Motley Gathering—Superstition and Licentiousness," June 29, 1850, p. 3, c. 1.

"The Voudou Humbug," July 25, 1850, p. 3, c. 1.

"The Louisiana Ball-Room Homicide," March 16, 1859, p. 1, c. 6.

"Murder and Its Punishment—Three Men Executed," March 19, 1859, p. 2, c. 3, 4, 5.

"Police Matters—Recorder Long's Court," July 12, 1859, p. 2, c. 5.

"Execution of James Mullen," July 30, 1859, p. 1, c. 4, 5.

"A Modern Lucretia Borgia—The Last Adventure of Fanny Sweet—An Extraordinary Conspiracy," December 8, 1861, p. 1, c. 1–5.

Democrat
"Marie Lavaux—Death of the Queen of the Voudous Just Before St. John's Eve," June 17, 1881, p. 8, c. 2.
"A Sainted Woman," June 18, 1881, p. 2, c. 1.

Gambit Weekly
Garry Boulard, "Pulp Nonfiction," December 20, 2002.

Le Courier de la Louisiane/Louisiana Courier
"Recorder Seuzeneau's Court," July 3, 1850, p. 1, c. 4.
"The Voudous in the First Municipality," July 30, 1850, p. 2, c. 5.

Louisiana Gazette
"Idolatry and Quackery," August 16, 1820, p. 2, c. 3.

Republican
"Voudouing a Wine Mark," February 26, 1871, p. 5, c. 1.
"Fate and Mystery," June 21, 1874, p. 5, c. 1.
"The Voudou Ceremonies," June 25, 1874, p. 3, c. 1.

States-Item
Roehl, Marjorie. "The Voodoo Queen Sleeps . . . There!" February 12, 1980, A1 and A4.

Times (New Orleans)
"The Voudous' Day," June 25, 1870, p. 6, c. 2.
"Voudouism Rampant in Louisiana," July 17, 1870, p. 3, c. 4–5.
"Making a Night of It—A Search for the Vous Dous Queen—An African Ball," June 26, 1872, p. 2, c. 1–2.
"The Vous Dous Incantation," June 28, 1872, p. 1, c. 6.
"Voudou Vagaries—The Worshipers of Obeah Turned Loose," June 26, 1874, p. 2, c. 2–4.
"Struck by the Sun," June 23, 1881, p. 7, c. 5.
"The Thermometer," June 23, 1881, p. 7, c. 3.
"Fetish Worship—St. John's Eve at Milneburg—A Voudou's Incantation—Midnight Scenes and Orgies," June 25, 1875, p. 2, c. 1 and 2.
"Voudou Vagaries—The Spirit of Marie Laveau to be Propitiated by Midnight Orgies on the Bayou," June 23, 1881, p. 7, c. 4.
"The Slaying Sun," June 24, 1881, p. 7, c. 5.
"The Voudous—What a *Times* Man Saw Last Night," June 24, 1881, p. 7, c. 4.

"The Departed Voudou Queen," June 24, 1881, p. 3, c. 2.

"St. John's Eve Celebrations," June 24, 1887, p. 6, c. 4.

Times (New York)

"The Dead Voudou Queen—Marie Laveau's Place in the History of New Orleans—The Early Life of the Beautiful Young Creole—The Prominent Men Who Sought Her Advice and Society—Her Charitable Work—How She Became an Object of Mystery," June 23, 1881, p. 2, c. 3–4.

Kinzer, Steven. "Interest Surges in Voodoo and Its Queen," November 30, 2003, section 1, p. 28, c. 1.

Times-Democrat

"A Voudou Dance—Revival on the Lake Shore of Voudou Mysteries—How the Eve of St. John was Celebrated Last Night by the Queen and Her Adherents," June 24, 1884, p. 2, c. 3.

"A Cungi Dance," June 24, 1887, p. 3, c. 3.

"A Voudou Orgie—Sensational Disclosure in the Third District," May 28, 1889, p. 4, c. 3.

Castellanos, Henry. "The Voudous: Their History, Mysteries, and Practices," June 24, 1894, p. 18, c. 3–5.

"Dance of the Voodoos—Outlandish Celebration of St. John's Eve," June 24, 1896, p. 2, c. 6–7.

Times-Picayune

Nott, G. William. "Marie Laveau, Long High Priestess of Voudouism in New Orleans: Some Hitherto Unpublished Stories of the Voudou Queen," Sunday magazine, November 19, 1922, p. 2.

Moore, Herbert. "Voodoo!" Sunday magazine, March 16, 1924, p. 1, 4.

LeBlanc, Doris Kent. "Beware These Closing Days of June," Sunday magazine, June 26, 1927, p. 2.

Hammond, Hilda Phelps. "Behind the Veil of Voodooism in America," Sunday magazine, October 5, 1930, p. 3.

"Cabildo Will Get Catlin Portrait," August 24, 1933, p. 23, c. 7.

"Repeal of 'Black Blood' Law Awaits Signature of Governor," June 23, 1983, section 2, p. 2, c. 2–3.

Mullener, Elizabeth. "California Creole," Sunday magazine, May 20, 1984, p. 9–16, cont. May 28, 1984, p. 8–18.

Roehl, Marjorie. "Marie Laveau: A Woman of Mystery," June 24, 1984, section 3, p. 4.

MacCash, Douglas. "Midsummer Rite—Voodoo devotees show the tourists how they celebrate a holy day," Living section, E1 and E4, June 30, 1999.

Jensen, Lynne. "The Lowdown on Laveau—1801 baptismal certificate holds long-lost truth about legendary voodoo priestess, researcher claims," February 17, 2002, Metro section, B1–2.

LaRose, Greg, and Richard A. Webster. "New Orleans Wants to Stop Laveau 'Desecration,'" Business Briefcase, May 26, 2005.

Jensen, Lynne. "Just Who Was Marie Laveau?" May 27, 2005, A1, A8.

Jensen, Lynne. "Voodon't—X used to mark the spot of Marie Laveau's tomb, but some local groups hope to lay the practice to rest," May 27, 2005, A1, A8.

Your Opinions, June 1, 2005.

Tribune
"Federal Agents Expose Business in Goofer Dust," May 14, 1927, p. 1, c. 3.

SECONDARY SOURCES

Accilien, Cécile, ed. *Revolutionary Freedoms: A History of Survival, Strength, and Imagination in Haiti*. Deerfield Beach, Fla.: Caribbean Studies Press, 2006.

Allain, Hélène d'Aquin. *Souvenirs d'Amerique et de France par une Créole*. Paris: Perisse Frères, 1883.

Alliot, Paul. "Historical and Political Reflections on Louisiana, Dedicated to His Excellency, Mr. Jefferson, President of the United States of America." In *Louisiana Under the Rule of Spain, France, and the United States 1785–1807*, vol. 1, edited and translated by James Alexander Robertson. 1910. Reprint, Freeport, N.Y.: Books for Libraries Press, 1969.

Anthony, Arthé. "Lost Boundaries: Racial Passing and Poverty in New Orleans." In *Creole*, edited by Sybil Kein, 295–316. Baton Rouge: Louisiana State University Press, 2000.

Arthur, Stanley Clisby. *Old Families of Louisiana*. 1931. Reprint, Baton Rouge: Claitor's Publishing, 1971.

Asbury, Herbert. *The French Quarter: An Informal History of the New Orleans Underworld*. 1936. Reprint, New York: Garden City Publishing, 1938.

Atkins, John. *A Voyage to Guinea, Brasil and the West Indies, with Remarks on the Gold, Ivory and Slave-Trade*. London: Caesar Ward and Richard Chandler, 1735.

Baade, Hans W. "The Law of Slavery in Spanish Luisiana 1769–1803." In *Louisiana's Legal Heritage*, edited by Edward F. Haas. New Orleans: Louisiana State Museum, 1983.

Baughman, James P. "A Southern Spa: Ante-Bellum Lake Pontchartrain." *Louisiana History* 3, no. 1 (Winter 1962): 5–31.

Bell, Caryn Cossé. *Revolution, Romanticism, and the Afro-Creole Protest Tradition in Louisiana 1718–1868*. Baton Rouge: Louisiana State University Press, 1997.

———. "Hermann-Grima House: A Window on Free Black Life and Urban Slavery in Creole New Orleans." *Louisiana Cultural Vistas* (Summer 2000): 68–78.

Berlin, Ira. *Slaves Without Masters: The Free Negro in the Antebellum South*. New York: New Press, 1974.

———. *Many Thousands Gone: The First Two Generations of Slavery in North America*. Cambridge: Harvard University Press, 1998.

Bibbs, Susheel. *Heritage of Power: Marie LaVeau—Mary Ellen Pleasant*. San Francisco: MEP, 1998.

Bisland, Elizabeth. *The Life and Letters of Lafcadio Hearn*. Boston: Houghton, Mifflin, 1906.

Bispham, Clarence. "Fray Antonio de Sedella." *Louisiana Historical Quarterly* 2 (January–October 1919): 24–37, 155–89.

Blessingame, John. *Black New Orleans: 1860–1880*. Chicago: University of Chicago Press, 1973.

Blier, Susanne Preston. "Vodun: West African Roots of Vodou." In *Sacred Arts of Haitian Vodou*, edited by Donald Cosentino. Los Angeles: University of California Fowler Museum of Cultural History, 1995.

Boyd, Valerie. *Wrapped in Rainbows: The Life of Zora Neale Hurston*. New York: Scribner, 2003.

Brandon, George. *Santería from Africa to the New World*. Bloomington: Indiana University Press, 1993.

Brasseaux, Carl A., and Glenn R. Conrad, eds. *Road to Louisiana: The Saint-Domingue Refugees 1792–1809*. Lafayette: University of Southwestern Louisiana Center for Louisiana Studies, 1992.

Brown, Karen McCarthy. *Mama Lola: A Vodou Priestess in Brooklyn*. Berkeley: University of California Press, 1991.

———. "Serving the Spirits." In *Sacred Arts of Haitian Vodou*, edited by Donald Cosentino. Los Angeles: University of California Fowler Museum of Cultural History, 1995.

Bryan, Violet Harrington. *The Myth of New Orleans in Literature: Dialogues of Race and Gender*. Knoxville: University of Tennessee Press, 1993.

Buckingham, J. S. *The Slave States of America*. Vol. 1. 1842. Reprint, New York: Negro Universities Press, 1968.

Buel, James William. *Metropolitan Life Unveiled; or the Mysteries and Miseries of America's Great Cities, Embracing New York, Washington City, San Francisco, Salt Lake City, and New Orleans*. St. Louis: Historical Publishing Company, 1882.

Bundy, David S., comp. *Painting in the South 1564–1980*. Richmond: Virginia Museum, 1983.

Cable, George Washington. *Old Creole Days*. 1879. Reprint, Gretna, La.: Pelican, 1990.

———. *The Grandissimes: A Story of Creole Life*. 1880. Reprint, New York: Penguin Classics, 1988.

———. *The Creoles of Louisiana*. New York: Charles Scribner's Sons, 1884.

———. "The Dance in Place Congo." *The Century Magazine* 31, no. 4 (February 1886): 517–32.

———. "Creole Slave Songs." *The Century Magazine* 31, no. 6 (April 1886): 807–28.

Canizares, Raul. *The Life and Works of Marie Laveau: Gris-gris, Cleansings, Charms, Hexes*. Plainview, N.Y.: Original Publications, 2001.

Carter, Edwin Clarence, ed. and comp. *The Territorial Papers of the United States—Territory of Orleans, 1803–1812*. Washington, D.C.: Government Printing Office, 1940.

Castellanos, Henry C. *New Orleans As It Was: Episodes of Louisiana Life*. 1895. Reprint, Gretna, La.: Pelican, 1990.

Churchill, C. Robert, compiler. *Men Under General Don Bernardo de Galves and Other Records from the Archives of the Indies, Seville, Spain, in the Spanish-English War, 1779–1783*. New Orleans: Louisianna Society Sons of the American Revolution, 1925.

Clapp, Theodore. *Autobiographical Sketches and Recollections during a Thirty-Five Years' Residence in New Orleans*. 1857. Reprint, Freeport, N.Y.: Books for Libraries Press, 1972.

Clark, Emily, and Virginia Meacham Gould. "The Feminine Face of Afro-Catholicism in New Orleans, 1727–1852." *William and Mary Quarterly* (April 2002): 409–48.

Clinton, Catherine, and Michele Gillespie, eds. *The Devil's Lane: Sex and Race in the Early South*. New York: Oxford University Press, 1997.

Conrad, Glenn R., ed. *Dictionary of Louisiana Biography*. New Orleans: Louisiana Historical Association, 1988.

Cosentino, Donald, ed. *Sacred Arts of Haitian Vodou*. Los Angeles: University of California Fowler Museum of Cultural History, 1995.

Cott, Jonathan. *Wandering Ghost: The Odyssey of Lafcadio Hearn*. New York: Alfred A. Knopf, 1990.

Courlander, Harold. *The Drum and the Hoe: Life and Lore of the Haitian People*. Berkeley: University of California Press, 1960.

Craige, John Houston. *Black Bagdad*. New York: Minton, Balch, & Co., 1933.

———. *Cannibal Cousins*. New York: Minton, Balch, & Co., 1934.

Cruzat, Heloise. "Sidelights on Louisiana History—Slave Ordinances." *Louisiana Historical Quarterly* 1, no. 3 (January 1918), 108–10.

Cuming, Fortescue. *Sketches of a Tour to the Western Country . . . Together with A Notice of an Expedition Through Louisiana*. Pittsburgh: Cramer, Spear, & Bichbaum, 1810. Reprinted in *Early Western Travels 1748–1846*, edited by Reuben Gold Thwaites. Cleveland: A. H. Clark, 1904.

Curry, Leonard C. *The Free Black in Urban America, 1800–1850: The Shadow of the Dream*. Chicago: University of Chicago Press, 1981.

Dargo, George. *Jefferson's Louisiana: Politics and the Clash of Legal Traditions*. Cambridge: Harvard University Press, 1975.

Davis, Wade. *Passage of Darkness: The Ethnobiology of the Haitian Zombie*, Chapel Hill: University of North Carolina Press, 1988.

Dayan, Joan. *Haiti, History, and the Gods*. Berkeley: University of California Press, 1995.

Debien, Gabriel, and René Le Gardeur. "The Saint-Domingue Refugees in Louisiana," translated by David Cheramie. In *Road to Louisiana: The Saint-Domingue Refugees 1792–1809*, edited by Carl A. Brasseaux and Glenn R. Conrad, 113–243. Lafayette: University of Southwestern Louisiana Center for Louisiana Studies, 1992.

Deggs, Sister Mary Bernard. *No Cross, No Crown: Black Nuns in Nineteenth-Century New Orleans*. Edited by Virginia Meachem Gould and Charles E. Nolan. Bloomington: University of Indiana Press, 2001.

Desdunes, Rodolphe Lucien. *Nos Hommes et Notre Histoire*. 1911. Edited and translated by Sister Dorothea McCants, Daughter of the Cross, as *Our People and Our History: A Tribute to the Creole People of Color in Memory of the Great Men they Have Given Us and of the Good Works They Have Accomplished*. Baton Rouge: Louisiana State University Press, 1973.

Din, Gilbert C., and John E. Harkins. *The New Orleans Cabildo: Colonial Louisiana's First City Government, 1769–1803*. Baton Rouge: Louisiana State University Press, 1996.

Domínguez, Virginia R. *White by Definition: Social Classification in Creole Louisiana*. New Brunswick, N.J.: Rutgers University Press, 1986.

Duffy, William McFadden. "Voodoo Queen." *Roosevelt Review* 1, no. 8 (1938): 17, 45–50.

Duggal, Barbara Rosendale. "Marie Laveau: The Voodoo Queen Repossessed." *Folklore and Mythology Studies* 15 (1991): 37–58. Reprinted in *Creole*, edited by Sybil Kein.

Estes, David C. "Traditional Dances and Processions of Blacks in New Orleans as Witnessed by Antebellum Travelers." *Louisiana Folklore Miscellany* 6, no. 3 (1990): 1–14.

Evans, Sally Kittredge. "Free Persons of Color." In *New Orleans Architecture: The Creole Faubourgs*, vol. 4, edited by Roulhac Toledano, Sally Evans, and Mary Louise Christovich. New Orleans: Friends of the Cabildo, 1984.

Fandrich, Ina Johanna. "Mysterious Voodoo Queen Marie Laveaux: A Study of Spiritual Power and Female Leadership in Nineteenth-Century New Orleans." Ph.D. diss., Temple University, 1994.

———. "The Birth of New Orleans' Voodoo Queen: A Long-Held Mystery Resolved." *Louisiana History* 46, no. 3 (Summer 2005): 294–309.

———. *The Mysterious Voodoo Queen, Marie Laveaux: A Study of Powerful Female Leadership in Nineteenth-Century New Orleans*. New York: Routledge, 2005.

Ferguson, Leland. *Uncommon Ground: Archeology and Early African America*. Washington, D.C.: Smithsonian Institution Press, 1992.

Ficklen, John F. *Art Work of New Orleans*. Chicago: W. H. Parish, 1895.

Florence, Robert. *City of the Dead: A Journey Through St. Louis Cemetery #1*. Lafayette, La.: Center for Louisiana Studies, University of Southwestern Louisiana, 1996.

Florence, Robert, and Mason Florence. *New Orleans Cemeteries: Life in the Cities of the Dead*, New Orleans: Batture Press, 1997.

Frazer, James George. *The Golden Bough: A Study in Magic and Religion*. 1922. Reprint, New York: Macmillan Company, 1951.

French, Benjamin Franklin. *Historical Memoirs of Louisiana, from the First Settlement of the Colony to the Departure of Governor O'Reilly in 1770*. New York: Lamport, Blakeman & Law, 1853.

Gandolfo, Charles, and Jerry Gandolfo. *Le Voodoo à la Nouvelle Orleans: A Strolling Tour of Voodoo in the Vieux Carré*. New Orleans: New Orleans Historic Voodoo Museum, 1975.

Gayarré, Charles. *Louisiana: Its History as a French Colony*. New York: John Wiley, 1852.

Gehman, Mary. *The Free People of Color of New Orleans*. New Orleans: Margaret Media, 1994.

Gill, James. *Lords of Misrule: Mardi Gras and the Politics of Race in New Orleans*. Jackson: University Press of Mississippi, 1997.

Glassman, Sallie Ann. *Vodou Visions: An Encounter with Divine Mystery*. New York: Villard Books, 2000.

Gomez, Michael A. *Exchanging Our Country Marks: The Transformation of African Identities in the Colonial and Antebellum South*. Chapel Hill: University of North Carolina Press, 1998.

Gould, Virginia Meacham. "In Full Enjoyment of Their Liberty: The Free Women of Color of the Gulf Ports of New Orleans, Mobile, and Pensacola, 1769–1860." Ph.D. diss., Emory University, 1991.

———. "A Chaos of Iniquity and Discord: Slave and Free Women of Color in the Spanish Ports of New Orleans, Mobile, and Pensacola." In *The Devil's Lane: Sex and Race in the Early South*, edited by Catherine Clinton and Michele Gillespie. New York: Oxford University Press, 1997.

Haas, Edward F., ed. *Louisiana's Legal Heritage*. New Orleans: Louisiana State Museum, 1983.

Hall, Gwendolyn Midlo. *Africans in Colonial Louisiana: The Development of Afro-Creole Culture in the Eighteenth Century*. Baton Rouge: Louisiana State University Press, 1992.

———. "The Formation of Afro-Creole Culture." In *Creole New Orleans: Race and Americanization*, edited by Arnold R. Hirsch and Joseph Logsdon. Baton Rouge: Louisiana State University Press, 1992.

———. "African Women in French and Spanish Louisiana: Origins, Roles, Family, Work, Treatment." In *The Devil's Lane: Sex and Race in the Early South*, edited by Catherine Clinton and Michele Gillespie. New York: Oxford University Press, 1997.

Hanger, Kimberly. "*Persones de varias clases y colores*: Free People of Color in Spanish New Orleans, 1769–1803." Ph.D. diss., University of Florida, 1991.

———. *Bounded Lives, Bounded Places: Free Black Society in Colonial New Orleans, 1769–1803*. Durham, N.C.: Duke University Press, 1997.

———. "Coping in a Complex World." In *The Devil's Lane: Sex and Race in the Early South*, edited by Catherine Clinton and Michele Gillespie. New York: Oxford University Press, 1997.

Harms, Robert. *The Diligent: A Voyage Through the Worlds of the Slave Trade*. New York: Basic Books, 2002.

Harvey, Chance. *The Life and Selected Letters of Lyle Saxon*. Gretna, La.: Pelican, 2003.

Heard, Malcolm. *French Quarter Manual: An Architectural Guide to New Orleans' Vieux Carré*. New Orleans: Tulane University School of Architecture, 1997.

Hearn, Lafcadio. "Scenes of Cable's Romances." *The Century Magazine* 27 (November 1883): 40–47.

———. "The Last of the Voudoos." *Harper's Weekly Magazine* 24, no. 1507 (November 7, 1885): 726–27.

———. "El Vomito." In *Fantastics and Other Fancies*, edited by Charles Woodward Hutson. 1914. New York: Arno, 1976.

Herskovits, Melville. *Dahomey: An Ancient West African Kingdom*. Vol. 2. New York: J. J. Augustin, 1938.

———. *The Myth of the Negro Past*. 1941. Reprint, Boston: Beacon, 1990.

Hirsch, Arnold R., and Joseph Logsdon. *Creole New Orleans: Race and Americanization*. Baton Rouge: Louisiana State University Press, 1992.

Historical Sketch Book and Guide to New Orleans and Environs. New York: W. H. Coleman, 1885.

Holdredge, Helen. *Mammy Pleasant*. New York: Putnam's Sons, 1953.

Hollandsworth, James G. "Death and Disease Among Union Soldiers in New Orleans During the Civil War." Paper delivered at the annual meeting of the Louisiana Historical Association, Lafayette, March 28, 2003.

Holmes, Jack D. L. "Do It! Don't Do It!: Spanish Laws on Sex and Marriage." In *Louisiana's Legal Heritage*, edited by Edward F. Haas. New Orleans: Louisiana State Museum, 1983.

Huber, Leonard. *New Orleans: A Pictorial History*. New York: Crown, 1971.

Huber, Leonard, Peggy McDowell, and Mary Louise Christovich, eds. *New Orleans Architecture: The Cemeteries*. Vol. 3. New Orleans: Friends of the Cabildo, 1974.

Hurston, Zora Neale. "Hoodoo in America." *Journal of American Folklore* 44, no. 174 (October–December 1931): 320–414.

———. *Mules and Men*. 1935. Reprint, New York: Harper Perennial Library, 1990.

———. Book review of Robert Tallant's *Voodoo in New Orleans*. *Journal of American Folklore* 60, no. 238 (1947): 436–38.

Ingersoll, Thomas. "Slave Codes and Judicial Practice in New Orleans." *Law and History Review* 13, no. 1 (Spring 1995): 23–62.

———. *Mammon and Manon in Early New Orleans: The First Slave Society in the Deep South, 1718–1819*. Knoxville: University of Tennessee Press, 1999.

James, C.R.L. *The Black Jacobins: Toussaint L'Ouverture and the San Domingo Revolution*. 1938. Reprint, New York: Vintage Books, 1989.

Johnson, Jerah. "New Orleans's Congo Square: An Urban Setting for Early Afro-American Culture Formation." *Louisiana History* 32, no. 2 (Spring 1991): 140–47. This article was reprinted, along with "Notes on the Drawings of Benjamin Henry Latrobe" and "Notes on the Illustrations of E. W. Kemble" by John Joyce in *Congo Square in New Orleans* (New Orleans: Louisiana Landmarks Society, 1995).

———. "Colonial New Orleans: A Fragment of the Eighteenth-Century French

Ethos." In *Creole New Orleans: Race and Americanization*, edited by Arnold Hirsch and Joseph Logsdon. Baton Rouge: Louisiana State University Press, 1992.

Johnson, Walter. *Soul by Soul: Life Inside the Antebellum Slave Market*. Cambridge: Harvard University Press, 1999.

Jones, Robert R. "Race Relations in Louisiana, 1877–98." *Louisiana History* 9, no. 4 (Fall 1968): 301–23.

Jordan, Rosan Augusta, and Frank de Caro. "'In This Folk-Lore Land': Race, Class, Identity, and Folklore Studies in Louisiana." *Journal of American Folklore* 109, no. 431 (Winter 1996): 31–59.

Joyaux, George J., ed. and trans. "Forest's *Voyageaux États-Unis de l'Amérique en 1831*." *Louisiana Historical Quarterly* 39, no. 4 (October 1956): 457–72.

Joyce, John. "Notes on the Drawings of Benjamin Henry Latrobe" and "Notes on the Illustrations of E. W. Kemble." In *Congo Square in New Orleans*. New Orleans: Louisiana Landmarks Society, 1995.

Kaplan, Carla, ed. *Zora Neale Hurston: A Life in Letters*. New York: Anchor Books, 2003.

Kein, Sybil, ed. *Creole: The History and Legacy of Louisiana's Free People of Color*. Baton Rouge: Louisiana State University Press, 2000.

———. *Gumbo People*. New Orleans: Margaret Media, 1999.

Kendall, John S. "Old New Orleans Houses and Some of the People Who Lived in Them." *Louisiana Historical Quarterly* 20 (January–October 1937): 794–820.

Kennard, Nina H. *Lafcadio Hearn: Containing Some Letters from Lafcadio Hearn to His Half-Sister, Mrs. Atkinson*. New York: D. Appleton & Co., 1912.

Keyes, Frances Parkinson. *Madame Castel's Lodger*. New York: Farrar, Straus & Co., 1962.

Kilbourne, Richard H. "An Overview of the Work of the Territorial Court, 1804–1808." In *Louisiana's Legal Heritage*, edited by Edward F. Haas. New Orleans: Louisiana State Museum, 1983.

Labbé, Dolores Egger. *Jim Crow Comes to Church: The Establishment of Segregated Catholic Parishes in South Louisiana*. Lafayette: University of Southwestern Louisiana, 1971. Reprint, New York: Arno, 1978.

Lachance, Paul. "The 1809 Immigration of Saint-Domingue Refugees to New Orleans: Reception, Integration, and Impact." *Louisiana History* 29 (Spring 1988): 110–42.

———. "The Foreign French." In *Creole New Orleans: Race and Americanization*, edited by Arnold R. Hirsch and Joseph Logsdon. Baton Rouge: Louisiana State University Press, 1992.

Latrobe, Benjamin Henry Boneval. *Impressions Respecting New Orleans, Diary and Sketches 1818–1820*. Edited by Samuel Wilson, Jr. New York: Columbia University Press, 1951.

Laussat, Pierre Clément. *Memoirs of My Life*. Translated by Agnes-Josephine Pastwa. Baton Rouge: Louisiana State University Press, 2003.

Lawrence, John. "Picture Perfect: The New Orleans of Pierre Clément Laussat, 1803–04." *Louisiana Cultural Vistas* (Summer 2003): 45.

Lebsock, Suzanne. *The Free Women of Petersburg: Status and Culture in a Southern Town, 1784–1860*. New York: W. W. Norton, 1984.

Leglaunec, Jean-Pierre. "Slave Migrations in Spanish and Early American Louisiana: New Sources and New Estimates," and "A Directory of Ships with Slave Cargoes, Louisiana, 1772–1808." *Louisiana History* 66, no. 2 (Spring 2005): 204–5, 211–30.

Le Page du Pratz, Antoine-Simon. *Histoire de la Louisiane*. 1758. Translated as *The History of Luisiana or of The Western Parts of Virginia and Carolina, with an Account of the Settlements, Inhabitants, Soil, Climate, and Products*. London: Beckett, 1774.

Loederer, Richard. *Voodoo Fire in Haiti*. New York: Literary Guild, 1935.

Logsdon, Joseph, and Caryn Cossé Bell. "The Americanization of Black New Orleans." In *Creole New Orleans: Race and Americanization*, edited by Arnold R. Hirsch and Joseph Logsdon. Baton Rouge: Louisiana State University Press, 1992.

Long, Carolyn Morrow. "Voodoo-Influenced Rituals in New Orleans Cemeteries and the Tomb of Marie Laveau." *Louisiana Folklore Miscellany* 14 (1999): 1–14.

———. *Spiritual Merchants: Religion, Magic, and Commerce*. Knoxville: University of Tennessee Press, 2001.

———. "Haitian Vodou and New Orleans Voudou: A Comparision." In *Revolutionary Freedoms: A History of Survival, Strength and Imagination in Haiti*. Edited by Cécile Accilien. Deerfield Beach, Fla.: Caribbean Studies Press, 2006.

Loomis, Rosemarie Fay. *Negro Soldiers—Free Men of Color in the Battle of New Orleans—War of 1812*. New Orleans: Aux Quatres Vents, 1991.

Macdonald, Robert R., John R. Kemp, and Edward F. Haas, eds. *Louisiana's Black Heritage*. Proceedings of the 1977 Louisiana Black Heritage Symposium. New Orleans: Louisiana State Museum, 1979.

MacGaffey, Wyatt. *Religion and Society in Central Africa; Art and Healing of the BaKongo*. Stockholm: Folkens Museum-Ethnografiska, 1991.

———. "The Eyes of Understanding: Kongo Minkisi." In *Astonishment and Power*. Washington, D.C.: Smithsonian Institution, National Museum of African Art, 1993.

Mackey, Albert G., ed. *An Encyclopedia of Freemasonry and Its Kindred Sciences*. Vol. 1. New York: Masonic History Company, 1918.

Magill, John. "Oblivion's Blight: Girod Street Cemetery 1822–1957." Exhibition catalog. Williams Research Center, The Historic New Orleans Collection, 2001.

Martin, Joan. "*Plaçage* and the Louisiana *Gens de Couleur Libres*: How Race and Sex Defined the Lifestyles of Free Women of Color." In *Creole*, edited by Sybil Kein. Baton Rouge: Louisiana State University Press, 2000.

Martineau, Harriet. *Retrospect of Western Travel*. Vol. 1. London: Saunders and Otley, 1838.

Martinez, Raymond J. *Mysterious Marie Laveau, Voodoo Queen, and Folktales Along the Mississippi*. New Orleans: Hope Publications, 1956.

Matthews, John R. N., *A voyage to the river Sierra-Leone, on the coast of Africa*. London: B. White and Son, 1791.

McAlister, Elizabeth. "A Sorcerer's Bottle: The Visual Art of Magic in Haiti." In *Sa-

cred Arts of Haitian Vodou, edited by Donald Cosentino. Los Angeles: University of California Fowler Museum of Cultural History, 1995.

Medley, Keith Weldon. *We as Freemen: Plessy v. Ferguson*. Gretna, La.: Pelican, 2003.

Métraux, Alfred. *Voodoo in Haiti*. 1959. English translation, New York: Schocken Books, 1972.

Moreau de Saint-Méry, Medric Louis. *Description Topographique, Physique, Civile, Politique, et Historic de la Partie Francaise de l'Isle Saint-Domingue*. Philadelphia: Moreau de Saint-Méry, 1797. Translated by Ivor Spencer as *A Civilization that Perished: The Last Years of White Colonial Rule in Haiti*. Lanham, Md.: University Press of America, 1985.

Mulira, Jessie Gaston. "The Case of Voodoo in New Orleans." In *Africanisms in American Culture*, edited by Joseph E. Holloway. Bloomington: Indiana University Press, 1990.

Murray, Paul. *A Fantastic Journey: The Life and Literature of Lafcadio Hearn*. Sandgate, England: Japan Library, 1993.

Nolan, Charles E. *A History of the Archdiocese of New Orleans*. New Orleans: Archdiocese of New Orleans, 2000.

Olmsted, Frederick Law. *Journeys and Explorations in the Cotton Kingdom: A Traveller's Observations on Cotton and Slavery in the American Slave States*. London: S. Low & Son, 1862.

Owen, Nicholas. *Journal of a Slave Dealer: A View of Some Remarkable Axedents in the Life of Nics. Owen from the Year 1746 to the Year 1757*. London: George Routledge & Sons, 1930.

Palmié, Stephan. "Conventionalization, Distortion, and Plagiarism in the Historiography of Afro-Caribbean Religion in New Orleans." In *Creoles and Cajuns: French Louisiana—La Louisiane Française*, edited by Wolfgang Binder. Frankfurt, Germany: Peter Lang, 1998.

Perrin du Lac, François-Marie. *Voyage dans les Deux Louisianes*. In *Louisiana Under the Rule of Spain, France, and the United States 1785–1807*, vol. 1, edited and translated by James Alexander Robertson. 1910. Reprint, Freeport, N.Y.: Books for Libraries Press, 1969.

Pitkin, Helen. *An Angel by Brevet: A Story of Modern New Orleans*. Philadelphia: J. B. Lippincott, 1904.

Porteous, Laura, "Renunciation made by Daniel Fagot of his office of Regidor and receiver of fines forfeited to the Royal Treasury of this city to Don Cristoval de Glapion, 1776, translated from the original in the Cabildo at New Orleans." *Louisiana Historical Quarterly* 14 (July 1931): 372–82.

———. "The Gri-Gri Case, A Criminal Trial in Louisiana During the Spanish Regime, 1773." *Louisiana Historical Quarterly* 17, no. 1 (1934): 48–63.

Potter, Eliza. *A Hairdresser's Experience in High Life*. 1859. Reprint, New York: Oxford University Press, 1991.

Prose, Francine. *Marie Laveau*. New York: Berkley Publishing, 1977.

Puckett, Newbell Niles. *Folk Beliefs of the Southern Negro*. 1926. Reprint, Montclair, N.J.: Patterson Smith Reprint Series, 1968.

Raboteau, Albert. *Slave Religion: The "Invisible Institution" in the Antebellum South*. New York: Oxford University Press, 1978.

Rankin, David. "The Politics of Caste: Free Colored Leadership in New Orleans During the Civil War." In *Louisiana's Black Heritage*, edited by Robert Macdonald, John Kemp, and Edward Haas. New Orleans: Louisiana State Museum, 1979.

Rebennack, Mac. *Under a Hoodoo Moon: The Life of the Night Tripper*. New York: St. Martin's, 1994.

Reed, Ishmael. *The Last Days of Louisiana Red*. 1974. Reprint, Normal, Ill.: Dalkey Archive Press, 2000.

Reinders, Robert C. *End of an Era: New Orleans, 1850–1860*. 1964. Reprint, Gretna, La.: Pelican, 1998.

———. "The Free Negro in the New Orleans Economy, 1850–1860." *Louisiana History* 6, no. 3 (Summer 1965): 273–85.

Renda, Mary A. *Taking Haiti: Military Occupation and the Culture of U.S. Imperialism, 1915–1940*. Chapel Hill: University of North Carolina Press, 2001.

Rhodes, Jewell Parker. *Voodoo Dreams: A Novel of Marie Laveau*. New York: Picador, 1995.

Rice, C. Duncan. *The Rise and Fall of Black Slavery*. Baton Rouge: Louisiana State University Press, 1975.

Richardson, Lillie. "The Admission of Louisiana into the Union." *Louisiana Historical Quarterly* 1, no. 4 (April 1918): 333–51.

Rightor, Henry, ed. *Standard History of New Orleans, Louisiana*. Chicago: Lewis Publishing, 1900.

Robertson, James Alexander, ed. and trans. *Louisiana Under the Rule of Spain, France, and the United States 1785–1807: Social, Economic, and Political Conditions of the Territory Represented in the Louisiana Purchase, as portrayed in hitherto unpublished contemporary accounts by Dr. Paul Alliot and various Spanish, French, English, and American Officials*. 2 vols. Cleveland: Arthur H. Clark, 1911.

Robin, Claude-Cézar. *Voyages dans l'interieur de la Louisiane*. 1807. Translated by Stuart Landry as *Voyages to Louisiana*. Gretna, La.: Pelican, 2000.

Rose, Al. *Storyville, New Orleans: An Authentic, Illustrated Account of the Notorious Red-Light District*. Tuscaloosa: University of Alabama Press, 1974.

Rousséve, Charles Barthelemy. *The Negro in Louisiana: Aspects of His History and His Literature*. New Orleans: Xavier University Press, 1937.

Saxon, Lyle. *Fabulous New Orleans*. 1928. Reprint, Gretna, La.: Pelican, 1988.

———. *Old Louisiana*. 1929. Reprint, Gretna, La.: Pelican, 1988.

Saxon, Lyle, Edward Dreyer, and Robert Tallant, eds. *Gumbo Ya-Ya: Folk Tales of Louisiana*. 1945. Reprint, Gretna, La.: Pelican, 1986.

Schafer, Judith K. *Slavery, the Civil Law, and the Supreme Court of Louisiana*. Baton Rouge: Louisiana State University Press, 1994.

———. *Becoming Free, Remaining Free: Manumission and Enslavement in New Orleans, 1846–1862*. Baton Rouge, Louisiana State University Press, 2003.

Schultz, Christian. *Travels on an Inland Voyage in the Years 1807 and 1808*. New York: Isaac Riley, 1810.

Seabrook, William. *The Magic Island*. New York: Literary Guild of America, 1929.

Smith, Michael P. *Spirit World—Photographs and Journal: Pattern in the Expressive Folk Culture of Afro-American New Orleans*. Gretna, La.: Pelican, 1984.

———. *Mardi Gras Indians*. Gretna, La.: Pelican, 1994.

Snelgrave, William. *A New Account of Some Parts of Guinea and the Slave-Trade*. 1731. Reprint, London: Frank Cass & Co., 1971.

Spear, Jennifer M. "Colonial Intimacies: Legislating Sex in French Louisiana." *William and Mary Quarterly* 110, no. 1 (January 2003): 75–98.

Starr, S. Frederick, ed. *Inventing New Orleans: Writing of Lafcadio Hearn*. Jackson: University Press of Mississippi, 2001.

Sussman, Rachelle. "Conjuring Marie Laveau: The Syncretic Life of a Nineteenth-Century Voodoo Priestess in America." Master's thesis, Sarah Lawrence College, 1998.

Tallant, Robert. *Voodoo in New Orleans*. 1946. Reprint, Gretna, La.: Pelican, 1983.

———. *The Voodoo Queen*. 1956. Reprint, Gretna, La.: Pelican, 1983.

Taylor, Joe Gray. "The Foreign Slave Trade After 1808." *Louisiana History* 1 (Winter 1960): 36–43.

———. *Louisiana Reconstructed, 1863–1877*. Baton Rouge: Louisiana State University Press, 1974.

Thompson, Robert Farris. *Flash of the Spirit: African and Afro-American Art and Philosophy*. New York: Vintage Books, 1983.

———. "From the Isle Beneath the Sea: Haiti's Africanizing Vodou Art." In *Sacred Arts of Haitian Vodou*, edited by Donald Cosentino. Los Angeles: University of California Fowler Museum of Cultural History, 1995.

Thornton, John. *Africa and Africans in the Making of the Atlantic World, 1400–1680*. Cambridge: Cambridge University Press, 1992.

Tinker, Edward Larocque. *Lafcadio Hearn's American Days*. New York: Dodd, Mead, & Co., 1924.

———. "Cable and the Creoles." *American Literature* 5, no. 4 (January 1934): 313–26.

Toledano, Roulhac, Sally Kittredge Evans, and Mary Louise Christovich, eds. *New Orleans Architecture: The Creole Faubourgs*. Vol. 4. New Orleans: Friends of the Cabildo, 1984.

Toledano, Roulhac, and Mary Louise Christovich, eds. *New Orleans Architecture: Faubourg Tremé and the Bayou Road*. Vol. 6. New Orleans: Friends of the Cabildo, 1980.

Touchstone, Blake. "Voodoo in New Orleans." *Louisiana History* 13 (Fall 1972): 371–86.

Tregle, Joseph. "Creoles and Americans." In *Creole New Orleans: Race and Americanization*, edited by Arnold R. Hirsch and Joseph Logsdon. Baton Rouge: Louisiana State University Press, 1992.

Trevigne, Barbara. "Prominent People and Places in New Orleans." In *Gumbo People*, edited by Sybil Kein. New Orleans: Margaret Media, 1999.

Turner, Arlin. *George W. Cable: A Biography*. Durham, N.C.: Duke University Press, 1956.

Vella, Christina. *Imitate Enemies: The Two Worlds of the Baroness Pontalba*. Baton Rouge: Louisiana State University Press, 1997.

Ward, Martha. *Voodoo Queen: The Spirited Lives of Marie Laveau*. Jackson: University Press of Mississippi, 2004.

Warner, Charles Dudley. "A Voodoo Dance." *Harper's Weekly Magazine* 31, no. 1592 (June 25, 1887): 454–55.

Wiesandanger, Martin, and Margaret Wiesandanger. *Nineteenth-Century Louisiana Painters and Paintings from the Collection of W. E. Groves*. New Orleans: W. E. Groves Gallery, 1971.

Williams, Marie B. "A Night with the Voudous." *Appleton's Journal* 13 (March 27, 1875): 403–4.

Wilson, Charles Reagan, and William Ferris, eds. *The Encyclopedia of Southern Culture*. 1 vol. Chapel Hill: University of North Carolina Press, 1989.

Wilson, Samuel, Jr. "Early History." In *New Orleans Architecture: The Creole Faubourgs*, vol. 4, edited by Roulhac Toledano, Sally Kittredge Evans, and Mary Louise Christovich. New Orleans: Friends of the Cabildo, 1984.

Wilson, Samuel, Jr., and Leonard Huber. *The St. Louis Cemeteries of New Orleans*. New Orleans: St. Louis Cathedral, 1962.

Wirkus, Faustin, and Taney Dudley. *The White King of La Gonave*. Garden City, N.Y.: Doubleday, Doran & Co., 1931.

Woodward, C. Vann. *The Strange Career of Jim Crow: A Brief Account of Segregation*. New York: Oxford University Press, 1955.

Musical and Theatrical Works

Carbon, John Joseph. "Marie Laveau: A Full-Length Voodoo Opera." Ph.D. diss., University of California, Santa Barbara, 1983.

Chambers, Wendy Mae. "Voodoo on the Bayou." Play script, 2000. Not yet performed.

Du Plantis, Daniel. *Gris-Gris*. Play script, 1998. Performed by the African Continuum Theater Company at Source Theater, Washington, D.C., January 24–February 11, 2001.

Hank, Steven, dir. *The Widow Paris*. Film. New Orleans, UNO productions, 1991.

Index

Page numbers in italics indicate illustrations.

Carolyn Morrow Long studied studio art and art history at Auburn University, the University of Missouri, and the University of Mississippi. During her career she has been a painter, a collage artist, a potter, an art teacher, a photographer, and a writer. She was employed for eighteen years as a conservator of paper artifacts and photographs at the Smithsonian Institution's National Museum of American History and retired in 2001. Long is the author of *Spiritual Merchants: Religion, Magic, and Commerce* and has written articles on New Orleans, Voudou, and Marie Laveau. Since 1978 she has been a frequent visitor to New Orleans and considers it her second home. She lives with her husband in Washington, D.C.